GW00578021

Fiona Ross, born in Durban 1950, grew up in the Drakensberg Mountains of KwaZulu-Natal, one of four girls of a dysfunctional family in paradise. She attended a boarding school, a Swiss finishing school, married three times, worked as a wildlife veterinary nurse, a bush camp manager in the Okavango, and now lives in Wisbech, England.

Further information can be found on the author's website: www.whitezulubook.com.

~~~

This book is dedicated to Fred,
the love of my life

NON OMNIS MORIAR

("I shall not wholly die!")

**Part One of a Two-part autobiography**

# Fiona Ross

## White Zulu

## - A White woman's story of her African heritage

# White Zulu                                    Fiona Ross

A CIP catalogue record for this title is available from the British Library.

ISBN 9781786292537 (Paperback)
ISBN 9781786292544 (Hardback)
ISBN 9781786292551 (e-Book)

First Published (2016)
Austin Macauley Publishers Ltd.
25 Canada Square
Canary Wharf
London
E14 5LQ
www.austinmacauley.com

Second edition (in two parts) published by Worldwide Books and Art,
South Africa in 2018.
Editor: Fanus Bothma
Cover design by the author.

Note by the author: All Zulu words, names and meanings need to be read as "seen in context", during the time-frame of the story.

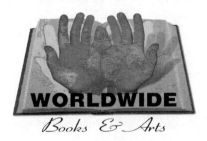

# Acknowledgement

My acknowledgements go to Peter Buchan, my initial editor, who made this book possible by wading through, and unravelling, the jumble of short stories I handed to him, and making sense of it all, and who made so many helpful suggestions as to how to improve the writing.

This book couldn't have been written without Kelly Prendergast, who looks after me every single day, making it possible for me to be able to plough on with my book. She is the backbone of my daily life, and I simply couldn't manage without her.

My two sons, Alastair Mackay-James and Justin Whitsitt, who both encouraged me to write this book from the word go, and have given me their unwavering support.

My acknowledgements go to Jenny Fowler for helping me ease the pain of ME (otherwise known as *Myalgic encephalomyelitis* - a debilitating, painful and terminal condition of unknown cause, with fever, aching, and prolonged tiredness and depression, to name but a few of the many symptoms) by giving me weekly reflexology sessions, Dr L de Gray, my Pain Specialist who assists in my pain relief, and Dr Danie Treurnicht, my dentist, for looking after me for the past 18 years, helping me through so many dental crises.

# Contents

Picture section (i) to (xx) - middle of book.

# *1*
# The beginning ...

"For God's sake Mum! Give the baboons a break!" I pleaded.

It was December, 2000, and I was sitting in the glassed-in veranda at home, writing an e-mail on my laptop. This was to be my last visit to the farm before emigrating to the United Kingdom, and I was reflecting upon leaving Africa, my mind filled with images of the old days on the farm.

Earlier on, I'd been alerted by a baboon bark, and seen a troop of about forty baboons crossing the river that runs alongside the dense, dark forest in front of the house. They sauntered up through our paddocks after negotiating the river. Once across, they became silent and more cautious, dropping their usual insolent, front-paws-crossed swagger. They were on a dangerous mission: to pick the sweet fruit that hung like bunches of rubies from an ornamental cherry tree growing just in front of the May hedge that divided the garden from the paddocks.

The first big male reached the tree and began picking up fallen berries, murmuring in soft grunts to the others to join him. Soon the tree was alive with furry grey bodies whose long dark tails dangled while they picked fruit with their hand-like front paws, gripping the branches tightly with the long toes on their flexible hind feet. As their feast progressed, one young male became too enthusiastic, and, in reaching for a particularly big cluster of berries, broke off the branch with a loud snap. The baboons froze, and even I held my breath as they waited. Nothing. Silence. And after a minute or two they resumed stuffing the berries into their cheek pouches.

A floorboard creaked next to me, and I looked up to see my eighty-three-year-old mother creeping stealthily, crouched and carrying the 4.10 shotgun low by her side, stalking towards the open window. She slowly raised the gun to her shoulder, rested the barrel on the window ledge, took aim and pulled the trigger.

There was a deafening explosion as she fired a single blast of birdshot. The tree erupted as, with terrified screams, every baboon in the troop leapt out and dashed down the paddock, back to the safety of the forest. They disappeared into the shadows, to vanish up one of the tallest Yellowwood trees growing in the bush. At the base of the cherry tree I could see little piles of wet dung lying scattered on the ground. Mum had, in every sense of the word, quite literally scared the shit out of them.

Mum had a fairly good aim, but only ever used bird-shot. In spite of the fact that they were terrified out of their wits, the baboons were perfectly safe, and all she achieved was a major scare and the satisfaction of watching them scattering and running away screaming.

"Do you still have to do this at your age?" I rolled my eyes in exasperation.

"Bloody baboons!" she muttered. "They didn't even give me time to reload, and now I've got to clean the damn gun."

Mum dropped the shotgun and a handful of cartridges onto the sofa, picked up her knitting, and sat down in her favourite padded cane chair - the one with the best view of the two roads approaching the house, and from where she could monitor everything that went on. She crossed her feet, shod in her favourite comfortable old Kudu buckskin veldskoens worn with rolled down khaki socks, and tucked them neatly under her chair. Sitting there with her knitting she looked the archetypical gentleman landowner's wife. Her figure was still trim under the knee-length, sky blue, A-line denim skirt she always wore for gardening, and she had on a crisp, pin-tucked, capped-sleeve cotton blouse, patterned with pale blue forget-me-nots, tucked into her skirt to emphasise her slender waist.

As long as I could remember, people had remarked upon how much like Grace Kelly my mother looked. Unlike the former, she'd sailed gracefully into old age with hardly a line to be seen on her silken, peaches-and-cream complexion. Her glossy, wavy hair had only recently faded almost imperceptibly from spun gold to sleek silver. As Mum had reached her eighties, the only concession she gave to the passing years was mild arthritis in her hands, which gnarled her fingers enough for her fine white gold wedding and engagement rings to swivel loosely at the knuckles, and a slight tendency for her shoulders to stoop. The arthritis had stiffened her right shoulder, too, and reluctantly she'd relinquished the old farm shotgun – the twelve-bore – complaining that it kicked too hard on the recoil and hurt her shoulder when she took a pot shot at the baboons. She'd always preferred the 4.10 anyway – "It's a more ladylike weapon, and easier to hide with" was her opinion. The cane chair creaked as my mother leaned forward to look at the glistening turds where they lay among discarded half-chewed berries, and narrowed her cornflower blue eyes to a steely glare.

'Curtain twitching' my sisters and I called it, when Mum would leap to her feet to peer over the hedge whenever a vehicle passed by in a cloud of pale dust on the District Road or if one of our bakkies drove up the lane behind our house, towards the sheds.

"What's he doing now?" she'd mutter under her breath, as she recognised a white farm manager behind the wheel, one of the many Dad had employed over the years. "He's not supposed to be down here at this time of day. I bet he's forgotten something, and it's our petrol he's wasting!" She could keep this up all day long, and it drove my father mad when she constantly insisted on drawing his attention to every imagined transgression on the part of their current manager.

"I don't want to hear another thing about it!"

Then he'd pick up the newspaper and snap it open as a barrier between himself, her, and the rest of the world.

Mum's attitude to farm managers, baboons, and her garden – among many other subjects – were a source of amusement or mild irritation to us all, depending on how far she pursued them.

During our childhood, her obsessions had had a deep and lasting impact on our lives, and affected us to such an extent that we had all seized the first opportunity to get away from the farm. This might have been her intention of course, as, either deliberately or subliminally, she and Dad had made sure that none of their daughters lingered at home after we left school.

Our parents really wanted boys, on the basis of a rather Victorian view that only a son would be entitled to inherit the ranch and continue the line of wealthy gentleman farmers like my father, who had inherited the ranch from his parents. The last straw for our parents was when another girl arrived after me, the third, and they gave up trying for a boy altogether. As each daughter was born our mother immediately lost interest, handed us over to be raised by Zulu nannies, and turned back to her real passion – gardening. It felt to us that every day since we'd been born, we girls were subjected to her genuinely heartfelt lament "if only you lot had been boys, our lives would have been so much easier!"

Thus the Zulus became an integral part of me and my sisters' lives. From infancy, we were absorbed into the lives of the house and farm staff. Our upbringing was haphazard: speaking pure Zulu, we learned all the ways of our local African tribe, their folklore, beliefs, superstitions and many other traditions, as well as the skills of tracking game and the uses of indigenous plants in witchcraft and healing. Since none of the staff spoke any English, Zulu was the only language used on the farm. We four girls had two nannies to look after us, and, on the very few occasions our parents spoke directly to us, they used a combination of a little bit of English, but mostly Zulu, as those rare interactions were usually in the form of instructions to be passed on to our nannies.

Each time I went back to the farm, I felt a growing excitement and anticipation – particularly during absences from boarding school, having not previously left the farm for any lengthy period. My heart would leap with joy on seeing each familiar landmark on reaching my home town – the small village of Nottingham Road (which the Zulus called *mTuleni* – The Place of Dust). Then comes the craggy, pointed Drakensberg mountain range looming in the distance, covered by a mantle of snow in winter, and, when the *iNhlosane* mountain, a cone-shaped peak and the twin of our own *inHlezela*, meaning Maiden's Breast, due to its shape, came into view, it was time to turn off the disintegrating tarmac road and drive the last ten miles of dirt track.

Each time I had done this journey, it had evoked the thought of the freedom to come.

No more school for a few weeks, no more early morning prep, and I could get out and ride, swim and play tennis to my heart's content. Even now, forty years later, I felt a delicious thrill of pleasure. Then I'd be on the farm, driving past fields that I knew so well – I'd ridden past every tree, every tuft of grass, and opened and closed all those gates so often. Being back on the farm with my parents, this time for a final, short visit, brought back so many memories of my early life.

On my arrival from Durban earlier that day, Mum and Dad had walked out to meet me at the garage and given me a peck on the cheek before we went into the house for a cup of tea, while Lefina, (iNdlovu, meaning elephant), Evalina's now middle-aged daughter, and Lokatia (we and the other Zulu staff called her "Kati" – pronounced "Kaahti") brought my bags in. We had caught up on news, mine first, and then Mum started telling me what had been going on in their lives on the farm. This is when I felt the familiar slide of my spirits going downhill, just as surely as one drives down the hill into the valley.

My earliest recollections are of Evalina, my Zulu nanny, singing a quiet lullaby while she did the ironing – I would have been about two years old: *Thula thula wemTwana, musuKala.* ("Hush hush baby, do not cry.")

*iZo figa uBaba, musuKala.* ("Daddy will come, do not cry.").

Her voice was as rich as dark treacle and she swayed her hips slightly as she sang. She'd tied me to her back the way Zulu women traditionally carry their infants – piggyback and strapped on with a big woollen shawl – while she rhythmically took the flat irons in turn off the fiercely hot *biyela* (wood stove) and thumped them, gently hissing, onto the still-damp linen.

My little legs stuck out on either side of her plump back as I rested on her warm, cushiony rump. My head was nestled on her shoulder, and sleepily I savoured her familiar faint African smell – slightly musky with a touch of cinnamon and wood smoke – which I loved so much. It was almost overwhelmed, though, by the sharper scent of *Lifebuoy* soap with which my mother insisted her house-servants bathed every day, since she couldn't stand the smell of them. She'd wrinkle her nose: "They stink – especially the farm ones." The farm staff weren't allowed in the house, and had to stand outside on the back lawn beyond the kitchen veranda, twisting their khaki cotton hats in their black hands, waiting anxiously while the house staff (the team of Zulus, including a cook, a houseboy and three cleaning women, who doubled as nannies, formed the "house staff'" and the rest were referred to as "the farm staff'") relayed their messages or requests to one of my parents.

Another childhood memory is of a late-winter afternoon when I was still very young, probably three, as Evalina and I sat under a huge wattle (mimosa) tree on the sandy bank of our District Road, an ambitious name for the rutted track that was carved out of the red earth by the big, yellow Roads Party grader.

The District Road ran below our garden and led to the

Umgeni Poort Convent, a retreat for Roman Catholic nuns. As well as a tiny chapel in which they held missionary services, the nuns had a small clinic at the back of the convent, and Zulu people walked there from surrounding farms many miles away to receive treatment for various ailments.

The turn-off from the road to our sheds was a favourite place for the house-servants, especially our nannies. They put a grass mat in the shade and sat with their backs against a convenient tree trunk, legs straight out in front, ankles crossed, while they did their beadwork or wove more grass mats. I remember so well the slanting rays of our winter afternoon sun warming my back as, aged three, I squatted and ate sand happily, while Evalina chatted to her friends.

Every now and then a small group of Zulu passers-by appeared over the rise in the road, coming to or from *amaLomeni* (their name for 'the Romans'). There's no 'r' in the Zulu language, so, like the Chinese, they pronounced it 'l' when they tried to speak English. We were called *amaLosi* – the Rosses). As they came into view, Evalina would call a greeting, her voice echoing throughout the valley. *Sanbonani!* ("I see you all") she'd shout.

There'd be a *Saubona!* in response, and they'd carry on a conversation in this hilltop-calling fashion until the travellers arrived to shake both her hands, and sit down next to her.

Everybody knew one another in those parts, and of course they all knew who we were. There were clucks and murmurs of admiration as Evalina showed me off. "What a beautiful white child," the strangers said, "is she well behaved?"

"Mostly," replied Evalina proudly.

"So no sons yet?" was always the next question.

"No. *nKosane* (this was my father – meaning Son of the Chief. Grandpa was *nKosi* – Chief) is sad, but he should be happy. He'll get a lot of *uLobola* (bride price) for his four girls. *Au yebo!*" and Evalina clapped her hands together, laughing delightedly at the prospect of all these riches coming to *nKosane*. As my mother produced each of their four daughters, the Zulus on the farm rejoiced and congratulated my father on how many cattle he was eventually going to receive as *uLobola*. He just shook his head grimly. "We are *aBelungu* (white people). I have to pay for four damned expensive weddings to get rid of my girls. No *uLobola* for me."."

"Hau!" they said in astonishment, clapping their hands over their mouths in dismay. "So it is bad luck to have so many girls then?" and he'd nod gloomily.

"None of them are too naughty either, not like some white children I've seen," Evalina would boast to the now-settled Zulu passers-by. "Some of them at the polo run away from their nannies and scream at them." She clicked disapprovingly and shook her head neatly clad in its white *doek* – a headscarf tied turban-like, with the ends twisted and tucked neatly inside. This was what all married, widowed or mature Zulu women wore; Zulu maidens and unmarried girls were allowed to go bareheaded, but an older woman without a doek on had to be a slut or *isiFeba* – a whore. The white doek was part of our nannies' uniform of navy blue overall and white pinafore.

The gathering moved on to other subjects: their health, and their relatives back in iMpendhle (a large settlement of round, thatched African huts on the other side of the mountain behind our farmstead, where all the other Zulu tribal members lived, and was called a 'location' by the white farmers).

I was brought out of my childhood reverie with a jolt when Dad came into the room, having just woken up from his daily afternoon snooze and saw I was still there. The sight of me was enough to put him into one of his sour moods; he was of the 'guests and fish go off after three days' school, but in his case it was after three hours. He ignored me, snapped at Mum to call Lefina to bring in the afternoon tea, and retreated behind his newspaper. This made my heart sink, as I knew I was spending a couple of nights there – and he wanted me gone already, even though I was soon to depart the country.

This utopia, this paradise onto which we gazed right now, held a constant undercurrent of discontent and bitterness. Mum had such a negative outlook on life that my joy at being home gradually turned into an inward groan of despair as she complained about all the shortcomings of their latest white farm manager and how dreadfully useless he was.

Dad had already lost interest, and he'd what my sisters and I described as 'run out of nice'. We four had always agreed that it only took a couple of hours for Dad to be thinking "When are they going to leave?" He hated any breaks in his rigid routine, and ideally guests, including his daughters, ought to leave straight after lunch, so he could get on to his bed for his afternoon nap. He'd looked at me with genuine surprise when he'd seen me later on, sitting with Mum in the glassed-in veranda, waiting for Dad to appear before Lefina produced the tea tray. 'Are you still here?' was the look on his face. From then on, things got worse. During the interminably long evenings he wanted nobody around, so he could enjoy his three measured Imperial tots of whiskey in peace without having to make any effort at conversation.

I felt I ought to have left them and driven the gruelling two hours back to Durban after lunch that first day. No matter the age I currently was, the situation went instantly back to the old days on the farm when I had to amuse myself, by myself, spending all my time keeping out of both their ways: by running off to join the Zulu labourers' children in my childhood years – if it was good weather, or in the chilly nursery if it was particularly bad, and reading one of the books I'd already read for the umpteenth time. This particular day I was longing for the moment I could pack up and leave – this time for ever.

Often I did cut my visit short and would leave a day or even two earlier than I'd planned to. The relief on both Mum and Dad's faces made it clear to me that I was making the right decision. They didn't even try to hide it, and Mum would enthusiastically help me pack, to speed up my departure.

Mum never took a rest after lunch, even if the temperature outside was 35°C. As usual she'd taken me for a walk around the garden and down to the sawmill, perhaps even as far as the old cattle-dipping tank.

"We've had to sell most of our cattle," she had said bitterly as we stood under the gum-trees looking at the weed-infested ruins of the concrete tank. To the right, at ground level, lay a smaller, round sheep-dipping tank, now filled with rainwater blackened by fallen, rotting gum-leaves.

"They were being stolen twenty at a time, and Dad sold the rest while he could. The thieving bastards come with trucks now, and the police don't do anything about it. They're all in cahoots up there in *iMpendhle*. Since the ANC took over, this country has gone to the dogs."

"Your garden's looking lovely," I said, hoping for a moment to deflect her from her litany of complaints.

"Oh no! It's gone over now. I wish you'd come up to see it last week, it was looking so much nicer then. Everything was flowering at its best, then we had another hailstorm which flattened everything," she gesticulated at the waist-high blaze of bright colours everywhere. "There's nothing left – it's all been ruined. I don't know why I bother really, it's such hard work keeping this old place looking nice."

And so she carried on, as she had done for so many years, until I'd heard enough depressing talk. I wondered why I had come. It was always the same and it didn't take long before I came to the conclusion that I didn't want to be trapped there a moment longer. I mentally counted how many nights I'd be spending in my uninviting and unchanged old bedroom, still with its clown and balloon wallpaper put up for Dine when she'd been about five, and wished I could leave there and then, driving the hazardous hundred miles back to Durban, abandoning my ageing parents to wallow in their own self-created despondency. Mum, especially, couldn't look past all the problems – some real and others only imagined, and see the sheer beauty, the uniqueness of this exquisite, pristine part of the Natal Midlands (now called KwaZulu-Natal). Like the serpent in Paradise, she always succeeded in souring it for all of us by taking such a pleasure in her negativity.

Besides this undercurrent, my sisters and I had always been subjected to constant disapproval. On the rare occasions Mum lifted her head from her garden and noticed us, it was to look us over critically, along with disappointment. Nothing we ever did was good enough, and she held up various cousins of ours as role models.

"Why can't you be more like Jacquie?" she'd complain to me at the end of every school term. "She's in the A-stream at school and plays for the tennis team. She tries so much harder than you do. You just don't make any effort to be good at anything."

This was true. Apart from the fact that my cousins had the advantages of proper schooling instead of my sorely lacking early education, I couldn't see the point of attempting to ape my eager beaver cousins just to please my parents. Rather the reverse. I'd given up years ago.

My sisters and I had always clearly been a dismal failure to Mum and Dad simply by being born the wrong gender. They made no secret of the fact that they'd wanted sons to continue their bloodline and take over the farm, thus perpetuating their self-appointed tradition of being polo-playing gentleman ranchers. Even the prestigious Ross surname would die with us, as it was a given that we would all marry well.

They'd had four daughters instead, and none of us, especially since we'd never had any grounding or encouragement, had been particularly good at anything on either sporting or academic lines. We'd plodded through high school and apart from myself, left as soon as possible. My three sisters had dropped out of school early, eschewing tertiary education to escape from our parents' disapproval, which hung over us as inexorably as the dense white mist hangs over the mountains around us.

Every time without fail, I'd feel happy to be home, then disappointed at Dad's dismissal, and finally angry that I'd taken the trouble to come up at all, driving my little car for so many miles through those huge hippo-wallow potholes on the dirt roads, just to be given the brush-off. Nothing ever changes, I always told myself, and why did I ever expect it to? Gloom always settled on me after the first few hours of being there, and the only way I could shake it off was by leaving. The only difference this time was that I was leaving the farm, Mum and Dad, and Africa forever. I was never to see my parents again.

~~~

# *2*
# My heritage

**M**y ancestry is an unusual mixture, half Scottish and half Boer, which is a formidable combination of stubborn Highlanders and other equally uncompromising and intractable settlers who dragged their wagons doggedly over near impassable mountains to get away from British rule.

Mum and Dad always assumed an aristocratic air that was entirely self-appointed, and they kept very quiet about the fact that their wealth had been created by trade. Dad's ancestry reveals nothing more than a family of canny Scots who had owned a woollen mill and a cast-iron foundry in the highlands of Ross and Cromarty in Scotland; Dad always told us proudly "there's nothing but Scottish blood running through my veins." This was true as, although both his parents had been born in South Africa; all four of his grandparents were Scottish born and bred: having come out to Natal as settlers in one way or another, during the 1820s.

Mum is half English and half Boer, although she'd never admit to the latter. She somehow always managed to airbrush the Afrikaner-side right out of her ancestry. Her maternal grandmother wasn't even an Afrikaner, but of such strong Boer stock that she still spoke only the old style 'pure Dutch', as opposed to 'kitchen Dutch' that became the (much despised by my parents) Afrikaans language spoken by the majority of white South Africans, and was also the mother tongue of all the Coloured people of the Cape. The Coloureds are the dusky, mixed-race offspring that resulted from the early white settlers interbreeding with local indigenous people such as the Khoisan Strandlopers, a small, lean, yellow-skinned people roaming along the coast living off the seafood and small fish that they gathered, (they looked rather like the Kalahari Bushmen of today), Hottentots, (another coastal dwelling people), Malayan slaves, and African Xhosa tribes. This was altogether too murky a past for Mum to ever admit to, even though Gran's maiden name of Cloete crops up as frequently among the Coloureds as it does among white people in the Cape.

My family's history on my mother's side thus begins in the early days of what is now The Cape Province, and is joined by my father's side nearly two hundred years later, entering the east coast of what is now Kwazulu-Natal.

Mum comes from a long line of Dutch settlers to the Cape. The first one, a man called Jacob Clueten, profession unknown, but possibly a mercenary soldier, in 1652 stepped off a sailing ship (one of three: Drommedaris, the Reijger, and De Goede Hoope) under the command of Jan van Riebeeck, a representative of the Dutch East India Company; the very first Europeans to settle permanently in the Cape.

Mum's maternal grandfather, Henry Cloete, was the last of a succession of Cloetes who owned huge vineyards in Constantia behind the Table Mountain range in the Cape. In 1778 Hendrik Cloete acquired Groot Constantia estate (part of a much larger estate established in 1684 by the Dutch Colonial Governor of Cape Town, Simon van der Stel), and spent 14 years rebuilding the dilapidated farm. In 1854, Dirk Cloete bought the classically elegant manor house, Alphen, at the north-eastern end of the valley, which has been passed down through a succession of Cloetes.

The first considered himself a Renaissance man and employed a fiddler to wake him up every morning; the second established the Constantia wines which found their way into the cellars of Napoleon and that of the Duke of Northumberland; and the third, Dirk's son, adopted the British way of life, changing his name to Henry and studying law at the Bar in England.

Mum's maternal grandmother, Deliana van Warmelo, (known to us as Ouma), was a feisty young Boer girl, and she met Henry Cloete while he was practicing law in Pretoria (where they were married). They returned to Alphen, where they had four daughters: Nicolette (Mum's Aunt Ninky), Reniera (Mum's Aunt Bogey), Deliana (Gran), and Mary. Henry was appointed Acting British Agent at the outbreak of the Boer war after the British had left, and in fact he was awarded the CMG (the Most Distinguished Order of Saint Michael and Saint George; a British order of chivalry founded on 28 April 1818 by George, Prince Regent, later King George IV), for being Acting British Agent for his services to the British throughout the Anglo Boer War.

While he entertained the British generals (such as lords Kitchener and Roberts) in the Agterkamer (dining-room), Ouma would spy on him by listening through the slats of the teak and yellowwood screen. She is supposed to have written notes in invisible ink and put them in a hollow oak for collection by Boer commandos who'd slip by on horseback that night, under cover of darkness. The notes would then be smuggled to her mother in Pretoria (who ran a spy network from her home there) in false suitcase bottoms and once in a doll whose head had been broken off to insert the letter. On one occasion instructions came back from her mother in the head of one of three dolls for the three children (Mary wasn't born yet). Deliana had to break the head off the doll to retrieve the letter. (There is a photograph in the Alphen archives of the three girls with their dolls and the nanny. My Great Aunt Ninky became the owner of the naked doll with the broken head, which she was given because she was the eldest.) Sadly, I don't have a copy. The information would then be passed on to the Transvaal Boers to help them in their fight against the British. If the British had discovered these extraordinarily bold and risky operations, Ouma, along with her mother, would have been instantly shot for treason. This Boer underground rebellion, consisting of mainly women, was called the "Petticoat Commando" and there are several books available, written by members or their descendants.

There is a family story about Ouma snubbing the Prince of Wales. After the Anglo Boer War had been won by the British, Prince Edward, the then Prince of Wales (the thirty-six-year-old son of King George V and Queen Mary, and the future King George VI), toured South Africa on a Royal visit. There was to be a magnificent function held at Government House in Cape Town to which all the illuminati of Cape Town had been invited, including Henry Cloete and his Boer wife, Deliana.

When the time came to get dressed and leave for this Royal function, Henry went upstairs to prepare himself in his best white tie. To his surprise however, when he came back downstairs, he saw his wife still sitting in the drawing room and wearing the clothes she had had on all day.

"Go and get changed, my dear," he said to her, "it's getting late and we need to be there on time." She ignored him and resumed her needlepoint. He glared at her. "Come on Deliana, we do not have much time."

Deliana very deliberately lowered her needlework, and turning towards Henry said, "You know exactly how I feel about the British and having lost my beloved country in the War to them. I refuse to go."

Henry was near an apoplectic fit. "I represent my Colonial duties at this evening's function, and I need you at my side. You are my wife and as so, it is your duty to attend the Reception with me. Go and get ready as I will hear no more about it!"

Without a further word Deliana rose to her feet, put her needlework on a side table, and walked very deliberately past her husband and up the staircase. After a long wait, while Henry paced the drawing room fuming, she reappeared at the top of the stairs and walked slowly down them. She was dressed in all her finery: a long silk dress with matching elbow length gloves, her hair piled up elegantly with glittering, bejewelled clips to keep it so, and round her slender, long neck she wore her best strand of pearls. In her hand she carried an ivory fan, along with a large hat dressed with ostrich plumes. She looked stunningly beautiful. With some relief Henry escorted Deliana out to the waiting Daimler, and handed her into the car.

When they arrived at Government House Deliana walked up the steps to where there was a reception committee of both Royal and Colonial representatives. When their names were called out Deliana walked regally down the receiving line, her head held high and looking neither left nor right, while her husband followed a step or two behind her. When she reached the Prince of Wales she continued walking, brushing aside his outstretched hand; she ignored him completely. When she reached the end of the reception line, just beyond where the Prince stood, she turned around and loudly announced to her husband "I have done my duty as your wife. Now please take me home!"

Henry was speechless with mortification, and was about to stumble out some sort of apology to His Royal Highness, when he realised that the Prince was laughing. "I love it!" roared the Prince, wiping tears of laughter from his eyes. "We have a few of those in my own family and it's most refreshing to see. I enjoyed every moment and that was the highlight of my evening."

Cloete property had to be passed down the male line of the family, and because there were only daughters there was no one to inherit it. So when Nicolette met Hugh Bairnsfather he changed his surname to Bairnsfather-Cloete so that on their marriage Nicolette was able to inherit Alphen in trust until a male heir was born, and Alphen would remain in the Cloete family. When Henry died, Nicolette and Hugh's son Pieter inherited the farm, but as he was still a child his parents managed it for him until he came of age. Sadly, Pieter was killed in the Second World War and never actually inherited Alphen, which was then inherited by his younger brother

Sandy. (Ouma stayed on there in a wing as the South African version of a dowager.) A widow with a title or property derived from her late husband. The other three sisters (of which Deliana was one) were destined to be married off with only a lavish dowry. As I write, Alphen remains in the Bairnsfather-Cloete family. It has been turned into a luxurious hotel, and one can still find the foundation stone to the Great Cellar laid by Deliana Cloete (Ouma) and engraved with her name and the date of the occasion.

The only time I remember meeting Ouma was when we made a visit in 1953 - when I was three. Mum took all four of us girls without Dad (or our nannies, as a couple of Coloured maids had been enlisted at the other end to look after us) on a plane - an old Dakota DC3 - from Durban to Port Elizabeth, where Ouma was staying with Mum's parents. We spent a couple of weeks in their house in George, in a part of the Cape called 'The Wilderness' (a trip after which Mum repeated adamantly, "I don't know what I was thinking. I must have been stark staring mad!" every time the subject came up.)

My clearest recollection of that trip was that, after we'd boarded, and I'd fought for my seat at the window, I could see Dad, with Evalina hovering nervously behind him, standing close to the runway next to our car waiting to wave us off. As the mighty engines cranked deafeningly into life and the massive plane began to taxi, I saw Evalina sink to her knees in the short grass, throw her pinny over her head and begin keening in that wailing, ululating fashion so typical of a Zulu woman in mourning. It might have been my imagination, but I swear I could hear her wailing over the noise of the engines. After we'd returned weeks later, Evalina told me that she'd been convinced that that would be the last time she'd ever see any of us again – that we'd been swallowed up into a huge silver bird and taken off into the sky and out of sight.

I remember Ouma looking very old and wizened, with a walnut-like wrinkled face, sitting in a rocking chair in the corner of the sitting-room. Being a widow, she was always dressed from head to foot in black, including an old-fashioned Boer-style bonnet. Dine's (then aged five years) recollection of our visit to Gran and Grandpa in George was (in her words): "I only remember very faintly seeing Ouma as a very old lady living with Gran and Grandpa. I seem to recall her crying out in pain - poor old thing. I was very young, but do remember you (me) crayoning on the walls, and us rocking Delia, still an infant, in an old wooden cradle on rockers," something we hadn't come across before and which we pushed to its very limit before she could actually take to the air and fly out. Sometimes it was a close shave before we got caught by one of the Cape nannies who knew nothing of the lengths Dine and I could go to, using our baby sister as a plaything. Our Zulu nannies were far more sussed to the extent of our mischievous ways and would have nipped it in the bud. Dine said, "I remember Grandpa being proud of his pullets, which he kept in a run in the back garden. To get us four unruly children out of the older women's hair, he took us to a beach where we looked for Pansy shells for Mum, but didn't find even one. Oh, and licking a piggy bank I had been given on the airport bus and wondering why it smelt so horrid."

Deliana (Gran), to judge from a miniature portrait of her at the age of 19, was an exquisitely lovely young girl. While her sisters married into Cape aristocracy (Nicolette married Hugh Bairnsfather, Reniera married Sir Herbert Stanley, and Mary married the 7th Earl of Strafford), she married a struggling ostrich farmer named Charles Southey who owned many thousands of acres of scrubland in the Karoo desert. They had a daughter – my mother – and a son, James.

They suffered a serious setback when, with the invention of the motor car, ostrich feather boas and big-brimmed elaborately trimmed hats decorated with fine feathers rapidly went out of fashion to be replaced by dust coats and goggles. He was stuck with large tracts of arid land perfect for rearing ostriches, but not much good for any other form of husbandry. He turned to sheep farming in a rather desultory fashion as the very sparse grazing could support only a few hundred sheep.

When Mum reached school age she was sent from their remote farm to live at Alphen with her aunt Nicolette. From there she attended Wynberg Girls' School, learned to waltz, play tennis, and acquire all the other essential social requirements desirable for a privileged young lady. Because Mum was so beautiful she was surrounded by young men at tennis and lunch parties, all seeking her attention and possibly her hand in marriage.

When the Second World War broke out, Mum joined the WAAFs (the Women's Auxiliary Air Force), where she met and fell in love with Dad, who was flying Maryland bombers for the South African Air Force and based in Cape Town.

Great-grandmother Ouma was a formidable woman, and so anti-British that she had supported the Germans during the Second World War, so it was with some trepidation that Dad, with his pure Scottish blood and British ancestry, and having already asked Charles Southey, also had to ask her (as was the tradition) for the hand of her favourite and most precious youngest granddaughter.

Dad's maternal grandfather (my great-grandfather) William George Brown (always known as WG) and his family owned two thriving industries near Aberdeen in Scotland. One was a woollen mill and the other an iron foundry. In the 1870s my great-grandfather discovered a lucrative trade in wool and iron goods to the 'natives' in South Africa, as well as settlers, both Boer and British. They had realised that what both the newly arrived and the indigenous populations needed most was three-legged cooking pots, stoves, and blankets, and the cast-iron wood-burning stoves especially became a much sought-after necessity for Afrikaner and English colonial families alike. 'Dover' stoves of all shapes and sizes, as well as buckets, pots and blankets were shipped out in great quantities.

WG Brown was a tough Highland Scot from the East Coast of Scotland and an astute businessman. His second wife, Elizabeth, a music teacher from Aberdeen, whom he married in 1922, identified in him a "hard-headed Scottish capacity for driving good bargains." WG was as parsimonious as he was plucky, and he was unsentimental in as personal relationships – both with his older son and his clients.

He moved to South Africa from Scotland in the late 1870s and opened a trading store in a small settlement called Rietvlei above the densely forested Karkloof Valley in the Natal Midlands. From there he settled in Pietermaritzburg, the capital of the Crown Colony of Natal and became a minor importer and wholesaler. As this enterprise grew, he decided to relocate to the commercial hub of the colony, Durban, where he opened WG Brown and Co.

WG Brown's first wife was called Dollie, who bore him four children, namely Helen (Nellie), who married Henry Anderson Barnby (known as Barnie).

Then came Hugh (the oldest son) born on 24 December, 1924. He married Helen Mary (affectionately known to the family as Aunt Maisie). She was a daughter of Archibald McKenzie and his wife, Helen Jesse Weddel. Maisie was the fourth child in a family of ten daughters and one son (he was the firstborn), an expansive brood, explaining Archibald's nickname of "ten-to-one McKenzie."

Hugh died pursuing his greatest passion: polo. This death was the result of an accident. He was playing in a semi-final at the South African polo championships in Pietermaritzburg. He collided with two other players, was thrown off his pony and hit the back of his head on the ground. Hugh Brown was rushed unconscious to Grey's Hospital, but it was too late to save him. His skull was badly fractured and he died of internal bleeding that night.

The third child, also a boy, was George (Bongo), who died tragically at the beginning of the First World War at the age of 21.

The youngest, a girl, was my grandmother, Grace Mary, known as "Mollie" who married Allen Ross.

After the death of Dolly, WG Brown remarried, this time to

Elizabeth Christie from Aberdeenshire and clearly a talented musician. WG bought her a Bechstein piano and she seems to have been very happy with him in their short period of married life. Five years after their wedding, WG succumbed to blood poisoning.

The export business prospered so well that, to save the high cost of shipping small amounts of their goods on slow and usually unreliable steamships, they built an enormous warehouse in Durban, (a small, newly-established settlement on the Natal and Zululand coast) which was flourishing so rapidly that it had grown into being the principal town and port.

The Browns quickly filled their giant three-story warehouse to its maximum capacity. The family became a registered company, and also began accumulating and selling other stock; necessities such as linen, crockery, cutlery and other items from gunpowder and dynamite, to sweets, clothes, shoes and saucepans, wax candles and matches, as well as saddles, tents and all manner of goods that were essential to anyone who was trying to carve a new living out in the African bush. When the very prosperous WG Brown business was firmly established, he bought Monaltrie (a beautiful Victorian three-story mansion) built on the cool slopes of the Berea in Durban – a leafy hillside overlooking the Indian Ocean and the beautiful blue Durban bay, and out of range of the swampy, mosquito-ridden mangroves of Durban harbour. Framed by rows of palms and flamboyants, the Browns' home, Monaltrie, was built in 1897 for the Consul of Belgium. Designed in the Queen Anne revivalist style with red face brick, white painted balustrades, half-timbered gables, several verandas and entrance portico. The three-storey villa, 59 Musgrave Road, was set on a large property that extended all the way up to Essenwood Road above. Today it is a national monument.

As soon as the house was bought, and after the defeat of the Boers in the war that established that it was the British who would rule the country, WG decided to settle permanently in South Africa, and enjoy the benefits of the boom of a developing nation, as well as a much kinder climate.

Sugar farmers, cattle and sheep ranchers, and of course the many African tribes needed essential provisions, anything from a saddle to a pin, all of which could be provided by the massive WG Brown warehouse, and that far-sighted man was only too happy to supply all the small trading stores that mushroomed up all over the country, wherever there was a settlement of farmers. As a result, WG's youngest (and clearly his favourite) daughter, Grace Mary (always known as Molly), my father's mother, was a privileged young lady from an extremely wealthy and doting family; when she came of courting age there was no shortage of hopeful suitors.

On Dad's father's side, his great-great-grandfather, George Ross of Knockbreck House in Tain, Scotland, is an enigma. It's clear, since the original 'big house' is still there, that he was also born into a wealthy family. As Dad was always very vocal when it came to our highly successful Brown family history, it was odd that he always clammed up whenever we asked him about Grandpa Ross's background, and how he'd come to be born in South Africa to a cattle-farming settler. We got nothing from Dad, and it was always interesting to us that he appeared to treat Grandpa, his own father, with some degree of contempt. He never, ever went to visit him, even when Mum took us four girls over to spend almost every Sunday afternoon with him at his smallholding at Fort Nottingham. Circumstances became a lot clearer when I read a book, written by Pat McKenzie (a cousin-by-marriage to Dad), who has done extensive research into the settlers of Zululand and the Natal Midlands. He reveals that the Ross's did indeed come out to South Africa, and, along with so many of the 1820 settlers, had fallen upon hard times.

George Ross, of Knockbreck House in Tain in the Scottish Highlands, had nine surviving offspring (there were thirteen born altogether to his long-suffering wife Christine, but four children in various stages of infancy died in those extremely hard times, a common occurrence among the settlers). Although most of George and Christine's surviving children were daughters, there were two sons, the older of whom was James Ross, and my great-grandfather George.

In the 1840s, disillusioned and fed up by all the Bushmen raids on their livestock, a lot of the Boers who tried but failed ranching in Zululand and the Midlands, sold their farms to new, raw and unsuspecting Scottish and English settlers, who then had to endure the same, and worsening, deprivations. The Boers moved on in their covered wagons, up over the formidably difficult Drakensberg mountain range, to the vast, flat and arable plateaus of the Orange Free State where there were no mountains or thick mist for the Bushmen to hide in. Times were so hard that a farm of several thousand acres could be sold for next to nothing, and, in more than one instance, traded for a bottle of whisky.

The Bushmen raiders in the foothills of the Drakensberg Mountains, where the new settlers' ranches were situated, began to team up with Africans from the umKomasi valley, and they formed even bigger, stronger raiding parties, taking up to 100 head of cattle or more plus horses to use in the next raids, off a single farmer in one night. James Ross was one of these unsuspecting settlers, and had built a beautiful stone farm-house on a large property originally called 'Vlakplaats' which he'd bought from a Boer farmer. James renamed his home 'Greystones', and it changed hands a couple of times, each time the land being divided into smaller and smaller parcels, until they became effectively non-viable for grazing enough stock to keep a family alive, let alone make a profit. There were no alternatives such as growing crops either, as nightly damage by baboons, bush pigs, monkeys and antelope made it impossible to get any kind of crop past the seedling stage, let alone be able to harvest them.

Great-grandfather George was born in Pietermaritzburg, and married a Miss Anne Chadwick. They farmed at 'Onverwacht' (between Fort Nottingham and the village of Nottingham Road), another ex-Boer piece of land, which also changed hands frequently (until it eventually became the experimental station for chicken 'factory farming' – a new and pioneering venture in the 1970s). In 1883 George and Anne produced Allen, Dad's father (our grandfather). There are no exact records of how many surviving siblings Grandpa had, but Dad said that Grandpa had eleven of them. There wasn't enough land for anyone other than Allen, being the oldest son, to be able to farm the land successfully; his brothers had to make their own way in the world, with no family fortune to fall back on. This was when Dad always stopped any more talk of Ross ancestry.

I discovered that the younger Ross brothers teamed up and became haulage contractors – known then as transport riders. They moved to Pietermaritzburg (the capital city of Natal), the city nearest to 'Onverwacht', and there they settled, to build ox-wagons using local hardwood cut from the surrounding forests. They loaded the wagons with gum-tree poles, specially grown in Natal and Zululand as pit props for the gold, diamond and coal-mines, because they grew to the right size within five years and were straight and strong. There were also goods such as blasting equipment for all the flourishing mines that were burgeoning everywhere on the young subcontinent. Sacks of sugar, now being grown on the Zululand coast, and even crates of liquor - in fact anything that came in from overseas into Durban harbour and was destined for Jo'burg - had to be sent up by ox-wagon.

The brothers hauled their goods up through Natal, the Orange Free State, and all the way to the Transvaal, (about 400 miles), usually using a span of sixteen oxen, plus a few spare in tow. They employed a 'voorloper' (usually a young barefoot Zulu boy walking in front) to walk at the head of the team leading the two front oxen that were yoked together. There was an Afrikaner driver who wielded a long hippo-hide stock whip, walking alongside, to keep the oxen pulling evenly, and as one. One of the brothers would ride alongside on horseback, frequently going ahead to scout the easiest routes and ascertain where the best crossings could be found over the numerous, and often flooded, rivers in their way. All their own supplies had to be taken along, as well as plenty of gunpowder and bullets to shoot game, which they badly needed to augment their meagre provisions. Poultry went along on the wagons, to be let out of their travelling *hoks* (coops) at dusk when the team outspanned, usually near a river crossing where the oxen could drink and, hobbled with riempie (rawhide straps), graze the veld. Sheep were let loose as well, to eat and drink, while the fowls pecked busily around and under the wagon, feasting on the bounty of insect life in the long grass.

The Ross brothers would often take their entire families along with them, because, for one reason, it cost too much to put them up in rented lodgings in the towns, and also the men could be away for anything up to a year, first delivering the goods to their various customers up on the Gold Reef, and then having to round up enough of a consignment to cover the costs of making a return trip worthwhile. So, the wives of the wagon owners or in some cases hired transport riders, and those of the Afrikaner drivers, went along, too - some of them giving birth to their babies en route. They had with them their children of all ages, and some took Zulu or other unattached African tribal women and girls to help with the little ones, and give a hand with collecting firewood, and cooking using the very same three-legged pots as those sold by WG Brown. If the transport riders could afford it, their families travelled in separate, canvas-covered wagons, otherwise they trundled along perched uncomfortably on top of the freight and, when the heavens opened or the frost bit into them during the brief, but harsh winters (the temperature could drop to -16°C on some nights up on the Highveld), taking shelter huddled under the tarpaulin that protected the goods.

Every evening, as the sun set, the little outspan would be a hive of activity, as the men hacked thorn branches off surrounding trees (usually the Umbrella Thorn Acacia which grows so profusely all over the veld), and stacked them in a circle to make a makeshift *boma* (thorn enclosure) to protect their cattle, a milk cow or two to provide fresh milk, as well as the sheep and most importantly of all, their very scarce and valuable horses. It had to be high enough to prevent a lion or leopard from clearing it, grabbing an animal, and carrying it off. There were also hungry hyenas and packs of wild dogs to be seen off, too; every man, woman and child had to join in to help with the work. They would build big bonfires all around the outer perimeter of the encampment and enclosure as it took more than a wall of thorns to deter a pride of hungry lions. The women gathered firewood, slaughtered and prepared a chicken, made *uPhutu* (a form of "thick mealie porridge") in the pots, milked the cow, saw to the children and generally scurried about, getting food ready for everybody. One of the brothers would take a rifle and go out to see if he could shoot antelope for much-needed meat, and whatever they didn't consume they cut into strips, salted and hung on the wagons to dry, to eat later as biltong. They would also scout for predators, and, if they could, shot one or two, if not, they fired at them as a deterrent, to prevent them from coming any closer.

After their meal prayers were said, and when all the animals were safely enclosed in the *boma* the women and youngest children settled to sleep on makeshift beds in the wagons. There had been instances when young boys had been snatched and carried off by hyenas - for lack of space in the wagon and who were thought old enough to sleep with the men under the wagons. The men took turns on guard duty, well-armed as they patrolled the outer perimeters of their tiny and vulnerable encampment. They had to be on the lookout for eyes glowing from the light of their bonfires, which they carefully tended all night feeding them with wood cut from the same thorn trees. Those men not on duty either slept under the wagons, or, if they had that luxury, inside the covered one with their wives and children. Almost every summer's night the sky would erupt in a blitzkrieg of a violent thunderstorm, and everybody cowered under the wagons, sheltering from hailstones as big as pigeons' eggs that clattered down on them with a ferocity that often killed some of their livestock. Bolts of lightning darted down too, like arrows of fire all around them. Occasionally wagons were struck, including their contents and those sheltering beneath; carnage ensued if they were carrying a load of gunpowder or dynamite. These same storms flooded every river, which in normal conditions would have been laborious to ford, so that the water overflowed its steep banks and became a massive, muddy, foaming, thundering torrent.

The biggest dangers lay unseen and hidden. The Anopheles mosquito, which thrives in marshy conditions, would feast on the travellers as they tried to sleep. Adults and children alike suffered from the, often fatal, malaria that they carried in their bite. Ticks, another almost invisible hazard, carry 'tick bite fever', a rickettsia-type of disease that leaves the sufferer feverish with blinding headaches that go on for weeks, and completely incapacitates them, much as malaria does; if the victim survived they were left weak and often permanently debilitated. The ticks attached themselves to the stock as well, and killed oxen with rinderpest, (also known as cattle plague), an infectious viral disease of cattle, which could almost wipe out a team of over sixteen oxen within days. Tsetse-flies, large biting flies that inhabit lowland veld areas and prefer moist conditions such as river valleys, feed on the blood of both animals and humans causing sleeping sickness (human African trypanosomiasis, otherwise known as 'African lethargy') in people, and *nagana*, a deadly and terminal parasitic disease in the animals. There was also lung sickness, (parasites that cause fatal pneumonia), blackwater fever, and redwater fever (caused by the same mos-quitoes that carried malaria). 'Salted' cattle and horses (the animals that had survived the various diseases, and had built some sort of resistance to the parasites carried by ticks, flies and mosquitoes), were a valuable commodity in South Africa in those days. Humans, especially European settlers, weren't so lucky, and more of them were carried off by tropical diseases than by any wars or conflicts that occurred in this developing country.

I suppose you could say that the Ross brothers were the original truckers, making themselves a fair sum of money in the process. It was a long, hard, trek, though, and the roads were no more than rutted tracks. Every river, if it was in flood (as it would be throughout the wet season, which is about ten months long), had to be crossed by swimming the oxen across. This meant off-loading the wagons on one bank and portering the cargo through strong currents perched on the heads of African porters, none of whom could swim, enlisted from tribesmen from local kraals, and happy to receive a haunch of venison or a pound or two of beads in exchange for a day's labour. Then the empty wagons had to be floated across, one by one, using 'buoys' made from cattle hides sewn together and somehow semi-inflated. Sometimes, when the rivers and streams were in full flood and the currents were strong, cattle, porters, wagons, and everything and everybody got swept away, some to drown, others to scramble to safety on a bank much further downstream. In those cases, the cargo (sometimes highly valuable items such as gold bullion and diamonds) was either lost forever, or spoilt if it was things such as sugar, flour, tobacco, gunpowder. The rivers were infested with crocodiles, hippos, and the parasite bilharzia, unseen and much more dangerous, which attacked one's liver and, in those days, was usually fatal.

In 1879, as a very young man barely out of his teens, Great-grandpa George Ross fought in the Anglo-Zulu War between the British Empire and the Zulu Kingdom. The ruling Zulu chief, Cetshwayo, (son of Zulu king kaMpande and half-nephew of the infamous and bloodthirsty King Shaka), had refused to comply with certain conditions laid out by Sir Henry Bartle Edward Frere (1815 – 1884), the British colonial administrator at the time, who then sent

# White Zulu                                      Fiona Ross

Lord Chelmsford (better known as Frederic Augustus Thesiger, second Baron Chelmsford – from 1844 – 1905) to invade Zululand. That war was notable for several particularly bloody battles, including a devastating victory by the Zulu at Isandlwana, as well as for being a landmark in the timeline of imperialism in the region. Great-grandpa didn't get embroiled in the notorious Battle of Isandlwana, but fought in small and ferocious skirmishes around the Northern Natal area, and when he wasn't fighting he had to return to 'Onverwacht' and carry on farming. These battles, however big or small, were to the death, and Great-grandpa would wade in to a tide of warriors, sometimes up to a thousand determined Zulus, all screaming and seeing the 'red mist' (a kind of battle fever that came upon them fuelled by intensive training and a mysterious witchdoctor's herbal remedy that gave them the strength to do a running march for three days at a time covering a hundred or more miles without stopping for rest, food, or water), firing his rifle frantically with one hand, and trying to manoeuvre his horse, (just a shaggy little Basutu pony) with the other. If he was dragged off, or his horse was stabbed and fell, then he was on foot, fighting bayonet to assegai, or even hand to hand until the rest of the impi was dead or ran away. Not many Europeans survived this kind of close combat. Debilitated from the countless diseases, scorched raw by the sun, and, unlike the crafty Boers who wore khaki and practiced clever guerrilla tactics, the soldiers in their scarlet woollen uniforms were a soft target. Eventually the war was a victory for the British and the end of the Zulu nation's independence.

I remember, and I couldn't have been much older than four at the time, Grandpa sitting comfortably in a cane armchair on our front veranda at New Forest, a cup of tea in his hand, regaling us girls with stories of his father's battles against Zulu warriors in various skirmishes that took place mainly in Northern Natal and Zululand. And this is one I remember.

It was midsummer and very hot. Great-grandpa was riding

back to where his fellow troops were camped out in the veld, somewhere near Ladysmith. He and his horse were tired and thirsty after several encounters with members of a Zulu impi, and, having dispatched them, had become separated from the rest of his commando (a squad of up to eight men). He saw a stream and dismounted, to lead his horse down the sloping bank for a long drink. He knelt down and scooped some water up in his hands and, as he drank, he thought the water tasted odd. He looked up, to see that a few yards further upstream, lying almost covered by the rippling water, was the corpse of a Zulu warrior. Unperturbed, Great-grandpa simply led his horse a little way upstream of the dead body to drink the clean water before remounting to continue his ride back to camp. We loved these stories and couldn't get enough of them, begging him to retell them over and over again, until we knew them by heart.

Grandpa Ross, as a rancher working alongside his father on 'Onverwacht', was a restless young man and loved to ride over to parties and dances at neighbouring farms. He became the original DJ, as he had a gift for music and played the piano by ear; he could pick up a tune if somebody whistled it or he heard a gramophone record, and so he was invited to all the dances. Grandpa, and often any of his brothers who might be visiting home, as well as any sisters he had (most of them ended up marrying local, young McKenzie farmers), would roll their dance clothes up carefully Zulu fashion so they wouldn't crease, and put them into saddlebags. Then they would get up at first light and ride for a day to a neighbouring farm, where the dance was to be held. There they would meet cousins and friends, and, with Grandpa at the piano, dance the whole night. Gramophones and records were a brand new fashion and the young farmers danced to those as well. All the farmers, some of them women, would dance until dawn and, after a hearty breakfast, collected their horses from the paddocks where they'd been turned out for the night, often in winter, scraping frost off their saddles. Then they'd ride the long journey back to their farmsteads to start another day's hard work on their far-flung ranches.

WG Brown, to get away from the oppressive Durban summer heat, would rent rooms in a hotel in the Dargle area for a month or two in January and February, and take his family up there by horse and carriage. When he tired of renting rooms, he bought a large piece of land at the top end of the Dargle valley, at the foot of a peak called the *iNhlosane*, and built a sturdy stone house, which he called Beverly.

That was how, at a dance in the Dargle district, a handsome young rancher from the Nottingham Road district, Allen Ross (Grandpa), caught Molly Brown's (Grandma) eye. They were married with a lavish wedding reception at Monaltrie (WG's house in Durban). WG Brown arranged for five thousand acres of fine ranching land in the foothills of the Drakensberg mountains (named by the early Boer settlers, because the outline, covered in snow except for six months in the summer, were so sharp and jagged that they resembled the scaly back of a dragon) to be pegged out by the bridegroom. (This was the standard method of land purchase in South Africa at the turn of the century: a day's ride out across the countryside and a peg placed in the ground at the furthest point, followed by a second day to set the other two pegs; was roughly five thousand acres.) WG then paid 20 guineas to the Crown, and gave the land to Allen and his beloved Molly as a wedding present. This privileged young couple named their land 'New Forest'.

As Grandpa was farming Beverly at the time, he used the land at New Forest to support and graze several thousand head of cattle and sheep, using Zulu herdboys to look after them. He had them build a kraal of huts for themselves and their families, and he also arranged to have a small fishing cottage built. This was a very functional small, square house built with homemade bricks, a corrugated iron roof, and had a deep veranda on the three sides that caught the full brunt of the African sun. The 'kitchen' was a Dover stove on the open back veranda, and the dwelling was perfect for

Grandpa to be able to go over there, taking Molly with him, and spend a few nights, seeing to his stock, as well as enjoying the magnificent trout fishing the river offered. The huge tracts of dense natural bush also offered good hunting, and the Rosses often arranged hunting parties there, where local and neighbouring farmers could spend the day, using their Zulu labourers as beaters, to shoot majestic *nKonka* (Bushbuck bulls) as well as Mountain Reedbuck, and even the tiny Grey and Blue Duikers, known locally as the 'Piti' Buck and no larger than a fox-terrier.

Dad was born in 1915 in his grandparents' home Monaltrie in Durban, and his sister Josephine was born there in 1918. His parents lived and farmed at Beverley until 1925 when they moved to New Forest. By the time of the Second World War, Grandpa and his Zulu farm labourers had built additions on to it by enclosing half the back stoep to make a kitchen, and adding bedrooms to both sides of the main hut part. Dad had enlisted to fly bombers for the South African Air Force, and at the end of the war arrived back with his new bride to claim his farm (New Forest, which he had mysteriously inherited directly from his mother Molly before she died, shortly after the war, in her late forties. This mystery as to why WG bought New Forest in Molly's name so that she held all the title deeds rather than her husband, has never been discussed or cleared up). Although Grandpa, with my gradually ailing grandmother, had gamely and very successfully run New Forest, with its 5,000-acre sheep and cattle ranch, he never got any thanks, recognition or appreciation from Dad, even though he'd made huge improvements to the place by building vast, thatched outbuildings, a water-mill, and carving a road into the steep hillside, which would allow ox-wagons and the jeep to get up the top part which held the majority of the best grazing on the plateau. Since he'd now been disinherited, Grandpa discretely moved into a small cottage in Fort Nottingham (about 12 miles away), remarried to a mature lady I only ever knew as 'Val', and they lived out their days in peace and quiet together. Beverly was sold, and the money invested in adding on to the house at New Forest, as well as buying more livestock.

Dad had no more to do with his father, other than to allow Mum to invite him and Val over for afternoon tea with us on the occasional Sunday. It all seemed very strange to me, to treat one's father effectively as an unpaid farm manager and then dismiss him without any thanks or acknowledgement.

~~~

# *3*
# The homestead

**I**n typical South African white-settler style, the farm house is built of timber cut from the forest, with a steeply pitched corrugated iron roof that extends over huge, deep verandas on the front and back, so as to cool and shade the rooms. To the right of the sitting-room, was a big dining-room with a heavy stinkwood chest of drawers taking up one wall, a fireplace and a long stinkwood sideboard along the opposite wall (stinkwood is a rich-looking, dark heavy wood, and was cut from the bush in front of the house. The wood has a pungent-smelling sap that gives it its name). We had a long, French-polished table that seated eight. Occasionally our midday meals in the dining-room were enlivened by a rustle and a thud as a snake, climbing through the variegated ivy that festooned the entire front of the house, arrived at the open sash window and slithered over the window-sill to fall onto the wooden floor inside the room. We would all jump to our feet and Mum would ring the bell for Makhaye or Masango. *iNyoka*! (snake!) she would call, and one, or both, of them would run in carrying a pair of iron tongs from the sitting-room fireplace. We moved out onto the front veranda while the snake was cornered and removed, and then went back to our seats to resume our meal.

In front of the house are lawns, garden, and paddocks that lead right down to the river bank, and on the other side of the river is another mountainside, which rises steeply forming the east side of our valley, and is covered by the dense, evergreen indigenous forest we call the bush. The house faces the bush, and between the two bottom paddocks, there is the dirt District Road that belongs to the

Government and runs the length of the valley. Early on my grandmother (Molly) planted a thick May hedge to block out the sight of the road, even though the only people who used it, were the nuns from the Roman Catholic Convent at Umgeni Poort, and a few Zulus on foot, bicycles, or horseback. Grandpa would tell us how he used to sit on the big wide front veranda when he and my grandmother were living there. He would have his feet up, a tall glass of chilled lager (courtesy of the cooler in the dairy) in his hand, and the twelve-bore shotgun loaded with rock salt propped against the arm of his white cane armchair.

On Saturday and Sunday afternoons, merrily drunk Zulus would come staggering past along the District Road, just out of sight below the hedge. They sang raucously at the tops of their voices, the songs echoing up and down the valley, which annoyed Grandpa.

"I don't want them making all that racket while I'm enjoying a well-earned pre-lunch drink," he would grumble. On these occasions, raising the shotgun to his shoulder, he fired both barrels over the hedge. Voices were cut short in mid-song, and there'd be a long silence, as the report echoed off the sides of the valley, then a sudden flurry and the thudding sound of bare feet running away in both directions as the singers bolted off down the road. After which there was terrified shrieking and howling at a safe distance from the house, and Grandpa would take a satisfied swig from his glass.

"That'll teach 'em to disturb my peace."

Sometimes we heard singing throughout the night as Zulu passers-by walked along the road in the pitch dark. "They sing because they're frightened," explained Grandpa. "They think the noise keeps away evil spirits and anything else that might pounce on them." It annoyed my parents as well, but they never went so far as to shoot over the Zulus' heads as Grandpa had done.

When Mum arrived on the farm as a bride in 1945, she'd naïvely had a clear vision of her future. Five thousand acres of excellent grazing promised a large herd of fine cattle and sheep; she could already picture her strapping young sons riding over the hills on their polo ponies, admiring the stock. But, as their daughters relentlessly arrived one by one, my father was forced to have a wing of four bedrooms and two bathrooms added on, ensuring that we four children were effectively well out of earshot. If any of us took ill or needed our parents in the middle of the night for any reason, and it had to be a very good one, we had to traipse all the way up the long passage, past the spare room, through Dad's dressing room and knock or called timidly through their shut door.

The dining, sitting and all the bedrooms had Bakelite bells hanging from the ceiling, all of which were wired to a panel in the kitchen. Obviously imported from a supplier to a large country house, each panel was numbered and labelled to drop down when the correct bell was rung. Even we children had bells in our rooms, but these had to be tied up one by one, out of reach of our mischievous little fingers as we got old enough to ring them, bringing an irate Masango shouting in angry Zulu at us for wasting his time. He was the only one in the house who could read a little English, but Makhaye had memorised them correctly, allowing him to bring early morning tea-trays in, or answer their summons to announce that supper was on the table or we needed more firewood in the sitting-room.

Beyond the dining-room was the *iGluzini* or *gluzeen* – the Zulu's version of a glassed-in veranda which, being north-facing, was always the warmest place in winter as it had the afternoon sun streaming in and a wonderful view up the length of the valley with the *inHlezela* peak standing sentinel at the north end. Just behind the house, my Grandmother had planted gum- (eucalyptus) trees in a semicircle, as a windbreak, and these had grown extremely rapidly, as gums do. They shot up to well over a hundred feet high, from where they loomed, towering over the house, rustling their dangling, dry, pungently eucalyptus-scented, pale bluish-green leaves in the very slightest of breezes. The stronger winds whipped their foliage to a constant roar, like waves breaking into rough surf, and I used to lie in bed in the dark on stormy nights imagining I was at the beach listening to the sound of the sea. It was only the regular thump-thump of their drums coming from the staff kraal that reminded me I was at home.

The gums were the bane of Mum's life, as they cast long shadows over the house well before the sun sank below the mountain, and it was almost impossible to grow anything underneath them. Their pungent sap drives off any other plant competition, and they were so enormous and thirsty that no other plants could survive in their vicinity. The gums also shed long strips of cardboard-like grey bark that dropped all year round onto the sparse kikuyu lawns that my mother had managed to coax out of the dusty, eucalyptus-saturated soil beneath the trees. After a big storm or high winds, their bark and leaves would lay scattered all over the garden, forcing her to take her team of garden girls off more important jobs to rake up the debris. "Bloody gums!" she would mutter almost every day. During one particularly fierce thunderstorm, a bolt of lightning hit a gum-tree instead of the tall lightning conductors on the roof of our house. The tree exploded in the most spectacular fashion as eucalyptus sap boiled through the trunk, and split it in half down the centre, blazing and spitting. Mum was delighted, and from then on hoped to get rid of the remaining gums in the same fashion, but (as the saying goes) 'lightning doesn't strike twice in the same place'.

So, after much nagging, Mum eventually persuaded Dad to arrange for a contractor to come and fell the worst offenders that remained.

The fact that they were so close as to be almost on top of the house, made the job of dropping these massive trees in just the right place extremely difficult, and Mum made us all go and stand as far away as possible, beyond the sheds behind the house, while the felling took place. The fact that the slightest miscalculation, or even a soft breeze, would cause one of the trees to drop onto the house, flattening it completely, didn't seem to concern her. Just so long as she got her way and rid of the gums was enough. Apparently, Dad felt it was worth risking the homestead just to get Mum off his case.

There was a big double garage with a storeroom alongside the saddle room, where Dad kept his tack and polo equipment, and at the back of the garage were two rooms where Masango slept. Makhaye had his own hut in the kraal, where he lived with one of his wives. Like most of the Zulus on the farm, they lived in iMpendhle, the settlement over the back of the mountain behind our house, and went home to their families for one long weekend a month. Next to the servants' rooms was another storeroom in which farm rations (sacks of government-subsidised sugar and mealie meal) were locked up, and there was an open lean-to workshop with a big vice and a huge anvil in an open shed beside the storeroom. In this there was a makeshift forge in which the farm manager shaped pieces of metal to repair the ox-drawn ploughs and mowers.

The smaller outbuildings, such as our dairy and laundry, and all the round huts in which the Zulus lived, were made from wattle and daub and were thatched in their traditional way, and stood at the very feet of the gum-trees, to take advantage of their cool shade. Just behind the kitchen there was a little wooden generator hut on stilts that housed the oily black Lister diesel generator, which provided electricity for the house until Escom, the national electricity supply commission (established in 1923 and later changed its name to Eskom) brought mains electricity to the house in the 1930s. However, we kept the generator operational because our mains electricity could always go down for several days at a time.

Big stables with a very high-pitched thatched roof were built behind the garage, and had about six or seven loose boxes in which the polo ponies stood every winter night, blankets on and contentedly munching warm, scalded oats. Snug and cosy, they were sheltered from the frost that settled everywhere at night. The grooms let them out as soon as the sun came over the bush-covered mountains, melting the frost within minutes, and the ponies galloped, kicking and cavorting, to their green winter kikuyu grazing in paddocks near the house. Sadly, one night in 1960, the massive thatched stable roof caught fire and burned it and its big adjacent shearing shed to the ground. The horses were out to summer grass at the time, and although my father didn't have the stables rebuilt, he had a corrugated iron roof put over the shell of what had been the shearing shed and much later parked his tractors there.

Beyond the stables, about a hundred yards further along the road, was the kraal - our compound where all our Zulu staff lived in various huts of their own along with their rangy fowls scratching about in the swept, bare earth.

Our labourers had their own wives and young children living there with them, although they also had homes in iMpendhle, the nearest African settlement way beyond the mountain behind our own homestead. There the rest of their family members, like elderly parents, extra wives and older children lived, along with their stock, including dogs, goats and donkeys which Dad did not allow on the farm.

There were always our dogs, though. When Mum and Dad first arrived on the farm, they brought two of the most incongruous pets (for them anyway) – a Pekinese called 'Feny Roo', and a Siamese cat. And then, before I was born, Dad bred Pointers. He had a lovely kennel and run built for them; it was a long, whitewashed, waist-high building with about six arched doorways and a deep thatched roof. As a toddler, I could crawl into each separate section and lie down with the puppies in their soft, warm, straw-filled (and, of course, flea-ridden) sack beds. We always had Pointers, and after Grandpa died in 1962, his Pointer, Spot, came to live with us.

When she was about twelve, Nicolette was given a puppy, a golden Cocker Spaniel, and about as brainless as dogs come; she named him Mups. When I was about seven, on coming home from a cattle sale, Dad told me to go and look in the office. It was lunchtime, and I went in there to find a small bundle of fluff in a cardboard box on the grass mat in front of his desk. He was a cross between a Peke and a Pomeranian, and we called him Pitz.

He was my dog, and a better one I couldn't have had. He was a constant and devoted companion, small as he was. His character was such that he immediately became the top dog among our pack of three. At that stage we were down to one Pointer, Grandpa's Spot. Spot and Mups submitted to Pitz, as he had brains enough for the three of them.

Whenever the baboons came into the garden it was Pitz who tore after them, barking in his high-pitched squeaky little yap, setting the others off. He could be apparently fast asleep at my feet while I read a book, curled up in a cane armchair on the front veranda, just out of reach of the baking heat of the morning sun. Suddenly, he would take off, yapping furiously, and race down to the May hedge, and there would be an explosion of grey furry bodies as the troop exploded from the long grass in the paddock below the garden. He'd chase the entire lot, seventy or more of them, across the field, and he was so small that he disappeared completely in the long grass. All I could see was the troop bolting back down to the river, and Pitz's progress given away by the waving of grass stems as he tore after them. I don't know what the baboons thought he was, but they never turned on him.

They could so easily have done it, too, and torn him to pieces without hesitation, as they did to some of the dogs in the pack that came with the 'baboon boy' (the local baboon pest control man). But in Pitz's case they always ran away from him as fast as they could, and he often managed to tree the entire troop, circling them on the ground underneath, growling and with his hackles raised, waiting for one of us to come and finish them off.

Another of Pitz's favourite activities was pig weighing. When Mum's pigs were ready for sale, she'd have them weighed. This involved a hessian sack, a scale with a hook on it hung from a gum-tree branch near the pigsty, and the pigs. The method was for our labourers to grab a pig by the back leg, stuff it head first into a sack and then hang the sack on the hook. Mum would stand there with her notebook, taking down each pig's weight. The squealing was deafening. Pitz normally gave the pigs a wide berth, although he could slip under the poles and into their sty with ease if he'd wanted to. But now they were in such distress he loved it, and spent a happy morning snapping at their heels as they were grabbed, and circling them when they were hanging upside down from the scales, yapping and snarling. He must have driven everyone crazy and got underfoot in the worst possible way, but our farm boys had enormous respect for Pitz, and even Mum was amused by his antics, and didn't have him banished.

When I went out on a ride, the dogs nearly always came with me, unless I was working with cattle or sheep, when Makhaye locked them up in the dairy until I was long gone. They ran along next to me, and if Pitz got tired, as he often did with his short little legs and extra heavy coat, I'd stop, let him catch up, take my foot out of the stirrup and let it dangle down near his head. He knew to jump up on my foot and I'd then lean down and grab his scruff and manhandle him onto the saddle. There he'd sit for the rest of my ride, on the pommel, regally taking in the scenery, while the others had to tag along behind in the dust and heat. If we came to a stream, a dam or the river, then everybody went in for a swim. My horse and the dogs would always slip in for a dip, and often I would as well, if it wasn't too close to the District Road.

Pitz, being so small, wasn't daunted by deep water, and swam with the best of them. He was weighed down by his extremely thick coat, but it didn't seem to slow him. The best thing about Pitz was that when I was eventually sent away to school, he didn't switch allegiance to Dad like the others did; he'd wait for me to come back, Dad told me. When I finally came home for a day out, after what seemed like years to both of us, he jumped into my arms to lick me and whimper with delight. Pitz spent many happy years on the farm until he died in his sleep at the ripe old age of fifteen.

~~~

# 4

# The shearing gang

Every spring the shearing gang arrived. This was a motley collection of up to fifteen rough-looking Basotho men. Quite unlike our familiar and more fastidious Zulus, who looked down their noses at them with unconcealed distaste, these strangers had beards and rather shaggy hair. They were tribesmen from Basutuland (now called Lesotho), a little-known African kingdom high up in the mountains beyond the Drakensberg range.

Tied around their shoulders were blankets of ochre and mustard coloured wool, intricately patterned with black symbols, and on their heads conical straw hats, the same shape as the thatched roofs of the mud huts behind our house, and they moved around the district from farm to farm to do the spring shearing. They had a young white man in charge, who drove the lorry they travelled in, and did all the wool sorting. I don't know where the Basothos slept, but their overseer was billeted in our thatched laundry, as far away from the house as possible. Masango carried his food down on trays, and he used the bathroom at our end of the house to shave and wash.

We children were deliriously excited when the shearing gang arrived, as it was quite an event in our rather under-stimulated, uneventful lives. We weren't allowed anywhere near the gang and especially not to speak to the overseer, or to hang around him whatsoever. "He's a very ordinary little man," sniffed Mum, and he wasn't invited to set foot inside the house, other than to come and go through the outside door of the end bathroom to wash, but I remember trying to spy on him through the keyhole of our bathroom while he shaved at the washbasin, not for prurient reasons, but simply because it was something to do.

"Just watch out!" warned Dad, the day the gang arrived.

"Basothos eat cats, so you'd better hide yours!" With terrified squeals my sisters and I would race off to find our cats. Dine had a big, grumpy, pitch-black cat called Vespa, after the evening star, because he had a tiny white patch on his chest. He was bad tempered simply because Dine and I couldn't resist dressing him up in our dolls' dresses; we would stuff his black paws into little pink cardigans, cram a knitted bonnet over his furious, flattened-back ears and pin him down, yowling in protest, in our dolls' pram with a shawl tucked firmly in under the little mattress, and push him around over the bumpy ground. These games always ended in tears as he finally struggled free, hissing and growling, and clawed us savagely when we tried to retrieve the clothes from his furry black body as he bolted off down the driveway.

Delia had a cat called 'Birds Bath'. She was given a grey and white kitten for her sixth birthday and we were all sitting on the front veranda before lunch, admiring it. "What are you going to call it?" asked Mum. Delia looked nonplussed and then gazed around at our enquiring faces looking for help. Frantically she searched around in her head for a name, and finally, in desperation, she looked around her.

"Birds Bath!" she said triumphantly as her eye fell on a stone basin placed on a pedestal in a flowerbed at the bottom of our big lawn for that very purpose. "Birds Bath?" Dine and I had simultaneously exclaimed with delighted disbelief, but then we caught Mum's eye and she just pressed her lips together and shook her head.

We exploded into ill-concealed mirth and had to stagger off snorting and giggling, to re-compose ourselves out of sight behind a bush of sweetly scented red Salvia.

So, Dine and Delia ran to find Vespa and Birds Bath, and I

headed for the sheds to try and round up the half-dozen or so semi-wild stable cats that lived outside, earning their place in the hierarchy of our farm animals by keeping the rat population down. Scratched, bloodied, and struggling with our cats, we staggered into the dairy where we thought we could keep them locked up for the next ten days. In the ensuing excitement, as the gang of Basothos settled in and the shearing went into full swing, we forgot all about our cats, which was just as well, because Makhaye had already let them out when he went in to operate the hand-turned separator to get some cream for supper.

Our five thousand or so Merino sheep were rounded up from all corners of the farm and herded into the shed, a hundred at a time. Each Basotho shearer grabbed one, manhandled it into the stables next door and wrestled it to the ground. There he expertly gripped his sheep between his knees while, with lightning speed, he clipped its wool away with a pair of hand shears. Within minutes the bewildered and newly shorn sheep, now looking skinny, half their previous size, and sporting a brand new pale cream-coloured suede-looking skin, was allowed to scramble to its feet and was then promptly grabbed by one of our Zulu labourers who branded it with R for Ross in silver paint. It then had its mouth wrenched open with a special, but rather crude-looking long oval metal instrument, and a dollop of bright turquoise powder – some sort of copper sulphate treatment against internal parasites – was unceremoniously shoved into its mouth, and released.

The sheep then bounded off to join its shorn mates, leaping high like a startled antelope, unused to the new feeling of antigravity without its heavy fleece to encumber it. My and my sisters' contribution to shearing was to help our labourers trample wool. About ten enormous hessian sacks were each suspended by four strong hooks from beams that criss-crossed under the stable's thatch, and had bundles of wool tossed into them by the sorter's assistant. Each sack was marked in red paint, with letters and numbers stencilled on its side to show what grade of wool it contained. The sorter stood at a long slatted wooden table, greasy from many years of lanolin, and graded each fleece as his Basotho assistant flung it open along the table, creamy-white shorn side up. They both trimmed the rough edge by simultaneously moving around the table pulling the dirty wool off with their hands, and the assistant then bundled it up, still shorn side up, ran to the sack and threw it in.

We climbed up into the sacks, pulling ourselves up the sides like monkeys, and jumped in onto the soft, warm wool. We spent hours in there, ostensibly tramping round and round in our bare feet compacting the wool to make room for more, but in reality we sat there in the semi-dark, our sacks rocking gently to and fro as more and more fleeces were dumped on top of us. The slightly dusty hessian sack scent mingled nicely with the sweet hay-and-sheep smell of the wool, and we found the constant clip-clip-clipping sounds of sheep-shears pleasantly soporific. We dozed comfortably to the background of constant baa-ing and the Basotho shearers singing softly, their deep voices rising and falling in harmony, enchanting unknown melodies sung in a strange language. When we were eventually flushed out by Evalina at bath-time our legs and feet were covered in lanolin from the wool and felt deliciously soft and smooth.

~~~

# 5

# The baboons

In 1945 Mum got the Zulu women to dig a quarter of an acre of the rich, dark soil behind the house, and began growing vegetables. As the mealies (maize) grew silky tufts to their soft, green ears, the baboon troop slipped silently in at dawn and wrenched the plants out, eating the mealies and trashing what was left. They also dug up her new potatoes and stripped the vines of pea pods. She was outraged, and Dad offered to fence the plot with strong chicken wire, including the top, to prevent any more such raids. For reasons best known to herself, Mum refused this offer, thinking, I suppose, that she wasn't going to let any baboon get the better of her, and for the next sixty years the baboons led her a merry dance.

When my great-grandfather bought the 5,000 acres, the baboons had already been there for centuries; a troop of about 80 chacma baboons live in the rocky outcrops high in the hills, and forage in the dense natural forests that carpet the valley.

The baboons developed a strategy of stealth around the new humans who had encroached upon their territory, and of course had all day in which to monitor the house while Grandpa built, and after the War ended, Mum went about the business of creating a home. She started to get up even earlier in the morning than the baboons, lying in wait for them in the long grass behind her veggie patch, with the 4:10 shotgun. Dad told her she'd never get a baboon with birdshot, but she proved him wrong. Early one morning in 1955 she somehow managed to tree the whole troop. Several baboons were cowering high up in a pine tree, having pulled the branches around them for cover.

She saw a grey paw reaching out to pull some more pine needles across to camouflage its fur, and fired into the tree. A medium-sized baboon dropped out of the tree, having let go in fright, and fell heavily, breaking its neck instantly.

Mum was thrilled. Delighted with her victory, she rang the local newspaper, the *Natal Witness,* who sent a reporter the hour and a half journey on dirt roads to take a photo of her, wearing a blue cotton shirt, a denim skirt and veldskoens and holding the shotgun, triumphantly posed next to the dead baboon. She kept the picture framed on her dressing table. The troop continued to plague her though, and we were often woken at the crack of dawn by shotgun reports rending the still, tranquil dawn air and echoing around the valley.

Mum had another goal: to exterminate the flocks of fluffy, grey Speckled Mousebirds (*iziNdlazi*) that swooped in flocks on to her Namaqualand daisies and nipped the buds off before they flowered. She would lie in wait in their bedroom at dawn, elbows resting on the windowsill, and blast them as they settled – the noise causing us to leap from our beds in surprise. On meeting Mum, people saw her as a slender, blonde blue-eyed beauty, with exquisite manners that revealed her aristocratic background – a lady with a privileged upbringing. When the war broke out and she joined the WAAFs (Womens' Auxiliary Air Force) she was in her early twenties. Because of her steely determination, Mum rose to the rank of Sergeant-major and became an excellent shot. This same resolve was now directed to creating her version of a perfect home and garden in the lovely valley, with the river a silver ribbon winding through the dark green forest. With her single-minded obsessive passion, she planted fruit trees, ornamental cherry trees and masses of shrubs, all of which bore ripe, succulent, scarlet berries in the autumn. The baboons were drawn to this bounty, and every year, silently like brown ghosts, they would creep into the garden and strip the fruit and berries off the trees, breaking off big branches and often uprooting the bushes in their enthusiasm.

We loved the baboons. I enjoyed watching them as they frolicked in the paddocks just beyond the garden, and on the banks of the river. They would graze happily on the rye grass that Dad had sown for green winter-feed for the livestock, pulling up great tufts of the sweet, juicy shoots and stuffing them into their cheek pouches. The baby baboons would jump and play while the adults gorged themselves. One or two of the older males sat on boulders and kept watch while the troop moved quietly along the peaceful valley.

My sisters and I could choose whether to lie on the lawn, gazing at the tranquil scene unfolding below us, or have some sport. We would race across to where Mum was bent over in a border, weeds flying out behind her, along with a small cloud of dust and earth, and whisper "Baboons in the paddock, Mum."

The effect was immensely satisfying as she'd rip off her gardening gloves, throw them onto the lawn and run into the house for her 4.10 shotgun. Quickly she'd load it with cartridges, and then start her leopard crawl towards the hedge that shielded the garden from the paddocks. Slowly she'd rise to her feet, the weapon to her shoulder. We'd always have a last-minute pang of conscience, and, as Mum was about to squeeze the trigger, one of us would manufacture a loud sneeze to warn the troop. The startled baboons would scatter in all directions, and, with loud warning barks amid shrieks of terror, scamper as fast as they could into the depths of the forest. Mum would lower her weapon and round on us as we prepared to melt away with the same alacrity as our primate cousins had. "Why did you have to scare them off?" she'd demand indignantly. "I could've got one."

"nKosizana – did you see the baboons this morning?" Makhaye would ask me conversationally, as he was clearing away the breakfast dishes. "They were down in the paddock, there," and he pointed out towards the river. "I saw them pulling up and eating the new rye grass shoots *nKonsane* (Dad; literally 'Chief's son) planted for the cattle." He'd pause and started to cackle, shaking his head ruefully. "Then your mother saw them, and she shouted for the dogs to chase them. Those dogs ..." By now he had both hands on his bent knees he was laughing so much "... they were barking, and they ran down and chased the baboons off. Fast. Right into the bush." He was gasping for breath between gales of laughter as he demonstrated the scene with both hands. With his left, he depicted baboons running along by galloping his black fingers, chased by his right-hand paddling the air to represent our dogs in pursuit, all accompanied by the caterwauling noise he made in his expert mimicry of terrified, shrieking baboons. "... even your dog, Pitz. That dog, small as he is, was out in front chasing those baboons!" Makhaye stood for a moment, shaking his head and clicking his tongue in admiration. None of our farm staff ever got over the discrepancy between the size of Pitz and his capacity for bravery – or, more to the point, recklessness.

Makhaye would put his hands down, picked up the big wicker tray again and, still chuckling with mirth, make his way slowly and rather reluctantly back to the kitchen. I loved these interludes. I got as much pleasure out of the baboons' antics as the Zulus did, especially Makhaye, and always enjoyed his imitation of their behaviour, copied from his years of covertly watching them when he was outside doing chores such as fetching firewood from the sawmill, or collecting veggies from our garden.

Grandpa had been aware of the baboons' nuisance value as soon as he first settled and started grazing sheep on the farm. To supplement the sparse winter grazing he would put troughs in the paddocks and fill them with mealie kernels. Immediately the troop started raiding, eating all the mealies as soon as it was put there. Grandpa employed *umfaans* (Zulu boys) to stand guard over the troughs and throw stones at the baboons to chase them off, and so allow the sheep to eat their fill each day.

This system worked well enough, until Grandpa was at a stock sale in our nearest village, and, while comparing notes with other farmers, was told by an old Afrikaner Boer that there's a simple way to rid any farm of baboons: you build a trap and bait it with ears of mealies, and when you have caught a baboon, you paint it white and release it again. The baboon would race off to join its troop, but the rest of the animals would run away from it as they wouldn't recognise it as one of them. Thus, the entire troop would just keep on running, off the farm and into the Drakensberg mountains, never to be seen again.

So, Grandpa built a sturdy baboon trap out of strong timber, right near the edge of the bush, alongside the river, where they were often seen foraging for food. It had a gate that dropped down firmly once the mealies were disturbed – but all he ever caught was guinea-fowl, which are also partial to mealie kernels.

Many years later, Mum developed her own version of the baboon trap. This was a big wire cage from an old bakkie that was used to take sheep to the stockyards, propped up on bricks on one side. This contraption was placed carefully just outside a mud hut, home to Mattheus, our Zulu tractor driver. He was to bait the trap with mealies, last thing at night and then lie hidden on his bed at dawn, holding a long piece of string leading from the trap into his hut. When a baboon crept into the cage to steal the mealies Mattheus would yank the string hard, pulling the cage down off the bricks. Amazingly, this worked. At five the next morning an excited Lefina arrived, panting, at my parents' bedroom door to tell them that Mattheus had caught a big baboon. Mum was delighted, and, waking Dad, said, "Go and shoot it!" Grumpily, he put on his dressing gown and sheepskin flying boots, loaded the 12-bore and trudged up to Mattheus's hut on the hill behind our homestead.

There he found a crowd of interested Zulu farmhands gathered round the trap. A terrified baboon cowered in the corner, shivering with fright, its paws clamped over its face. Without a word

# White Zulu                                            Fiona Ross

Dad lifted the corner of the trap, shoved the baboon out with his foot, and, as it raced over the horizon to freedom, he raised the gun and fired both barrels into the sky. Then he turned to his staff and put his finger to his lips. Nobody would tell. This was a vendetta between Mum and the baboons. He had no quarrel with them.

Then he went back to bed, saying curtly to Mum: "I've done it. Just don't ever ask me to shoot a trapped baboon first thing in the morning again. If you want them dead, you must shoot them yourself."

For several years the trap lay unused, but when Mum started to have further, and more brazenly impudent baboon trouble, she and Mattheus resurrected the trap and set it up again. By this time, in the late 1970s, we had all married and were living in various parts of the country, raising our own children. Often, at weekends, we came up to the farm to spend time with Mum and Dad and indulge our sons in their favourite pursuit – trout fishing. It was late on a warm Saturday afternoon, and our entire family was up at the lake fishing.

John, married to my older sister, Diana, was by himself in the house, watching a rugby match on television. He was disturbed by a small, noisy group of farm workers banging on the kitchen door and all trying to tell him something. John grew up in Johannesburg and is a townie. He can't speak a word of Zulu, but was told by Lefina, in her few words of halting English, that Mattheus had caught a baboon in the trap, and he must come and shoot it. John knew the guns were all locked away in the gun safe, but he had no idea where the key was kept. Then he remembered the old Boer story about painting a baboon white and letting it go, so he asked Lefina, in sign language, whether there was any white paint in the house. After a thorough hunt through Mum's storeroom, she eventually reappeared triumphantly holding an aerosol can of silver spray paint, which we used to decorate fir-cones at Christmas time.

John is a Chartered Accountant, a tall, fastidious man with a gentle soul and impeccable manners. Much loved by our family, he's always willing to please, especially Mum. So, followed by an excited, chattering entourage of the entire farm labour force of about forty Zulu men, women, and a large number of whooping, jumping children, John ran up the hill to the trap. Shaking the can vigorously, he advanced on the cowering baboon, and proceeded to start spraying the animal with silver paint. Understandably the baboon took fright and ran round and round the wire cage, trying to escape the terrifying hiss and spray coming from the can. John had to run round and round as well, attempting short bursts from the nozzle at intervals. There was silver paint everywhere. Every time he managed to get a direct jet onto the animal, it shook itself vigorously, splattering him and the cage with paint. The terrified baboon also lost control of its bowels, and its loose, stinking dung became mixed in with the silver paint. Eventually the can ran dry. Panting but triumphant, John stood back to admire his handiwork. There was a small amount of silver paint on its fur, but most of it covered John and the cage. He told the onlookers to lift the cage to release the baboon, which took off at speed, stopping only to pick clumps of silver dung off its coat and flick it to the ground. By the time it reached the brow of the hill it was almost clean again. John, covered from head to foot in silver and holding the empty can, had to trudge, defeated, back to the house for a turpentine clean-up and a long bath.

# THE MINKEY

In 1985 my husband, George, as manager of a small branch of Barclays Bank in Pietermaritzburg, was approached by the curator of the Natural History Museum for an overdraft in order to fund some very necessary renovations to their exhibits, some of which had been on display since the turn of the century. As a child I had loved visiting the museum, and once or twice Dad had taken us as small girls. Overawed and clutching his hand tightly, we'd gaze at the live, writhing, venomous snakes in their glass case in the foyer, and crane our necks to stare up at the massive, lifelike stuffed bull elephant that took up the entire floor space of the main hall.

The curator offered George a tour of the museum, including a look behind the scenes at their taxidermy workshop, to show how the money he intended to borrow, would be spent. When George mentioned this visit I asked if I could come too, and bring our two boys who were on holiday from prep school. On the day, George wasn't able to get away from the office, so the boys and I spent an interesting morning seeing how the exhibits were prepared and displayed.

Just before we were to be ushered out of the workshop for a cup of tea, I saw the foot of a primate, half-covered in sawdust, sticking out from under a workbench. Intrigued, I asked the curator what it was, and he told me they were about to throw it out. It was an adult chimpanzee, and well past its best. It had been on display for seventy years, some of the fur was starting to fall out, and it was looking a bit mangy. The museum had applied for a new specimen from the Far East and they were going to renovate the display niche with its painted jungle-like surroundings, putting the new ape in place of this one.

I was suddenly struck with an idea. On the spur of the moment I asked, if they were going to throw it away, could I have it? Surprised, the curator said, yes of course. We pulled it out, brushed the sawdust off it and I had a better look at my new acquisition. Frozen in a half crouch, with its long arms dangling, it stood about four and a half feet high, and had a rather distant gaze to its soulful, brown glass eyes.

It was too big for us to carry, so the curator arranged to have it sent over to the bank later that afternoon.

As promised the chimpanzee was delivered by a Zulu messenger, and since George was still out, the bank staff seated it in his chair behind the huge desk in the manager's office. Apparently he was more than astonished to find it sitting there when he arrived back, and being a good sport, he put it in the front passenger seat of his car, the seat belt strapped over its shoulder, and drove home.

I wrapped it up as best I could, with colourful birthday paper, wrote a card and, with Mum's birthday the following Saturday, the boys and I took it up to the farm to present her with it.

She was thrilled with her gift. She called it "the Minkey" after a Pink Panther movie she'd seen on television, in which Peter Sellers, as Inspector Clouseau, had chastised an organ grinder in the street, saying, as he scraped dung off his shoe onto the cobbles, "Get your feelthy minkey off the street!".

Mum got Jomela to put up a sturdy pole in the middle of the veggie patch, and between them they mounted this large, stuffed ape, posed upright and if one didn't look too closely at it, appearing very realistic.

The arrival of this new ape created quite a stir among the Zulu farm staff. During their midday lunch hour, they all gathered at the veggie patch to have a look at it. Dad was there as well.

"Have any of you seen an *umFeni* (baboon) like this before?" He enquired of the enthralled group in Zulu.

"Yes! I've seen one of these before." Said one of the older men. "I saw it at the circus riding a bicycle."

"Hau! An *umFeni* like this riding a bicycle?" The rest of them gasped and clicked in awe, clapping their hands over their mouths. It had been a long time since the Boswell Wilkie Circus had come to Nottingham Road.

In the 60's it had been the tradition every year for the circus to arrive on the Durban to Johannesburg train, stopping off at a field next to the Nottingham Road stockyards next to the railway station, to raise their big top for three or four nights, enabling all the local farming communities to attend a show. Each farmer, including Dad, packed his family into the car and arranged for a tractor and trailer to take their Zulu staff along for this treat.

In our case, since we didn't have a tractor, we used the old ex-army Willys Jeep to pull a trailer load of our excited house and farm staff to Nottingham Road to see the circus.

Eventually, the novelty wore off, the labourers went back to work, and the minkey kept solitary vigil in the veggie garden. Not a single baboon went near that garden for the next five years.

Mum was delighted with her new acquisition, and every time I spoke to her on the phone she crowed happily about the success of my birthday present to her. She was able to plant mealies, pumpkins and even raspberries, something she'd never been able to do before the minkey arrived. She looked after it carefully. In the summer, if a thunderstorm threatened, she sent Jomela running to cover the minkey with a plastic fertilizer bag.

During the short, dry winter season when nothing was growing for the baboons to raid, it had a place in the corner of the cool, thatched dairy, where it was kept safe, carefully wrapped in a sack. Mum even sprinkled the interior of the sack with Rattex poison pellets in case it was nibbled by rodents.

In early spring Mum and Jomela would pull the Minkey out again, brush it down and reinstate it on the pole. Now and again a seam would split and some of the sawdust stuffing would start to ooze out. Mum painstakingly stitched it back up as one would a favourite, but tattered old teddy bear, mending the rips with a big curved needle and baling twine (left over from sewing up wool bales in the days when Dad had the Basuto shearing gang in to shear our sheep and shipped the wool to Durban).

Mum loved to entertain. She'd have friends to stay, held lunch and tennis parties and, once a year even hosted a visit from the local garden club. As every visitor or family member replaced their teacups on the saucers after having arrived, after sometimes enduring a hot, two-hour drive from Durban, Mum would drag them off to the veggie garden to admire her Minkey.

One summer afternoon there was a tremendous thunder-storm. Hailstones, the size of golf balls came hurtling out of the sky and, despite its waterproof cover, the minkey's head was knocked right off by a big hailstone and fell to the ground. Mum was devastated and tried everything she could to reattach the head. Nothing worked, so, sadly, she stuck the severed head on an upright post at the gate and walked forlornly back to the house. The following morning, at first light, the entire troop of baboons crept silently in to the veggie garden and stripped it bare.

The troop of 80-plus baboons resumed their endless and systematic raids on Mum's vegetables, the orchard and especially the berries on her ornamental fruit trees, breaking branches off to leave the trees misshapen and damaged. Mum even went so far as to plant her pumpkin seeds in among the rose bushes to try and fool them. When the time came to harvest the pumpkins, I happened to be staying at the farm, and when Mum was showing me her roses, complete with big, fat nearly-ripe pumpkins semi-hidden among them. I voiced my doubt that the baboons would be that easily fooled and had probably been eyeing them until they were ripe, but my opinion was summarily dismissed.

A year beforehand, I'd become a member and secretary of the Natal Midlands Bird Club, a bird-watching society, and to engage with Dad, worked very hard to raise his interest in bird identification as we had a plethora of, often rare, species all over the ranch. To help him get to know our multitude of garden birds, my young boys made him a wooden bird table, which we hung from the tree directly outside the *gluzeen*, where he could see every avian visitor from the comfort of his favourite armchair. This was a resounding success, so much so that even Dad started putting out food for the birds himself, instead of getting the servants to do it. This was too much for Mum. Instead of allowing her aging husband this pleasurable little hobby, Mum had Jomela make a trap out of chicken wire, a cunningly clever thing, into which the, mainly mouse-birds, whose crime it was to nip the buds off her Namaqualand Daisies, preventing them from flowering, could creep in, but not out. She not only carefully placed the trap *on* the bird feeding table, but paid her three garden girls 50 cents per bird, for every mouse-bird they caught and wrung its neck. Every unfortunate little bird that went into that trap came to a sticky end. I remember seeing dead White-eyes, mouse-birds as well as so many other pretty little firefinches (a small African songbird of the waxbill family) and rare sparrows; their corpses all laid out neatly in a row on that huge wooden table on the back veranda which we called the 'polo ground'. They'd been carefully put there so that Mum could count them and pay up. She was unstoppable. Then Karma took over.

I was on my way from my bedroom to eat breakfast when Lefina came to me quietly, and with her finger to her lips said, "Come and look". She led me to the back veranda where the 'polo ground table' was covered with some plastic tarpaulin. she lifted it up and I saw that it was laden with the pumpkins I'd seen the afternoon before, now harvested. She picked one up to reveal a huge bite taken out of it from underneath. They had all been bitten in this way. There, laid out in rows, were about nine big, but not quite ripe pumpkins, each one with just one single, but enormous bite taken out from underneath it. She had stealthily placed all the damaged pumpkins on the table, bitten sides down, on our back veranda and was waiting to tell Mum the news.

I went into the dining-room to join the family for breakfast, but when I got to the table, only Dad sat there eating his porridge. I looked at him, and before I could say anything he asked,

"Have you seen the pumpkins?" I nodded.

"Well, your mother hasn't seen them yet, she's out there, weeding in the front border, and don't say a word. I want to see her face when she comes in after seeing that lot on the back veranda".

We sat eating while Mum did her usual performance of rushing around with a piece of toast in one hand, a coffee cup in the other, hunting for her reading glasses so that she could make a shopping list; she never actually sat down to breakfast. Our system of grocery shopping was rather haphazard. If anyone was going to be driving the thirteen miles into Nottingham Road, Mum would ring up Hoosen's (the Indian general dealer), on our party telephone line shared by eleven other farms, and place an order, which would be collected, along with our post and the newspaper. This involved Mum impatiently snatching up the phone at intervals, only to find someone already talking. She'd curse and storm off to the pantry to add items to her list. Eventually, she would find the line free and place her order. By this time, she'd be in a state of exasperation and would return to the breakfast table to dump her coffee cup. This was the moment Dad chose to tell her to go and look on the back veranda. We both sat there and waited until we heard the inevitable eruption from the back, and Mum yelling at the garden girls to "Go and pick every single unripe pumpkin that's left in the garden. Now! And put them all on the roof of the back veranda, where the baboons can't get at them!" while Dad and I wiped tears of laughter from our eyes with our table napkins.

~~~

# *6*
# Routines and rituals

**M**um barely tolerated us in the house. On the rare occasions that the weather was wet, and we were allowed indoors during the daytime, we had to play in the nursery where we ate all our meals. As we grew older Mum grudgingly permitted us to sit in the armchairs in the *gluzeen*, but yelled at us if we dared put our bare feet on the covers. I remember many occasions when I would be curled up, happily absorbed in a good book, to find Mum bearing down on me with a fly swatter, shouting, "Get your filthy feet off my covers!"

Every waking hour, and unhindered by domestic chores (because she had a full-time cook, a houseboy who did all the housework, maids to do the laundry and work in the garden, as well as nannies to look after the children), Mum was always on the warpath over one thing or another. She even raged over the weather, trying to control the elements. Being a perfectionist, she would have the garden looking immaculate, then, as storm clouds darkened the sky and the first rumble of thunder rattled the windows, she would frantically pace the veranda, throwing salt out of the doors (according to the Zulu superstition that it prevents hail), all the time muttering furiously about all her hard work that was about to be destroyed.

Dad had obsessions, too. Or rather, delusions. He and Mum were convinced that they were superior in breeding and education to practically everybody on the planet. They cut themselves – and as a result also their four daughters – off from everybody in the neighbourhood. After leaving his private boarding school (Balgowan College in Balgowan in the Dargle Valley, Dad had spent three years at Cambridge University in England doing a rather ordinary agricultural degree. As her only son, his mother indulged him and arranged for unlimited funds, enabling him to buy a car and travel extensively while he was there. He mixed with other privileged young rakes, and when he came back to South Africa was under the impression that he was the equivalent of an Upper-Class English gentleman surrounded by colonials.

Dad didn't like women particularly and constantly bemoaned the travesty that allowed women into Cambridge after he'd left.

Both my parents judged people solely on how they spoke, dressed and, most importantly to them, their wealth and breeding. Loyally and blindly Mum agreed with all his decisions and opinions. Backgrounds such as the correct private education and how people they met earned their living would be weighed against whether they were 'old' or 'new' money. Acquaintances were ruled out on the strength of their table manners, whether they said, "Pleased to meet you" instead of the more correct (in their view) "How do you do?" Some people were ruled out simply because they had the wrong accent or held a knife incorrectly, "Like a pencil" scorned Mum, and deemed them socially unacceptable.

Wealthy people could break the rules as, for example, in the case of beards. Dad hated beards on men, saying they looked scruffy, and he called them beatniks, but when Harry Oppenheimer's son grew a beard, it was 'distinguished'. Similarly, a very rich friend of theirs, a widow, was overweight and wore too much make-up. Normally she would have been vilified by my parents, but they fawned around her and made a weekly phone call to her to chat, something they hardly ever did with their own family members.

Dad despised Afrikaners, called them *Boets*, and refused on principle to learn a word of their language, although he spoke Zulu fluently. He disliked the Afrikaner Nationalist government, but he also hated and despised English-speaking white liberals. Because he had spent the war bombing the Italians, he hated them as much as he hated the Germans. Together with the former, he dismissed all Europeans as 'Eurotrash'. Unsurprisingly he was anti-Semitic, and the only Jews he would associate with were Harry Oppenheimer, who owned and controlled all the gold and diamond industries in the country, and another Jewish friend who was nearly as wealthy.

Catholics were on his blacklist as well as Christians, because he scoffed at the fact that they believed in a God that didn't exist. Both my parents were openly atheist but, oddly, Communists were anathema to him as well. Dad could spit the word 'Priests' with alarming venom. The Chinese and other Eastern races were dismissed, and Muslims he lumped together with Arabs, as 'disgusting and filthy'.

Dad had no time for the Africans. As a race they were, in his words, "useless bloody coons," and his favourite expression was "at least they're not running the country," although he relied on them entirely to raise his children, work the farm, and make his home comfortable. Dad didn't like Indians, he said they were all cheats, although he dealt exclusively with the polite Hoosen family, who allowed him to run up a monthly account at their store, because it suited him not to carry cash. He also dismissed the mixed-race Coloureds with the sweeping statement "they all drink." He would have nothing to do with what he called "the common English," and labelled practically every white South African a 'peasant'. These included all our nearest neighbours in the remote ranching community, and we were forbidden to associate with them.

Naturally, this arrogance and appalling snobbery left very few people acceptable, and these were mostly cousins or people he'd been to private school with; "not out of the top drawer" or "not one of us" served to dismiss everybody else. It sounds laughable and shouldn't have been taken seriously, but my parents' arrogance and bigoted attitudes were to create serious problems for us later, when we started bringing potential boyfriends home to be assessed.

Dad would play 18 holes of golf twice a week with the same

few selected old school chums he'd played with since before the
Second World War, and Mum played tennis with their wives or other
carefully picked friends, but neither he nor Mum made any effort to
organise any sort of social life for their daughters. Apart from the
occasional visits from cousins, we were completely isolated on the
ranch. Now and again we trekked our ponies across the hills to
compete in a gymkhana on somebody's farm, and Mum would drive
over to make sure we behaved ourselves correctly. She made us sit
on a rug as far away as possible from the 'common' children, and at
the end insisted we rode home before the fun event of a barbecue and
dance for all the young riders who had participated. As a result, we
never got to know our contemporaries on the surrounding farms.

Although Mum made all the decisions in our upbringing, she
always used Dad as her ultimate weapon and threatened to call him
in to decide our punishment if we disobeyed her. None of us wanted
to incur his wrath, so the threats worked instantly. If we'd been
caught doing something wrong, we feared his cold lectures far more
than the odd swipe that Mum gave us with her hairbrush, although
most of the time I was out of sight and earshot playing with the Zulu
children.

We were absolutely forbidden to play with the '*munt*' (an
abbreviation of *uMuntu*, the Zulu word for a black person) children
on the farm but, since Mum ignored us, concentrating her entire
attention on her garden and leaving us to spend our young lives in
the sole care of our nannies, I found it easy to slip away from Evalina
every day and play with them. The children were not allowed
anywhere near the house, though, and I had to shed them at the back
gate when I was called to meals by Evalina. Our parents didn't mind
if we spent the entire day out in the garden, out of sight and earshot
with our Zulu nannies, in fact Mum insisted we did so, the reasoning
being, I think, that they didn't consider Africans as people.

Where Mum had her garden and her battles with the
baboons, Dad had his routines; for 70 years every second of his day

was accounted for. He was the only son, and as such was expected to take over the farm when his mother died at the onset of the Second World War. He had been thrust into the role of rancher, although he didn't particularly like the idea of a career in farming. By 1955, my father had increased his cattle herd to over a thousand head, as well as running about five thousand Merino sheep. He wanted to spend less time farming and more time on the polo ground, golf course, and other gentlemanly pursuits, so he decided to employ a white farm manager.

Mr Bannatyne was a tall, middle-aged man with a large belly, and a greasy leather bush hat. A four-bedroomed cottage was built for him on the farm boundary, and he settled in with his wife, a shapeless woman with meagre, stringy hair that had once possibly been straw-coloured and was now a faded off-white, tied in a sparse bun at the nape of her neck and held at the sides with tortoise-shell combs. She wore loosely-knitted beige wool cardigans with pockets and sensible brown lace-up shoes with what we called 'lavatory heels' – those thick, chunky heels that look like the part of the loo that stands on the bathroom floor – the kind of heels that old ladies wore in the 1950s. Her teeth were large and prominent, reminding me of Chanter's, Dad's polo pony who bit ferociously at people and horses alike.

Answerable to no one, Dad's most difficult decision to make every morning was whether to go off and play golf or polo, and so, after breakfast he would have a brief meeting with his manager, ring his accountant to discuss his financial affairs, and then go out to his practice polo ground, where we had already exercised his ponies. Toto, Petrus, Shorty and myself would exercise them every day and deliver them, all ready and kitted out for his practice session, with me relinquishing the job to the three Zulu grooms when I went to boarding school. I played as well, perfecting my skills in horsemanship and ball control, but was not allowed to compete in tournaments; Dad refused to consider the idea, saying "It's not ladylike."

Dad could spend the morning sitting on the front veranda, with his legs propped up on a soft footstool in the sun, reading and have a tray of tea brought to him at ten thirty.

At exactly 12:30, because by then the sun had moved around, Dad would sit in his favourite armchair in the *gluzeen* to read the newspaper (often two or three days old because no one had been in to collect the latest edition from the station). One of the servants would bring in a polished silver tray of crystal glasses, slices of lemon, and ice cubes clinking gently in a silver bucket, placed alongside a Waterford Crystal glass jug of fresh spring water. Dad would then proceed to sip his pink gin, the first of three that he allowed himself every day.

Mum saw to it that his favourite food, a hot meat-and-two-veg lunch, was served in the dining-room at exactly twenty past one, after which he shuffled off to his bed for an hour's snooze. Nothing was to disturb his afternoon rest, so he'd even pull the plug out of the telephone, consistently forgetting to replace the jack, leaving the farm out of contact for days. Everybody else had to keep quiet for that hour as well.

Looking back, I feel as though we spent our entire young lives tiptoeing about and trying to keep out of Dad's way.

After the rest there was the exertion of an afternoon of driving around the valley in his Land Rover with the dogs in the back, muzzles thrust into the breeze and wet, pink tongues hanging out with delight. If there wasn't a daughter around to hop out and open the gates for him, he sent Makhaye to call for a farm boy to jump up and join the dogs at the back of his vehicle to do the job. If the dogs didn't know the man, there was a flurry of growling and snarling as the Zulu labourer unfamiliar to them approached the tailgate.

"Hau nKosi – *isInja!* (dogs!)," he'd call, and stood back at a safe distance, while Dad cursed and leaned over to open the cab's passenger-door. The dogs would leap down, using the tailgate as a springboard, and run around to jump in the front, snapping at each other good naturedly as they fought for prime position on the cracked leather passenger-seat, while others had to make do with crouching uncomfortably in the hot foot-well.

The farm boy then hopped over the tailgate and stood up at the back, holding on to the roof of the cab to steady himself as the vehicle rocked over ruts and potholes.

It never occurred to Dad to leave the dogs in the back and let the Zulu ride up front in the cab with him. "Too whiffy," he'd have explained, if someone had asked him. "And anyway, the dogs would have a go at him every time I stopped to let him get out to open the damn gate."

Some of the dogs could stink, though, especially if they'd found a polecat and rolled in its disgustingly, pungent eye-watering scent, and the Land Rover cab windows would have to be pushed open to their limit while dog snouts jostled for the privilege of getting the best place in the breeze.

When Dad went to check on the cattle on their summer grazing up on top, he would take the bakkie up the steep, winding road that Grandpa had blasted out of the mountainside with dynamite, to a plateau where most of the grazing lay. He'd stop at the first gate to let the dogs out to run beside the bakkie, and we had to open and close the many gates separating the paddocks, and during the summer Dad would take a couple of trout-rods with him for a leisurely cast over the glassy waters of one of the dams in the valley, either the bass dam near the boundary where the weaver birds hung their nests, or the small dam in a hollow at the top of the bush, where a Purple Heron stood sentinel, waiting for an unwary frog, hiding in the deep imprint left by a cow's hoof on the silty bottom, to give away its position. We stood on the bank of the dam watching the sun set behind the mountain range as we cast our flies over the mirror-like water, gnats and mayflies dancing just above the surface.

As night fell we would stand up at the back of the bakkie on the way back to the house. There is no twilight in that part of Africa, so near the Tropic of Capricorn, and, as warm wind blew onto our flushed faces, we could see the first stars spangle the black velvety sky.

Sometimes there would be a pair of Mountain Reedbuck grazing unconcernedly in a corner of the pasture near the dense wattle plantation, keeping to the shade, which camouflaged their greyish coats. They would stop and lift their heads to give a sharp whistle of alarm as the vehicle creaked up, drew to a halt and the dogs tumbled out. Dad tried to teach them as puppies not to chase buck, and most of them were fairly obedient. There was always one though, the smallest, my dog Pitz who took off like a grey hairy streak, deaf to shouts and sticks being flung after his retreating backside as he raced after the big, graceful antelope.

The male turned his ridged horns, which rose majestically from the top of his head almost straight back with black tips hooked sharply forward, to look disdainfully at the small dog, and then he followed his mate with an exaggerated rocking-horse action and his tail curled up to show the fluffy white underside, to vanish between the impenetrable wattle saplings. Pitz always came wagging his way back to the Land Rover, grinning from ear to ear, but wriggling lower to the ground and more ingratiatingly as Dad's enraged shouts eventually reached his ears and it sank home that he was in trouble. He rolled on to his back in the long grass, legs sticking up and wrists hanging limply, exposing his filthy belly, long hair matted with grass and mud, to subject himself resignedly to a smack or two over his fluffy ears and "You useless bloody dog! I know you're not stupid – you could learn if you wanted to!" And he'd do it again the next time he felt it was worth it.

After a typically onerous day in Dad's working life, back at the house there was always a game or two of tennis, if Mum could be dragged out of her flower-beds. With six of us, there was always somebody to make up enough for a set, although Dad played the sneakiest game, cutting the ball so that it reared off the soft, dampish grass and up at us like a cobra as we swiped at it with our racquets, groaning "Da-ad!"

His days always ended with a warm bath and a change of clothes, after which he settled down in his armchair in the sitting-room with the radio on, tuned to the *World Service* and preparing the first of his three whiskies, carefully poured out using an imperial tot measure. He never drank any more than that, but neither did he ever go without his twice-daily 'noggins'. At 9 o'clock, he ate sparingly of a light supper and went to bed at 10. His morning tea was taken to him on a tray by one of the servants at seven every morning. For 70 years this routine never wavered.

If we had guests staying, they had to fit in with Dad's rigid routine. If he went on holiday, he refused to stay with other people, always choosing a hotel just in case he would have to adapt. Mum and Dad certainly looked the part of upper-class County gentlefolk. Every day Dad, with his slightly florid complexion, wore cavalry twill trousers with tweed jackets patched at the elbows with leather, and a deerstalker. If he was going to town, he wore a Savile Row suit and a Jesus College, Cambridge, Old Boy's tie, his impeccable outfit looking rather incongruous amongst the khaki shorts and shirts favoured by the other farmers. Mum dressed in tasteful linen shirtwaisters, carefully hand-stitched by her dressmaker (a 'little Afrikaner woman' in Pietermaritzburg, our nearest city an hour and a half's drive away). The dress material was tasteful cream-coloured backgrounds sprigged with pastel spring flowers, imported from Liberty's of London.

Mum's silken 'peaches and cream' complexion with her high cheekbones, golden blonde hair, and cornflower blue eyes gave her an extraordinary likeness to Princess Grace of Monaco. When she was gardening, Mum wore jeans, which set off her slender, willowy figure, but if she drove the Land Rover into 'the station' (Nottingham Road) she would always change into a dress, putting on her make-up and pretty sandals before she got into the dust-covered vehicle. Even if she was only going to collect the post and farm rations, she still made sure she looked perfect in every way. Like Dad she was a serial charmer, sweeping people off their feet with her easy, elegant manner. He had a disarmingly courteous demeanour, which successfully concealed his complete contempt of people in general.

At polo tournaments, Mum sat in the pavilion, wearing a beautifully cut tweed suit with a diamond brooch on the lapel, dressed exactly like she had seen Queen Elizabeth in a photograph in a copy of the *Woman's Weekly* during the 1950s.

Her name, Dorothea, was shortened to Doffie in a manner reminiscent of fluffy socialites at smart cocktail parties. In her usual idealistic manner, my Mum had us dressed up in her idea of what English country children wore: woollen kilts, fawn Fair Isle jerseys, long fawn woollen stockings and Clark's sandals, all of which were carefully copied from pictures of young Princess Anne in the same magazine. Various cousins who lived in England, sent out crates of their outgrown clothes; perfect for an English climate, but far too heavy and irritating for the African heat.

We hated being dressed up by our nannies for an outing, usually a polo tournament in which Dad was competing. We scratched resentfully at our tormenting clothing and fidgeted sullenly. On arrival, we ran off to play with the other white children, an opportunity we seldom had. What Mum didn't realise was what un-socialised little savages we had become. Her wrath, on the many occasions when she discovered me covered in red earth and panting happily after a vigorous clay fight, was severe. She seemed unaware that we spoke hardly any English, as on the few occasions she told us to do something, she spoke in Zulu as well.

When I think back, my mother never really knew what to do with us. Very occasionally we were taken to a children's birthday party on a farm in the district, wearing our horrible outfits. How we envied the little girls who arrived in frilly party dresses, wearing lacy white ankle socks and black patent leather shoes. When we begged Mum for similar dresses, she snapped, "Certainly not – you'd just look common." We had no idea how to behave amongst our peers, and on more than one occasion I got into a fistfight with a boy who had underestimated my level of tolerance. I kicked a younger male cousin hard in the testicles during a particularly rough game, and wondered why he staggered off, wailing and clutching his groin, to complain to his mother, who then kicked up a fuss to my mother. Bewildered, I was dragged off – her fingernails biting into my arm, to sit in the car until it was time to go home.

At home on the farm we wore shorts and T-shirts, ran around barefoot all year round, and only pulled on a woollen jersey when our nannies thought we felt cold. At an altitude of over six thousand feet up in the mountains, our climate was far less steamy than the coastal towns like Durban with its sauna-like summers and warm winters. We had regular, thick frost early in the mornings in June and July, our mid-winter, and we'd race barefoot down to the grass tennis-court where we'd skate around on the ice-covered grass, drawing figures of eight and trying to spin like the performers we'd once seen when Mum had taken us to see *Cinderella on Ice* in Durban.

Our skating always got us into trouble, because the fine grass with which the court was carefully sown, became easily bruised, leaving traces of our manoeuvres on the immaculate lawn. Mum would hunt us down and drag us by the arm to the scene of our crime, yelling at us that we were inconsiderate little brutes, and we'd stand there mutinously, agreeing never to skate again. These promises lasted only until the next frosts though, and we'd be twirling around again, humming what we thought was appropriate music for skating.

Our upbringing had certain similarities to that of the Mitford girls, but where their 'Farve' (a nickname they gave their father;

short for and a corruption of 'father') roared from the end of their long dining table, "Sewers – they're all sewers!" of the young men the girls brought home for approval, Dad disguised his distaste for our young friends behind a façade of impeccable but patronising good manners, then he would fix them with his cold green eyes in a cobra-like stare and lift his newspaper to terminate the greeting, only to vociferously reveal his dislike for them and their shortcomings after they'd left. We would rather have had Farve's ranting than the insidiously poisonous remarks from Dad.

Unlike 'Muv' in Nancy Mitford's autobiography, Mum showed no interest in doing good works around the village or surrounding district, but preferred to isolate herself, and us, to immerse herself in her passion for her garden. Pouring all her energy and devotion into making the place look good, she spent every waking moment creating a magnificent and enormous expanse of sweeping lawns and herbaceous borders, all blazing with colour.

By the mid-1960s her garden filled five or six acres and consumed every second of her day, every ounce of her energy, and all her attention. It didn't worry Mum at all if, as was often the case, three weeks could go by without her ever leaving the farm.

We hardly ever saw our parents. We ate all our meals in the 'nursery'; a playroom tacked on to the house beyond the kitchen and supervised by our nannies. Masango cooked our meals under instruction from Mum who, when she could be distracted from her garden, decided what we would eat. Normally he would have to track her down, and when he eventually found her - usually in a flower-bed pulling out weeds so ferociously that there was a cloud of dust around her and clumps of earth lay scattered on the lawn - would ask her what to prepare for the children's supper.

Distractedly she'd rack her brains and finally come up with a suggestion.

Mum had never shown any interest in food, considering eating decadent and a waste of good gardening time.

She would reluctantly drag herself away from her planting to sit down for a desultory lunch at the dining-room table, ritually laid for every meal as if for a dinner party, and which gleamed with silver cutlery, serving dishes and candelabra that had been carefully polished by Makhaye, the houseboy. She'd eat whatever the servants put in front of her, served from the correct side by Makhaye in his uniform of dazzling white tunic with long trousers, red sash over one shoulder and rakish little white fez-like cap perched jauntily on his black, closely-shorn woolly curls. Dad ate heartily at his end of the long French-polished table, with the wireless next to his place mat, tuned to a dour-sounding local news broadcast that gave the latest beef market prices.

So, we grew up, becoming more and more lonely; resentful of the isolation imposed by our parents. One by one we went to boarding school and began to spend our school holidays as far away from the farm as possible. We desperately wanted to invite our school friends home, to share the wonderful, paradise-like valley with them. We had polo ponies to ride, a lawn tennis-court, a river to swim in, and trout to catch. But we didn't dare. We knew better than to subject them to the chilly disapproval they would encounter from Mum and Dad during their stay, and we didn't want to hear for the rest of the holidays how common they were, and a blow-by-blow account of how bad their manners were.

Nicolette and Dine went away to the Prep School very early on while Delia and I stayed behind on the farm. Mum needed me to remain as company for my little sister, three-and-a-half years younger than me, as she thought Delia would be lonely all on her own. This was a classical demonstration on how little our mother knew about her children. I believed that boarding school was the answer to all my problems of loneliness. It would be a nirvana of the jolly japes and endless fun I had read about in Enid Blyton books, and overlooking all the moans and complaints by my older sisters of how awful being incarcerated in such a place actually was, I looked forward to joining them there. I had absolutely nothing in common with my little sister. We were poles apart in our interests as she was effectively still a baby, content to lie around with the nannies, sucking her thumb and occasionally looking at the pictures in her *Robin Annual* as she hadn't learned to read yet.

On the other hand, I had become a typical tomboy. I strived to be the son that Mum and Dad had never had. As soon as I could walk and then ride, I threw myself wholeheartedly into farm life. Whatever was going on, be it herding the cattle and sheep, burning fire breaks, hay-making or whatever activity was happening at the time, I would be in the midst of it. I knew the name of everybody on the farm, and of all the oxen, horses and the dogs, and there was very little that I missed as I jumped out of bed to race up to the huts and eat a clandestine breakfast with my Zulu playmates.

My only problem was not being able to share my activities with a like-minded sibling, and most of all, not having anybody as company on my rides. As a result, I resented Delia for holding me back, forcing me to stay behind with the nannies, passing interminable days doing nothing. I took out my frustrations on her at any and every opportunity. I found ways of tormenting her – an easy task, as she was terrified of everything and it only took a handful of spider web to be brushed casually onto her hair to send her into a total meltdown of hysterics and, naturally, running to tell tales on me, which culminated in my receiving a hiding with Mum's Mason and Pearson hairbrush. Seven years passed in this fashion. I rode around the farm consumed by loneliness, or took up an illegal and secret alliance with the Zulu children, with whom I spent the rest of my time, flying under Mum's radar and risking Evalina's job for her on a daily basis.

We kids had a curfew, and the rules were rigid – my mother insisted that we were out of the house straight after breakfast.

"Frowsting away in your rooms reading!" she shouted when she caught me, once again, lying, half-dressed and engrossed in my third read of *Reach for the Sky* about Douglas Bader. "You're not sick and it's not raining or anything. Go outside and play!" aiming a vicious slap at my bare legs in her rage. Define 'play', I would wonder to myself.

Sometimes I'd smuggle a book out, and go and sit up in a tree house I'd made in a gnarled old apple tree by nailing some pine planks to a branch, but it was neither comfortable nor private. The very best place of all was a nest I'd made for myself in a giant fern. It was about ten feet tall, and, by using a boulder right next to it as a step up, I could climb up the woolly trunk and lie comfortably curled up in the soft, almost papery centre where the new leaves appear. The huge fern leaves that grew profusely outwards made me completely invisible, and I never told anyone other than my Zulu friends about it.

We weren't allowed to play with '*munt*' children at all. Ever. Similarly, they called a white person, *uMlungu*. Neither term is particularly derogatory, nor is it polite, even though *uMlungu* translates as "dog shit that has turned white in the sun," but since very few whites spoke or understood pure Zulu, they didn't know that, and we, who knew the language, never used either term to each other. We could say to one another "*Nansi uMuntu*" meaning "There's a black person." The same way as they'd refer to having seen a strange *uMlungu* driving up the back to the sheds. 'Kaffir' was the very worst word a white could call a black to his face or about him, and even Mum and Dad didn't use the word in front of us children, they referred to them as "K's" or "The K word" – even "the K factor" when any machinery broke when the Zulus were operating it.

~~~

# 7
# Zulu conversations

Every day after breakfast we were escorted by Evalina and Lisha out to the back, to a big shady area of soft green (and tick infested) kikuyu grass near the big rubbish pit under the biggest gums. There they settled down, Evalina making herself comfortable as she wriggled her large rump into the dappled, shaded grass, and they resumed an ongoing and rowdy gossip with the two washing and ironing girls. The four Zulu women shrieked with laughter and slapped their substantial thighs at delicious titbits of scandal.

The wash girls had a huge oval zinc bathtub with handles at each end, and scrubbed our clothes and linen with soft, mottled blue soap that came in long bars, and always looked to me as if they could be good to eat. They would have done the washing at the river, pounding the soapy clothes with stones on the rocks, like they did their own on Sundays, well out of sight of her disapproving eyes, but my mother wasn't going to copy the Africans to that extent. On ration days Mum would unlock her store cupboard, pull out a two-foot long bar of the delicious-looking soap, and hack off four inches or so with a sharp knife. She doled out the house servants' food and cleaning rations, such as *Vim*, *Brasso* and *Cobra Floor* polish, once a week with the same grace as she did everything involving the servants (and us children).

"Don't waste it!" she said briskly to the staff as they stood in front of her in the big pantry. The four women in the front with their eyes respectfully lowered, and Masango and Makhaye at the back. The men's uniform hats off their heads, being twisted nervously in their hands as they bent their greying heads to look politely at the ground.

Underneath the gum-trees, while the Zulu women gossiped, I became instantly bored. "I'm going to look for *donny* balls," I told Evalina, looking earnestly into her face. They were Grandpa's name for pine cones, and we used them as toys, like skittles, and painted the biggest ones silver to hang on our tree as Christmas decorations.

"Don't go far!" she'd say automatically, distracted by the ongoing, scurrilous conversation taking place next to her, and I bolted off, up into the pine plantation and then made a quick detour around the back of the hill to the huts.

There I gathered my small gang of Zulu friends and we set off to play in the river, and then to hunt in the paddock below the house, which had been planted with rye grass for cattle winter feed. We hunted *mBibas* – striped field mice. With practised ease, Dumi bashed them on their tiny heads with the scaled down *iwisi* (knobkierie) he'd made for himself. We all had an *iwisa*, (make him fall down) and acted as beaters to chase the mice. With lots of yelling "*Vimba*! *Vimba*! ("head them off!"), we pounded the ground vigorously with the heads of our *iwisas*. The thumping noises herded the delicately patterned little rodents through the long grass in a gradually funnelling V until they made a dash past Dumi who stood stock still, like a heron, his *kierie* poised for the lightning strike.

He threaded the limp little corpses on a long plaited grass string, and we could collect up to twenty on a good morning. They were enchanting little creatures, with greyish buff fur and had four distinct black, white, black-and-buff stripes running down their backs. Their bellies were pure white, and the backs of their tiny round ears were black, as were their long furry tails. "They're delicious," he told me, "we skin them and roast them whole in the ashes."

I never tried roasted *mBiba* as I was far too squeamish about the idea of eating them. Privately I loved mice and would much rather have kept the *mBibas* as pets - they were so pretty. Once, when he was out with the gang burning fire breaks, nGidi (our *Induna* chief of our farm Zulus. He was chief of all the Zulus in iMpendhle, working as a foreman, but acted as chief over all our staff) had found a nest of baby *mBibas* in the hollow of a forked tree and had given them to me to raise. But they were too young; still hairless, pink and blind, and I was only about five and had no way of feeding them or keeping them warm, so—they all died. I was heartbroken and kept pestering nGidi to find me a nest of older mice that I could keep and play with.

I was allowed to run free and loved every minute of my days.

Dumi and company kept an ear out for the sound of the farm bell, which signalled the end of the working day, and, packing up our clay oxen, the *mBiba* corpses, or a tightly woven reed basket oozing sweet honey that we'd smoked out of a wild beehive, we made our way back home – they to their cosy-looking huts with their smiling mothers stirring *uPhutu* with a long stick over a smoky open fire, and me back to an anxious, scolding Evalina who still had to hustle me into the bathtub, get me dressed in my pyjamas and into the nursery for whatever insipid spaghetti supper Ben had made for us.     As far as Mum was concerned, we had been 'playing nicely and keeping clean' all day, watched over by our nannies.

~~~

# Lunch parties and dances

**M**um and Dad regularly (at least every month during the summer) held tennis and lunch parties. Sometimes they'd invite neighbouring ranchers over for a few sets on our grass court with drinks on the veranda afterwards, followed by a hearty lunch of roast mutton from one of our merino sheep, accompanied by roast potatoes and vegetables from our garden. Sometimes, they would have a weekend for adults only. On these occasions we were to be neither seen nor heard (I was seven, Nicolette and Dine were at boarding school , and Delia was four) and Delia and I would play quietly all morning, out of sight, usually out by the stables behind the homestead, hearing the occasional pok pok of tennis balls and shouts and laughter from the players.

Evalina would give us lunch in our nursery/play-room behind the kitchen, and when Mum gave Masango the signal to serve lunch in the dining-room, we'd race round the lawns that skirted the house to the front veranda to drink the dregs from all the glasses, before Evalina, who was helping wash pots in the kitchen, could catch us. Feeling slightly woozy from the snatched mouthfuls of pink gin, lager, and whisky and soda, we would trail after her as she took us to her home, a cluster of mud huts on a hill behind the farmhouse, beneath the tall, rustling gum-trees.

There we'd find a different kind of party. The Zulu women had swept a large area of bare earth in front of their huts with brooms made from twigs tied together. They had dragged logs into a pile in the centre and made a big fire, adding eucalyptus branches to create leaping flames, filling the compound with its unique spicy, aromatic, blue smoke. The women all sat round the fire in a wide circle, on grass mats, and with their palms two of them beat drums made from carved hollow logs with animal hide tightened over it. The men sat on their haunches in a group, passing around a *calabash* (a gourd) filled with *Mahewu* (corn beer).

We children danced, while the women sang in harmony and clapped their hands to the rhythm of the drum. Jabu, Thandi, Nobuhlwe, Dumisane, Maqulaza and I did the traditional Zulu Jiga dance; arms outstretched in front of us, fists clenched stiffly and knees bent, we kicked our legs high, bringing our bare feet thumping down on the earth. As the afternoon wore on the pace would quicken and the drumbeats would become more and more frenzied as orange flame-sprites jumped higher into the dusk, sparks flying as one of the women kicked a log into the centre of the blaze.

While Delia dozed in Evalina's lap we whirled and crouched at a dizzying speed as our dancing became more abandoned. Puffs of red dust flew up as I stamped my small bare feet on the hard, dry ground. I whirled in circles around the big fire, kicking so high my feet were sometimes above my head, as I and my fellow dancers were spurred on by the faster-beating drums and hand-clapping. Eventually, panting and dusty, I was led quickly back to the house, my sleepy sister tied on to Evalina's back in a woollen shawl, to be bathed and given supper. Then, scrubbed pink and glowing and in our cotton pyjamas, we spent our obligatory hour in the sitting-room sitting quietly.

This was the only social time we spent with our parents, at the end of the day with our storybooks on our laps. Mum would look at Dad over her reading glasses, the ice cubes tinkling in her cut glass tumbler as she took a sip of her whiskey and water, and say to him crossly, "Do you hear those blasted drums? They go on and on all night you know. They drive me mad!"

Dad rustled his newspaper impatiently and replied curtly

"They're off duty, and anyway there's nothing I can do." I kept quiet. Late into the night I would listen to the drums letting their quick thump-thump-thump lull me into sleep. All the years I spent on the farm, every Saturday and Sunday night, I fell asleep to the comforting sound of drumming up at the huts, knowing that everybody there was dancing around the big open fire.

~~~

# *9*

# Duck hunting

Some evenings my father would pick up his trout rod and, calling us and the dogs to hop into the Land Rover, drive up the mountain behind the house. We had to open all the gates – something else to squabble over: "It's your turn – I did the last one."

"She did the last one, it's your turn and if you don't hurry up and jump back in, I'm gonna tell Dad to drive off without you and the leopards can eat you."

Discussions like this were kept to hissed whispers because if my father heard us he jammed on his brakes, turned the engine off and roared at us: "If you blasted girls don't shut up and stop fighting I'll chuck you all out here and you can walk home!"

One memorable summer evening he took his shotgun with us up to the vleis on the moor-land at the top of the mountain, to shoot some wild duck for the pot. On board was our motley crew of dogs: Spot to flush them out, a young and not-too-bright Mups that he was attempting to train to retrieve, and Pitz, who was gun shy and a troublemaker of note. After the first few shots my father discovered that Mups was cowering with Pitz under the dashboard in the cab.

"Now I've got two useless bloody dogs – one's taught the other to become gun shy!" he complained. "You girls will have to retrieve the ducks."

So, very reluctantly, we took off our shorts and T-shirts and, while Spot (the Pointer) ran excitedly over the marshes, pointing with his tail stiffened at ducks (which my father shot with unerring aim), we had to flounder through waist-high water – it was too reed-choked to swim – in just our pants, slipping and scrabbling to grab the ducks. We were covered in mosquitoes, bitten on every part of exposed flesh, and our legs and arms scratched by razor-edged reed grasses. When we got back to the Land Rover with our ducks, some dead and others wounded, and complaining bitterly, my father just said, "Now wring the necks of the live ones." With distaste, and at arm's length using just our fingertips, we twisted their heads round and round on their rubbery necks, only to find them unwinding with speed, and the duck fixing us with a baleful and resentful stare.

Eventually my father lost patience with his feeble, wishy-washy daughters, and wrung the ducks' necks himself. After this my father dragged the two cowering dogs out of the cab by their scruffs and threw them into the back of the vehicle where we were sitting glumly, and when Spot jumped in Pitz attacked him in a jealous rage, and a monumental dogfight broke out in the back. We scrambled out using the back wheels for toe-hold, shrieking with alarm, but not before Mups had sunk his teeth into the back of Nicolette's heel (he was supposed to be her dog) leaving deep punctures that bled profusely. Cursing, my father drove back down the long, steep and twisting road, bouncing crossly over the ruts and bumps with his cargo of cringing dogs, dead ducks (that slithered from side to side), and sullen daughters, one of whom was crying and dripping blood everywhere.

"That's the last time I take you lot out hunting. You're more of a liability than those damn dogs," he said bitterly as we arrived back at the house.

~~~

# *10*

# Fairyland

The farmhouse was filled with books, and Dine and I had taught ourselves to read very early on. Grandpa was an ardent and omnivorous reader; after he'd moved on to the farm he had crates of books sent up from Durban by ox-wagon. There were most of the classics, as well as less digestible works. When I was able to read, I started on the bookshelves that lined the long passage to our bedrooms. All the heaviest books lay on the bottom shelves, and, at the age of about four, I dragged out a large tome of Tolstoy's *War and Peace* and hauled it down to my bedroom to devour hungrily.

My father's taste in literature was inclined to works, factual and fictional, on both world wars, particularly about flying as he'd been a bomber pilot in the South African Air Force. I loved reading autobiographies of men who had served in the British and South African armed forces, picturing their bravery as they fired at the Jerries while they were under fierce attack themselves, although I did wonder why the British servicemen used the words 'muck' and 'mucking' so often. I enjoyed all the works of CS Forester and read the Hornblower series over and over again. PG Wodehouse was another favourite as my father had the entire collection.

On the top shelves stood the children's books, and were the last books we read, having to stand on the big war books to reach them. Various aunts and cousins, most of whom were English, posted us books on our birthdays and for Christmas. I found them disappointing and childish. *The Famous Five*, in our opinion, were simpering Poms, and we couldn't relate to their weedy antics with smugglers and gypsies. We jeered at their manners of speech, and mocked the way they pulled on coats and boots before going out of doors, but secretly I envied them their exciting-sounding schools and being able to play in the snow with friends.

One year an English aunt had sent us a copy of Cicely Mary Barker's *Fairies of the Flowers and Trees*, with its exquisite illustrations of elves and fairies, and we were obsessed by fairies from that time onwards. We would draw them in all the flyleaves of our books – the only blank paper we could find – which drove my mother into a rage. She called it scribbling in our books and ruining them; it never occurred to her to buy us blank drawing books or even sheets of plain paper, so we drew on any blank pages we found. Although we often received colouring-in books at Christmas or on birthdays, we both loved to draw freehand, and Dine showed budding talent as an artist.

We'd scamper down the front lawn to the cattle grid spanning a small stream that flowed from a spring in the pine plantation on the mountainside behind the house, and down into the big paddock below the garden. Trees and flowering shrubs had grown up alongside the permanent trickle of water, making a pleasant little oasis. The best part of it was that it wasn't in the garden, and thus out of range of our mother's prowling. She didn't like us playing in the garden as we pulled the heads off flowers and turned them into fairies by sticking them onto twigs to play with, and she always chased us out. "You've got five thousand acres to play on, for God's sake. Why do you have to ruin my garden?" she'd mutter as we slunk off sullenly.

But down here we could sneak up, raid her biggest flowers and bring them back to play with undetected. What gave our private little glade added appeal was its resemblance to pictures of Bluebell Wood in our Pookie books, where he and his woodland friends frolicked so happily. (Pookie, the little white rabbit with wings, was a set of classic stories for children published from 1945 by Ivy

Wallace.) We often took our dolls down there as well and played contentedly until we heard Evalina calling us for lunch. We spent so much time down there that we'd had to create Goblin Land. As we hopped out of bed and left the house as soon as possible every day, we didn't go near the bathroom to wash or brush our teeth – although we always said yes to any questions Evalina asked us about whether we'd done so. It never occurred to her to actually check if we were lying – we didn't find time to answer the call of nature either. So, if we were caught short we simply moved a few yards downstream and squatted to *bosha* (widdle) in a less attractive, rather boggy area overgrown with weeds:

# GOBLIN LAND

There was a Bonga-Bonga tree (the Zulu word *bonga* means 'to thank') growing conveniently down there on the bank. This had nice big strong leaves, shiny on one side and soft, fluffy and marginally more absorbent on the other, perfect for using as lavatory paper, and they were pleasantly scented in a medicinal sort of way. When we were out on an all-day ride we always looked out for a Bonga-Bonga tree early on, so that we could pull off a few leaves and stuff them into our pockets for emergency use later.

We made fairies out of the flower heads, and declared any darker green circles appearing on the kikuyu lawns to be enchanted fairy rings, and stuck our homemade fairies into the soft, springy grass around the edges of these circles. We laid out little picnics for them with tiny, flat, round Nasturtium leaves for plates and acorn caps for tea-cups. We filled these with coloured water that we'd made by crushing petals into an old glass jar we'd found at the rubbish heap, and topping it up with water.

Delia was fascinated by all this, and we allowed her to watch our elaborate and exciting party preparations until, being the youngest, she was hauled off by Evalina, protesting loudly, to be bathed first. We described to our entranced little sister all the wonderful tea parties we'd witnessed at sundown, after she'd been taken away to be bathed, embellishing our stories with descriptions of a beautiful Fairy Queen called Rosebud, and her handsome escort, a prince dressed in green, like the Willow fairy. There was an entourage of delicate little courtiers, including a pretty little fairy called Bluebell, all of whom got to their dainty feet and danced around our enchanted ring before taking to the evening sky on their transparent gossamer wings and turning into those fragile, shining fireflies that flitted about after dark on still warm nights.

One evening, a week or so before, Dine, to make our stories even more convincing, decided to write a letter to Delia from the Fairy Queen. She'd swiped a sheet of our mother's airmail writing paper from the desk in the office, and cut it into quarters with pinking shears purloined from the sewing room. With finely sharpened different coloured pencils from her colouring box a letter was created by Dine. She folded it into a square, drew microscopic hearts and flowers on it, addressed it to 'Dear Delia' and very early the next morning, just as the rising sun touched the front lawn, she and I crept out of the house and placed it carefully in the centre of the dew-sparkling fairy ring, still festooned with its circle of stick fairies, and tea-party leaf crockery in the middle. Then we'd raced down the passage and burst excitedly into Delia's room. "Come and look at the fairy ring!" we exclaimed. "Quick!" She scrambled out of bed and, still in her pyjamas, ran ahead of us out onto the front lawn. She snatched up the letter and looked at it with delight.

"Is it really for me?" We both nodded. "Can you read it to me?" Although she was getting on for four years old, she hadn't taught herself to read like we had (it turned out that she was struggling with dyslexia but nobody seemed to notice – there was no such condition then, and my mother thought she was just 'slow') and still just looked at the pictures in books.

"Dear Delia," read Dine. "You are a very good, sweet little

girl. We the fairy folk will watch over you to keep you safe while you sleep at night. With all my love, from Rosebud the Fairy Queen."

Delia was thrilled and carried the letter around with her all day, asking us or my mother to read it over and over again.

After that Delia checked every fairy ring she found each morning, and, to oblige, Dine would write the odd letter and leave it there. They were all in the same vein, but I could tell Dine was getting bored with the whole thing, and it wasn't long before Delia did something to annoy her. To this day I'm not sure what the transgression was, but I suspect Delia took something of Dine's and either broke it or lost it, but I do know that Dine was furious. That night she penned another letter.

"Dear Delia," it started. "You are a very BAD little girl! You have made the Fairy Queen very cross and she has told me to come over tonight when you are asleep and pinch your toes! Signed, Fish-Grab, the Goblin."

Delia was devastated. And terrified. She was a bit of a scaredy-cat about going to sleep at night anyway, and it didn't help that Dine and I often apple-pie'd her bed with prickly branches pulled from a big old Monkey Puzzle tree, which my grandmother had planted near the house. And once we'd carried a large toad in and placed it carefully under her top sheet just before bed-time, at which point it crawled up and piddled on her pillow.

She was too petrified to go to bed and begged Dine to be able to sleep with her. "Bugger off!" was the reply. Then she pleaded with me to allow her to spend the night in my bed.

"No!" I retorted. "Sleep in your own bed." And so, after bedtime, while I read by the dim yellow glow coming through a crack in my bedroom door, I could hear her whimpering and sobbing from under her bedclothes in her room next to mine. Callously both Dine and I ignored her, and from then on we only had to hiss "Fish-Grab" at her to get her to run, wailing in distress, to Evalina.

It wasn't only Delia that was the victim of Dine's teasing – I didn't trust her either.

Once she managed to persuade me to get into the big double horse-box that was parked out at the back next to the stables, and in which my father took polo ponies to those tournaments too far away to get to on horseback. Naively I'd climbed in, only to hear her slam the small groom's door behind me; lock it and run away cackling triumphantly. I spent the entire morning sitting in there in the dark on a clump of dusty hay until midday, when Evalina had heard my calls for help when she'd come out to ring the lunchtime gong.

~~~

# *11*

# Chocolate pudding

**B**ut sometimes I got myself into trouble through my own efforts. All summer long the big kitchen, with its two open sash windows, filled up with flies (it never occurred to my parents to put wire fly-screens in). Masango asked Mum to order yellow sticky arsenic-covered fly paper from Hoosen's, which he hung from the ceiling, and which soon became black with dead flies, but the rest clustered everywhere, on the floor, the work surfaces and hundreds of them danced in the air.

That particular afternoon, in the dead-time between two and four when every person and other living creature on the farm fell into a heat-induced stupor and dozed until an explosive thunderstorm broke the silence and relieved the stifling, baked atmosphere, I had got off my bed where I was supposed to be resting, bored and feeling a little peckish after having listlessly pushed my congealing, greasy mutton stew and boiled potatoes around my plate at lunchtime. Now I fancied something to eat, so I crept through the silent house to the deserted kitchen, to be greeted by swarms of flies buzzing languidly around.

I picked up one of the wire swatters that lay in every room and began to lay about me, whacking clumps of flies that had clustered on the work-tops, until all the remaining survivors were air born. Not wanting to be beaten by a bunch of flies, I looked around for a better weapon and saw the sprayer on a high shelf in the big, walk-through pantry between the kitchen and the back veranda, so I climbed up to grab it. Long before the days of aerosol spray cans this was nothing more than a little drum, into which one poured the spray, on the end of a tin cylinder filled with *DDT*, and a thick wire pump handle, which I now pumped vigorously as I chased the flies around the kitchen, knocking them out of the air with the skill and enthusiasm of a fighter pilot attacking those Jerry planes about which I'd recently and avidly read in Dad's war books.

Eventually there was nothing left but a scattering of twitching, buzzing casualties and corpses lying around on the floor and, satisfied with my handiwork, I left the now empty spray can in a prominent place on a scrubbed wooden tabletop next to a large cut glass bowl which was standing there with a fly cover over it.

Then, having forgotten my intended snack, and pleased at how grateful Masango would be with me for having single-handedly eradicated his fly problem, I tiptoed back to my bedroom to wait for him or Makhaye to hammer on the bell – the rusty old ploughshare that hung from a tree branch on a piece of wire, announcing four o'clock and the signal for the somnolent farm to drag itself back into activity.

I was roused from my reading by raised voices – Masango's and Mum's, and I jumped up and skipped happily along the passage to receive my well-deserved accolade. I arrived in the dining-room to discover my entire family standing around our irate cook as he ranted in Zulu, waving the cut glass bowl around angrily. Dine dug me in the ribs as I joined them. "You're in big trouble," she said with glee. "That was our pudding you sprayed." And, sure enough, the big bowl contained a chocolate mousse that he'd whipped up, using lots of fresh farm cream and sugared cocoa paste, and had left out to cool before placing it in the fridge for tonight's supper.

In those days all the insecticides were *DDT* based and extremely toxic, and I'd succeeded in contaminating the dish so thoroughly that it had to be thrown out. I made myself scarce for the rest of the day and pretended not to notice when my sisters ostentatiously pinched their noses at the tinned fruit Evalina put in front of us as we sat at the nursery table at suppertime, waiting for our pudding.

"We want chocolate PUD-ding!" they chorused, and dissolved into mocking laughter.

~~~

# *12*

# Zulu legislation and traditions

To me Evalina was old, but I think she must have only been about 35 when she became my nanny. Traditionally Zulu maidens became brides at the age of 13 or 14, normally in exchange for cattle, and bore their first children soon afterwards. So Evalina could have had anything up to five children (infant mortality was as high as the birth rate) of her own back in iMpendhle, being cared for by her own mother.

Evalina's age was difficult to determine. She was illiterate, as were all our staff, and Zulus, in those times anyway, didn't register the births of their children – the villages are too remote for a newly-delivered mother to trudge over 40 miles of mountainous, and sometimes leopard inhabited, country to the closest municipal registry (our nearest was in Lions River, about 50 miles away), burdened down by her previous baby, now a year old, strapped to her back in a shawl, her new-born infant in her arms, and often with several other very small children in tow.

The mother might even already be pregnant with her next baby, as the only form of birth control among rural Zulus was a very high infant mortality. Anyway, the Africans didn't see the point of this *uMlungu* number-keeping – they knew who was in their tribe, and, as they did with their cattle, they knew them by the shade of their skins instead of by counting, which they couldn't do unless they'd been taught at a mission school.

As an old-age pension was issued to all natives over the age of 60, the recipient had to produce some kind of physical identification to receive it. There was the official system whereby every month the pensioner would be taken by their relatives to Lions River (often in a wheelbarrow, on a journey taking several days) and *faga uStupe* their pension book (place an inked thumbprint under an x instead of a signature) to collect the pitiful allowance of a few pounds Sterling. Wily older relatives over their late 30s would cut off the right thumb of their parent's corpse before they performed the three-day burial ceremony, pickle the thumb in meths, and, by secreting the legitimate digit under their own, kept drawing pensions for their long deceased elders for years as it was very difficult to determine the age of a Zulu; they don't wrinkle or lose their hair, and only some of them turn a little bit grey at the temples.

The logistics of the Afrikaner Government officials keeping track of the numbers of births and deaths (those weren't registered either) on 'natives' (their collective word for Africans, although we and the Afrikaner clerks were all born in South Africa as well) in the rural areas were too much to overcome. The Afrikaner officials became suspicious and did some investigation only when some of these old Zulus reached ages that surpassed any of those in the Guinness Book of Records. Jomela, our herdboy, was old, because his thinning curls were grizzled white at the temples like nGidi's and Makhaye's, and he'd lost most of his teeth. Like Makhaye and Lokatia, he didn't have a Christian name, and he lived in his own hut up on top of the farm and looked after the 5,000 head of sheep that grazed on the veldt up there all year round, except when there was a forecast of heavy snow in the winter when Dad sent a message via one of the farm boys to him to bring them all down into the valley where the bush afforded them good shelter and browsing.

Evalina loved me as if I were one of her own children, and I loved her, too, but my mother's rules had to be strictly enforced, and Evalina was so terrified of Mum's volatile temper, and the fact that she could be fired on the spot and replaced with any of the other Zulu women who worked on the farm. I wouldn't sit still, or play games with my younger sister's dolls, so Evalina turned a blind eye to my slipping away, and then spent the whole day worrying she'd lose her job. Very occasionally my mother prowled around to check on us, perhaps once or twice a year, and early one day she crept up on Evalina to find her testing the temperature of the milk in Delia's bottle by taking a swig from the teat instead of putting a few drops onto the inside of her wrist as she'd been taught. My mother exploded, Evalina nearly jumped out of her skin with fright and, although she didn't get the sack, for the rest of her time as our nanny it must have preyed on her mind that her job was hanging by a thread.

Fortunately for me, my mother was too engrossed in her gardening to check on me, and for my first eleven years she never knew what I was up to. If there was any need for me to be called back to the house, Evalina left Delia with Lisha and came to look for me, calling in that special hill-top-calling voice all the Zulus used to communicate over long distances. Her voice carried along the valley and bounced off the mountainsides, and I was able to sense by the urgency in the tone of her cries to hurry and meet her. I didn't want either of us to get into trouble.

Our staff came from iMpendhle, the Zulu settlement (bigger than a normal sized village) of round, thatched huts, perched on a hillside that lay on the escarpment behind our farm. All their front entrances faced the East, and it looked as if the huts were peering out over the valley into the sunrise. Up there lived the chief, the *Induna*, who ruled over the tribe, and it was to him that everybody deferred.

When Makhaye wanted a wife, for instance, he dressed up in his best clothes (I remember a well-cut brown tweed shooting-jacket with discretely understated suede elbow patches, and baggy, khaki drill long trousers – cast-offs from my father's 1930s Jesus College, Cambridge wardrobe).

On another occasion, I recall a perfectly tailored dark Savile Row suit, with an almost imperceptible pinstripe.

Since he and my father had a similar, slight build, it looked as though Makhaye himself had stood to be measured for the suit in that London tailor's fitting rooms. Now he was ready to spend his weekend-off in his kraal, going hat in hand to see the chief to ask his permission to marry the girl he'd been courting. He carefully wrapped his hand-me-down brogues, polished to a mirror shine, in a couple of sheets of old newspaper and packed them into a satchel he'd made for himself from the skin of a Bushbuck with a pattern of black and white porcupine quills he'd threaded through eyelet holes bored into the hide. He'd added a trim of speckled Guinea fowl feathers to complete the festive effect.

He placed his rather battered and definitely faded old brown felt trilby hat (another sartorial treasure from my father's university days) on his closely-shorn peppercorn curls, bent over to roll up the cuffs of his trouser legs, to reveal skinny black ankles and horny bare feet, and carefully padlocked shut the door of his little room built onto the back of our garage. He hoisted his cheerfully fluttering bag over his shoulder and strode off, with me following closely at his heels.

We listened to the calls coming from the other Zulu men, and he answered so that his voice ricocheted around the valley, arranging where to meet up with the other members of our farm staff who were going home for the weekend. They collected at the cow byre; about seven of our staff, men and women, all dressed in their best clothes, some of the younger girls wore the traditional Zulu *uBeshu* (a small apron of beads, or an animal skin hand sewn and covered in rainbow-like, eye-catchingly colourful beadwork around the waist), bare breasts, and many, equally colourful bracelets and necklaces.

I was left standing at the farm boundary to watch them disappear up the mountainside behind our milking shed, feeling like a puppy that had been told to stay at home. I would have given anything to follow that cheerful chattering group home to iMpendhle, to see their grandparents who had worked for Grandpa, and were now retired, sitting comfortably on woollen blankets, backs leaning against the sun-baked mud and dung walls of their huts, while their daughters brought home rations from Dad, carrying the big sacks on their heads – mealie meal to make *aMahewu* (corn beer) and *uPhutu*, sacks of brown sugar, tea, coffee and meat as well as gallons of skimmed milk. There would be other treats too: sweets for their grandchildren, bread, and *Coca Cola* bought with their wages from the local store up there.

"Please can I come with you?" I pleaded.

"No, we're sorry, nKosizana." They seemed genuinely regretful. "You have to stay here at home with Lisha."

Sadly, I watched them move into single file to walk through *uMgeni Poort* pass (just a steep, rocky single pony track that took them above the nuns and Wakefield) and finally along the back of the *iNhlosane* peak to their home in iMpendhle. Then I walked slowly and reluctantly back to the farmhouse, moodily scuffing my bare feet in the dust.

When permission was granted for Makhaye to marry the girl (and it usually was after some sort of gift – usually money – had been handed over to the prospective father-in-law, and often the tribal chief as well), Makhaye then had to go to see the father of his intended bride. There he sat with the older man, in his hut, and they discussed *uLobola* – the bride price. In those days twenty head of cattle was an acceptable price for a good, strong and beautiful young woman. It was a very proud moment when the father and his future son-in-law shook hands on the deal, and that was the signal for the women of that kraal to bring in *calabashes* of *aMahewu* – some of them wives of the bride's father, and any sisters she might have still living there. The bride-to-be shyly came in to join them and, kneeling obediently, offered her future husband the first swig from the gourd of beer she carried. Finally a goat was slaughtered and roasted to seal the pact and celebrate the betrothal, and everybody feasted and drank to the happy event.

After the weekend of joy and celebrations, Makhaye had to slither over a loose surface and scrabble his way down the steep mountain, and walk back to the farm to have a quiet word with my father. It was arranged that, in lieu of some of his salary, he could have two new-born bull calves and a couple of heifers from my father's stock. This worked well, as our herd was a particularly good one – a cross between Aberdeen Angus (good hardy beasts carrying a lot of meat), and Swiss Simmentaler, which were huge. There was also a strain of Brahmin added in to produce strong and really heavy cattle with great, powerful humps, which would have won prizes at the Royal Agricultural Show in Pietermaritzburg if my father had been bothered enough to enter them. Historically and traditionally Zulus kept *Nguni* – scrub cattle – smaller, rangy beasts with long horns and an attractive pale mottled hide.

These were resistant to most bush-, tick-, and fly-carried diseases, and they seemed to manage on fairly poor grazing, but they didn't carry much meat on their bony bodies. My father's cattle needed a fair bit of attention with regular dipping and inoculations, and on those days Makhaye could bring his own little herd along to be treated immediately after the farm boys had finished with my father's and the nuns' cattle. Once interbred, the herd became a good stock of large, hardy beasts and of great value to any Zulu cattle owner.

~~~

# 13

# Witch-doctors

**O**nce, as the Zulus went about their work, there was a flurry of excitement and the buzz of conversation about a Sangoma coming. "What's a *Sangoma*?" I asked Evalina that evening as she bathed Delia and me.

"It's the witch-doctor," she said, scrubbing at my feet, which were ingrained with dirt from running about barefoot all the time. I squirmed as the nail-brush tickled my leathery soles.

"We're getting a visit from a *Sangoma* from iMpendhle. Somebody has asked one to come here to give them some information. Perhaps they've lost something precious or they have a problem they want fixed. The *Sangoma* will throw the bones and they will show them what they need to know."

"What sort of bones?"

"I don't know – it's all to do with *uMuti*." She shuddered involuntary although the bathroom was warm and steamy. "We will soon find out though."

"Will I be able to go and see them doing the bone *umuthi*?" I persisted, but Evalina wasn't to be drawn any further.

She inspected the soles of my feet – she was short-sighted and had to peer at them closely. "Keep still!"

"Where will the *Sangoma* stay?" I enjoyed anything new that cropped up in our uneventful day-to-day lives, however irrelevant it was to me.

"I don't know yet – perhaps in somebody's hut – the person who has called them. Now jump out so I can dry you."

# White Zulu

Fiona Ross

As I lay in bed that night I recalled a dim, distant memory of a witch-doctor that Grandpa had summoned to sort out a stock theft problem he'd had once, long ago. I must have been about three years old, and I remember it was a crisp winter's morning.

Although the sun's rays had warmed the farmyard, there was still sparkling white frost lying on the long grass in the shade of the old dry-stone wall that enclosed his fowl run. A cow had mysteriously gone missing from Grandpa's herd, and he'd assumed it had been stolen, so he sent word to a local witch-doctor to come and find the culprit.

My older sisters and I stood well back behind him as his five farm labourers, summoned from their morning jobs, shuffled nervously to form a line in front of him. They had respectfully removed their faded cotton hats, which they now twisted anxiously in their calloused black hands. Waving his walking stick to indicate the low stone wall, Grandpa told them to sit in a row and keep still. Still wielding his stick expansively, to illustrate various points, Grandpa proceeded (in his fluent Zulu) to tell the little group lined up on the stone wall how he'd discovered his cow was missing, and what he was about to do to find out who'd stolen it. Tension built up perceptibly as he carried on describing what he'd planned. The men shifted nervously on the wall, showing the whites of their eyes as they glanced at one another, hoping, I suppose, that somebody would own up before the ordeal began. Then the medicine-man appeared in full regalia, with feathers and blown-up dried sheeps' bladders flapping from his head and body, to stand in front of the group, next to my grandfather.

Quietly the witch-doctor said to Grandpa, "The guilty one will fall off the wall backwards." The arrival of the witch-doctor seemed to strike terror into the five Zulus, who sat on the stone wall, statue-still in their ragged overalls and worn gumboots, eyes fixed in front of them like condemned men. The interrogation began in rapid Zulu, during which the man with special powers flung his hand out at the group several times, indicating that he was putting *mTagati* (his own spells) on them. He might even have thrown some substance like a powder at them, I don't remember. Suddenly one man plummeted backwards off the wall with a frightened yell, landing on his back in the fowl run behind them. We all gave a startled jump, especially the men on either side of him.

"Guilty!" said the witch-doctor succinctly.

Grandpa was delighted that the money he'd spent on the procedure had had such a good outcome, and happily paid the witch-doctor his fee. The cattle thief had revealed himself, Grandpa recovered his stolen cow, and the whole event served to deter any other would-be cattle thieves.

The following morning, I ran off to play with Kupane, the Cook-woman's boy. He was eight and lived with his parents in one of the small round mud huts up at the kraal. His father was a labourer, and his mother cooked the food for all the single male workers that lived in a long oblong hut, called the *'phuthu khaya'*, a sort of dormitory, where they slept and ate. We'd been told by both our parents, Mrs Bannatyne, and even Evalina, that we were never allowed ever to go anywhere near there, not even to walk along the road that passed in front of the *phuthu khaya* – but I'd nipped in once anyway, purely out of curiosity to see why it was so expressly forbidden.

It was almost pitch dark and extremely smoky in there, as there were no windows at all, and certainly no chimney, just the small front opening that served as an entrance, with the homemade door propped open. As my eyes adjusted to the gloom all I could see were two rows of makeshift wooden beds, each covered in an army blanket and with pillows made from hessian sacking stuffed with hay. The beds were ranged against the long walls, all the legs set in jam tins and then propped up on bricks to keep the Tokoloshe away. I'd long ago asked Evalina and Lisha why they insisted on raising the legs of their beds on bricks. "To keep away the Tokoloshe" was the emphatic reply.

"What's a Tokoloshe?" I'd asked.

"It's a small, black, mischievous demon that comes out at night when you're asleep, and does bad, bad things to you! They can't climb up bricks though, so that's why we put them under the bed legs."

"What sort of bad things?" I persisted, but everybody just pressed their lips together, shook their heads and changed the subject. Each of the four wooden hand-cut legs were placed first in a used tin (some with the baked beans or pilchards in tomato sauce label still on) filled with an unidentifiable liquid – probably paraffin – to keep ants, scorpions and other creepy-crawlies from climbing up into the bed.

A woodfire burned in a circle of big stones in the middle of the dung floor, and as my eyes began to sting and weep from the dense smoke coming off it, I felt something tickling and then biting my ankles, and ran quickly outside again into the bright morning sunlight. Looking down I saw what appeared to be crawling black socks over my bare feet and ankles. Fleas! Hundreds of them had latched on and were biting my skin. The itching was unbearable, and I fled to the standpipe to run icy cold water over my legs and ankles, frantically scrubbing them off.

Half a dozen of the *khaya* residents were sitting on a log, backs to the sun-warmed wall of their hut, enjoying their breakfast (a plate of *phuthu* scooped from the big, black, iron three-legged pot over the fire in front of the doorway – this was one of the two daily meals of *phuthu* Kupane's mother made for them – with a dollop of *amasi* on top. A tin cup of well-brewed coffee was placed carefully on the hard-baked clean-swept ground next to each man), and they all burst out laughing as I danced and hopped, scraping at the fleas in disgust.

"*Hau!* nKosizana – that's why nKosikazi and Zuma told you never to go in there!" And they slapped their thighs and cackled and shook their heads, wiping away tears of mirth, some of them mimicking my slapping motions with their brown, work-hardened hands.

Still chuckling, they eased themselves to their feet as the farm bell rang for them to start their day's work, showing pink gums as they yawned widely, stretching their arms over their heads and arching their backs, and, still chuckling, they made their way to collect their *pangas* (machetes) for a long morning's slog hacking pungent-smelling *Bonga-Bonga* from the river banks.

Kupane and I each had a Dinky car (I'd given him one of mine) and the previous afternoon he'd said that they needed servicing.

He was waiting for me at the workshop, and we both poked around in all the tins and containers on the wooden work-bench looking for axle grease. "Nothing here," said Kupane, "we'll have to go and look under the jeep." He crawled under our old war-issue American Willy's jeep and scraped some black grease off the back axle. "Right. Now we must do our cars."

We were squatting under the gum-trees next to the standpipe up at the huts, in the shade, working grease into our cars' axles, when I saw somebody approaching slowly up the path. It was the strangest apparition I'd ever seen in my life. She was a large middle-aged Zulu woman, and there was nothing uncommon in that – it was what she was wearing that made me stop what I was doing and stare, my mouth open in astonishment. She wore several animal skins (some of which I recognised as those of Spotted Genets and Banded Mongooses), sewn together to make a voluminous, flapping skirt. Over her shoulders she had draped a cape of Black Backed Jackal skin, long, bushy black tail and all, and pinned to her shoulder, like a brooch, was the head of a recently-killed chicken.

She wore a bizarre head-dress of other strange materials of which I recognised only one – a python skin.

Festooned around her neck and waist, were strings onto

which she'd threaded the dried vertebrae of many different small wild animals, seed pods that looked like dried, bloated blue ticks, scarlet carapaces of beetles, ladybirds, and more pieces of snake skin. She had necklaces of traditional Zulu beads, too, but not in any patterns and colours I'd ever seen before. The strangest effect of all was the dried sheep's bladders. She'd blown up about a dozen of them so that they looked like grey, semi-opaque balloons, and tied them to her head-dress and around her upper body and waist. They flapped alarmingly as she walked, and the bones rattled loudly with every movement she made.

I stood there gaping at her. "Kupane!" I turned to my friend, but he was gone. He must have bolted into the nearest hut. I stood up to greet this apparition. I may have been slightly apprehensive but I still had my Zulu manners.

I put both hands forward, the right one just behind the left to *Xhawula* (shake hands) as is the custom, and bent my knees in a little bob.

"*Saubona*," I said. I didn't know what title to use to address this stranger, so I left it at that. "*Sawubona inGana wUmlungu*." ("Greetings child of a white man.") An odd way to describe me since everybody on and even off the farm called me nKosizana (the chief's daughter). This person obviously didn't know anything about us. She looked imperiously around at our surroundings – the cluster of round, thatched mud huts in which the farm staff lived. As she turned her head, the sheep's bladders bobbed and her skins rustled with a crackling noise.

"Where is everybody?" she asked. I looked around as well, and discovered the place was deserted. That was odd. Normally there was lots of activity going on in and around the huts – children playing, mothers sweeping around the front steps or stirring big pots of *phuthu* on the fires that burned constantly in front of their dwellings.

There wasn't a soul about.

"I'll find somebody," I replied, and ran into Kupane's hut. I suspected I'd find him in there. He was cowering under his parents' bed with just the whites of his eyes visible in the gloom.

I noticed that the legs of their bed were also set up on bricks to keep the Tokoloshe away.

"Kupane!" I hissed. "What's going on? What are you doing?"

"That's the witch-doctor," he whispered back, his teeth chattering with fright. "Tell her there's nobody here." I'd never seen him this frightened before. I peered at him closely: his face was beaded with sweat and his skin had a greyish pallor. Then I remembered what Evalina had said.

"Somebody called the Sangoma to come here," I said to Kupane in a whisper.

I could smell his fear – a pungent, musky, almost polecat-like stink coming off him. "We can't send her away."

"I'm not going out there," he hissed emphatically, and I realised that I would have to drag him bodily, probably screaming, out of his bolthole if I wanted him to deal with this situation.

"Stay there then, you coward, and I'll go and call Evalina." I ran back to the oddly-dressed woman and asked her politely to wait while I fetched someone, then I trotted back past the stables and sheds to the house. Evalina was kneeling on a piece of sheepskin in the sitting-room, polishing the crystal knob of the door that led to the dining-room. "The *Sangoma*'s here," I said quietly in her ear. She froze, the soft cloth dropped out of her hand and onto the floor, and her eyes widened, the whites showing as they swivelled about in terror.

"Where?" she gasped. I noticed that she too had beads of sweat that suddenly appeared on her brow and top lip, and her skin was going grey like Kupane's.

"She's up at the huts," I said. "She's waiting up there and I can't find anybody."

"I can't leave my work. nKosikazi would be very angry. What shall I do?"

She remained where she was, still on her knees, a middle-aged mother and probably grandmother, torn between her fear of the witch-doctor and that of my mother. "Go and tell Makhaye. He's up at the back chopping firewood. He'll be able to slip away and go and greet her." I did as I was told, and then stood in the road as I watched Makhaye hurry nervously up the path towards their huts.

The Zulus would never have involved me in whatever transpired, and for me the remainder of these proceedings were a closed door.

I knew very little about this witchcraft business.

Incidents in our daily lives regularly revealed themselves as *mTagati*. For instance, when we had boiled or fried eggs, and Evalina saw a minute blood clot (as often appears in eggs), she'd fuss and very carefully scrape the offending particle out with a spoon, then she'd go and throw it out of the window very quickly, muttering to herself. Zulus believe that's a sign that someone's put a spell on the intended egg-eater. She would have thrown the whole egg away, I know, if she hadn't been so afraid of my mother.

Chameleons, too, threw them all into a state of sheer terror, and we could achieve some satisfying results by walking casually up to anybody on the farm and suddenly thrusting a hand out to show them a live chameleon clinging there, with its tail wrapped around one of our fingers. If the startled creature opened its mouth to hiss, it showed a bright orange interior where its tongue lay coiled, and this could produce an actual fit among the women. "It'll bite you and you'll die!" they pleaded.

"*Unwabo* is venomous!" Frogs and toads produced a similar reaction, although not quite as dramatic. Zulus believe that chameleons, toads, and frogs are all as deadly as snakes, if not more so. The Zulus believe implicitly that they carry venom and can strike just like any snake. The latter on the other hand caused an excited shout of "*iNyoka!*" whenever one was seen slithering around or lying in wait, as puff-adders do, and everybody gathered around to kill it. Finally, an argument usually arose as to who would claim it as theirs to use for *umuti*. It seems that one could apply snake fat and the oil to one's joints to reduce pain and arthritis, and that qualified as medicine, but without the terror associated with witchcraft.

~~~

# *14*

# Zulu folklore and friends

One day we were sitting next to where the washing and ironing girls hung our laundry out to dry on a sagging wire line strung between two wonky poles. Our sheets, which were too big to hang up, were draped over the shaggy kikuyu grass along the path. Minute red ticks climbed into the warm, damp seams and settled there until the sheets were back on our beds, when they crept out again to lodge their mandibles into our warm flesh. For years and years we all suffered from hundreds of tiny itching bites around our pulse points, until our GP (family doctor) asked my father (when his bites had gone septic and turned into a huge abscess) "Where do your servants dry your laundry?" and he had explained about the ticks. So my mother had rather grudgingly arranged for Jomela to put up another couple of wire lines for our sheets. It was bliss to be able to get into a bed after our baths without itching so badly that I sometimes scratched my ankles raw. Oddly enough, ticks never seemed to bother my mother much.

"I was reading a book about war last night," I said to Evalina as we sat in the shade of the gum-trees. I didn't know the Zulu for 'war' so I used the English word.

"What is this thing 'war'?" she asked, two vertical lines wrinkling her gleaming brown forehead in puzzlement, as she threaded a long line of tiny scarlet coloured beads on to a piece of cotton with an embroidery needle.

"It's when two countries fight over some land, I think," I said uncertainly. "Anyway, I was reading this book called *The Great*

*Escape* about prisoners of war."

"What are 'pleesoners'?" She carefully tied a knot in the thread and began picking up some yellow beads with her needle.

"A prisoner is when a man gets caught by others. They put him in a place where he can't escape, and they keep him there for years even, and they give him very little food ..." I expounded, warming to my subject.

"Why?" interrupted Evalina. "We Zulus don't do that. When we catch a man who has done something wrong, we kill him," she said, biting off the thread, her strong white teeth making a sharp 'snap!', then she turned her beadwork over in her pink palms, inspecting with satisfaction the small square of red, yellow, green and blue beads woven into an intricate pattern {she was making a *uBeshu* – a little modesty panel worn by Zulu maidens over the *nQutu* (the private parts) – for one of her young daughters}.

"Hau! Do you kill them all?" I asked, surprised at this revelation. "Why?" Evalina put the *uBeshu* down on her lap and leaned her back against the warm trunk of the gum-tree. Its bark hung down in strips, like peeling wallpaper, to reveal the smooth delicate pinkish, grey-green skin underneath. Pungent eucalyptus leaves rustled dryly overhead in the hot breeze that meandered through the valley at this time of the afternoon. The rest of the farm lay in its usual soporific state while everybody slept through the worst of the heat. The Christmas Beetles were the only creatures that made any noise as they screamed incessantly.

"Well now. If a man steals something from a member of the tribe, or hurts somebody for no good reason, he's brought before the chief who, with the other elders, questions him. If he won't speak they'll fetch the *Sangoma* – the healer – or even *mTagati* – the witch-doctor who casts evil spells." She stopped speaking and shuddered for a moment, disturbed by the very thought.

"The witch-doctor puts a curse on the man so that he has to tell the council all his wrongdoings, and the chief then speaks to his elders, and they hold an *umhlangano* (meeting or council) and decide whether they should punish him or not. If the crime is not a bad one, they let the man go, making sure he is very frightened. But if it is a serious one, they put him to death. The *Induna* tells one of his warriors to run a spear through his heart. Or sometimes they throw him off a cliff to his death, like King Chaka used to do with his enemies in my great- grandfather's day."

"Isn't that very cruel?" I asked; my eyes big with alarm.

"No!" said Evalina emphatically. "That means the end of the problem. Just think about it. If the tribe has to keep a man prisoner they would have to first dig a deep pit. One with very steep sides that he cannot climb out of and run away. Then somebody – a woman – has to cook food for him and take it to him three times a day. She also has to take away his waste."

She pulled down her mouth and shook her head at the thought.

"It would be a drain on the strength of the tribe, especially as, as you know, every few months we have to move on to find better grazing and game. If the prisoner does manage to escape, he will have a grudge against his people forever and he will be a very dangerous man. No, it's better that he's put to death straight away."

"It's the same with old people – those who are too weak to help gather food or hunt. When they can no longer walk, we carry them out beyond the *boma* (the thorn enclosure), out to where the hyenas will take them during the night." Evalina sat there for a moment, deep in thought, and then with one hand picked up her *uBeshu* again and with the other she began scratching around in her rush basket for another packet of beads.

"Every member of a Zulu tribe has to serve a purpose," she said, holding a cellophane bag of white beads up to the light and scrutinising it through narrowed eyes. She then selected a handful and began to thread them carefully onto her needle and cotton.

"They have to be able to move on with the others to new

hunting grounds, and bring food back to the huts. If they can't, then they are useless and make the tribe vulnerable, having to stay behind to look after them. The weak and frail have to be despatched. Sick people, very old people, and even babies, get taken out beyond the *boma* as night falls."

"Babies!" I exclaimed in horror. "Why babies?" I sat up from the soft tuft of kikuyu grass where I'd been lying, forgetting that I was almost certainly attracting those tiny red pepper ticks that lurked on its blades just waiting for such an opportunity.

"Twin babies," explained Evalina impassively. "If a woman gives birth to twins, the tribe sees it as a curse, put on her by *mTagati*. They'll take away the smaller or weaker baby, wrap it in a grass mat, and leave it out beyond the *boma* for the night predators to take away."

I wriggled uneasily on the grass tussock, and it was not from the thought of ticks crawling into my broeks. That explained why I'd never seen twins among the numerous Zulu children I played with every day. I had twin cousins though, whom I met now and again at polo tournaments, a boy and a girl about two years younger than I was. Wow! I thought. Imagine if they'd been Zulus …

"What if the mother of the twins wanted to keep both babies?" I asked, perplexed. "Could she hide one of her babies and say she'd had only one?"

"Hau! No!" exclaimed Evalina. "The mother of those twins would be as frightened as the rest of the tribe. And anyway – how could she hide a baby away for ever? The people would soon find it. Come now. The sun is getting low in the sky. It's getting on for your bath time. We must see if you've picked up any ticks where you've been sitting in that long grass."

She packed away her beadwork and heaved herself to her feet, brushing dust off the seat of her navy uniform skirt with both hands. I followed her down the narrow earth path, carved over the years by the bare feet of so many of our workers: the washerwoman,

Masango when he walked up to the chicken run to fetch a fowl for lunch; Makhaye who fed the fowls and then put them to bed each night (secure behind strong wire netting in the corrugated iron hut, so that they would be safe from Genets and Water Mongoose, who could slip in though the tiniest hole in a wire cage and kill the lot).

Another of my best friends was our *Induna*, Robert nGidi, who had led an almost parallel life to Dad's. nGidi arrived at New Forest in 1925, when Dad's parents moved across from their ranch, Beverly, in the Dargle, about 15 miles away. His father was Grandpa's *Induna* at Beverly, and naturally came across to New Forest with his wives and children, including Robert, who was ten at the time (the same age as Dad). The two boys became close friends and playmates; there was none of the peculiar snobbery that made Mum insist that we girls never play with '*munt*' children. Dad and nGidi spent all their time together, until Dad went to boarding school at King's School in Nottingham Road, and then a couple of years later on to a College, at Balgowan, about 30 miles away from the farm.

They continued to play together during the school holidays though, although nGidi must have gone back to iMpendhle at some stage during those years, as he had had some schooling, was able to read and write, and thus pass his driving test in Mooi River.

After the Second World War (when Dad came home to live at New Forest with his new bride), nGidi senior retired. Robert nGidi took his place as the head boy on the farm, and, like Mum and Dad, he produced four daughters; he never had a son, just these four girls. Of course nGidi was delighted as each new girl arrived, as it meant he would receive many head of good cattle as *uLobola*, and each birth was a cause for rejoicing: rather the opposite of what was happening in the big farmhouse five hundred yards away, where Mum and Dad received the news of the gender of each of their children with such dismay.

nGidi had his own hut, bigger than any of the others, except the *uPhutu Kaya* (the dormitory accommodation for bachelor farm labourers), which was a long, oblong thatched hut with several doors. His hut was round, like the others, but bigger. His most senior wife lived with him, but none of his daughters – they lived with the rest of his other wives in iMpendhle, and had some sort of schooling, as nGidi earned a better salary than the rest of our Zulus, being in charge of all of them. The hierarchy went upwards from him, to the white manager, and then to Dad who had to finally settle disputes or make the most crucial decisions.

All the farm staff liked and respected him immensely, and he was a valuable asset to the smooth running of the farm. His wife kept a *hok* with some fowls, and had a flourishing veggie patch, growing pumpkin, sorghum, potato, and mealie.

To Mum's disgust the baboons never went near nGidi's veggies.

That was because, wisely, his wife used to hire an *umfaan* for pocket money of a few pennies a day, to spend the day throwing sticks or stones at them to keep them away, a solution that Dad had suggested to Mum when the problem of baboons trashing her garden first arose, and which she greeted with a snort of disgust and the comment, "I don't want any idle *umfaans* around, getting up to mischief."

And so the baboons regularly laid waste to her veggie and flower gardens for the best part of sixty years.

To add insult to injury, nGidi's wife used to bring a huge woven basket, filled with prize vegetables, over to Mum as a gift now and again. nGidi also ran some cattle (*uLobola* for his daughters) with Dad's herd, and had them dipped and inoculated at no cost to himself, other than all the effort he put into running the farm efficiently for Dad. nGidi was, as was only proper in a chief, quite portly, with a big belly. He ferried the labourers about, carted winter supplement feed for the stock, and oversaw everything. He was the intermediary between the staff and the white farm manager.

Mr Bannatyne (our farm manager) was the buffer between Dad and his labourers. Our Zulus hated him with a deadly loathing.

They called him *mDhloloti* ('cattle tulip', an indigenous, poisonous species of lily, toxic and deadly to cattle), and watched him warily as he strutted around among them, giving orders by gesticulating with the short handled, long *riempie* whip he always carried in his right hand. His cruel little red eyes constantly darting around to see what trouble he could nip in the bud.

When nGidi gained his driving licence, Dad had an immaculate white chauffeur's coat and white cap (like yachtsmen wear) with a shiny black peak sent up for him from WG Brown's, to wear on special occasions. Otherwise he drove the jeep and trailer all over the farm wearing faded denim bib-overalls. When (for a year) all four of us were at boarding school *Prep and College* at Hilton Road, nGidi would drive the enormous Pontiac, called Gig (back seat and boot filled with our four school trunks), over the day before, so there would be enough room for Mum and the four of us, plus our own small overnight cases, in the car the following day when she fetched us herself.

When the time came for us to get married, nGidi proudly drove Dad and each bride to the church, the car beribboned with white satin, and our *Induna* proudly at the wheel in his smart chauffeur's uniform. He beamed back at the waving crowds of Zulus who screamed, "*Umkoti!*" (bride) as the car sailed by, his broad smile revealing about half a dozen rickety-looking teeth higgledy-piggledy in his shining pink gums.

When we girls had married and left home, and time came for nGidi to retire, he left the farm to live out his days in his hut in his kraal in iMpendhle. He had plenty of wives to look after him, and no shortage of daughters, either, to do the same.

As he and his wife could live for nothing at New Forest (because there was such an abundance of food, blankets, gumboots and overalls), and because he'd received a good salary as *Induna*, all his money was intact, so he had been able to save almost all his salary to pay for his daughters to have an education, and they became teachers and nurses and clerks. They, in turn, were able to support their parents in a comfortable retirement. If only Dad had been similarly enlightened, things would have turned out for him as well as they did for old nGidi.

Jomela had spent nearly all his life herding sheep and cattle at the top of the farm. He had a hut in the shelter of a clump of old gum-trees on the ridge of the escarpment that divided the top farm from the rest of the valley. It was built from corrugated iron, and had several sheep pens surrounding it in which kikuyu grass grew in lush profusion as additional grazing for any sick or lame animals that he rounded up on horseback and brought in for treatment. He had a bony, shaggy old Basutu pony that he rode over the veldt all summer long while he checked on the stock, and occasionally he rode down into the valley to report losses to Dad or the manager.

Black Backed Jackal took the opportunity during the lambing season to snatch the odd lamb when they were casting about, competing with our big, pitch black and noisily vocal African crows for the placentas they felt were rightfully theirs; if jackals became too numerous and posed a real problem, Dad sent a message for the *Jackal Pack*.

This was vermin control in the form of a Zulu hunter and his pack of toast-rack-ribbed curs – *iziGodoyi* – who arrived at the back gate amid a frenzy of barking and snarling from our own dogs, who had to be shut up in the dairy while a transaction went on between Dad and the Jackal man. The state offered a bounty of fifteen rand on each tail that could be produced at the Nottingham Road police station. I expect Dad offered another small sum over and above the bounty fee, a ration of *uPhutu* and our plentiful skimmed milk for the hunter and his dogs, and free run of the farm until jackal numbers were reduced to an acceptable level.

I was horrified at the sight of so many undernourished and

desperate-looking dogs.

I hated the way they cringed round their master's legs, lips curled ingratiatingly, skinny tails tucked under their concave bellies, and the way they shivered when our sleek, well-fed Pointers, Radar and Rufous, bayed at them. Of course, I followed at a safe distance to sit on the bank to watch the jackal hunter make his preparations.

When he'd received his ration – a big bucket of *uPhutu* from our cook-woman, he asked for a wheelbarrow. He tipped a portion of *uPhutu* for himself into a billy-can he kept in a sack he had slung over his shoulder, and the rest into the filthy wheelbarrow.

The cook-woman brought him the same bucket filled with separated milk, and he poured some into an empty whisky bottle from his sack for his tea, and the rest on top of the *uPhutu* in the wheelbarrow. Then he stood back, and the pack of about fifteen dogs fell on the food wolfing down *uPhutu* and milk in great choking gulps.

I'd never seen starving animals before, and felt ashamed at my disgust as I watched these creatures eating for their very lives. The jackal skins were lovely: black and tan and white, and I'd have loved one for my very own to put at the foot of my bed, but the hunter shook his head and said he could sell them for good money in mTuleni (Nottingham Road).

During the winter Jomela and the stock came down into the valley to spend the short (two to three months) season safe from the sudden snowfalls that fell each year and covered the top of the farm, painting it white as far as the eye could see, joining our farm to the Drakensberg Mountains, which were already snow-covered from April onwards.

Jomela lived down in the valley now. The sheep had long ago been sold, as wool prices plummeted in the 1960s, after the invention of cheaper, synthetic substitutes such as acrylics and polyester, and now somebody else herded cattle up on top.

He was enlisted as a spare on Mum's team of garden girls.

He washed both cars and the Land Rover every morning, although
Dad often got into the car and said dryly, "Jomela's given it a Jewish
wash. He's only cleaned all the bits I can see from the driver's seat."
Jomela also did most of the watering and various other small jobs
that younger Zulu women and girls thought were beneath their
dignity, and more suited to withered old men.

Picking up after the baboons was one of them. It meant
replanting the potato or pumpkins vines torn up by them, or trudging
up the hill behind the house to replace the water pipes they'd pulled
up leaving our supply to trickle impotently into the soil that the
baboons had grubbed through looking for *songololos* (millipedes)
instead of into the reservoir.

Edging the lawn took up most of his time, and he kept up a
lively, animated conversation with himself as he slowly inched his
way along the endless sweep of kikuyu grass with his shears. Now
and again he'd give a loud hyena-like cackle of laughter at one of his
own jokes, and we found it quite unnerving if we were lying in a
cane easy chair on the front veranda with our legs in the sun, reading
and relishing the peace, or idly watching purple and golden
butterflies sipping from dangling red Fuchsia flowers hanging from
the big white pots at the veranda's edge. Greater Double Collared
Sunbirds flocked to sip from scarlet Salvia and the males especially,
in their iridescent plumage of emerald heads and scarlet bodies with
a band of bright blue across the breast, hanging tentatively, almost
hovering as their long curled tongues searched down the floral tubes
for sweet nectar.

In the middle of our hottest summer days, all we could do
was to retire to the deepest shade of the very back of our front
veranda and lie there, bare feet up on the cushioned footstool and
read, or gaze into the dense bush on the other side of the river. Our
thoughts would be miles away when we'd hear a hissing from just
the other side of the flowers and then a high-pitched cackling that
subsided to wheezing chuckles, making us jump with fright, only to

stand up and, peering over the shrubs, see Jomela's tattered old hat going slowly by. We were fairly accustomed to Jomela, but he could make visitors jump out of their skins, expecting a puff-adder when his hissing began.

~~~

# *15*

# Lyndhurst (up on top)

Shortly after he moved in to New Forest, Grandpa bought the adjacent ranch, Lyndhurst, which was on the plateau at the top of the mountain behind our house. Lyndhurst was an immense, 3,000-acre, treeless stretch of grassland, including the four vast main marshes that formed the sponge of the Umgeni River. It was the breeding habitat of South Africa's only three crane species – the rare and highly endangered Wattled Crane, as well as the Blue Crane, which is our National Bird, and the Crowned Crane.

It is most unusual, if not almost unknown, for all three types of crane to occur in one place in South Africa.

Getting to Lyndhurst is a climb of 1,000 feet, and Grandpa had put his engineering skills to use, building a narrow road that zigzagged up the nearly vertical mountainside. He'd used Zulu labourers, and oxen pulling a homemade metal blade to scour out the road, which was wide enough to accommodate an ox-wagon and a team of 16 oxen. At one bend in the road, which he called 'Devil's Corner', he'd encountered several massive boulders (rather like the ones we called 'elephant rocks' as they were the same size, texture and colour). Some of the smaller rocks he managed to split by the simple means of lighting a fire on top of the boulder, getting it as hot as possible and then getting his Zulus to pour buckets of ice cold water from the nearby mountain stream over them. The rocks cracked cleanly through their weakest places, and he repeated the process until the pieces were small enough to be hauled away by his team of oxen.

The huge boulders were almost insurmountable obstructions, but Grandpa, typically undaunted, sent a letter to WG Brown & Co (his father-in-law's warehouse) in Durban and asked for some sticks of dynamite to be sent up by rail to New Forest. He duly received these in a (presumably) carefully packed wooden box, fuses included. He instructed one of his labourers to drill the correct sized hole in each boulder (by hand, so this must have been quite some job as the rocks are solid granite). Grandpa placed the sticks of dynamite into the holes, gave his *Induna* (nGidi's father) a box of matches, and said, "Go and light the bit of string and then *balega* as fast as you can to the furthest boulder and hide behind it" (he already having placed himself well out of reach of any possible flying debris). The technique worked, and as far as I know nobody got hurt, and one can see the exact spot on each boulder where the dynamite blasted the rock in half, or quarters. The road is passable in any weather.

As soon as you crested the final rise in the road leading up from the steep valley, all that was visible was rolling veldt and marshes as far as the eye could see, with the distant range of the Drakensberg Mountains as the backdrop. It was lovely to ride there in the summer months, over the long, soft grass, looking at the heifers grazing the luscious green fodder, with their skippity calves at their heels, and then having a glorious extended gallop along the extra-long, closely mown airstrip with its faded, ragged, khaki canvas windsock on the corner. Our strip was at the same altitude as Johannesburg Airport's main take-off runway, and even the small planes that used our strip needed an extra amount of runway to be able to take-off into the thin air at 6,000 feet.

The airstrip was the bane of Dad's life. The Department of Defence insisted it was kept closely mown and operational, and that the windsock was up and flying at all times, in case there was any 'unrest' from iMpendhle. This was during the forty-odd years of living under Apartheid, and our strip, as well as our new bridge over the Umgeni, were vital access routes to strategic points overlooking that large African settlement where all our staff came from. Guests and relations who decided to visit us by plane regularly landed on our lovely extra-long airstrip.

One early summer afternoon, just as the pale green grass was getting longer, a group of us, Mum and Dad, some of my sisters, an English cousin in his early twenties who was staying with us, and the dogs, were enjoying a pleasant stroll along the airstrip. Dad had parked the Land Rover at the very edge of the strip and was doing a routine check for molehills, which would need to be scraped flat before they became hummocks and dangerous to aircraft taking off or landing. He also needed to check for antbear holes; the Aardvarks would come out at night and dig deep holes in the ground as they searched for the delicious termites (to them and the Zulus anyway – apparently according to Dumasane they tasted of nice, fatty marrow). These deep holes also posed a hazard, and needed to be filled in by hand, with shovels, by his labourers. He also needed to see when the grass strip next needed cutting by a small team of oxen and the old mower.

We heard a strange whistling sound high above our heads, but it didn't sound like any bird-call we knew, and we all looked up. There was a glider circling gracefully, the whistling coming from its wire-wing struts. The pilot circled lower as we craned our necks to see who it was, and we hurried off the airstrip, grabbing the dogs and hustling them into the cab of our vehicle. The beautiful aircraft landed as silently as it had flown over, and we hurried over to find Brian Walters, a friend of ours, climbing out of the cockpit. We all embraced, and Brian, who'd just qualified and was working as an architect in Durban, told us that he'd flown up from the gliding club's airfield near Midmar Dam.

It was such a perfect day, and the thermals so good that he'd been able to come up to over 6,000 feet, and thought he'd drop in on us, on the off-chance that one or more of the Ross family would be fishing for trout, checking the cattle as it was calving time, or just taking advantage of the beautiful, settled weather for a day out on Lyndhurst. Mum invited him to stay, but he declined, telling us that the weather forecast was for possible thunderstorms in the Berg area, and he certainly couldn't afford to take any chances of being caught up in one of those in his fragile craft. So. he asked us to help him turn his glider around to face the mild, warm breeze that was blowing, and started up a tiny engine with a small propeller.

"Now comes the tricky bit," he said. "Since the glider only has two wheels, one at the front, and a very small one at the back, two people have to hold the wings up, off the ground and run like mad, so that I'm at an even keel for take-off."

I jumped at the chance to show off, and our cousin, rather more reluctantly, volunteered to hold the other wing. And off we went. Brian had his engine at full throttle, and as the glider gathered speed we runners had to really pick up the pace and *balega* to keep up with him. Just as I thought I couldn't manage any more speed and was racing along barefoot through the grass, Brian gave us the hand signal to let go, and the craft soared up and away into the sky, as gracefully and as silently as it had arrived. Brian banked and gave us a thank you wing-waggle, before he turned the nose towards Midmar, and the plane became a tiny white speck in the distance.

The real problem with the airstrip was our climate. We lived in the 'mist belt', which meant that when it was overcast over the rest of the KwaZulu-Natal midlands, we would be sitting in dense mist, so thick that you couldn't see your hand in front of your face. The mist was always accompanied by a fine, cold, drizzle, and could go on for five days at a time, meaning that anyone who landed was stuck on the farm with no means of getting out until the mist cleared, which could be nearly a week.

Dad hated having anyone to stay at the best of times, but sometimes they were complete strangers – people used to pop down on our strip on a nice day out, looking at the beauty of the Drakensberg Mountains, and suddenly find themselves stranded.

The mist could come rolling down over the escarpment within the space of an hour or so, and if we were out walking, riding or driving on the veldt, even we, who knew the area so well, knew we had to find a road quickly or we could become totally lost for five or more days. The temperature dropped immediately the sun was obliterated by the mist, and it could get as low as freezing-point at night. The upshot was that suddenly Dad would find himself playing host for an indefinite length of time to people he neither knew nor liked – his worst nightmare. He'd sit there glowering resentfully while 'these people' made free with his good whisky, wine and sherry, and Mum panicked about provisions running out in the kitchen. Fortunately, we usually had a good supply of food off the farm itself, but there could be a danger of running out of things like tea and coffee, or flour and sugar, the items that she would have to order from Hoosen's.

Up on top (as we always called Lyndhurst) had more distinctive seasons than we had in the valley. It was a very bleak place in winter as, with the autumn frosts, the green veldt turned a pale, tawny yellow, exactly the colour of a lion; there was not a speck of green anywhere, and a bitterly cold wind knifed down from the 'Berg, bringing with it snow blizzards every winter.

Through meticulous meteorological records, kept every day - first by Grandpa and then by Dad - it has been recorded that snow fell up on top during every month of the last 80 years, and frost has also been recorded every month of every season since records began in 1925. Even on most Christmas Eves, which is our midsummer, we'd sit around a roaring log fire, knowing that it could be snowing up on top, or a thick layer of frost was settling up there.

In the valley, too there was frost all through the winter, and snow every winter, but it usually melted away by mid-morning, and we could run around in shorts and T-shirts and bare feet until sundown, when the frost began to settle again.

Lyndhurst offered excellent and almost all year round

grazing and water, and it was where Dad ran his 1,000 head of cattle. These were overseen by a couple of herdboys on horseback, who supervised the calving and kept an eye out for jackal problems.

Grandpa had been determined to grow mealies as winter feed for his stock somewhere on the farm during the summer, instead of having to buy it in. Anywhere in the valley was hopeless, for, as soon as the little green shoots broke through the ground, they would have been nibbled away by baboons and vervet monkeys who would strip away every mealie cob if it survived the buck and bush pig, which loved to root through ploughed fields, crunching up the juicy mealie stalks. So, unless the fields were protected by an electric fence, growing any form of crops was a non-starter.

But up there on the plateau of Lyndhurst there were no trees, and very few really big boulders or crags, and hence no baboons, bush pigs or monkeys, all of which need both for cover and habitat. Here lived another variety of small antelope species, sparsely scattered, and in too small numbers to do much damage to a young mealie crop. These are the very rare Red Hartebeest, living in a solitary state and very well-hidden. These are only found in southern Africa. Only 130,000 individuals are left. Males and females look alike, and they only pair up to mate before separating again. Hartebeests have an excellent sense of hearing and smell although their sense of sight is poor. When alarmed, Hartebeests elude confusion before running, by which they can reach a maximum speed of 55 km/h. Their evasion tactic is to run in a zigzag pattern, making them difficult for predators to catch.

Our other resident buck up on top, are the Oribi antelope, known as 'South Africa's Tiny Bouncing Antelope' which roam on the several thousand acres of veldt up there. A very rare species, the population is at best scattered and sparse in Southern Africa. There are about four rams, distinguished by their short, straight horns, ringed at the base. Each has their two ewes, and they live high up in the hills, right at the very top corner vlei of Lyndhurst.

They are almost impossible to see, unless one of the dogs puts them up, to scatter and bolt from their hiding places in the long grass. One would then be entertained by watching them display their distinctive 'stotting' action when alarmed or excited, which entails vertical, forward-leaning leaps with straight legs. Early Boer settlers named this bouncing action 'Pronking'.

They have comical oval-shaped ears, a long, slender neck, and thin, slim legs. Their hindquarters are slightly higher than their forequarters, their tiny tails are black, and there are white accents around their snouts. The coat of an Oribi is tinted from brownish to yellowish hues with white under-parts, which allows the animal to better hide from the many infamous African predators in the region, especially jackal. Occasionally, we'd see gigantic Eland (antelope the same size as full-grown cattle), which are specific browsers of the *nChichi* bush that grows in profusion in the gullies up there. Not nearly so obvious, but also extremely rare, is the Golden Mole which lives up there.

Taxonomically distinct from true moles, which they resemble due to independent evolution of similar species, the Golden Moles bear a remarkable resemblance to the marsupial moles of Australia, so much so that arguments can be made that they are related, possibly because of the similar, very primitive placentals. This demonstrates proof that at some point in the earth's history, all the present continents were joined in the "super continent" known as "Gondwanaland." Their giveaway is that they make shallow, raised tunnels that hump out of the surface of the soil, rather than the deep, downward burrows of true moles.

So, Grandpa, in his usual indomitable way, drained the marshland by using most of his labour, a team of 16 oxen, and a homemade ditch-digger for a scoop. He created furrows all around the vlei that drained the water off into the stream that became the Umgeni River, and then ploughed up the entire, now dried out, vlei of about 200 acres. These days this would be seen as ecological vandalism, but at that time it was a case of a settler making his land arable. His mealie crops were so successful that he built a mill in the valley so as to be able to grind the corn to make mealie meal flour for our bread, and lovely coarse yellow porridge, which we ate for breakfast, slathered in rich cream.

The mealie meal supplemented our staff rations, too, and our pigs, ducks, and fowls feasted on the remains. Even the stable cats and our farm dogs had a huge enamel washing-up bowl brimming with home grown *uPhutu* and skimmed milk, put outside for them every morning by Makhaye. Everyone had to share that bowl, and Mups (our rather dim-witted Golden Cocker Spaniel) resented the fact that he had to share his food with the Muscovy ducks that had free roam of the garden. He'd spend most of the morning lying in wait for the leader, a huge drake called Patrick, who'd come waddling along to the *uPhutu* bowl with all his wives in tow. Once Patrick had dipped his beak into the dish, Mups would charge him, and then run, yelping, back to his cover with Patrick tightly attached by his beak to Mups's long floppy ear. This drama went on every morning, even though there was plenty of food to go round. It was just a principle Mups wasn't prepared to abandon.

In May up on top, when the shadows grew longer and there were the first signs of frost, red, white and pink everlasting flowers appeared in profusion, and we picked them by the armful, bringing them down to the house to be stuffed into any dry receptacle, where they gave off the sweet dry scent of freshly cut hay, and lasted for years. The leaves of the *mlotjezane* bush (wild raspberries) turned russet red and came into fruit; a wild raspberry with berries far more delicious and sweeter than any garden raspberry, and up there there were no baboons to strip them. Mum asked the farm girls to fill their enamel bowls with this fruit and they would arrive at the kitchen for Masango to make jars and jars of *mlotjezane* jam for us to eat on our buttery toast all year round.

At that time of the year Dad would take his Pointers up and

train them to find Red Legged Francolin, Natal Francolin, partridges, quail, and even Guinea Fowl that had strayed over from the Rolls farm mealie fields. All these types of game bird he shot and brought home for Masango to roast or casserole with apple jelly, bacon, and red wine. We called them *nyonis* and they were delicious beyond words.

~~~

# *16*

# Burning fire breaks

**O**nce the grass had turned tawny brown and dried off, Dad would get his winter fire breaks burnt. This was to protect his pine plantations and good winter grazing from being burned off by runaway bush-fires, of which there were plenty every year.

Once the end of July passed, and the dry winter season supposedly reached its end, Dad finished off his burning by setting controlled fires on windless days, carefully allowing the grass to burn slowly, and keeping control of the situation.

We children loved the burning season, and were allowed to set the line where he wanted the fire break burned by walking along with a small tin of paraffin with a handle in one hand, and in the other a straight length of baling-wire bent around a mealie cob on one end. We dipped the cob into the paraffin, and then put it into the previous patch of burning grass and walked along in the designated straight line, dotting flames into the dry veldt as we walked. Now and again, we'd have to dunk our corn cob back into the paraffin and then back into the last fire (sometimes we'd get it wrong and dunk a flaming cob into the paraffin, but there was always an adult, usually nGidi, nearby to put out the fire in the pot by smothering it with a wet sack.)

Behind the fire-setter walked a team of Zulu men and women, each carrying a wet sack stitched to a wattle pole, like a flag, and their job was to put out the fire once a sufficiently wide strip of grass had been burned. Things got tricky for me once, at the age of about six, when, as fire-setter I had to climb through a barbed-wire fence with my paraffin tin and cob stick. I didn't have the brains to put everything down, carefully dowsing the flaming cob, before I tackled the fence, which was standing in long grass where the cattle hadn't been able to reach through to graze it down.

The next thing I knew, I was tangled up in the barbed wire, and all the veldt around me was six feet high in roaring flames. I could see no escape, so I screamed for help, and it was nGidi who came stamping through the fire in his gumboots, to lift me carefully out of the barbs and set me down on a rock, safely away from the fire, while he went back to retrieve the pot and my cob on its wire.

In August the fire breaks all turned green, and Dad turned the stock onto them for some early fresh grazing after their four months' diet of hay and commercial feed, supplemented by browsing in the bush and a bit of silage.

Once the blackened veldt had turned to green (usually within a few weeks of the first soft rains), the wild flowers began to bloom, and up on top the entire veldt was a painter's palette of different colours. There were the pale pink gladioli-like dierama everywhere, interspersed with scarlet amaryllis, yellow flowers, blue flowers, veldt flame lilies, white and gold arums in the vleis and snowy St Joseph's lilies on the banks. Near the streams were red mombresia and blue agapanthus. Dine and I could walk for twenty yards along the gently sloping bank that led into a vlei, and pick anything up to thirty different wild flowers in that short distance. We always had to stop long before we'd completed a collection as we couldn't hold the bunches in our hands, there were so many different colours and varieties, and that included the teeniest 'Granny Bonnets' as we called them.

So we'd sit down in the grass and make ourselves coronets out of the sweetly scented strands of wild peppermint herb, which grew in long, pretty tendrils, with tiny, pale green leaves, and we always knew where to find them, because as we walked along, barefoot as usual, through the soft grass, the strong minty scent would waft up from our toes, and we'd stop and collect some to tie up our bundles of multi-coloured flowers, and the rest were twisted into sweet, minty crowns for our heads. We felt like princesses, walking sedately along with our heads adorned and carrying our armfuls of posies like brides.

There was a plethora of birds, too. Greater Double-collared Sunbirds; little iridescent emerald, scarlet, and purple hummingbird-like creatures that sipped the nectar from the trumpets of wild flowers. There were Malachite Sunbirds, too, slightly bigger, that drank from wild red Salvia flowers.

White-bellied Sunbirds flitted about, and the Black Sunbird with its gorgeous breast of lustrous purple feathers drank from the endless variety of flowers. Lower down in the valley where the sugar bushes grew, were the Cape Sugarbirds with their long fawn tails.

Over the vleis the *Sakabulas* (the Long-Tailed Widow birds), fluttered, dangling their magnificent broad and long, pitch black tails temptingly just above the grass in a mating display. There were Red-Throated Widows with shorter tails displaying over the veldt, and Red Shouldered Widows swooped and danced over the vleis with Golden and Scarlet Bishops - also Orange Throated Longclaws running along in the grass in front of our horses or vehicles.

The sky above the veldt was filled with the snapping noise of the wings of the tiny brown Ayres' Cisticola in their display flight. There were all the different songs of larks, and finally, swooping gracefully in trailing squadrons, came all the white European storks from their long and perilous migration down from the Northern Hemisphere. They would spend the summer here with our three different types of cranes, eating the endless supply of frogs and grasshoppers. We also had White-backed Vultures circling overhead, a short swoop from their roosts in the Drakensberg, and occasionally the lammergeyer (the Bearded Vulture, famous for its bone-dropping techniques to get at the fatty marrow of carcasses), made an appearance, circling overhead.

Great big solitary Stanley Bustard strutted around the drier parts, sometime just their heads visible above the summer grass.

They were very large birds in the bustard family, and resident all year round. Their backs were brown, darker and plainer in the male, and the underparts were white, and the male inflated his throat when displaying, to show a conspicuous balloon of white feathers. This species was always silent and are a very rare sight in South Africa today, having suffered population declines through much, if not all, of its range. Hunting is the primary cause of declines across southern Africa, and conversion of grassland to agriculture is a greater threat.

Whenever we rode or drove around the vast acreage of the veld and vleis, we always saw Secretary Birds; large, very long-legged, mostly terrestrial birds of prey. Endemic to Africa, and also very rare, it's a member of the diurnal raptors such as kites, buzzards, vultures, and harriers. It gets its name from a tuft of feathers on the nape (which looks like the old secretaries carrying their pencils behind their ear), which is spread when attacking and misleads a snake's attack.

The Secretary Birds' favourite prey is snakes. The bird usually kills the snake with strong and precise kicks with its very long legs and, if it can't kill the snake on the ground, it raises it in the air and drops it over stones. It was enormous fun to watch one with a big, long snake like the Cape Cobra, which can be up to six feet long, hurling the unfortunate reptile around like a lasso.

There were plenty of cuckoos in the summer months. My favourite was the aptly named Emerald Cuckoo with its green plumage, beautifully offset by a pale yellow belly. There was the green and white speckled Diederiks Cuckoo with its distinctive three note call. The Klaas's Cuckoo was also green, but had a snow-white belly. The European Cuckoo arrived from its northern hemisphere home for our bountiful summer's feeding, and there was the Black Cuckoo with its plaintive call.

We also frequently heard Burchell's Coucal, which called before the rain, and was thus known as the 'Rainbird'. It had an extraordinary bubbling call that sounded like somebody emptying water out of a hot-water bottle. And there were hawks, harriers, kites, swifts and swallows everywhere. During the fish-spawning season we often saw Ospreys carrying trout, nose forward, unlike African Fish Eagles (our old friend *nKwazi*, which Evalina had told us was a dragon) these magnificent birds are very distinctive in appearance with a mostly brown body and large, powerful, black wings. The head, breast, and tail of African Fish Eagles are snow white, with the exception of the featherless face, which is yellow.

The eyes are dark brown in colour. The hook-shaped beak, ideal for a carnivorous lifestyle, is yellow with a black tip.

Their feet have rough soles and are equipped with powerful talons in order to enable the eagle to grasp slippery aquatic prey, and we loved to watch them swooping into the water-filled vleis and streams to snatch up a big, wriggling trout and carry it off to eat in a willow tree, planted by Grandpa along the banks of the stream that flowed from a beautiful, pristine waterfall at the top corner boundary, and joined up the three or four vleis like beads on a string; the true source of the Umgeni River, which eventually spills into the Indian ocean a hundred miles downstream - brown, filthy and polluted.

The only trouble with this paradise were the sudden and ferocious summer thunderstorms that loomed out of the Drakensberg; their grumbling, blackening anvil-shaped clouds forming at top speed, so rapidly that, when the storm broke, there was nowhere to take cover. According to Grandpa, the land up there was full of iron ore, and this is what attracted the lightning, and to prove it he drove us around in the old jeep, showing us places where the earth had been torn up in great furrows as if a giant had taken a plough to them, with large pieces thrown over like one would kick a carpet over, revealing the earthy underneath and the grass still rooted and alive.

"That's what lightning does if there aren't any trees around," he said. "But you're safe in a car. It's when you're out on horseback that you're in real trouble."

I was frequently caught out on a horse in these crackerjack thunderstorms, and had to resort to Grandpa's instructions, which were to jump off one's horse, pull off the saddle and bridle, and chase him as far away from you as possible. Then I had to yank out the stirrup leathers, containing the steel stirrups, and, along with the bridle and its steel bit, drop them quickly on the ground. With just the saddle over my head to protect myself from big hailstones, I had to run away from the steel in the bridle and stirrups, and in the opposite direction of my horse, and lie on the grass in a foetal position, using the saddle to cover my head. Sometimes these storms went on for hours, as they'd wander away and then suddenly come back when the wind changed, and often the hailstones were the size of golf balls or bigger. Neither I nor my horses ever came to any harm, but we lost a lot of other stock to lightning.

When a storm began brewing, cattle automatically turned their tails to the wind, rain and hail, bunching their heads and shoulders together, in a central, communal circle, and got the best protection that way. Because their heads and shoulders were so tightly packed together it only took one big bolt of lightning to hit the group, killing anything up to 20 head of cattle with one strike. The same happened with sheep, too, as they tended to hunch together the same way as cattle do, and Dad had even greater losses with his sheep.

These were real blows to any farmer, as the carcasses began to putrefy rapidly once the hot sun had reappeared after the storm, and the electrocution had made the insides and guts of the animals boil and explode.

There was no way the meat could be salvaged, so the only recourse was for the farmer to have them buried.

This brought another problem, as Zulus are too superstitious to touch anything that's been struck by lightning. They have a god of lightning, and they never want to anger him in any way, assuming he wanted the meat for a feast of his own. Burying these huge quantities of sheep or cattle corpses with no manual labour was a real problem, and I remember Dad had to go over and borrow a mechanical digger and front-end loader from his neighbour, Mike, and then had to get Mr Bannatyne to dig deep furrows and tip the dead beasts in, finally covering them with a thick layer of earth.

The Zulus were also superstitious about their huts getting struck by lightning, and they had a ritual before each impending storm. The women would tie knots in the long grass around their huts, chase all their poultry into their little wooden *hoks*, and lock them in, and then gather all their families inside the main hut. They'd close the few wooden shutters that served as windows, throw a handful of salt out of the door to appease the god of lightning, and finally cower in the pitch dark, mumbling incantations to their ancestors, begging them not to allow the tribe to come to any harm.

Now and again, we'd read in our local newspaper that a cluster of native huts had been struck by lightning, the thatch catching fire, and all the occupants, anything up to 30 people, had perished. Our house in the valley had extra tall lightning conductors, and the towering gum-trees also acted as conductors, so we should have felt safe, except that our Zulu nannies didn't understand conductors, and kept to the same terrified, cowering ritual as they did in their huts, thereby frightening the life out of us children.

There were accident reports from neighbours and friends who'd been on the 'phone when the line was struck by lightning and had been horribly burned, or even killed. Others, foolish enough to be in the bath during a storm, had been electrocuted by having the house struck by lightning, the bathroom pipes acting as conductors straight into the bath water.

In September, once we'd had our first thunderstorm, the farm sprouted veldt mushrooms, especially up on top; it looked as if there had been a snowfall - there were so many. The rest of the year round we wouldn't touch any mushrooms, as there was no way of knowing if they were safe or not. Although during the mushroom season there appeared giant versions of the veldt mushroom, some about a foot or two in diameter, (the Zulus called them *aMakowe*), which Masango would cook for us – anything he didn't recognise he threw away. They were utterly delicious, and Masango cooked them every way possible: fried for our breakfast, omelettes, soups, and gorgeous rich stews with a small amount of onion chopped in farm butter, lots of mushrooms, with milk added instead of stock, and thickened with cream.

The crops could go on for weeks, or not appear at all for a couple of years, depending on when we got our first rains and if there'd been an early thunderstorm. When we had a bumper crop the Zulu women on the farm used to come to our kitchen door with big enamel washing up bowls full of them, balanced on their heads, and Mum would buy the mushrooms from them.

When we went out riding, we'd take a jersey with us, not just for warmth but to use as bags. We'd tie up the hole where the head goes, knot the wrists, turn them upside down and fill them with mushrooms, finally to snag the bulging sack-like jersey onto the saddle. Often we'd have to ignore the bounty and just ride through drifts of the snowy white caps, as the deep freezes were full to the brim with cooked mushrooms, and there were more overflowing bowls in the pantries waiting to be eaten. We never got tired of them and even the sheep and cattle ate them too, as did all the wild life, especially the baboons.

~~~

# 17

# The scrub hares

**D**ad once received a message from Jomela via one of the cattle herdboys that there was a problem with a couple of our sheep, and he was driving the old Willy's Jeep up, taking me in the back to open the gates. We went to Jomela's hut where it stood right on the escarpment overlooking the Durrants' farm and right over to Lions Bush and Fort Nottingham where Grandpa lived by then.

The hut with its few pens and a crush tacked on behind (for lambing ewes, and sheep that needed treatment), was half surrounded by a very necessary windbreak of massive gum-trees, planted by Grandpa at the same time as he'd planted those around our house. This gave some shelter from the icy winds that came whipping down from the snow covered Drakensberg in winter, and also prevented Jomela's hut from being buried in snow, as he had a couple of wives and several children living with him who stayed there all year round, too, and remained behind when he brought the sheep down into the valley for inoculations, shearing, dipping and for sale.

Jomela was waiting to meet us and showed us the two sheep he'd found in trouble, and had carried over his shoulders to the pens behind his hut. The first had been attacked by one or more Black Backed Jackals. Because they're smallish predators, about half the size of a sheep, their method of killing was to hamstring the back leg of the animal and then, once it was down, eat as much flesh as it could manage (in the spring, which was now, they carried meat back in their bellies for their pups, disgorging it once they'd reached the den), all this time the poor unfortunate sheep was still alive. There it lay with one back leg eaten almost right off, leaving just the white shin bone, tendon and hoof, still kicking. After a nod from Dad, Jomela quickly cut its throat and hung it upside down from a wire hook on a nearby gum-tree branch to drain the blood out. The rest of the meat could be salvaged and shared out among our family, the Bannatynes, and the farm staff.

The second sheep had fly-strike (also called blowfly). This was uncommon up in the cooler veldt of Lyndhurst, as the blowflies preferred the moister heat of the valley, but the sheep had had diarrhoea, and blowflies had laid their eggs in the matted wool and faecal matter under the tail. We always cropped the tails of our lambs for this very reason, snipped off with a pair of sheep-shears just after they were born. The maggots had eaten their way right into the sheep's flesh, leaving a deep and wide hole in its backside and groin. The entire wound was a heaving mass of wriggling white maggots.

Jomela fetched a tin of *Jeyes Fluid* and diluted it with a little water from the nearby rain barrel. He poured the mixture over the maggots and they began to fall off and writhe on the grass. He repeated this procedure until there were a mere hundred or so maggots left in the gaping but clean pink wound. He then picked up a stick, round the end of which he had twisted a generous hank of sheep's wool. Using it like a paintbrush, he dipped the woolly end into the *Jeyes* and gently and carefully brushed out the last maggots. Dad told him to hoist both the jackal-eaten sheep and the blowfly one into the back of the jeep, and he got into the driver's seat and started the engine.

"Wait nKosizana, I have something for you," said Jomela softly to me, and he went back into his hut reappearing with a hessian sack loosely tied at the neck. "What is it?" I asked him.

"Wait and see when you get home," he said, and I thanked him before I climbed into the cab with Dad, and we set off bumping over the veldt and down the twisting steep road back down the valley.

The trip would take at least three quarters of an hour and I wasn't going to wait that long to look in my sack. I pried the string holding the sack open and stuck my hand in. I reached warm fur, almost woolly and softer than any kitten's, and feeling cautiously around I felt two tiny little forms that moved and nudged at my fingers. I opened the sack a little further, folding back the neck, and there sat two baby Scrub Hares. Not too young to have been taken from their mother, they had bright little eyes and lovely snuffly noses.

"Jomela must have hand-raised them," chuckled Dad when I showed him my treasure. "He's a decent old *munt* that one. Definitely got a gift with animals. I don't think I've ever lost an orphaned lamb since I've had him. He must have raised them on ewe's milk."

I was delighted with my two new pets and stroked them all the way home, luxuriating in the feel of their softness, and enjoying the fact that they were completely unafraid of me. Their breathing was normal and contented, not the rapid heaving panting of a terrified animal. "I love Jomela!" I said happily as we bounced down the road at crawling pace.

"*Munts* are funny things," mused Dad. For once, in spite of having lost a sheep to a jackal and almost one to blowfly, he was in a fairly expansive mood. We usually drove in silence if I was in the cab, that's why I always preferred to ride on the back with the dogs (we hadn't brought them this time as our trip up there was to work on sick sheep and they'd just have been a nuisance).

"If you're a white man, you'll never get to understand them unless you've grown up with them like your great-grandfather, Grandpa, and I did, and like you are now." His silence after that remark made me think he'd stopped talking, but when I stole a sideways glance at him he was looking into the distance, far beyond the rutted track in front of the jeep, and obviously thinking.

"You need to know their ways, as they do things completely opposite to us *aBelungu*." I nodded. I'd often seen Dad discussing matters with nGidi or other staff like his polo boys. He continued, "For instance, if you're interviewing a *munt* for a job, say, and he comes to your office, the first thing he'll do, when it's his turn to see you, is to sit down on the ground. Now, that's because in Zulu custom it's forbidden for anyone to be physically above his elder, especially his chief, who'll usually be sitting on some kind of stool. With a white man, when somebody important comes into his presence, he'll stand up. That's where the first problem occurs. The white thinks the *munt* is too lazy or cheeky to stand up." Again I nodded, fondling the tiny velvety ear I had between my fingers.

I'd always understood why the staff sat down on the grass in front of the office.

"The other thing is that a *munt* must never look an elder in the eye as that constitutes a challenge," continued Dad as he wrestled the play on the jeep's loose steering over the ruts and holes in the road, trying not to bump the maggoty sheep around in the back too badly. "Whites interpret that as looking shifty, and won't employ them. Even something as simple as a handshake between a white and a black man is complicated. We just shake hands, but *munts* have a triple grip handshake, and each manoeuvre has to be followed carefully. This leads to all kinds of problems unless either party knows the other's ritual."

"I know about the handshake," I said, "Dumasane taught me ages ago...." I was about to elaborate, but remembered that I wasn't supposed to associate with Dumi and his ilk, so I quickly stopped and let Dad continue. "If a *munt* gives you something – anything, like a piece of paper containing a reference, or the hat you've dropped, or anything for that matter, there is a ritual way in which he gives the item. He offers it in his left hand, with his right hand clasped on his arm, just under and behind the wrist. This is an ancient ritual, and they do it to one another, too. It indicates that he's not intending to harm you and that his right hand is visible and not holding a weapon."

"Evalina doesn't do that with us," I said.

"That's because, even though you're white, you're still a child. She'll follow the proper rituals when you get older," replied Dad.

"How much older?" I asked. This ought to have been my last question as I knew Dad could so easily become irritated by what he considered pestering.

"When you reach the age of about fifteen, I suppose. That's when Zulus consider their children to become adults." I kept quiet after that and only jumped out to open and close the three or four gates on the rest of the road home.

When we got back, Dad drove the jeep into its little thatched garage, and sent Makhaye off to the Bannatyne's cottage with a message about the sick sheep. I took my sack carefully back to the house to show Evalina my new pets. Mum was passing by and peered into the sack, too. "You'd better share them with your sisters. I'm sure Jomela didn't give them to you for yourself," she said briskly. "They'll be all you fours' pets as far as I'm concerned."

I was horrified. They were my baby Scrub Hares. Jomela had said nothing about sharing them with my sisters, but I knew better than to argue with Mum, so I nodded and continued showing them to Evalina. She was less than impressed, as baby hares were meant for the cooking pot as far as she was concerned, but she was pleased that I was so ecstatic with them.

"Go and show them to Makhaye and he'll make a place for them to live," she said kindly. "And then come back and have your bath – you're covered in sheep dung from that sack."

Once Makhaye had come back from his messenger's run, I intercepted him on the back veranda (there was no way I was taking the hares into the kitchen for Masango to see. He would have had their heads off and skinned ready for supper before I could blink my eyes). I showed him the contents of the sack.

"Hau! *nogwacha!*" he exclaimed. I told him that they were a gift to me from Jomela, and we needed a place to put them.

Even though it was late afternoon Makhaye quickly managed to knock up a wonderful *hok* made from pine planks; it was a square run, about the size of one of our big Persian rugs, with chicken wire all around it, even on the bottom, so the hares couldn't burrow out, neither could what Mum called 'hawks' (but were actually Yellow Billed Kites), swoop down from the gum-trees and snatch the little hares.

I helped him carry it down to the lawn next to our tennis-court, and he then put the finishing touches to it. A piece of corrugated iron was wired onto the top in one corner, for shelter from the rain, a wooden box underneath that, filled with lucerne and hay for food and warm bedding, as well as a square five-gallon tin, which had once contained sunflower cooking oil, which Makhaye had cut in half and carefully washed out. This he wired into another corner of the run for their drinking water.

Being square they wouldn't be able to knock it over, and we could fill it easily through the chicken wire. The best part of all, was that the lawn's lush, green kikuyu grass sprang through the wire on the bottom of the run and so the hares could nibble it to their hearts' content. Makhaye had also made a lift-up hatch in the wire on top of the run, so that I could climb in. This I did immediately, and gently placing my hares in their box, lay down and watched.

After a while the two little creatures hopped out, and I could finally get a proper look at them. They were enchanting, buff-coloured, with fine black speckles and pure white under-parts. Their fluffy tails were black on top and white underneath. Being nocturnal, they had large eyes, and their ears were bigger than a rabbit's. Their most distinguishing feature was a snow-white patch, about the size of a thumbprint, on their foreheads, exactly between their ears.

My sisters and I loved our new pet hares, and we spent many

happy hours with them. We cuddled the fluffy baby hares and played with them for hours as they were far more amenable than any of the cats, either our house cats or the even less docile stable cats, which slunk away into the sheds and hid among the bales of lucerne whenever they saw us.

Admittedly, we didn't try and dress the hares up in our dolls' clothes more than once, because, although they didn't lacerate us by ripping at us with their claws as the cats did, they wriggled straight out of the garments, lacking the proper kinds of legs to poke through the arms of little knitted blue cardigans, in the fashion of Beatrix Potter's Peter Rabbit.

After the novelty had worn off for Delia, and Nicolette had been sent back to Prep School, Dine and especially I, continued playing with them, giving them lucerne stalks to nibble and slivers of carrot and lettuce leaves filched from the veggie garden.

Every morning Makhaye dragged their enclosure a few yards along the lawn, leaving a square patch of manicured grass where they'd nibbled each blade through the netting underneath, revealing a bright green, fertilised, velvety surface like that of a bowling green, and he filled up their water can from the hose pipe.

Even Mum was quite impressed.

"I wish I could get the whole lawn to look that well cut – that blasted mower could never get such an even trim, however low Begindlhela, (our garden boy before Jomela retired from herding the stock and came down to take his place) sets it."

Once they were fully-grown, the hares became too restless to be kept in captivity, so with our permission Makhaye let them go, back into the veldt where they could find mates and raise babies of their own.

We were quite philosophical about it as we knew it was best for them, and when we were coming home from polo tournaments in the pitch dark in winter and saw a hare zigzagging in front of our car, too hypnotised by the headlights to have the sense to hop up onto the grassy bank and out of harm's way, we'd speculate as to whether those were our pets or, years later, their offspring.

~~~

# *18*

# Nun in gumboots

"Take them down to *umaLomeni* to buy some sweets," Mum had said to Evalina.

**D**elia and I were going down to see the nuns, and I had a penny clutched tightly in my hot little hand; my mother had given it to me at the gate behind the kitchen. And off we went, me hopping up and down next to Evalina in excited anticipation at this rare and unexpected treat of buying sweets. I padded along behind her as she walked unhurriedly down the hill. She moved majestically for such a large woman; her broad brown bare feet planted solidly on the dusty road as she carried herself with great dignity – back ramrod straight and her head gracefully poised as if balancing a *calabash* of water on it, as she'd done all her life. I was mesmerised by the undulation of her powerful buttocks – like those of a Percheron – as they moved beneath the skirt of her dark blue cotton uniform.

Delia, being only just a few months old, was tied to Evalina's broad back in a crocheted shawl; her white-blonde curls almost hiding her face as she rested her head on Evalina's shoulder-blade, her thumb plugged into her pink mouth.

The nuns lived in an old farmhouse on the District Road, way beyond our 'Far Boundary' of gum and wattle trees. The District Road that runs below our house crosses the Umgeni Poort Stream and ends at a group of old buildings that had been the Roman Catholic Convent when the original owners of Umgeni Poort had found the steep, rough, bush-covered terrain too difficult to farm, and had sold up and moved to a smallholding at Curries' Post, a district near Lions River. The Catholic Church had bought the place and moved a small group of French and Irish nuns in.

Primarily a mission station, the convent also served as a retreat for novitiates. Apart from the old dining-room and front veranda being converted into a small chapel, the rest of the building had remained the same, and the nuns slept in a new wing of cells.

There was a tiny front parlour next to the chapel, into which guests were invited to sit and drink a cup of tea.

My mother, being their one and only neighbour, had been their first invited guest of honour, and she had arrived back at home quite agitated. "I was seated on a plain wooden chair and given a cup of tea on a saucer in one hand, and a rather leathery crumpet, with a fork, on a dainty little plate in the other. I had to sit there and try and manoeuvre this lot around, attempting to cut the tough old crumpet with this tiny little fork and juggle my teacup, while all the nuns sat around me and smiled and nodded. Only the Mother Superior spoke any English, and none of them ate or drank as it was Lent or something – they were fasting – so I struggled alone, as they all watched me. I had a hell of a time, and I hope I never have to go back there," she muttered crossly.

My father had refused to go anywhere near the nuns but, since he admired Sister Theophane, who was in charge of the dairy down there, he did offer to dip their cattle when he was doing ours.

"She's an amazing woman," he said, after she'd walked up from the convent one afternoon to ask him some advice on a cow with mastitis. "She comes from a very good French family – aristocrats, I believe. She goes back from time to time to visit them in their chateau, she tells me."

This went down very well with my parents. They loved the aristocracy, even if they were French.

"She's got those *munts* right under her thumb, too," Dad continued. "I've never seen them work so hard. Even old Boniface. When he worked here he was an idle bugger. That's why, when

Sister asked me if I knew of a herdboy, I said they could have him."
He chuckled admiringly and shook his head before he returned to his
newspaper.

The convent was at the very end of the District Road, on the
left side. As we walked, big wattle trees loomed up beside us,
looking slightly menacing with their rough, pitch-black bark, here
and there oozing sticky golden resin; Grandpa had planted them all
to mark the boundary of our farm when they bought New Forest.

Glossy black Fork-Tail Drongoes (*iziNtengu*) perched on the
twigs of these trees, flicking their wings, ready to swoop down on an
unwary grasshopper. The sun beat down quite fiercely on our heads
as we moved out of the shade of our boundary trees – it was 3
o'clock and the time that every creature lay still, except the cicadas
who scream like shrill static from the bush. We crossed the stream
and I stopped as usual on the bridge, which is simply a few logs
across the water, the gaps between them filled with earth. I dropped
down on my belly to peer over the edge of the bridge at the water
flowing swiftly beneath at this time of the year, and Evalina called to
me, exasperated.

"Haai! *Suguma*! Get up off the dusty ground! You'll be
filthy and the nuns won't let you in." I skipped off again and she
quickened her stride, her square white pinafore billowing over the
front of her ample bosom, giving the impression of a ship in full sail.
I followed her large navy-blue-clad bulk as we walked the last few
yards up the back drive of the mission station to the steps that led
down to the big kitchen. Opposite the steps was a thatched mud hut
which was '*iClinici*' – a dispensary where the nuns held a daily
clinic giving inoculations and dealing with minor ailments, handing
out cough medicine, *Disprin*, and worming remedies (but, as I
learned later, not contraceptives) to the steady stream of Zulus who
come every day for treatment, bringing their children and carrying
their babies on their backs.

They came from far away – sometimes as much as ten miles,

because the next nearest dispensary was our GP in Nottingham Road, twenty miles from the mission. The nuns had a few jars of sweets on a shelf in the hut, and Evalina and I joined the already large throng of waiting women, whose chattering sounded like a flock of starlings. Some had untied their babies and were suckling them, seated straight-legged on grass mats they had unrolled from bundles. The older children peeped shyly from behind their mothers' long, full skirts, or stared boldly out of shiny black eyes at me in my shorts, grubby T-shirt and bare feet. I was probably the first *uMlungu* child they've ever seen. I stared back.

A bell rang from the chapel and the women gathered up their babies, grass mats, and bundles, and started making their way down the steps towards the sound of the bell. I saw a nun in a flowing, snowy-white habit, her wimple covering everything but her pale-pink, wrinkled face. Her robe reached down to her feet, and she had a soft, silky, dark-brown rope tied around her waist, from the end of which dangled a big wooden cross. She walked out of the dark kitchen jangling the brass handbell, and I wanted to join the stream of Zulus walking down the steps, but Evalina stopped me.

"You can't go with them. They're going to Mass," she explained.

"Who's Mass?" I asked.

"Shush! They go and talk to *nKulunkulu* (God) with the nuns. We must wait here to buy sweets," she insisted.

"I want to go with them," I replied.

"We can't," she said firmly. "You are not *Lomeni* (Roman Catholic – Zulus can't pronounce 'R') and your mother will be very angry."

"I won't tell her." I was pleading now, but Evalina was adamant.

She was terrified of my mother and would not risk any trouble if she were found out taking us to a Roman Catholic service; none of the Zulus on our farm had been to the mission to be converted for the same reason. They believed in various gods and spirits, especially the evil one, the Tokoloshe.

As we waited, I could hear the women singing and then murmuring, and a bell rang now and again. I would have crept away to have a peep in the chapel if Evalina hadn't had her eagle eye on me all the time. She'd been resting her bulk on the low wall, in the outside shade of the hut, her dusty bare feet crossed and her head bent forward, but I knew she was watching me. The bell rang again, and I heard women's voices rise to a wailing sort of song.

Then there was murmuring, chanting and finally more singing, all interspersed by the jangle of that brass bell. After what seemed like an eternity, all the women and their children began to trickle back to the clinic, and another nun arrived with a large brass key tied to a wooden block by a piece of string. She unlocked the door of the *iClinici*, and gestured to the waiting women to form a queue. Evalina moved forward, holding me by the hand, and the nun smiled at us.

"Ah! Mrs Ross's cheeldren. 'Ave you come to buy some sweeties?" I nodded shyly and handed her my warm penny. The nun went to reach into an enormous glass jar standing on a shelf, and came back with a small brown paper packet. I looked inside and there were several flat chalky-looking sweets in the shape of hearts and flowers all in pastel shades of pink, yellow, and green. Stamped on each sweet, in curly red writing, were words in Zulu. "*nGiya Thanda Wena*"; I knew that means "I love you," and I would later ask Mum what the others meant, since Evalina could not read, even in Zulu.

After thanking the nun, I asked her if I could go down to see Sister Theophane. "Yes, of course, ma petite. She weel be down at the meelking now."

Handing my precious bag of sweets to Evalina, I ran down the track to the tin-roofed sheds below the convent. Evalina followed me at her own pace, and settled down under a tall gum-tree at the side of the track. She untied the shawl holding Delia and spread it out in the shade, laying the sleepy little girl gently down. Then she leaned back against the tree and closed her eyes.

"Sister!" I called, and a small, elderly nun popped her head out from the dark interior of a room next to the cow byre.

"Come in ma petite – I am separating the cream." She was in her full white habit, exactly like the other nuns, but she had tied a voluminous apron, made from faded denim, around her slight frame. She had then somehow pinned up the hem of her pristine white habit to reveal a pair of very muddy gumboots on her small feet.

She was slowly turning the handle of the separator. Perched on top of her head over the wimple, was a wide-brimmed straw hat neatly woven from grass for her by one of the Zulu women patients.

"I 'ave a new calf. Would you like to see 'im when I have finished this?"

I jumped with joy. "Yes please, Sister. What have you called him?"

"Eez name is Challenger. He eez a cheeky one," she chuckled.

At that moment Boniface, the nuns' Zulu cow-man, put his head in at the door and asked Sister Theophane to come and check a cow's teats.

"I'll be there in a minute," she replied in her strange, mangled Zulu, spoken with a strong French accent. I could barely understand her, but all the staff on the convent farm jumped to it when Sister gave them orders, so they must have been tuned in to her peculiar accent.

"Can I turn the handle then?" I asked. "I do it with ours at home to help Makhaye." She looked uncertain. "Please, Sister!" I begged. "I know how – I promise."

"All right. But remember to turn the handle slowly and not to stop," and she hurried off, holding up her skirts, her boots clumping through the mud that always collected after Boniface had been hosing out the milking shed.

Diligently, I slowly turned the handle of the separator, at the same pace I'd seen her doing it. Time passed, and I turned and turned. It seemed that nothing was happening. After a little while longer, I decided to investigate, to see whether I was actually getting any cream from the trickle of milk that was running into the galvanised metal bucket under the spout. Nothing much appeared to be flowing into the silvery little cream urn – just a drop or two. Carefully, and still turning the handle slowly, I raised my free hand to the shiny metal pin at the very top of the separator, unscrewed it, and lifted it up. It came away in my hand, and at the same time there was an eruption as a pale fountain spurted into the air and cascaded over me, covering me from head to foot in rich, yellowish Jersey cream.

With a gasp, I let go of the handle and stood there dripping, still with the pin in my hand.

All the metal filter cones had flown off with the centrifugal force, like small tin flying saucers, crashing into and ricocheting off the walls, leaving little pale half-moon splats, and then dropping noisily down onto the wet concrete floor in a pool of cream.

"Ah Mon Dieu!" shouted Sister Theophane as she walked back into the room. I panicked and, dropping the pin, tried to run, blinded by cream and slipping and sliding in my bare feet on the slick floor. "Tu est très méchant!" she scolded me, but I could hear a chuckle in her voice, and I stopped.

"I'm very sorry, Sister, I didn't mean to pull that pin out. Please don't be cross," I pleaded, almost in tears.

"It eez all right, ma petite, I can see it was not meant. Go now and get Evalina to help you clean up," she replied.

So we stood there at the tap outside the sheds, me in my *broeks*, (underpants) while Evalina rinsed and wrung out my cream-sodden shorts and top in cold water. Good-natured Sister Theophane flapped them out and hung them on a nearby barbed-wire fence to dry.

"Come with me. Let us go and see that leetle calf now," said Sister Theophane.

And there, in the byre, standing in a shaft of late afternoon sunlight on his wobbly legs was the most enchanting newborn calf I have ever seen. Golden and fluffy, he had great big liquid dark eyes with a fringe of beautiful long eyelashes. His tiny tail swished vigorously as he turned to butt his placid mother in the udder. Evalina was getting impatient as I stroked the calf's soft ears. "Come on! It's time to go home," she called from her place in the shade. "The sun will be going down soon and it will be too dark to see."

So we said goodbye to Sister, and plodded home along the cooling road. My clothes were still damp, but I didn't care, I would be given a bath when we got home anyway. I suspected that Sister Theophane, when she finished overseeing the cows' evening feeds, rushed back up to the chapel, shed her gumboots and fell to her knees at the altar, to pray fervently that the 'leetle Ross girl' stayed away from her dairy, preferably for ever.

~~~

# *19*

# Our Governess, Mrs Bannatyne

**B**y law, after the age of five, we had to receive schooling of some sort, and Mrs Bannatyne, the farm manager's wife (who professed to be a retired school-teacher), seemed to be the perfect solution to the problem of our education, so my parents arranged that she would become our governess. I doubt that they ever checked her credentials. When my mother took us along to the manager's cottage to hand us over for our first day's schooling, Mrs Bannatyne looked indulgently at us both and said warmly, "Oh, of course I'll be able to teach them, Mrs Ross! We shall have such fun learning, won't we girls?" and wrung her hands ecstatically in front of her sagging bosom.

As she rubbed her pale, dry, hands together her skin made a rustling noise that reminded me of a snake's scales, and she smiled at us, baring her rather large yellowish teeth. I was slightly alarmed and shrank back as she bent forward to have a closer look at us. She smelt of mothballs.

The minute my mother left and walked off, back up the driveway to go home, Mrs Bannatyne turned to us and narrowed her eyes. "Go into the schoolroom," she snapped. We looked at her blankly – we had only rudimentary English. "The schoolroom!" she repeated loudly and pushed us none too gently towards a bedroom, their spare room at the back of the house, which had been turned into a schoolroom.

"Sit at your desks," she barked, and we stared around the room. There were two small tables with hard wooden chairs set against them. We slunk into the chairs. "Now sit there and fold your hands – we shall start with *All Things Bright and Beautiful*," and she struck up a chord on an old upright piano in the corner of the room. We'd never even seen a piano, let alone knew what to sing, so we just stood there gaping like goldfish and after a minute or two she slammed the lid shut and sighed in exasperation. "I had no idea you were so ignorant!"

This was an inauspicious start and did not bode well for our future, especially as I'd already developed a hooded-eyed, challenging look about me. I was five years old and knew everything there was to know in the world. She mistook this as cheeky. "Take that insolent look off your face this instant!" she snapped.

I continued to stare at her, wondering what insolent meant. "What?" I asked.

"What do you mean 'what'?" she demanded furiously, her face inches from mine, so close that I could feel her spit settling on me like fine mist.

"What did you say?" I faltered.

"You mean 'I beg your pardon'!" she yelled. "It's so rude to say 'what'!"

Later, after that interminable ordeal of our first morning in her schoolroom, we went forlornly home and spent the rest of the afternoon kicking sullenly around at the back of the house, hating Mrs Bannatyne. In the evening we were sitting on the big chintz sofa in the sitting-room with my mother and my father while they enjoyed their first whiskies and Dine said something to me in a low voice. "I beg your pardon," I replied. My mother's head snapped up from her knitting where she was counting stitches, and she looked at me over her reading glasses, eyes narrowed.

"What did you say?" she demanded.

"I said 'I beg your pardon'," I replied.

"Never, ever use that expression! It's common!" She pointed one of her pink knitting needles at me for emphasis.

"But Mrs. Bannatyne says …"

"I don't care what Mrs Bannatyne says, it's vulgar and you're never to use it in this house. If you haven't heard properly say 'what'."

"But …"

Mrs Bannatyne had never had children of her own. Apparently, she'd had very little to do with children either, giving lie to her claim that she was a schoolteacher. She was impatient, bad-tempered, and scathing. She was also sarcastic and disparaging about our shortcomings, particularly in arithmetic. We'd never heard of the times tables, and try as she might, making us chant "One and one is two, two and two is four…" over and over again, we never got them into our heads. Her thin, dry beige lips were set in a permanent slit of disapproval, and her pale blue, gimlet-like eyes cast a contemptuous examination over our admittedly rather wild-looking appearance. Our dark hair – mine was almost pitch black, and Dine's a lighter brown – although it was kept short, invariably became shaggy between sporadic trips to our nearest hairdresser, way out in Mooi River. We also managed to get covered in red dust during the short walk to her house, and we had big, startled eyes, the whites showing as we looked suspiciously around us and wondered about an escape.

In retrospect she must have been lonely, stuck out on a remote ranch in Zululand. She was certainly bitter. English by origin, she had come out ostensibly to teach in East Griqualand where she'd met and married a farm manager. She had learned to speak a few words of kitchen Zulu, but had refused to integrate any further into African life.

Dine and I would be dressed and given breakfast by Evalina, and then sent over the hill to walk the half mile to school every morning. We walked past the pigsty on our way over there and it was tempting to stop, climb through the barbed-wire fence, (ripping our dresses that were worn at Mrs Bannatyne's insistence – she said it wasn't ladylike to wear shorts to school) and throw handfuls of rich green kikuyu grass into the pen for them. We loved the pigs, and often went over to spend an hour or two there, watching them squabble and squeal as they competed for the delicacies we threw in for them. Then we scratched their pink, hairy backs with a long stick that we'd picked up from underneath one of the gum-trees nearby. We went reluctantly, dragging our shoes in the dust. They were another insult; Mrs Bannatyne insisted that we wore shoes to school.

On our arrival we were minutely inspected: "Go and wash the dirt off your faces," she told us, with distaste. "And tidy your hair!" So we tramped off to her bathroom and wet our hands, scraped them over our faces and tried to flatten our hair.

She had two mean, snappy, fox-terriers, J.T. and Rosette, whose unclipped nails made a clicking, scrabbling noise as they trotted after her on the over-polished wooden floors. Once we'd sat down, they lay under our tables-turned-desks and rooted for fleas while we laboured reluctantly over sums. Their fleas hopped onto our ankles and worked their way up our legs, biting us all over. We scratched at the itchy spots and were told sharply not to fidget, as she droned on with our lessons.

Days later, I couldn't bear the itching any more, and I pulled up my dress on arrival for our lessons to reveal a circle of angry-looking raised red weals around my waist. The fleas had had to negotiate the waistband of my pants, and paused there to feed even more voraciously. Mrs Bannatyne was shocked at my audacity to suggest that her dogs had given us fleas.

"Those marks are from constipation," she said, "that means you don't go to the lavatory properly and the result is that your jobs are trying to come out through your skin." How she came up with this explanation I have no idea, but from then on she made us each sit on the lavatory – as she called it – for half an hour before class. We weren't allowed off until we'd produced a 'job'. This meant that we had to strain, grunting and pushing, to get something, however small, out, in order to be released, and just added yet another aspect to our daily torment.

Her house had a strong smell of lavender furniture polish, which tried unsuccessfully to compete with the stink of whatever diabolical toxic-smelling concoction lay stewing in a black iron pot on the wood stove in her kitchen. Mrs Bannatyne had stuck doggedly to her native cuisine, and we giggled behind our books as we heard her trying to describe to her baffled cook-woman in her broken Zulu some complicated English recipe for their dinner. Horrible stews bubbled ominously on her hob, and casseroles of vegetables simmered to a pulp in the heat of our African summers.

There was a grandfather clock ticking away the seconds of our interminable mornings. Bluebottle flies buzzed frantically at the windowpanes, trying to escape, and, if we fidgeted or gazed out at the glorious freedom beyond the windows, she rapped us sharply over the knuckles with her wooden ruler.

During our morning break, we ate our 'luncheon' – her term for the *Marmite* sandwich Masango had been instructed to make for us each day, and which we carried to school wrapped in greaseproof paper.

She referred to what we called lunch at home as 'dinner'. Worst of all, she'd decided we were too thin, and didn't drink enough milk, so every day she made us sit and force down a teacup full of tepid milk. Like us, the Bannatynes had a bucket of fresh milk delivered to the house every morning by Petros, the milking boy. At home, ours went straight into the fridge, but hers lay in their hot kitchen until mid-morning, our two cupfuls sitting on the table beneath a crocheted fly cover that crawled with black flies. By our break-time it was just about to turn. I never drank milk at the best of times, even if it was offered to me ice-cold – I simply didn't like the taste of it – so this was a particularly cruel fate for me. Mrs Bannatyne's teacups hadn't been washed properly and smelt of rotten eggs, which added to my misery as I gagged and tried not to heave it all up.

The final straw was when I found a drowned fly in my cup of milk as I was sipping reluctantly one morning, and, unable to make it to the lavatory (as she insisted we call it), I threw up the lot, including my breakfast, all over her bathroom floor. She slapped me hard once or twice on my bare upper arm for this transgression, as well as then having to continue drinking my daily dose of milk.

I think Mrs Bannatyne was slightly mad, driven crazy by loneliness and boredom. She couldn't drive, had never driven, and didn't seem to have any friends, so she spent week after week stuck out on the farm, and only when her husband had a weekend off could she get a lift into Nottingham Road with him for a change of scenery. The village had nothing much to offer anyway. There was no coffee shop, no library, nothing but a couple of filling stations, a blacksmith, and the tiny post office. A filthy, fly infested butchery, Hoosen's General Dealer, and of course the bottle store – the Nottingham Road Hotel's off-licence – were the only shops. Apart from these attractions, there were the railway station and the stockyards.

Like ours, the Bannatyne's groceries were collected in a cardboard carton by whoever went by the store, either my mother on her way back from tennis or my father passing by on his way home from his twice weekly eighteen holes of golf at the Pietermaritzburg Country Club, and so Mrs Bannatyne had to ring Hoosen's on the party line to order her groceries like everybody else did.

She harried her servants mercilessly, standing over them to make sure they cleaned properly. The maid had to spread layers of lavender-scented *Cobra* floor polish every morning, and then, labouring on all fours with pads of sheepskin, one on each hand and one on each knee, had to polish the wood until it was slippery and mirror-like. Mrs Bannatyne seemed to have a blind spot when it came to her kitchen, however, because it was squalid. It was a small, stiflingly hot room off their cramped back veranda, so there was no proper ventilation. There was a black Dover wood stove taking up most of one side of the room, over which her perspiring cook woman toiled day after day.

A wooden table stood in the middle and a grubby, greyish fridge against the other wall. Piles of chipped enamel bowls, pans, and pie dishes lay stacked on a shelf beside the stove, and the whole room crawled with flies. There seemed to be so many more of them than in our kitchen at home, although that was far from spotless.

"Masango's a filthy bugger," my mother said at intervals, after having made one of her infrequent forays into the kitchen to tell him something. Once, after lunch when Masango was back in his room on his afternoon break, probably drawing deeply on a fat joint made from Boxer tobacco mixed with the finest home-grown dagga (marijuana) wrapped in newspaper, my mother smelled something odd emanating from the kitchen and went in to investigate. The oven was on and set to a low heat, and on opening the door she found his takkies – his trainers – drying off in there. The footwear part of Ben's uniform consisted of a pair of cheap tennis shoes bought from Hoosen's, and he was supposed to wear them in the kitchen only. Judging by the state of them it looked as though he'd walked in them back and forth to his home village, Impendhle, several times. They were filthy, encrusted with mud and had holes where some of his toes had burst through. I suspect that they were the only pair of shoes he owned, as, like most Zulus on the farm, he'd been barefoot all his life.

My mother was apoplectic with rage, switched the oven off and, picking the takkies up by the frayed laces, she hurled them out of the kitchen door, and glared at them as they bounced down the steps. When Masango came back at four that afternoon she waded into him with a tirade on cleanliness, and made him scrub the oven out. Years later my mother developed hypertension, which was discovered by chance during a routine visit to their GP in Howick for a health check-up for insurance purposes. He took her blood pressure, found it to be dangerously high, and told her she'd have to take medication for the rest of her life. "It's Masango's fault. I blame it on having to put up with his filthy habits for all those years," she said bitterly every time she had to swallow "all those damn pills."

For the rest of our break, Mrs Bannatyne sent us out into the garden. First, though, she handed us each a small tin filled with paraffin, which had homemade wire handles that bit into our palms, and into our other hand she thrust a small stick. Our task was to go around her garden knocking CMR beetles into the paraffin to kill them. These were black and yellow beetles about the size of rose beetles, and they fed on her plants, especially the flowers, gobbling them up and leaving great big holes in the leaves. (The CMR referred to the Colonial Mounted Rifles, an old established Durban regiment whose colours were black and yellow, and Grandpa had appropriated this name for them.) So, each morning we spent the best part of an hour trudging around the garden, in the blazing heat, slopping paraffin over ourselves, and dejectedly knocking beetles off our governess's plants and into the tins. We told my mother about this task when, after a couple of weeks she asked why we always stank of paraffin after school. She was outraged. "We're paying good money to her for your education, just so that she can get you to eradicate her garden pests!" she exclaimed furiously.

She never did anything about it though, and I suspect that privately my mother thought what a damned good idea, and when she had a CMR beetle infestation I noticed that her garden girls also went around with tins of paraffin and sticks.

We subjected ourselves to this ordeal for a few weeks longer, becoming more and more disillusioned about this wonderful idea of school we'd read about so avidly in our Enid Blyton books.

One morning, we set off for school as usual, and once over the brow of the hill kicked off our shoes into the grass and raced over to a path that led up the gum-tree-covered hill. We could hear the chatter of Zulu boys on their way to herd cattle on the mountainside behind the farmstead. We spent a wonderful morning with them, picking wild flowers, examining iridescent bluish-green beetles, and helping to smoke a swarm of bees out of a hive in a hollow tree trunk in the forest, nearly setting fire to a nearby pine plantation in the process.

When we heard the noon bell ring dangling on wire from a tree, on which Makhaye would go out and hammer with an iron bar, sounding the hours of noon and two, marking the farm lunch break) we raced back, grabbing our shoes, and reappeared sedately in the nursery for lunch.

The following morning we expected a sound reprimand from my mother for skipping school, but there was nothing. Silence.

And so we did our disappearing act again and spent the day herding cattle with the Zulus and making small clay oxen from mud near the river. From then on we continued our charade of getting dressed and trotting meekly over the hill on schooldays, apparently to Mrs Bannatyne, then peeling off barefooted to join the herdboys.

The Nationalist Government never made it compulsory for African children to attend school, so it was just us whites who had to go, which I felt was most unfair. I didn't see why I should sit in a dreary old classroom while they played outside in the sun, or ran off into the hills to herd cattle, so I remedied the situation by bunking off from our governess whenever possible.

Ironically, later on, when both our older sisters, Nicolette and Dine, were at boarding school, and Delia and I were supposed to be at Mrs Bannatyne's for our own lessons, we rounded up Bongi, Jabu, Danda and any other Zulu children who were mooching around at a loose end, and bunked off down to the river, where we played schools. Choosing a flattish upright boulder as a blackboard, a self-appointed teacher – usually me – wrote out lessons using soft, different coloured pebbles as chalk. Naturally, the teacher was bossy and dictatorial, yelling at her most recalcitrant pupil – invariably

Delia – and eventually making her stand in the corner for some invented misdemeanour. There was a carefully chosen boulder next to the deepest pool. Once her pupil's back was turned, the teacher selected a rock about the size of a rugby ball and hurled it into the water from head height, the resulting splash soaking the 'dunce' from head to foot. The classes invariably ended in a knockdown, maul-on-the-ground and drag-out fight with the white child stamping off crying, pelting the (white) teacher with clods of earth and muttering threats of terrible retribution. "I hate you – you bloody swine! I'll get you back and kill you when you're not looking." The Zulu children watched this spectacle of bad behaviour with some alarm, the whites of their big eyes showing nervously in their small brown faces. God knows what these kids thought school must be like, though, if our example was anything to go by – to be avoided at all costs, I suspect.

I can only surmise that our governess disliked us, and the prospect of drumming some sort of education into our reluctant craniums on a daily basis, so intensely that she was only too relieved whenever we stopped attending, and being slightly crazy anyway (her forcing us to rid her garden of pests, rather than teach us testifies to that) she couldn't care less if there were any consequences or repercussions. She must have continued to draw some kind of salary, about which nobody made any mention. My parents were too preoccupied to take any further interest in our education; they certainly never asked any questions or went over to the manager's cottage to see our work.

~~~

# *20*

# Polo season

**A**fter our baths, one late autumn evening, Delia and I were seated, clean and rosy-cheeked in our cotton dressing gowns, on the big chintz sofa in the sitting-room with our parents. Dad had the *BBC World Service* on, playing quietly from the portable wireless next to his armchair, and Mum was knitting as usual. They both had their cut-glass tumblers of whisky on small dark polished wood side tables, and took occasional sips, the ice clinking pleasantly. We had to read our books quietly. Delia looked at her picture book, and I was engrossed in a war book.

Dad put down his *Natal Witness* and took a sip of his whisky.

"I want you to go and see Toto first thing tomorrow morning", he said. "It'll be polo season in a couple of months, and I want him and Shortie to start getting the ponies fit. You can help them."

"Oh yes, please!" I was delighted. I loved all the preparations leading up to polo season. I fidgeted and wriggled on the sofa with excitement, knocking the annual out of Delia's hand by mistake. She kicked at me and I thumped her in the ribs.

"Cut it out you two!" said Mum fiercely. "Or you can go to bed right now." She glared at me over her reading glasses. "What's the matter with you? Why can't you sit still?"

"Ticks", I replied. "They've bitten me on my backside," (we were never allowed to say 'bum' in Dad's presence), "where I was sitting in the kikuyu with Evalina."

Mum sighed and said, "Ring the bell, Neil." Without taking his eyes off his paper Dad reached his hand up and pressed the white knob on a pear-shaped Bakelite bulb that hung, suspended from a wire in the ceiling, just behind his shoulder. This was the bell that was used to summon Makhaye to bring more firewood, Evalina (or Lisha or any other of the nannies we'd all had over the years) to take us to bed, or Ben to bring their evening meal into the dining-room.

"Evalina," said Mum, as the dining-room door opened timidly and a white doek appeared in the crack, "take the children to bed, and put some calamine lotion on their tick bites. There's some in my bathroom cupboard."

"Ehe, nKosikazi." She beckoned to us to follow her as she bustled through the sitting-room and through the big swing doors that led down the passage to our bedrooms, and so we hopped to our feet and said goodnight to our parents.

The next day I woke early and lay in bed, watching the curtains billow gently in the late autumn morning breeze, which promised another baking hot day. I could hear the Chorister Robin calling out his repertoire of mimicked bird songs. He could imitate so many of them so exactly that it was often impossible to tell it was him; the only give-away being that the call was coming from the depths of the hydrangea shrub under my window. He could even copy to a tee the baby Crowned Eagle who sat in his nest in the giant tree in the bush and called, "Pee wit! – pee wit!" All through the summer to his parents who circled above the valley, looking for vervet monkeys to feed him with. The robin made a few sad Diederik Cuckoo calls and then fell silent. I suddenly remembered why I was so excited. I was going to spend the morning with Toto, helping him with the polo ponies. I jumped out of bed and pulled on my jeans and a T-shirt, splashed a handful of water over my face in the end bathroom and ran out of the back door and straight over to the stables.

Toto had all the saddles out already, on the long hitching rail, seven of them, and he was applying saddle soap, his shadow against the whitewashed stable wall making him look like a giant in the early morning sun. There was a heap of bridles lying in the grass, the bits soaking in an enamel basin of warm water to loosen the chewed grass stuck to the metal. Toto was only about a foot taller than I, and I was seven. He was a Xhosa and had come to the farm as a boy of ten.

Toto had lived in a cluster of huts in the Transkei, overlooking a big, flat polo ground where his father worked, mowing the grass to keep it short, and looking after the red and white painted wicker goal posts during the summer months, when it was too hot to play polo. Toto was fascinated by the tournaments, and as soon as he was able to walk. he used to creep away to watch *aBelungu* racing their ponies about, hitting such a tiny white ball with long sticks. When he was ten, after hanging around with the grooms who came from all over the country, he'd decided that he wanted to be a horse boy. After one particular match, he climbed inside one of the big tack duffel bags and waited for it to be loaded onto the train back to Nottingham Road. It was only after the tack had reached our farm, along with the ponies, that he finally revealed himself by climbing out, to astonished shouts of *"Hau! uBani lo?"* (who is this?) from the farm boys unloading the truck. Toto refused to tell anybody where he'd come from and just repeated stout-heartedly to all questions, "I want to be a polo boy."

Dad shrugged and let him stay, saying, "Xhosas make good horse boys – Zulus are better at watching cattle." He was quite right about Toto. Through malnutrition in poverty-stricken Transkei the boy had suffered from rickets as a baby and was always going to be slightly built, he never grew from his ten-year-old height, so he had the proportions of a jockey. Incredibly strong, he was a natural rider and there wasn't a horse that could buck him off.

Even being a Xhosa didn't seem to matter and he settled into farm life with our Zulus with no trouble at all.

"Come," Toto said to me, "I've saddled up Pat and Squib – we must fetch the polo ponies from the field above the bush." I swung myself into the saddle and kicked Squib into a reluctant canter as I followed Toto's dust down the road. The ponies all raised their heads as we came into sight, whinnying a greeting, and from out of the long grass and over the horizon they began to assemble around us. There was Ronald, Dad's favourite, a strawberry roan gelding – his coat always had a pink tinge to it, and who had won the South African *National* 'Polo Pony of the Year Award' two years in a row – and Prince, a chestnut gelding with a white blaze on his face, who had come a close runner-up to that award on more than one occasion. There was Mac, a bay gelding with a good temperament, and then there was Chanter.

Chanter was a grey mare who flattened her ears and kicked viciously out at any other horse within reach. This made her very difficult to ride and we had to tie a red bow onto her tail as a warning to everybody else at gymkhanas, but she was a brilliant polo pony and Dad only kept her for that reason; "She's got a savage temper, but she stops and turns on a tickey," he said about her.

There was Phantom, another grey – Toto and I thought he was called Fanta after the lurid orange drink we'd seen advertised on a hoarding at Hoosen's store, and Klondyke – a mean-tempered horse, who only ever went backwards and didn't stay with us for very long; he was almost pitch black and moved into reverse at the drop of a hat, so Dad sold him to one of our neighbours.

We rounded up the herd and accompanied them, at a brisk jog, back along the road to the stables, their fat grass-bellies swaying from side to side. Ears pricked forward, they trotted up to the thatched building and milled around the doorway. By the time we'd climbed off our ponies they were all in their stalls, standing there patiently, waiting for their scoop of oats and bran. Each pony chose the same stall every winter season, and the pecking order never varied. They hung their heads over the half-doors nickering expectantly as we mixed their feed. They blew and snorted into their mangers while we dished out each helping of delicious-smelling warm mash. I loved the smell of their food and dipped my grubby finger into the mixture, only to be disappointed to find myself chewing on tasteless chaff.

Toto brought each pony clip-clopping, one by one, out into the sunshine again, tethering them by their halters to the hitching rail, and brushed their coats to a gloss, removing as much dust and grass seeds as he could, until they all stood, gleaming in the hot midday sun. Then he plugged the electric clippers into a light bulb socket that hung down from the stable wall for that purpose, and clipped them all. Ronald gradually turned pinker as his hair fell to the ground around his feet, and Prince's shiny golden chestnut coat became a peculiar pale orange suede-like texture. Chanter kicked out and fussed as she always did, and Toto dodged her lashing hooves and ducked when she flattened her ears, arched her neck and snapped savagely at him with her big yellow teeth as he worked the clippers over her. He cut their shaggy manes short with sheep-shears so they stood up like soft mohican brushes, and we both worked on trimming their tails in order to be easy to tie up into a knot for polo matches.

The next day the farrier – a tanned, stocky young white man – arrived in his battered white bakkie to shoe all the ponies before the polo season started in the cooler, dry winter. We had a small homemade iron forge and full-sized anvil in the tin-roofed shelter at the back of the garage that served as a workshop, and I spent the morning standing, holding waiting ponies by their halters and watching fascinated as he quickly prised off the old shoe, nails and all, briskly filed the hoof and then placed the new, red hot iron shoe there. There was a lot of hissing, and acrid grey smoke coiled up as the heated metal set into the horn of the hoof, and then the farrier would take it off again to hammer it into the perfect shape before he nailed the finished shoe on with expert ease. It was wonderful to watch, and the ponies stood there patiently as they did every year before the polo season, apparently resigned to the procedure.

Every day through the winter season Toto and Shortie brought all six ponies to the back gate, three of them saddled and the rest on bridles with lead reins, and I ran out to meet him. I mounted Ronald and Shortie rode Prince and led Mac.

Toto had the difficult ones. He rode Phantom and led Chanter and Klondyke on long reins, so they wouldn't fight with each other, and off we went. We kept to a brisk walk, only trotting them up the hills for the first few days so they could sweat off their summer grass-bellies and gradually build up fitness. To amuse ourselves, Toto asked me to teach him English songs and, as the only one I knew was the first verse of *Baa Baa Black Sheep*, we three sang it lustily as we jogged along and chorused, "Yassuh, yassuh, flea bags full!" at the tops of our voices.

After an hour or so of hacking over the farm we took them up to Dad's practice ground and waited for him to arrive, bumping over the veld in the Land Rover with another saddle, four polo sticks and a couple of balls in the back. Then the four of us practised playing up and down the grassy polo ground, hitting the ball along the ground with our sticks and weaving our ponies around each other. We galloped and pulled them to an abrupt halt so that they almost sat on their haunches, new shoes skidding on the dusty mown late summer grass, turned them and raced off to the other side, winding our sticks round and round, windmilling them by the straps and reaching under the ponies' necks to hit a shot across the field.

By the time we'd finished, they were sweating to a foamy lather around their leather trappings and their sides heaved as they gasped for air. It was almost as exciting as playing in a real polo match, but our only spectators were the baboons sitting up in the rocky krantz on the mountain behind us, and an occasional cluster of passers-by, usually Zulu women with their children on their way down the District Road to the nuns' convent. They stood or sat on the sandy bank at a safe distance and exclaimed "Hau!" now and again as one of us galloped along the field hitting the ball with a loud crack and whirling our mallet. Most of them knew Dad and me, but when strangers were told I was a girl there were clicks of amazement. With my short hair and jeans, riding at full tilt, my bare feet curled around the stirrups, I must have been an odd sight to them.

The ponies loved it. There was lots of snorting, they tossed their heads till their bits jingled, and foam flecks flew while they waited for their turn. As soon as I dismounted to give one a breather, the next pony surged forward, eager to join the fray on the field. Dad rode with very light hands and the gentlest types of bit, like simple thick snaffles which were the kindest available, he never used curb chains or straight bits, so all the polo ponies' mouths were beautifully soft. He insisted that we rode the same way, and it made for very pleasant polo as they were so responsive and we didn't have to yank them around.

The slightest tug on the reins brought them to an immediate stop, and a light nudge in the flanks sent them bounding forward at a gallop. Shortie, Toto, Petros and my older sisters and I all rode with the reins balanced lightly in one hand. Except with Squib of course; everybody refused to ride him at all, and the grooms only if they absolutely had to. Even if he was being led he stretched his hairy, mutinous chin out and dragged his feet reluctantly. As the sun started to dip towards the hills, we walked them home at a sedate pace, stopping at the river where they lowered their muzzles to the cool water, taking in long draughts to quench their thirst.

When we got them home, I jumped off at the back gate to run to the house, skidding in the back door, for my bath and supper in the nursery, and Toto and Shortie took the ponies on to their stable where they rubbed them all down with wisps of hay and prepared their evening feed of scalded oats and bran.

The horses were trekked to the closer tournaments, taken in a horsebox to those further away, and by goods-train to the more remote places such as Lusikisiki and Gingindlovu on the Zululand North Coast, or Matatiele and Kokstad in East Griqualand. When the ponies and grooms were sent ahead by rail, the ponies, with all their tack in big khaki duffel bags, would be loaded into a stock wagon at Nottingham Road station by Shortie and the other stable boy, Petrus, and they'd spend the night travelling slowly on the milk train to Matatiele, or Kokstad, or wherever it was.

We went in the car the next day and caught up with them at the polo grounds.

Grandpa, his brother Ken, and Dad's uncle Hugh Brown, (my grandmother, Molly's brother, and older son of WG Brown), dominated South African polo between the First and Second World Wars.

With Grandpa still holding the very high handicap of seven at the age of 47, these few but formidable players could easily have been among the best in the world when given the opportunity to find teams from other countries to play against.

On page 15 of *The History of Polo in South Africa* (a book written by two polo-playing McKenzie cousins of Dad's), there is a report about His Royal Highness Edward, Prince of Wales coming out on a royal visit to South Africa in 1925 (before he became involved with Wallis Simpson and had to abdicate). The Prince was a polo aficionado and a good player, and when, in Durban, he watched an exhibition match put on by some of our best players, he expressed enormous interest in having a game himself. And so it was arranged.

Because the Prince hadn't brought out any of his own players, (and this was long before air travel) it was decided that he would pick three players from the best on offer from the South African squad to be in his team. After much careful consideration, and by watching them play in his presence, he finally chose my grandfather Allan Ross (a seven-handicap) as his number three player (because he held the highest handicap, and was deemed the best player in the country). He also picked Jack McKenzie (Grandpa's cousin), and S.T. Amos. Ken Ross, Grandpa's brother, another outstandingly excellent player, was picked as reserve. Then one of the pre-selected ponies became unavailable, so the Prince of Wales rode one of Grandpa's.

They played against the Karkloof team (the reigning champions), consisting of Jack Otto, G. Norton, Eric Greene and Jack Shaw, (whose grandchildren I used to play with at polo tournaments).

And so in July, 1925, with great fanfare and publicity, the polo match was held at the Durban Polo Club, showcasing South Africa's best players to a massive crowd. The Prince's team won this illustrious tournament, thanks to him and Grandpa scoring very difficult shots, and enough goals to put them well in front.

In the Summer of 2013, I attended the Sandringham Flower Show on its opening day (Sandringham is the private country retreat of the Royal Family and their annual flower show is one of the most prestigious horticultural events in the East of England), and the Royal couple, Charles, Prince of Wales, and Camilla, Duchess of Cornwall, were opening it. They arrived by horse and carriage then went walkabout.

Prince Charles has always been a very good polo player, and passionate about the sport so I had with me my copy of *The History of Polo in South Africa*. When the Duchess of Cornwall saw the book she looked round for Charles.

"My husband would love to see that," she said. A minute later Charles came along, and when he saw the book his face lit up.

"Are you from South Africa?" he asked as he shook my hand, and I said I was.

I described how my grandfather and my great-uncle had been hand-picked by the then Prince of Wales to play as his fellow team members in an exhibition match against Karkloof, the reigning champions, and showed him the photo of his great-uncle seated on the loaned polo pony. "And they won!" I concluded.

"Oh they won!" the Prince burst out laughing, obviously delighted with this piece of living history.

In September 1933, a South African polo team was invited to Argentina to play a series of international tours against their, equally excellent, players. This was the first time the South African players had had the opportunity to play abroad. The Argentinians had offered to pay for shipping the horses, but due to lack of available space on the only vessel that would sail directly to Argentina, the South African team had to very reluctantly leave their own ponies behind and instead borrow mounts offered by the Argentinians. Playing on strange Argentinian ponies had a huge impact on the outcome of all the matches they played. According to my Great-uncle Hugh, who was the captain and team manager, "The Argentinian ponies were much bigger than the average South African pony, were schooled in an entirely different manner, and trained to a different type of polo from ours."

Another player, Ian Gibson, reported, "The only thing they are good at is pulling, and by Jove they do go and don't stop." Instead of the original offer of forty ponies, they found that there were a good deal less mounts available, and none of them up to the high standard of schooling their own ponies offered. In a newspaper report, one South African remarked that the Argentinian players must be exceptional horsemen to be able to play on these ponies, considering their total lack of finish. To add to their problems, all but a few of the borrowed ponies were very green and this was their first season.

Polo in Argentina was played at a much faster pace than in South Africa, and none of the ponies recognised any heel work. One heel meant the same as two heels to them, and stirrups were set far longer, noticeably changing the balance of the rider.

Argentinian horsemen held their reins high up, almost under their chins, and the touring side had to rapidly adjust their ways to suit those of their mounts, leaving them at a distinct disadvantage as to how to manage the reins up in the air, have no response to heels for manoeuvring, keep the new centre of gravity, and to top it all readjust their use of the stick by wielding it far higher, as it had to clear the reins.

The tour started off badly for South Africa with a series of injuries to players. The first was given an overfed mount (which should never have been used at all), and at the first turn it bucked its rider off, leaving him with an injured shoulder and out of play for two weeks. "I was the next victim," said Grandpa, "I was racing after an opponent and trying to hook his stick when my pony stopped dead. I went straight over his head, landing on my back." He damaged a bone in his back and was out for the rest of the tour. (Unfortunately, Grandpa had his fall during a "friendly" match before he was able to play in Springbok colours, and sadly never had the opportunity to do so, which was a great blow to him.) A third victim's horse rolled over him, leaving him concussed for five days, and then the fourth South African player's horse was knocked over and fell on top of him. By now, the South Africa team had only three fit players left, and the tour had barely started. Hugh finally had to resort to reinstating Ernest Greene, the first player to be injured, and, in spite of his shoulder still strapped up, the touring side, with just four players, managed to win all their matches, and emerged the victors of what could have been a disastrous trip.

After that resounding triumph, Grandpa and his brother carried on playing inter-provincial polo for a few more years before they both retired from competitive games altogether, and resorted to semi-retirement and playing the odd friendly match, often to make up numbers. The Second World War put a stop to any more international tournaments as all the younger players had enlisted, putting their ponies out to grass or into the hands of sons who were still schoolboys and would become the next generation of superb, skilled and courageous players.

The final blow to international polo was when South Africa became a Republic in 1961 and sanctions from all international sporting bodies ensured that they never had the opportunity to play anything but inter-provincial sports until Apartheid was lifted. This was only in 1994, so people like Dad, all our uncles from his generation, and cousins of my own age, missed out on tours to play countries overseas, or against any visitors who would normally come over to play against the renowned Springboks.

~~~

# *21*

# The Oyo

I was five going on six years old; it was a sweltering hot afternoon with no breeze to rustle the dry greenish-blue eucalyptus leaves, or give us some respite from the sun's scorching heat. Evalina and Lisha sat chatting on their grass mats just behind me, their sturdy dark brown legs stretched out in front with their ankles crossed and their backs resting against the massive, smooth grey tree trunk. They were threading tiny multi-coloured beads onto the outer edges of crocheted cotton circles, which they made to keep flies out of jugs and bowls, and sold them to Mum, Mrs Bannatyne, and the nuns for a few pennies each. They adorned every milk jug, jam and sugar bowl that appeared on tea-trays and the dining-room tables.

My little sister Delia, three and a half years younger than I, lay sleeping on a rug next to Lisha. She was wearing just a romper suit made from a pink cotton material sprigged with tiny scarlet rosebuds; her bare legs sprawled on the rough red and green tartan blanket, and her fine, white-blonde hair tousled and pale, twisted tendrils stuck to her damp cheek, flushed and moist from the searing heat that managed to bore between the gum-leaves, and radiate off the hard-baked ground.

I was in a pair of khaki shorts and a pale blue T-shirt, and I was bored. Delia looked very vulnerable lying there, and I toyed with the idea of tickling her ankle with a twig I'd picked up, to make her think there was something crawling on her bare skin. Amongst almost everything else, she was terrified of spiders. So much so, that even if she walked into a web she went hysterical, clawing at her face and screaming with terror. I always found this phobia of hers highly amusing, and laughed at her as she ran around in panicked circles, hands clutching frantically at her pink cheeks to rid herself of the fine, sticky silvery strands.

I looked at our nannies, chatting contentedly as their fingers worked busily through the rainbow of beads, and decided instead to draw an elaborate picture in the gingery-red dust with my twig whilst I listened to the Zulu conversation going on behind me.

"*We indlovu*, I heard the Oyo (type of grasshopper) again last night – it made me go cold with fright and start to shiver," said Evalina.

"*Hau*! *We nyaga, dadiwetu* – ("my sister, me too"). We'll have to bring the cattle closer to our huts or we'll have no milk," replied Lisha.

*We ndlovu* was Lisha's *uSpongo* – her tribal surname – meaning Elephant; Evalina's surname translated as The Moon, and this is how they always addressed each other. Zulus give their newborn babies a traditional Zulu name, often corresponding to the baby's surroundings or even weather conditions at the birth.

*Dumasane* is a common name for boys, *duma* meaning thunder.

Other names, like *Jabu*, or *Jabulani* for girls, describe joy or happiness, and there are variations such as *Tholiwe*, which means gift of God.

Then it's common practice for a mother to give her baby an English name as well. There are boys called Joseph, Ezekiel or Jeremiah, and many other Old Testament names. Other English names, such as Mary, Joseph, and so on, are taken from the New Testament. Happiness, Togetherness, Patience, and even Sixpence and Shorty are popular English names. On top of both names, English and Zulu, they all have *uSpongo* – a tribal surname. Thus people like our cook was Benjamin Bogiti Masango. Out of respect we white children had to call them by their Christian names. There were a few exceptions though, such as Makhaye and Lokatia who didn't have English names, but if we called Masango by his Zulu name, Bogiti, he reacted by threatening us with whatever kitchen utensil came to hand, and calling us cheeky little brats in Zulu, as we scampered out of his way.

I'd been lying on my front on my elbows in the dust, bare legs crossed up in the air and absorbed in my drawing. Hearing the conversation, I looked up, startled. "Why no milk?" I asked. I, too, had also heard the loud, echoing yelp of the Oyo repeating its name over and over through the darkness, becoming nearer and louder each time it called.

"My father told me that the Oyo is a big grasshopper with an inflated balloon-like abdomen. It makes its call by rubbing its back legs against its belly, which amplifies the noise and makes it carry so far," I intoned, parroting this information with all the importance of a precocious five-year-old. I didn't know the Zulu word for abdomen, so I said, "Buttocks."

"*Haai*! *Aaiybo*! A grasshopper with buttocks?" exclaimed Evalina. "No – everybody knows it's a big, big, black snake."

"Yes," added Lisha, "It carries a bright lamp on its head, and it comes sliding out of the river on the darkest nights."

I sat up, my twig discarded and my eyes wide. My blood had run cold.

"Why does it come out of the river?" I quavered nervously. "This snake is very, very big, and it likes milk," Evalina explained, putting down her beadwork and stretching her plump brown arms out wide to demonstrate the length of this huge snake they called the Oyo. Lisha gave an exaggerated shudder and drew her dusty bare feet back underneath her and onto her woven grass mat at the very thought of the snake.

"Is it a Black Mamba?" I asked. I had read about mambas in my father's snake book, which he kept on the telephone shelf in his office along with the snakebite kit – a tin box containing a rubber tourniquet, a razor blade, a large syringe and a rubber-sealed glass vial of polyvalent anti-venom (meaning it was effective for treating the two main snakebites of our particular region. The snake book showed all the most venomous snakes in southern Africa, in descending order of how lethal they are. The Black Mamba took pride of place on the frontispiece, followed in venomousness by the Green Mamba. The text under the picture of both snakes said, 'If bitten by either of these mambas the victim has ten minutes to find the antidote and inject it above the bite area before he becomes paralysed and dies.' Everybody called it the 'ten-minute snake'.

I was fascinated with the tin, which had a picture of a rearing Cape Cobra on the lid with its hood spread out, spitting, and when there was nobody about I dragged the swivel chair from its place at my father's big roll-top desk, and by climbing on it could reach the snakebite outfit. I went through the items in the tin box, and pored over all the colourful illustrations in the leaflet (one of my favourites, along with a huge tome called *Sheep Management and Diseases*, which had brightly coloured lurid photos of the many gruesome ailments that my father said his sheep were so very good at contracting). The leaflet also explained that polyvalent anti-venom is created by injecting minute amounts of venom into horses, which then generated the antidote in their blood, which was then drawn and the serum separated.

I'd decided that I was going to be a vet when I grew up, and read all this grisly information over and over again, saying the longer words out loud under my breath, whispering the wonderful, exciting medical terms to myself until I could repeat it all verbatim. I spent hours fantasising; imagining myself in a crisp white coat, stethoscope around my neck presiding over a gleaming, sterile veterinary surgery.

Mambas and cobras, among many other snakes, deliver neurotoxic venom, which attacks the victim's entire nervous system, shutting down vital organs by paralysing the lungs and thus immobilising the respiratory system. Quite quickly, the venom reaches the brain via the bloodstream and effectively paralyses it completely, killing the victim.

I read, too, that vipers, such as our common puff-adder and the more sinister night adders, insinuated themselves into houses at night to hunt for rodents, and could be found slithering silently alongside one's bed. An unwary bare foot could easily step on the snake as the victim got out of bed in the dark, for an innocuous visit to the bathroom, and in that way provoke a bite. This was designed to paralyse a rat or mouse and then turn their flesh to liquid, effectively pre-digesting the creature before the snake swallows it whole. In a human, this venom had the effect of turning the foot into a huge, swollen, purple mass as the weakened blood vessels leak blood into the surrounding flesh, which turns to soft jelly – an agonising process which, if not treated instantly, invariably culminates with the limb turning gangrenous and needing amputation as a lifesaving operation before the gangrene spreads further.

I'd questioned my father about mambas, and he reassured me that as they were coastal snakes and preferred a hotter climate to ours, neither he nor Grandpa had ever heard of one being seen around these parts. Now here I was, being told about this sinister black snake. I digested this piece of information for a while, abstractedly scratching an intricate pattern in the powdery red dust with my twig. The sun was setting below the mountain behind the house, and a cooler breeze was rustling the dry gum-leaves, releasing the pleasantly pungent aroma of eucalyptus. It was getting on for our bath time.

During the evening I was very quiet as Evalina bathed us; Delia first and then me, dressed us in cotton shortie pyjamas, then sent us running and skidding on the grass mats along the polished wooden floor of the wide passage that led to the sitting-room, where our parents were settled with their first whiskey and water of the evening.

I stopped halfway down the passage at the stable door that led out to the back veranda. There was a neat round chunk gouged out of the wooden step where, a year ago, Grandpa had blasted the head off *uBululu*, (a puff-adder), with his twelve bore shotgun. The snake had been trying to get into the house where it would be sheltered from the cooling night air.

Grandpa knew a lot about snakes. My heel fitted exactly into the hole in the step, and for a moment I stood there thoughtfully, picturing in my mind the thick, sluggish, zigzag patterned puff-adder. I knew the Zulus didn't mind snakes around their kraals – they kept the rat population down, but puff-adders were a different matter. Their ambush manner of lying, well camouflaged, in pathways, basking on the warm ground, combined with their lightning-quick and deadly strike at a careless foot, made them, according to the snake book, the most common cause of snakebite deaths in the country. Everybody on the farm killed puff-adders that they found around the farmstead, and I'd seen many desiccated skins nailed to the mud walls of the Zulus' round huts, to serve as a warning to other adders. The older Zulus used the snake fat to ease rheumatism in their joints, and they also took the poison glands out and dried and ground the contents into powder to use as *umuthi* – witchcraft medicine, and many of them wore the fangs for charms.

We sat with our parents for our obligatory half-hour before bedtime, listening to our mother read Pookie to us. The cosiness of the so-called adventures of those twee English woodland creatures of rabbits, squirrels, and elves only served to contrast now with my own alarming recollection of what Evalina had told me about the Oyo.

It was a warm night, and after I'd performed my ritual of simultaneously switching the light off at the wall near the door and leaping from the switch onto my bed, so that whatever hideous creature that lay in wait under the night frill wouldn't have a chance to grab my ankles. I lay down with just a cotton sheet over me and picked up a book from my bedside table.

# White Zulu

Fiona Ross

I spent as long as I could reading by the crack of light that came from the passage through my half-open door, until my eyes ached. My mother had confiscated my bedside lamp weeks ago when she'd discovered that I was reading all night, engrossed in one of my father's books about the Second World War. She'd wondered why I appeared so pale and red-eyed every morning, crabby and more quarrelsome than usual with Delia.

Finally the words began to dance in front of my eyes and the book slipped from my fingers.

Now I was wide-awake again, startled by the first call of the Oyo right beneath the big open sash window of my bedroom at the very end of the house. I pictured the enormous, thick black snake rising out of the waters of the river below the house, a glowing lamp shining a yellowish beam from its big head. I tightened my grip on the flimsy sheet that I'd pulled over my head and lay still, hardly daring to breathe. And what could it be that had disturbed the crickets? Usually, while the Oyo was yelping out its horrible call, crickets and tree frogs carried on their quiet background static. Now they were silent, which was most odd. I lay under my sheet rigid with fright. It was pitch dark outside and everything had sounded normal as I'd fallen asleep, with the usual shrill chirping of crickets and the peep peep song of tree frogs chiming outside my bedroom window. I'd woken with a jolt to find there wasn't a sound. There was an ominous quiet out there, which meant something big was close enough to frighten them into silence.

It was all very well, I thought frantically, Evalina telling me about the big black snake, but Zulu children went to bed in their huts and slept very close to their mothers; we white children had our bedrooms on the far side of the house, well out of our parents' earshot.

I heard a rustling noise in the hydrangea bush just beneath the window-sill and a loud snort. "Oh my God!" I whimpered to myself. Was it the snake or a leopard? I knew that leopards prowled around in the dark too, seeking out a tasty young baboon to drag out of the big treetops in which the troop cowered at night. The dogs usually warned us by barking furiously when they detected the unmistakable scent of the big cat, but they weren't making a sound.

My father and Grandpa had reassured us that the leopards didn't come into the garden, but stayed in the bush across the river, stalking through the darkness to snatch an unwary, sleeping baboon. But could they be wrong? Would a leopard drag me out of my bed and carry me off? I wondered if I should jump out of bed and race down the passage to our parents' room on the other side of the big, rambling house. This would be a last resort, as we knew that we were only ever to disturb them if one of us was very, very sick, or dying. I weighed up the consequences of knocking on their door and waking them, and decided to stick it out where I was. Then I heard a gushing noise, and something that sounded like water being poured onto the plants just outside my window. This didn't tie in with snakes or leopards, and while I was lying still, trying to puzzle out the sound, I fell asleep.

Early the next morning I was woken by my mother rampaging around outside, shouting for Jomela, her garden boy.

"That bloody great bull got into the garden last night!" she shouted crossly to me through my window. "Just look at those deep hoof prints in the lawn, and the mess he's made of the wall where he's splashed the whitewash by widdling next to it, and he's eaten most of my lovely herbaceous border! One of the farm boys must have left the gate open, dammit!"

And she went off, still ranting. I put the pillow over my head and tried to recapture that nice sleepy feeling I'd been experiencing before I'd been jerked awake, but it was no good; I was wide awake now.

~~~

# *22*

# Summer days

**I** got out of bed, dressed in my shorts and a cool cotton top, and ran down the long passage and out through the wooden stable door. I padded along the back veranda and skidded into the big kitchen, dodging Masango who was frying eggs for my father. He swiped at me with his metal egg lifter.

"*Hamba! Puma!*" ("Go! Get out!") he muttered, almost absent-mindedly. This was more of a ritual than a threat though – his way of discouraging us from getting underfoot or swiping food.

As a result, we always waited for him to go off to enjoy his morning and afternoon breaks before we sneaked in to pinch things out of the big fridge, such as raw bacon rinds, which we caught river crabs with. I ran off to the nursery to find Nicolette, Dine, and Delia already sitting there, eating their mealie meal porridge. We'd much rather have had bacon and eggs like my father did, but that sort of breakfast was for grown-ups, although we nearly always had scrambled eggs for supper because my mother could never think of anything else for Masango to cook for us.

Dine looked up at me as I sat down at the nursery table. She's two years older than I am. Her proper name is Diana, but we'd shortened it to Dine. My mother, Dorothea, but always known as 'Doffie' disapproved of our using nicknames, so Nicky for Nicolette and Di, Dee or Fi were not allowed. (Of course, once we were at boarding school those abbreviations became *de rigueur*.) But Dine seemed appropriate for some reason, and even our parents called her that. She was an inch or two taller than I was, although I'd recently shot up; growing very quickly into a long-limbed, coltish, rather gangly child, with skinny legs and bony knees. Her hair was dark brown, a shade lighter than mine, which was almost black. We two middle daughters had inherited our father's straight but shining dark hair, kept short by sporadic visits to the hairdresser in Mooi River. We all had his long, straight nose, and Nicolette and I had his green eyes too.

Dine and Delia had acquired our mother's intensely deep blue eyes, but Delia was the only child to be blessed by those luxuriant golden curls, until later when she reached the age of six, and to Mum's intense disappointment her hair darkened to a mousy brown and straightened out so that it looked just like ours. "None of you turned out to look like your mother" was frequently said by various friends or relations with more than a touch of dismay whenever they looked at the four of us – a self-conscious, defensive huddle of pre-adolescent girls.

It was early December, and summer was in full swing after our usual brief spring, with good rains having swollen the river to a manageable level. Later on, over the next four to five months, the water level would fluctuate. Most afternoons the skies would darken, and there'd be a crackerjack thunderstorm with torrential rain, and huge hailstones, turning the river into a roaring torrent, thundering and foaming over the rocks, and sending up spray that turned to rainbows in the bright sunshine.

The day, from a slightly misty start, had become sizzling hot and cicadas – we called them Christmas Beetles since they always began singing at the beginning of our Christmas holidays in early summer – shrilled from every tree. Red Chested Cuckoos repeated their "*Piet my vrou, Piet my vrou, Piet my vrou*" refrain over and over again from the tallest gum-trees, which towered over the lawn at the back of the house.

I sat down to join my sisters at the nursery breakfast table, and poked disinterestedly at the skin on my congealing white mealie meal porridge in its blue and white striped Corningware bowl. "What are we going to do today?" It was the beginning of the long Christmas holidays so we had no school for the next six weeks – not that that affected Dine and me much since we didn't go anyway. Our oldest sister, Nicolette, had come back the previous day from the Prep where she was a boarder, but we were already bored and at a loose end.

"Let's go for a swim," I shrugged indifferently.

"Can I come?" Delia looked at us expectantly, hoping as usual to be included in our daily activities. "No!" We both turned on her fiercely.

"You're too babyish!" I taunted. Her eyes filled with tears.

She cried easily, making it too tempting for us to pass up any opportunity.

"Please!" she pleaded forlornly. A large teardrop rolled off her round, pink cheek and plopped into her porridge. I don't know why she ever wanted to join in anything we did as we always managed early on to drive her home sobbing and stumbling, to tell on us to our mother or Evalina, and getting us into trouble when we eventually got home. "*Au, aaiybo!*" Evalina would say, clicking her tongue and shaking her head in exasperation, and "You've got to be nice to your little sister!" our mother would rage at us both, as we squirmed guiltily under her angry glare, with Delia's triumphant little face peering at us from behind her.

"No – you'll only get us into trouble again," said Dine firmly, and we abandoned our breakfast, noisily scraping our chairs back on the wooden floor, and clattering out of the nursery, ignoring Evalina's vain pleas for us to finish our porridge first. We'd go and scrounge some *uPhutu*" and *amasi* from the servants' breakfast later on, or, another favourite, a doorstop of bread squashed into a sausage shape with our grubby fingers, and dipped into an enamel mug of their delicious strong coffee, which bubbled in a battered iron saucepan for hours on the *biyela* – the closest word the Zulus could manage to describe the wood burner that heated the water in the kitchen – which we called the boiler.

We padded out on to the back veranda, followed by Delia at a cautious distance; she wasn't to be so easily brushed off, and we began to accumulate the equipment necessary for our swim.

"I hate you!" I gave Delia a shove. This was always how we started negotiations. "Bloody swine!" She poked me in the ribs.

"*umSimba kuNyoka!*" (Snake shit) This was the worst swear word I knew. I pronounced it *umZimba kuNyoga*. Years later I learned that *mZimba kuNyoga* was a Zulu retort referring in a most insulting way to one's mother's private parts. I'd always wondered why Evalina gave a small horrified scream and aimed a gentle slap at the back of my bare legs every time I uttered it.

We were negotiating a strategy, deciding on who would lead the procession down to the river; this happened every time. We'd changed into our bathing-costumes – a motley selection of styles, patterns, and colours. When Nicolette got a new costume, her old one was passed down to Dine and then to me. By the time I got it, the garment was faded and slightly raggedy from sliding down the huge boulders in the river, and being left out on the grass to dry in the baking sun. This had bleached what colours remained to a pale imitation of the original. To my disgust Delia, being the youngest, always got a new costume, as mine was beyond repair by the time I'd outgrown it. To my delight, she was still wearing those horrible shapeless floral-patterned bubble-type stretchy creations that only babies wore.

I could jeer at her while prancing around in my own worn-out, but slightly more fashionable, hand-me-down, wriggling my skinny backside at her with a taunting chant of, "You look like a bay-bee! You should wear a nap-pee," and any similar insults I could think of. Instead of ignoring me (a far better way to shut me up), she ran at me in a furious rage, hitting and scratching, but I was three and a half years older and could skip out of her reach with ease, cackling

# White Zulu

*Fiona Ross*

1. Mel Charles Southey, father of Grandpa Charles Southey
(our Great Grandfather).

2. Ouma Deliana von Warmelo (centre in black skirt).
Mum next to her (right).

*3. Great Grandfather WG Brown and his wife, Christianne,
in carriage – 1915.*

*4. Group photo of the staff of WG Brown.*

5. *Grandmother Deliana Cloete at 19.*

6. *Our Grandmother (Deliana Southey) on her wedding day.*
*(iii)*

*7.  Grandfather Charles Southey - 1916.*

*8.  Grandpa Charles Southey on the lagoon at Leisure Isle.*

**9.  Grandpa Allen Ross receiving a trophy for polo.**

**10.  Sketch of Monaltrie, WG Brown's home on the
Berea in Durban.**

**11. Mum and Dad after they were married and still in the SAAF – WAAF's respectively.**

**12. Portrait of Mum taken at 20.**

*13.  New Forest house – 1946.*

*14.  Studio portrait of us – self at the back.*

*15. Myself aged 2 years.*

*16. Lefina – Evelina's daughter, the spitting image of her mother.*

*17. Myself aged 5 on Sunny.*

*18. The polo ponies with Petrus and Toto –
stables and sheds behind.*

*19.  Myself aged 8.*

*20.  Myself and Delia dressed for polo.*

*(x)*

*21. Dine on Pat, myself on Squib and Nicolette on Chanter.*

*22. 'Gig' - the Pontiac.*

23.  *Myself and my sisters swimming in the Umgeni River.*

24.  *1958 – four sisters on the way down to the river for a swim.*

*25. Prep 'Stick Insect' – 2 months away from turning 12.*

*26. Masango (back) and Hlabesane (who replaced Makhaye*
*as houseboy) serving Christmas pudding.*

*27. Pitz (the reckless baboon chaser).*

*28. Andy.*

*29. Me in College uniform.*

*30. New Forest House – the front of our homestead.*

*31.  nHlezela – the view from the front verandah.*

*32.  The Oyo.*

*33. The Minkey with Lefina and Lokatia.*

*34. Dad in his favourite chair in the iGluzini (Gluzeen).*

*(xvii)*

*35. New Forest – view of iNhlosane in the summer.*

*36. Mum in her favourite chair – baboon look-out.*

**37.   Myself at 17 in school swimming costume, with
Dad at Southbroom.**

**38.   View of iNhlosane from on top.**

*39. Boulder dynamited by Grandpa.*

*40. Myself arriving at Madrid.*

*(xx)*

and still goading her.

"It's your turn to go in front," I told Delia.

"It was my turn last time," she whined. "It's always me who has to go in front." With a lot of arguing, we were establishing who would have to wear Dad's gumboots and walk at the head of the line, wielding his stick, which we'd appropriated without his permission. Dad was always annoyed if we borrowed his stick as we usually forgot to return it because we'd abandoned it somewhere in the long grass, to be lost forever.

The sister who got to walk behind the leader was the most vulnerable. Grandpa had his own theory, and because he knew the most about snakes, we believed him implicitly. "The first person wakes the snake up so that it's poised, angry, and ready to bite the second person," he'd said benignly, his hands folded over his khaki-clad belly as he sat comfortably on our front veranda, his feet propped up on a foot stool, having come over from Fort Nottingham for a morning cup of tea.

The sister that walked second, wielded a *knobkierie*, I've removed the translation and inserted at the firs mention, when hunting mBibas

The *kierie*, with its bulbous knob at the end of a two-foot long stick, was a favourite fighting weapon with Zulu men, who used it ferociously against an opponent while defending himself with an ordinary stick and a shield. The remaining sister could walk unimpeded and safely at the back. Dine thrust the stick and gumboots at Delia, and gave her a shove. "Just get on with it," she said irritably, and aimed a kick at her littlest sister's costume-clad backside. "I'm sick of all this arguing."

It always took a while to work out the pecking order, and on some occasions we ended up tackling each other, rolling into the grass and pinning each other down to be pummelled until someone gave in.

Eventually, hot and bothered, we formed a strange

procession down through the paddock. Walking in single file, in our bathing-costumes, towels slung over our shoulders and one of us carrying a lilo, with the sun sizzling the backs of our necks. The leader, in this case Delia, clomped along with her skinny long legs in the gumboots, many sizes too big for her. She swished the walking stick viciously from side to side in front of her, making as much noise as she could through the long, pale-green summer grass – snakes were a very real threat. Various types lay hidden in the grass, mainly puff-adders, which, in their lazy sluggish way, lay quite still, their yellowish scales with the distinctive chevron-shaped dark black bars creating a perfect camouflage on the sand in the shadows of the grass – until somebody trod on one, when it struck with lightning speed, sinking its fangs into a foot and injecting its venom, destroying blood cells and causing extensive tissue damage around the twin-fang punctures, usually on the lower leg. Puff-adder bites are common, and are responsible for most snakebite fatalities. Death usually results from kidney failure and other complications caused by the extensive swelling. If the victim was lucky, the limb could be amputated and he would survive. Occasionally, we would jump out of our skins when great big green grasshoppers with scarlet bellies and bright yellow legs leapt from the grass at our feet and flew off clumsily, their rustling wings clicking and whirring, to land with a thump in the grass a short distance away.

Fork-tailed drongoes sat on high perches on twigs in the wattle trees, their black wings flicking in anticipation, waiting to swoop hawk-like on the insects.

There were other reptiles too, harmless grass snakes and basking lizard-like skinks on rocks, which gave us just as much of a fright as they slithered rapidly out of our way and into the long grass. More rarely there were cobras, mainly the Rinkhals, which could rear up to the height of a child, the hood spread and showing its distinctive mark of a hook, when it spat a stream of poison into the eyes, temporarily blinding the victim before delivering a sometimes deadly bite.

In spite of all these drawbacks, and having safely run the gauntlet, we arrived at our favourite swimming pool, to lie and sunbathe on the huge, rounded elephant-coloured granite boulders, every now and again slipping into the chilly, fast-running water to cool off. Now and again we were startled by the leguaans anything up to seven feet long, which liked to bask on the bank. These coal black reptiles with their tough, glistening leathery skins covered in tiny yellow spots, jumped to their feet and raced for the water to disappear in a noisy splash. We knew there were no crocs this high in the mountains, but the croc-sized reptilian lizards so resembled those sinister creatures that instinctively the leader shrieked and ran back stumbling and knocking over the girls behind her, causing panic and mayhem.

When we'd collected our dropped towels, sticks, and lilo, someone would say "It's just a leguaan, stupid!" and we'd slide down the bank and onto our favourite rocks. There was a natural weir made by a ledge of rock that lay across the river, a small shallow pool on one side, and the big deep swimming pool below.

Glorious dark-blue wild agapanthus grew in profusion on the bank, among the rich green ferns and mosses and alongside the bright orange flowers of wild Mombresia and crimson wild Fuchsia. There were tall red-hot pokers with their many tiny bobble-like scarlet flowers, and creamy-white Arum lilies leaned in towards their reflections in the water. We picked giant rhubarb-like leaves and put them upside down on our hair, where they shaded our heads from the scorching sun, and if we stood on rocks on the bottom of the pool we had to keep moving our feet otherwise big brown river crabs scuttled over to pinch our pink toes hard enough for us to yelp and jump out of the water, cursing.

This was a pleasant way to spend a morning, but tempers became frayed towards one o'clock when we had to drag ourselves away, drunk from too much heat, feeling soporific, limp and lazy from overexposure to so much sun and swimming, drag on the hot sweaty gumboots again, hunt (usually unsuccessfully) for my father's walking stick where we'd thrown it into the long grass, and tramp wearily all the way up the hill at the very hottest time of day. Caring less about snakes by now, and resenting the broiling sun that bit into our already burnt shoulders as we trudged grumpily up, fought over whose turn it was to close the gate, and stamped crossly up the lawn to eat a hot meat-and-two-veg lunch in the stifling nursery.

My father refused to eat cold food – ever, so every day Ben cooked a proper English farmhouse-type of midday meal designed for a cold climate. We ate steak and kidney pie, cottage pie, stew, casserole, braised oxtail, liver, and even tripe and onions, all served up with mounds of boiled or mashed potatoes and two or three kinds of veg – whatever the baboons had left us – and all this despite the temperature outside being well over 35°C. Rice pudding, bread and butter pudding, and sago were my father's favourites, so we got those as well. They reminded him of the three years he spent at Cambridge University – "The happiest days of my life" he'd often say, a comment which predictably made my mother react with an indignant "What about when you met me?"

He referred to salads as 'rabbit-food' and wouldn't even entertain the thought of having them on his plate. Our preferences didn't feature at all in my mother's life; as long as my father got what he wanted, nothing else mattered - so unwillingly, we had to make do with what was put in front of us.

Since my mother never went near the kitchen it was up to Masango to collar her somewhere in a flowerbed and ask her what he should cook for lunch that day. She asked him what animal had been slaughtered on the farm that week, and which cuts were available. Masango would suggest a meat dish, and that was that, my mother could then concentrate on her priorities again. All our food came from the farm, except for commodities such as rice, sugar, flour, tea, coffee, salt, and spices like pepper and curry powder. My mother also had to buy cheese as the climate was too hot to make it in our dairy, although we had an endless supply of fresh milk, cream and butter from our cows.

After lunch, which we picked at disinterestedly, (it was no wonder we were all so skinny) we preferred to glean wild berries from the bush, or swipe a hunk of Masango's homemade bread from the kitchen while he was taking his lunchbreak back at his hut. We had to stay out of earshot until four, which was when my father woke up from his afternoon rest for a cup of tea on the veranda now that the day had cooled off a bit, and the mountains and gums were starting to cast a shadow over the garden.

My sisters and I emerged from our bedrooms, our short hair pillow-tousled and our faces damp with perspiration and flushed pink from the morning's exposure to the sun, and wandered aimlessly through the house. "It's cool enough for a game of tennis!" my mother called from her cane armchair on the front veranda as we mooched along inside the cool house, past the sitting-room window. She was leaning forward pouring out two cups of tea from the silver teapot, one of them for my father who sat in the other chair, which faced the garden and had the best view of the bush. He had his leather-slippered feet up on the matching footstool, and was reading the sports section of a two-day-old newspaper. His binoculars lay on the small glass-topped cane table next to him.

The prospect of tennis seemed quite attractive until I padded barefoot to the edge of the veranda steps and peered down at the grass court.

"Where's the net?" I asked. "I got Jomela to take it down because it looked like there was going to be a storm this afternoon, but I think it's passed over now. The net's in the garage – you can put it up again," said my mother. "I'll only put it up if the others help," I said plaintively. "It's heavy to carry down and we need two people to string it up," I added pointedly, looking round at the others who had collapsed into soft chairs on the veranda and were looking distinctly unenthusiastic. We'd had such a fight the last time we'd attempted to set up a game of tennis; the whole affair had ended with Delia stomping off back up the slope to the house crying and threatening to tell our mother on us, and Dine and I hurling tennis balls at each others' heads, then the wooden racquets, and finally trying to strangle one another with the net which had only got as far as being dragged halfway down the lawn to the court itself.

"I just don't know why I bother with you lot!" Mum had shouted at us as we trickled back to the house one by one, red-faced, tear stained and vindictive. "I was Eastern Province Junior Tennis champion when I was your age, and I used to practice every day with my cousins. All you girls do is fight and squabble. I'm sick of the lot of you!"

"What about a ride?" I said. "It's cool enough for a short one to the top of the bush."

Dine had slumped a little further down into the cushions of her chair and poked moodily at the wicker coffee table with her bare foot.

"All the polo ponies are out to grass. They'll be miles away." Her voice rose almost, but not quite, to a whine. "It'll take us ages ..."

"Your own ponies are in the pigsty field," snapped my father irritably. He'd had quite enough of this whingeing and wanted us off the veranda. There was nothing he hated more than seeing his daughters hanging around doing nothing, and the very first signs of our squabbling had already driven him into an another of his rages.

"Go and saddle them up and take them out. They've all got great big grass bellies on them so they need the exercise. Now!" And with a final snap of the page he returned to his paper.

Nicolette, Dine, and I slunk off quickly to the tack room to collect the bridles leaving Delia to curl up with a comic in the cushions of the chair I'd just vacated.

"Mine's gonna be a bugger to catch," I said gloomily. "He always runs off the minute he sees me bring his bridle out from behind my back. I'll have to use bait." On our way to the pigsty field I paused at the Dutch apple tree and snapped off a couple of the hard, russet-coloured little apples that grew on it in profusion in early summer. It would be a matter of days before they ripened sufficiently for the baboons to grab the lot. I took a crunching bite out of one; it was crisp and sweet, but rock hard, and I spat the mouthful out again, onto the grass. "This'll be perfect."

We stood at the gate and called, holding the apples out temptingly as each pony appeared from over the far side of the big field where they'd been grazing in the lush knee-high kikuyu grass, and walked towards us, ears pricked forward with interest.

Chanter, Dad's newest polo pony arrived first. He had just acquired her, and was going to start schooling her for the winter polo season in the autumn when it was cool enough to do so. Dine had a fat dun pony called Pat, and mine was Squib. A misnomer if ever I came across one; Squib was a Basutu pony – a hairy barrel on four stubborn legs. He had pigeon toes, knock-knees and a bottom lip that stuck out permanently giving him a mulish, half-baked look, and he had a temperament to match.

"I'm not bothering with a saddle!" I called to the others as I swung myself up on to Squib's dusty, spotted back. Technically he was a bay but he had tiny patches of white hair, like speckles, all over his back and rump, which gave him a flea-bitten look, and I dug my bare heels into his hairy ribs causing him to flatten his ears mutinously and tuck his tail into his rump. He refused to budge, so I collected up my reins in one hand and, using the spare dangling piece as a flat leather crop, I slapped him hard on his shaggy neck, raising a puff of dust.

The effect was spectacular as he bunched up his backside and sprang forward from standing into a canter. He kept up this gait for a minute or so, then it fizzled out into such a half-hearted reluctant jog that I had to keep drumming my heels on his rounded grass belly to keep him moving forward at all. Riding Squib was hard work.

"I'll meet you at the stables!" I yelled over my shoulder as the other two led their ponies more decorously up the dirt track to saddle up.

It was a glorious afternoon and the three of us clattered down the District Road at a trot, sending up a cloud of red dust. We turned in at the Brick Field. This was so called because that's where Grandpa had found the right kind of clay to mix with straw to make the bricks he had our house built with. He didn't actually do the building himself, but supervised his Zulu labourers in building it.

We struggled with the barbed-wire gate, which fought back and clawed our bare arms as we wrestled it shut again, and then coaxed the ponies to a full gallop up the long, grassy slope to the top of the hill that overlooked the house.

As we thundered up the incline, Squib puffing laboriously behind the others, we startled a pair of bushbuck that had been sleeping away the heat of the day in the long, cool veldt grass. The two dark brown antelope, with their beautiful paler rippled vertical stripes and distinctive white spots on their flanks, jumped to their feet, alarming Dine's pony who snorted and tossed his head, flecking her shirt with white specks of foam from his bit. The antelope bounded away gracefully – the regal bull angling his long, corkscrewed horns along the yellowish crest of hair on his back, as with consummate ease they cleared the fence that stood on the brow of the hill between the field and the dense forest, to evaporate into the bush as if by magic.

We drew our winded mounts to a standstill on the brow of the hill, where a cool breeze ruffled our hair and gently lifted our ponies' manes, to let them regain their breath. Their sides heaved from the exertion of their gallop, and lathers of sweat had formed under their girths and brow bands. "Wow! Look at that!" I said, and I pointed across the valley.

There, far away, on the side of *inHlezela* were some grey specks that looked like rocks, except that they were moving slowly up the mountainside. It's the baboons," said Dine. "They're making their way up to their sleeping place."

We sat on our ponies and watched the baboons climb up to their favourite cliff-face where they all huddled together at night, sleeping perched precariously on little ledges on the precipice, safely out of reach of our resident leopards. The sun had already set behind the mountain, there was still about half an hour before nightfall, and the baboons had a leisurely air about them as they picked their way up the steep slope, stopping every now and again to forage in the long grass. The little ones, typical of youngsters everywhere, had acquired a pre-bedtime burst of extra energy and were gambolling among the rocks, pouncing on one another, bowling teach other over so that they rolled quite a distance back down the steep incline only to jump back up and bounce, spring-legged up the hillside again.

"Come on, it'll be dark soon," said Nicolette. "We'd better get back." And we turned our ponies' heads towards home, and jogged back along the fence line until we reached the gate to the road.

"Phew! You stink of horse sweat," was our mother's only greeting, wrinkling her nose as we traipsed back into the house after releasing the ponies back into their paddock. "You'd better go and have your baths now and get into your pyjamas before supper."

~~~

# *23*

# The Christmas party

That December, a few days before Christmas, I woke with the cicadas' constant shrill shimmering through the air. The sun was already blazing high over the valley, and the day promised to be another scorcher. I hopped out of bed and ran down the long passage, and out onto the back veranda where Evalina was pressing a dress. I recognised it as one that had been handed down to me from a cousin in England; a Liberty Print smock with puffed sleeves and a sash. I hated it, and had already surreptitiously tried to ruin it by spending the afternoon at a polo tournament sliding down a bank with some other children, sitting on flat pieces of cardboard.

I was six years old. I had been told to stay within earshot because we were going out later, so I spent most of the morning mooching around at the back of the house, kicking aimlessly at the flowering shrubs, and playing with the equally bored Pointers, Rufus and Radar, because by that time we would have been far away, out in the bush looking for snares.

I found a long strip of silvery, paper-like bark that had unpeeled from one of the towering gum-trees that shaded the house, and I ran around in circles, dragging it behind me on the grass. The dogs good-naturedly chased the bark, jumping onto it with both front paws, growling and worrying it with their teeth.

Eventually the bark broke up and I grew dizzy, spinning now, with the short remainder in my hand. As I fell onto the grass Radar pounced onto the fragment I held and snapped at it. He accidentally bit my small fist, none too gently, and with a howl of rage I tackled him, pinned him down and bit hard on the loose skin at the back of his neck, making him yelp. His coat tasted horrible, a mixture of *Jeyes fluid* (with which the dogs were bathed regularly to control the many blue ticks they picked up every day), and muddy water from the small dam, green with algae, into which the dogs plunged on the way home from our long rides.

Instantly, I felt guilty at hurting Radar and stroked his soft, velvety ears, murmuring sweetly to him as we both lay, panting in the shade, Rufus sprawled out next to us, on his side with his head resting on the cool, matted green grass.

Evalina called me to come inside and get out of my shorts and T-shirt. I hopped excitedly around the room while she tried to wipe my face with a wet flannel and clicked in annoyance at the grass stains on my knees. Finally, I was wrestled into my dress, my short hair brushed, and, after strapping on a pair of sandals, I raced out to where the car was waiting.

Mum drove the big Chev, with both my older sisters sitting in the front, me on the back seat and Delia on Evalina's lap. We arrived at the Farmer's Hall in Nottingham Road, a big brick building with a corrugated iron roof and a veranda all the way round supported by wooden pillars. There were already quite a few cars and bakkies parked haphazardly in the shade of some gum-trees.

Mum stopped the car and we all climbed out, our clothes already creased and a film of red dust over our sweating faces from the half-hour drive from the farm.

Evalina carried Delia as we joined a cluster of other mothers and children standing and waiting on the shiny, red, polished concrete floor of the hall veranda. Everybody was watching a gap in the five-strand barbed-wire fence that surrounded the grounds of the hall, through which a strange procession was making its way. Leading a dejected looking droopy-eared old donkey was a clown with a big, bulbous red nose and huge feet, his white-painted make up glistening with sweat. The donkey was pulling a small cart, in which was seated another clown and Father Christmas holding a big bulging red sack. With a lot of shouting and gesticulating, the first clown pulled the donkey to a halt at the foot of the steps leading to the veranda. The clown in the cart stood up and wobbled about before he performed an untidy back somersault off the tailgate, landing unsteadily on his long, flappy shoes. There was a scattering of applause from the mothers, which was enough to encourage the other clown, standing at the bottom of the steps, to try a somersault of his own. He went down with a thud onto the hard, sun-baked earth, sending up a small cloud of red dust, and lay there laughing helplessly.

By now, I had shrunk back into Evalina's white pinafore. She was no less alarmed at seeing white men behaving in such an extraordinary and undignified manner, and I could feel her legs tense and hear her breathing fast. When I looked up at her face, all I could see were the whites of her eyes. One of the women called out, "Garth! Andy! Have you guys come via Notties?" (Notties is the pub attached to the Nottingham Road Hotel.) "Fortified yourselves a bit for this?" laughed another . Sheepishly, both clowns got up, dusted themselves off and helped Father Christmas out of the cart. He climbed the steps, the sack over his shoulder, and sat down on a wooden bench on the veranda. At the same time an apparition materialised in the open doorway leading to the cooler gloom of the hall. It was the Christmas Fairy; a girl I knew by sight, the local GP's daughter and the same age as myself.

She was dressed in a stiff, white net tutu, wore pink tights and had pink ballet slippers on with the silk ribbons criss-crossed up to her knees. Strapped to her back she had big, silvery gossamer wings and she wore a tinsel crown. In one hand she carried a silver wand topped by a glittering star. The fairy opened the sack, pulled out a present, read the label and whispered to Father Christmas. He called out each child's name and they came forward meekly, were handed a gift and returned to their mothers to unwrap it. When

Delia's name was called, Mum indicated to Evalina that she must take her to collect her present. Hesitantly our nanny walked forward to the seated figure.

"And what is your name little girl?" asked the bearded man, peering into Delia's face, his white whiskers slipping around on his ruddy face, slick with rivulets of perspiration which coursed into his beard, and his beery breath blowing her fine, pale hair off her terrified face.

It must have been 38 degrees Centigrade in the shade, and he was dressed in a red-hooded velvet robe and wore long red trousers tucked into black gumboots.

Whichever young dad had volunteered for this annual event, needed a medal. The clowns had a slightly better deal as they could jump around, even though their pancake make up was now streaked and blurred.

Delia let out a howl of terror and buried her face in Evalina's blue-overalled shoulder. Our nanny snatched the proffered gift and half ran back to where we stood watching.

"Take her to the car!" hissed Mum, and Evalina scuttled as fast as her bulk would allow, carrying the still wailing child to the safety of the parking area, to sit in the shade there.

All this time I had been staring, open-mouthed, at Helen Potter – the Fairy. Oh how I envied her! I'd often dreamed of wearing such an outfit. I wanted to learn ballet simply because I wanted to wear a little tutu, with the many layers of net standing proud from the shiny bodice, like I'd seen in one of my older sisters' books. I wrenched crossly at my own, flower-sprigged smock, hating it, hating Mum for making me wear it. I wanted frills, frothy petticoats, lacy ankle socks and dainty little slippers instead of these clumpy, clumsy brown Clark sandals with their thick rubber soles.

She even had long hair – something else I'd always hankered for, but Mum insisted that we had our hair cut short. Long hair on little girls was common.

After the last present had been handed out we were ushered into the hall where there was a wonderful spread of party food and many coloured bottles of *Sparletta* cool drinks with straws sticking out. There were *Iced Zoo Animal* biscuits and even crisps among the sausage rolls and tiny sandwiches. We never had these treats on the farm, and I ate and ate until my stomach hurt.

While I was shoving a handful of crisps into my mouth, I looked around, and, out of the window at the back of the hall I saw Father Christmas and both clowns lounging against the wooden poles that supported the back veranda, chatting, laughing and drinking from cans of cold *Castle lager*.

I turned my attention back to the hall and saw the Christmas fairy standing, nibbling daintily on a slice of cake while turning little pirouettes on the shiny floor. I walked up to her and stood in front of her, hands on my hips.

"Give me a go with your wand," I asked, firmly but reasonably politely for me.

"No," was the answer. I had a perverse nature, and when offered the option of behaving well or badly, I always chose the latter, perhaps because my sisters were so obedient and acquiescent, I always had an overwhelming urge to rebel.

I made a grab for the wand, too quickly for her to be able to snatch it away. I tried to wrestle it out of her hand, but she wouldn't let go and lost her footing on the slippery floor in those pretty little ballet pumps.

As she fell, I landed on top of her.

She still hung on tightly to the wand, so I sank my teeth into her hand and bit hard. She screamed, and half a dozen mothers rushed over to remove me and comfort her.

Tight-lipped, Mum dragged me out of the hall, her fingers clamped vice-like around my upper arm, and my feet paddling the air.

I was made to spend the rest of the afternoon sitting in the shade of the gum-trees with Evalina and Delia, in disgrace and awaiting the inevitable long lecture from Mum all the way home, on my appalling bad behaviour.

~~~

# *24*

# The honeyguide

**W**e were sitting outside in the shade as usual after lunch, during that still, baking hot, half-asleep time of the day between two and four in the afternoon, when almost every creature on the farm falls silent and even the flies slow down to a drowsy buzz.

Our parents were asleep: my father in their bedroom with the curtains firmly drawn against the fierce heat, and my mother on the cool front veranda, in a white cane armchair with her feet propped up on a footstool.

She resolutely fought against having an afternoon nap even on the very hottest days, but my father insisted, not concerned for her welfare but for his own sake.

If she did not take a nap, she would disturb him by having Jomela push the heavy, noisy petrol mower over the big kikuyu lawn at the front of the house, or get one of the garden girls to start hacking away at the lush undergrowth in the border just beneath his open window.

Nothing made my father grumpier than someone disturbing his after pink-gin-and-lunch snooze. He always pulled the phones out of their sockets in the office and their bedroom, and usually forgot to replace them, for a day or so until somebody managed to get through on the farm radio. This was equally difficult, as both my parents refused to have the CB radio on louder than a whisper – "Can't stand all that squawking," they said.

"I'm not tired – I've got loads to do in the garden," my mother would protest vehemently, but once she'd sat down with the newspaper it took mere seconds for her to fall fast asleep, the paper sliding to the floor, her reading glasses still perched crookedly on the end of her nose.

We were sent with Evalina out of earshot so there was no chance that we'd disturb anybody either, so on this sizzling hot afternoon she took Delia and me down to the lower lawn to lie on the grass in the shade of one of the tall plane trees.

I was seven years old and bored and frustrated with being lumped in with my little sister all the time. Being three years younger than I, as far as I was concerned she was too babyish and whiny to make good company. I had little to do, and so I amused myself by tormenting her at every opportunity.

I quite enjoyed playing with the knobbly bobbles that lay around the base of the vast trunk, dropped by the tree in the late summertime, but not enough to keep me out of mischief. I surreptitiously picked them apart and pulled tufts out of the golden hair-like centres. I decided the prickly fluff would make excellent itching powder, and suddenly I leaned over and stuffed it down the back of my sister's shirt, making her shriek in outrage and turn into a pummelling fury who pushed me to the ground, where I lay laughing and trying to grab her ankles as she kicked at me with her small bare feet.

Evalina, worried that the noise might wake my mother, and exasperated by our squabbling, pulled us apart and sat us down on either side of her bulky body. "*Aaiy*! Shh – listen," she said. "Can you hear that?" She looked up, head tilted to one side, her eyes squinting into the glare. We sat still and gazed up into the harshly brilliant blue sky. "Can you hear that?" she asked again. I could detect a shrill shrieking call from far above, so high that I couldn't see anything, not even a speck.

"What is it?" I asked nervously. It wasn't a call I knew.

"That's *iNkwazi*. You must be quiet and sit still now or he'll come and take you away." The thing screamed again and again, but I still couldn't see anything.

"Who's *iNkwazi*?" I was feeling slightly panicky now.

My sister was whimpering with fright and had clambered into Evalina's blue-uniformed lap, and pulled the white pinafore over her head.

"*Hau*! He's a great big black flying creature with a white head, and he swoops down and snatches up naughty children. He flies away with them to his lair high up there in the mountains and feeds them to his young." I sat very still and quiet, digesting this information.

I felt I ought to ask for more details of *iNkwazi*, but Evalina hadn't used the word 'bird' in her description, making this creature sound far more terrifying. I'd seen a picture of a fire-breathing dragon in one of our books, as well as a colour plate of Prometheus chained to a rock in another (a wonderful book called *Greek Myths and Legends*). A big, luridly illustrated page showed the half-man, half-god being punished for stealing fire from the gods.

He was semi-naked, bound tightly with chains to icy, snow covered rocks on a tiny ledge on a vertical, windswept precipice. There were two gruesome looking vultures in attendance, one flapping in to land and the other perched on a rock at Prometheus's head, about to begin pecking out his eyes. I wanted to ask Evalina if *iNkwazi* was a bird or a dragon, but there was no Zulu word for dragon (a northern concept – they don't feature in African folklore) and anyway I was far too frightened. My fertile imagination had generously amalgamated the two, dragon with vulture, and this was what I pictured *iNkwazi* to look like. I inched nearer her soft, comforting hip, and slipped my hand into the pocket of her pinny.

"He won't take you if you sit still now and be good," she reassured me. "He only takes very naughty children." I wriggled down so that I lay on the grass with my head on her leg, still staring into the sky to see if I could catch a glimpse of the terrifying dragon-bird. I trusted Evalina implicitly and I knew that, if we were in any danger from the creature, she'd run with us into the house where we'd be safe.

As I lay there I heard another call. This time it came from the thicket of bushes just beyond the lawn. "VIC-tor! VIC-tor!" the bird called over and over again.

I sat up again startled, eyes wide with alarm. "Who's that?" I asked Evalina anxiously.

"*Haai* – that's just *iNgede* (the Greater Honey guide)," she laughed.

"Will he harm us?" I asked again.

"He tried to kill me once." She smoothed her dark blue hem over her wide brown knees with satisfaction.

I scrambled to my feet terrified, ready to run back to the house, but she pulled me gently back onto the kikuyu grass.

"Sit still and I'll tell you." She patted her leg for me to put my head back on her thigh. Delia had fallen fast asleep, sprawled on Evalina's lap, her thumb plugged firmly into her mouth.

"It was long ago when I was still an *iNtombi* (a maiden). I was about fourteen years old and very beautiful. I was tall and had a slender waist and firm, budding young breasts.

"I came to the farm with my mother when I was still a child, and I grew up over there," and she pointed behind us to beyond the clump of massive gum-trees where the round thatched huts with their grey mud walls stood in a cluster. "My father was a herdboy for *nKosi* (what the Zulus called my grandfather). My mother cleared fire breaks in the dry season with the other women who live on the farm, and they hoed brambles out during the rest of the year. She tied me on her back with a blanket while she worked, just as I did with you when you were smaller, and when it was very hot, she placed me on that same blanket in the shade to sleep."

"Tell me about *iNgede*." I was impatient. I knew that Evalina's stories could drift off on another subject with ease, especially when she started reminiscing about her youth. Her once maidenly figure had ripened into the traditional, sturdy Zulu wife's build – that of a plump matron with big buttocks, ample thighs and huge breasts. These features were what a Zulu husband looked for in any woman he wanted to marry. Women of traditional build cost a lot of lobola, but they promised that his future wife would be able to bear him many children, as well as be able to work hard in the kraal, cutting firewood, fetching water from the valley, carrying the heavy container home on her head, and hoeing the sun-baked, dry veldt to plant sorghum for his beer. My mother said that fat Zulu women were lazy, but then to my mother a hummingbird on speed would have been considered slow and lazy.

"As I said, I was young – too young to marry, but old enough to perform some of the duties around the huts. I was sweeping the ground around our sleeping hut to keep it clear so that snakes wouldn't get too close without being seen, when I heard *iNgede* calling to tell me he had found a hive. We are all fond of honey so, running back into our hut to pick up a basket and a box of matches, I followed the call until I could see him perched on a tree near the river. I called back to him "VIC-tor! VIC-tor!" and he bobbed from his branch and flew a little way further, and then right into the thick bush on the other side of the river. I followed him and he led me to an old dead Yellowwood tree that had been struck by lightning years ago. There in the hollow of the tree wild bees had made a new hive." Evalina sighed with pleasure at the memory, and shifted her ample rump to make herself more comfortable on the rug. "I was so pleased and, lighting a wisp of dry grass mixed with a bunch of green leaves to make smoke, I climbed into the tree to collect the honey while *iNgede* sat nearby on a branch, watching.

"When the bees were drowsy enough, I took all the honeycombs out, and he flew down eagerly to look for his share. But there was so little from the small hive that there would be barely enough for our family, so I took all the honey, leaving him to look in vain.

"*iNgede* flew and landed on a tree in front of me, chattering anxiously. Then he followed me, calling more and more loudly, and finally threatening, but I ignored him and walked back down the path towards home, carrying all the honey in my basket on my head.

"As I got near our kraal a *Tegwane* (a Hamerkop) flew over the roof of our huts. This was a very bad sign – it always means there will be a death among one of our people living there, and that night as I lay awake far into the night I heard *isiKhovampondo*, (you know him – the owl with horns) hoot three times – another evil omen – it too means death would be coming to somebody in the kraal. When I finally fell asleep the honey-bird came to me in my dreams. He was angry, and sat silently while all sorts of terrible creatures came to look at me in my sleep." Evalina pushed her white *doek* back off her forehead to reveal her tight black curls, and rubbed vigorously at her brown skin where beads of perspiration tickled her temples.

"The next morning I rose very early, long before sunrise, aching and exhausted from my bad dreams and so little sleep, and I took my basket and a *panga* (a bush machete). I wanted to find a hive as soon as I could and give all the honey to *iNgede* to appease him and put things right between us. Down by the river, and on that same tree, I saw him sitting, and he called to me and flew off into the bush. I was so pleased. Now I could give him his honey. I ran after him along the path deep into the bush, still looking up at my guide when out of the corner of my eye I saw something on the ground, and I jumped back just as a big night-adder struck with the speed of lightning at the very place where my bare foot would have trodden. I ran back down the path as fast as I could, and I swear I heard *iNgede* laughing from his tree.

"He flew away and farther down towards the river again, chattering now, sounding exactly as if he knew where there was a hive, and, eager to please him, I ran after him, this time looking carefully where I trod. On the riverbank he stopped again, at the top of a very big old knob-thorn tree overlooking the water. He fluttered and chattered to me and, this time looking very carefully where I put my feet, I approached the broad tree trunk. As I pulled myself up to the first big branch, I found I was looking into a pair of slitted, glowing yellow-green eyes. There, lying stretched out along the branch, half-covered by foliage, was a full-grown leopard, his head resting on his great big front paws. I tore my eyes away from his, and as slowly as I could I slid back down the tree trunk, picked up my *panga* and basket and ran away, jumping from stone to stone across to the other side of the river.

"That whole day I spent following *iNgede*. He called me and fluttered temptingly slowly in front of me. But at each place he stopped I found something that wasn't honey. Once he took me to a termite mound and just as I put my hand in, thinking there was a hive, I saw a nest of those fierce little yellow scorpions that can kill a man with their sting. On another tree, a young one this time, there was a bright green, slender *boomslang* (a venomous tree-snake for which there is no antidote) its coils perfectly hidden among the green leaves. Finally I found the honey guide perched on a branch above a dry old tree stump. The middle of what had been the tree trunk was hollow, and, warily now, I peered cautiously down into the darkness of the hole before I put my hand in. There was a terrible hiss and *uVusamanzi* (the Spitting Cobra) reared up from where he was sleeping on his golden coils, his hood extended and his eyes blazing. I jumped back, shielding my eyes with my hands from his venom and again, before he had time to strike with his fangs I had to run away to save my life."

Evalina shook her head as she remembered the incident.

"It was as if it was yesterday. The sight of that terrible snake!" And she shuddered. "I knew I had to find honey that day or I would die. I had broken one of the laws of the bush, and I must somehow make it up to the honey guide. By nightfall I was still empty-handed, and *iNgede* was still leading me into danger. I went home in the dusk, leaving him chattering indignantly on the same tree next to the river. Again that night I hardly slept for the calls of *isiKhovampondo* (the Spotted Eagle Owl), and the Goat Sucker (*uZavolo* for Fiery Necked Nightjar). Everybody knows how terrifying the ghostly call of that bird is. In my dreams a puff-adder slithered over me, his forked tongue flickering and his eyes glinting like black beads in the starlight. A jackal howled incessantly, and all the time *iNgede* sat at the back of my dream, mocking me."

"The next morning I was up early again. I was too afraid to leave the kraal because he would surely kill me today, but I knew the only way to appease him was to find him some honey, so I woke my older sister, Thandi. She was a sweet, good girl and, unlike me, had never done *iNgede* any wrong. I gave her my basket and begged her to find a wild beehive, collect some honey and give it all to him.

"'I can't do that', she said. 'You were the one who wronged him – you have to make it right.' 'Please, Thandi', I begged. I was sobbing now. 'He will kill me for sure!' 'I tell you what I can do', she said, 'I can go out with *iNgede* and find a hive with his help. I can collect the honey, leaving behind some for him and some nice fat bee grubs in a comb, then I will bring the rest of the honey home to you and you can take it to him.'" Evalina sighed again, her head tilted back and eyes closed at the memory of her relief all those years ago.

"I was so grateful. I kissed her hands and hurried her off down the path to the river where *iNgede* sat waiting on that same tree.

"Thandi did as she said she would, and later that morning she returned to the kraal, and balanced on her head was my basket full of nice honeycombs. Thanking her, I snatched the basket, ran down to the riverbank and called for *iNgede*. He flew down to a branch of his favourite tree and I knelt down on the mossy ground and laid the basket of honey at the base of the tree. He flew down and began to eat. I was free again."

Evalina stroked my hair. The shadows had crept across the

grass and the sun was sinking below the mountain behind the house. "Come, it's nearly time for your baths," she said, stretching and yawning. And after she tied my still sleepy sister on her back with a shawl, she took my hand and we walked slowly back up, past the lawn tennis-court towards the house.

That night as I slept my own dreams were of small brown birds, their beaks filled with honeycombs, snakes with flicking forked tongues and a leopard with two great big green eyes that shone like twin-lamps from the dark bush. There was an eagle too, soaring high over the valley, that screamed as he swooped down to snatch me up. I jerked awake with a start and sat up in my bed, eyes wide with fright, my heart thudding. The thumping subsided as gradually I realised where I was, and that it was morning.

~~~

# *25*

# The Dragon's Nest

**T**hrough the big sash window I could see the pearl-coloured sky above the gum-trees, and the cicadas had already started their shrill skreeeee, which would escalate to background static as the day got hotter and hotter. A rooster crowed from the huts behind our sheds, where the farm staff kept their rangy fowls, a few hens with little clusters of fluffy chicks scuffling around their feet, and the proud father strutting around on his tough-looking legs, his tail plumes iridescent-green to contrast with his shining deep golden body and quivering scarlet comb. They scratched around the dusty bare earth surrounding the huts, and ate pot scrapings: crusty, slightly blackened *puthu* left at the bottom of the three-legged cast-iron pots after the families had eaten.

I hopped out of bed and pulled on a pair of shorts and a T-shirt. Then I ran down the passage and out of the door leading on to the back veranda, fitting my bare foot in to the gouge where Grandpa had blown a chunk out of the wooden step with his shotgun when he'd shot the puff-adder. I nearly collided with Evalina who was sweeping the veranda with a soft broom, her back to me.

"*Hau!* Where are you going in such a hurry? You should still be asleep in bed!" I dodged round her bulk and called airily over my shoulder as I scampered across the lawn towards the back gate.

"I'm going to see Bongi and Jabu. There's something I want to ask them."

"Be back soon then, or nKosikazi will be cross. Come back

when you hear the farm bell ring for breakfast."

I skipped through the narrow wire gateway and ran down the road past the sheds, my bare feet padding along, kicking up puffs of red dust. nGidi, our *Induna*, was filling the jeep's tank with petrol from a 44-gallon drum, and he raised his tattered khaki cotton hat to me in greeting.

"*Uyapi nKosizana*? (Where are you going so fast, Chief's daughter?) Is your house on fire?" and he guffawed at his joke, showing the few remaining teeth planted in his pink gums like crooked gravestones. I waved back and turned right to run up the sandy path that led to the compound where our Zulu labourers lived.

Lokatia was standing in front of her hut stirring steaming *uputhu* with a wooden spoon. She was tall and thin and had to stoop over the big black pot underneath which a fire crackled.

Branches of burning gum were stuck in through the pot legs and the fragrant eucalyptus-scented smoke mingled with steam from the stiff maize porridge, sending up a delicious aroma that made my mouth water.

"*Sawubona* nKosizana," she said, a little surprised to find me there so early. "Would you like some breakfast? The *uputhu* is almost ready. Jabu! Bongi! Come and eat your breakfast!" They appeared from the dark interior of their hut and whooped with delight to see me. Jabu was eight and wore a pair of ragged khaki shorts held up with string, and a tattered T-shirt. His younger sister was six, a year younger than me, and she was dressed in a faded cotton shift which might once have been pink.

We danced around excitedly while Lokatia took three enamel bowls from a rush mat near the pot, and placed a steaming heap of *uputhu* into each one. She poured a generous helping of *aMasi* (curdled sour milk) over the porridge and sprinkled a big spoonful of dark brown Government sugar on top. She gave us each a spoon and we sat down on a grass mat with our backs against the mud wall of their hut, to eat.

It was my favourite breakfast. The stiff, crumbly, yellow maize porridge soaked up the tart curdled milk, and the sugar gave the dish a sweet crunchiness.

We gobbled our *puthu*, scraped our bowls clean and handed them back to Lokatia. I thanked her politely, and, after declining her offer of strong coffee in an enamel mug, Jabu, Bongi and I skipped off down the path back to where it joined the road. We stopped.

"What are we going to do today?" asked Jabu.

"Listen," I whispered, "you know *iNkwazi*? Evalina was telling me about him yesterday." They both nodded warily. "Well there's a pair living in that big Yellowwood tree in the bush."

"They have a nest in the very top, I've seen them flying in to land there, and I've heard them screaming. There are young ones, too. They yelp and call when they see their parents arriving. My father says there are lots of bones and skulls lying on the ground at the bottom of the tree. They must be children's skulls. Do we dare go up there and look?"

We looked at each other apprehensively. Bongi and Jabu's eyes widened in alarm. They looked back at their huts, then down at their bare feet, which they shuffled nervously in the dust for a little while. "Do you know the way?" asked Bongi. "Is there a path?"

"I think so," I said. "Come on. Let's go a little way along the path, and if *iNkwazi* screams at us we'll run away and hide." I sounded braver than I felt, but my reputation as ringleader was at stake, and I needed to show them who was in charge.

We scurried down past the sheds, and, pausing only to pick up a sturdy stick from under the huge gum-trees that towered over us, we ran down to the District Road and crossed it to climb through a barbed-wire fence that surrounded the paddock next to the river.

Keeping a sharp eye out for snakes I swished and banged the stick from side to side in the long grass in front of me as we walked down to the riverbank. Dropping the stick, we squatted on our haunches and slipped down a wet recently used otter slide into the cool water. It was tempting to get side-tracked and spend some time splashing each other in the river, but I was determined to get a good look at the tree with its nest.

I was far too frightened to go on my own, and this was a good opportunity with two co-conspirators as back-up.

We paddled across briskly before the crabs could scuttle from their dens to pinch our toes, and entered the dense dark green forest on the far bank of the river. It was the exact spot from which *iNkwazi* had been calling yesterday. And this must be his favourite tree that Evalina had described. I stood and looked up into the leafy branches but could see nothing – I'd have to find and follow him some other day. We left the river behind us with its electric blue dragonflies dancing over their sparkling reflections among the reeds on the banks. The bright orange wild Mombresia leaned, nodding, over the ripples and eddies in rock pools. Pale-blue wild agapanthus clustered next to creamy-white arum lilies, and red-hot pokers stood tall among fine, lacy green maidenhair ferns.

The narrow path rose sharply up the steep forest-covered hillside. The forest, more of a jungle, consisted of masses of different evergreen trees growing closely together. There was thick under-growth to push through, and vines and lianas hung from branches, twisting around tree trunks and even around each other, forming great ropes that dangled in loops across the track.

Bushbuck had carved the path with their sharp hooves as they came down to the river every night to drink, and we could see their spoor on the slick, muddy ground. The bush stayed wet even during the dry winter season, and as a result remained untouched by the bush-fires that every year raged through gum, wattle and pine plantations everywhere in the Natal Midlands.

We slipped and slid in our bare feet, pulling ourselves up the steepest slopes by vine ropes that hung conveniently within reach; an action that was not without its own risks as big, red, and very fierce, biting ants used the ropes as their highways, carrying food to their nests, which hung in sinister black clumps in the forks of trees high up above. There wasn't nearly as much colour as on the river-banks; just grey-green, lime-green, apple-green, grass-green, dark-green, and emerald-green shiny leaves everywhere.

There was a creeper festooned over low bushes like Christmas decorations, growing prolifically with small, white sweet-scented star-shaped flowers like little pearls that gleamed against its jade leaves. Moss of all shades of green carpeted the forest floor, and covered every log and boulder, and long strands of greenish-grey lichen we called Old Man's Beard hung, dangling, from the branches of all but the smallest trees. In the occasional clearing big purple and blue butterflies with bright scarlet eyes on their wings rested in patches of the dappled sunlight, opening and closing their wings so that they looked as though they appeared from nowhere by magic, and then disappeared as they closed their wings again, revealing the dark blue underside.

We climbed higher and higher up the steep, thickly forested mountainside, pausing now and again to catch our breath. We were trying to walk silently, placing our feet carefully so as not to make any noise by snapping twigs. We breathed as quietly as our panting would allow. It was quite still, apart from the odd birdcall. A Natal Robin made its squeaky seesaw-like repetitive call, and Cinnamon Doves purred softly deep in the lush undergrowth. We were startled once or twice by the kok-kok-kok alarm call of the Knysna Loerie as it flew from a branch just above our heads, the scarlet beneath its wings flashing at us as it glided to another tree to perch and cackle at us indignantly. He raised his lime-green crest with its white edge and cocked his head to one side to inspect us.

We could hear a troop of Samango Monkeys chattering further down the valley, unaware that we were nearby. They were foraging in the treetops for insects. It was unusual to come across them here because, unlike Vervet Monkeys who preferred the bush, Samangos spent most of their time in our wattle plantations, feasting on resin, which they extracted by tearing off strips of bark with their sharp canine teeth. (They were a bit of a pest, my father said, because they could kill off quite a few trees by ring-barking them in this way.)

"We're nearly there." I stopped to wait for Jabu and Bongi to catch up, and to listen for any other sounds. We sat on a mossy boulder to rest and catch our breath. "Shhh! The tree's up there." I pointed up the slope to where a massive trunk rose out of the surrounding undergrowth. "Come on." Crouching and bent double, we crept closer. Bushes and brushwood gave way to thick, soft moss at the base of the towering tree. There was a lot of debris in the form of dry sticks and clumps of dead moss lying around – bits that had fallen from the nest over the years. Whitish objects lay among them. I stopped, and Jabu and Bongi bumped into me from behind. We squatted there, unsure now. I looked back at them. They stared at me – the whites of their eyes bright in the gloom of the dark forest. They were waiting for me to make the next move.

Holding my breath, I crawled forward slowly and reached out to touch the round off-white object lying on the moss. I picked it up. It was light, hard, and cold. With it in my hand I scrambled backwards on my bum into the undergrowth where my friends were hiding. I looked closely at the thing in my hand. It was a skull.

With a shriek of terror, I dropped it hurriedly, and, wiping my hand frantically on my shorts, I backed away from it, my heart thudding furiously in my throat. Jabu and Bongi had run a little way back down the path and were now cowering behind a mossy boulder. After crouching on the ground for a few minutes to catch my breath, and waiting for the churning in my stomach to subside, I crept forward and looked at the skull again. It was small, about half the size of my own head, and still had the jaw attached. It was lying on its side now, with the two gaping eye sockets staring at me. I shuddered. I sat and gazed at it while I thought about what I was going to do with this unexpected find.

I wanted to take it home to show Dad, but I didn't want to touch it again. I looked back to the moss at the base of the Yellowwood tree.

About half a dozen similar sized skulls lay there, and lots of long, curved objects the same colour, which, now that I looked at them more carefully, had to be ribs and leg bones from the same creature whose skull I'd picked up. There were other skulls too; smaller, flatter, and more as if they'd come from a very small dog, as well as a scattering of smaller bones of all shapes.

Then I had a brainwave, and stood up and took my shorts off.

There was no sign of Bongi and Jabu but I knew they were still hiding behind their rock. I took my broeks – my panties – off and pulled my shorts quickly back on. After that I broke a twig off the nearest bush and used it to roll the skull carefully into my broeks, which I held open like a bag. I picked them up with the skull inside and held the leg and waist holes in my fist. Now I could carry the skull home without actually touching it.

"*Wozani bo*," (come on) I called, and they crept out cautiously from their hiding place, their eyes fastened on the makeshift bag I was holding. "Leave it there!" pleaded Bongi. "We don't want to take it away. What if *iNkwazi* follows us and wants it back?"

"There's no meat left on it – that's why he threw it away," I said airily. I actually had no idea what *iNkwazi* would do, but bravado is my middle name, and I sauntered nonchalantly off down the mountainside with my broeks bag, and my companions treading carefully a safe distance behind me.

By the time we reached their hut, I knew there was some sort of uproar going on. I could hear Evalina calling for me, her voice echoing through the valley and bouncing back at us. Lokatia hurried anxiously out of her doorway as soon she saw us.

"You must run home quickly, nKosizana. Evalina has been calling for you all morning."

"Look," I said, and held out my broeks, letting them fall open to reveal the skull. "*Aaaaiy!*" she screamed and ran back into her hut. "Throw it away – it's *mTagati!*" she wailed from the dark interior where she was cowering.

I re-wrapped it and, saying goodbye to Bongi and Jabu who had run into their home the minute their mother screamed, and were hiding behind her, I padded along the road past the sheds, towards the house and Evalina's voice. She was standing at the back gate, her hand up to shield her eyes from the midday sun.

"*Hau!*" she shouted when she saw me coming up the road. "Where have you been? I told you to be back for breakfast and it's nearly lunchtime! nKosikazi will be very cross with me if she finds out that you missed breakfast! What have you been doing?" she scolded as I approached.

"Look!" I said, and held out my parcel again, revealing the skull. The effect on Evalina was even more dramatic than on Lokatia. She jumped backwards with her eyes popping out of her head like a cartoon character: if she'd had a hat on instead of her white *doek* it would have flown off her head.

"*Haaaibo!*" she screamed and turned and ran towards the kitchen as fast as her plump legs could carry her. Ben Masango and Makhaye came out of the kitchen doorway to see what the screaming was about.

"*mTagati!*" she cried. "nKosizana has brought *mTagati!*" They stopped in their tracks, and, instead of going back into the kitchen, the two men bolted toward the *tjaneen* – the thatched hut that served as a laundry. As they darted inside, Evalina barrelled past them and thundered into the hut, her bare feet pounding on the wooden floor. They slammed the door shut and Evalina appeared at the small window to shout, "*Susa lento!* (Take that thing away!)" just before she shut the window with a bang and started to wail.

I stood there on the back lawn, holding the skull, astonished at this reaction. I knew I could get a satisfactory result from the servants and farm labourers by sidling up to them, with my hand behind my back, and suddenly whip out a live chameleon.

They'd scream and jump and run away, but only far enough to shout at me to put it back in the bush. But this behaviour was unprecedented. I'd only ever once sprung a chameleon on Ben, because after he'd recovered from his fright he picked up a carving knife and chased me out of the kitchen with a terrible bellow, leaving me feeling quite alarmed; now he was cowering in the *tjaneen* as terrified as the others were.

I walked into the kitchen and through the house to the front veranda where Mum and Dad were sitting drinking their pre-lunch gins. I held out the skull to Dad. "Look what I found," I said.

He took it carefully and turned it over in his hands inspecting it with great interest. "It's a monkey skull – a Vervet, and quite a big one judging from the size. Where did you find it?"

"Under that big Yellowwood tree in the bush – the one with *iNkwazi*'s nest at the top."

"That's not *iNkwazi*'s nest," he said. "That's the Crowned Eagle's nest. They eat monkeys, Dassies, and even Blue Duikers."

"So it's only a monkey skull?" I was a little bit disappointed. "Why did the servants take off screaming like that when they saw it then?"

"They probably thought it was a child's skull. They believe that *iNkwazi* the Fish Eagle snatches small children and carries them off to feed their young." Dad was on his second pink gin and was feeling expansive. "But *iNkwazi* nests in trees up in the vleis where the best fishing is, not down here in the bush."

"They were shouting '*mTagati*' as they ran away," I explained.

"Ah! That means they definitely thought it was the skull of a child. One who was killed for *muti* – a spell. There's some bad witchcraft that goes on around these parts and now and again an innocent Zulu child gets murdered and parts of him are chopped up for *muti* against an enemy. Other parts get buried in certain places. They're a bunch of bloody savages, really," he said, and took a sip from his glass.

"I saw lots of other bones under the nest," I said. "Would those be Duiker bones?"

"Probably. I'll tell you what. When I've had my afternoon snooze we'll walk up there and take a proper look at the ground under the nest. I was planning to go into the bush anyway to look for snares. Those bastards can't resist putting snares in, or hunting with their kaffir dogs, no matter how much free meat they're given."

"Yes, please!" I said. "I'd love to look at all those bones," and skipped off for my lunch, only to find the kitchen deserted.

Mum called me back. "Don't forget your broeks! You'd better give them to Lisha to wash." The gin had mellowed her, too.

"And you'd better tell the servants that's only a monkey skull or we won't get any lunch," added Dad dryly.

I walked down the kitchen steps and over to the *tjaneen*.

"It was only the skull of *nKau* [the Vervet Monkey]," I called through the closed door. The Zulu name '*nKau*' is onomatopoeic and is exactly how Vervets sound when they give their alarm call: "*nKau!*" There was silence and then the door opened a crack.

An anxious brown face appeared. "Are you sure?" asked Ben.

"Yes. nKosane says it's *nKau's* skull." The door creaked open slowly and the three house servants came out cautiously, still not quite sure whether this was another of my tricks. "Where is it?"

"I left it on the veranda with nKosane," I said. "Can I have my lunch now?"

With a lot of dark muttering Ben stomped crossly up the steps into the kitchen to dish up lukewarm mince and mash for me.

Makhaye replaced his fez, which had fallen to the ground in his panic, and went back to laying the dining-room table. Evalina went off to call Lisha who was looking after Delia somewhere down by the tennis court.

At four Dad picked up his walking stick, whistled for the dogs, and we walked down the paddock, across the river and into the cool, dark green bush, retracing the steps I'd taken that morning with Bongi and Jabu. We followed the bushbuck path, Dad stopping every now and again to check the undergrowth on either side, looking for signs to indicate that a snare had been set.

"There's one!" he said, and poked a cunningly hidden circle of baling-wire with the tip of his stick. "The buck steps into the middle of that and look!" As he touched the inside of the noose, it suddenly shot upwards silently, attached to a strong, springy sapling, which the long strand of wire had been tied to. "That's strong enough to tighten round his leg or even his neck. He'll be trapped there until they come and check the snare in a few days' time. It's a horribly slow way for an animal to die," and he shook his head grimly.

"Barbarians!"

I pulled the noose off the sapling and looked at it closely. It was so neatly done that the thin wire looked exactly like the coiled dry end of a vine, of which there were plenty throughout the forest.

"Hang it on the branch over there." He pointed to a Knob Thorn tree growing at the edge of the path. "As high as you can reach, then they'll know I've found it. I'll put the word out tomorrow morning, warning the whole lot of them that I'm finding snares in the bush again, and I'll shoot any kaffir dog I find on this farm. I don't want them hunting in the bush, dammit."

We climbed up to the big Yellowwood tree, Dad making sure the dogs were well to heel in case they got caught in a snare.

"Here!" I called, pointing to the moss at the base of the massive trunk.

Dad walked around the tree and picked up one of the dog-shaped skulls. "This is a Blue Duiker skull. Look, it can't be bigger than a Fox-Terrier. It's amazing to think that there's an antelope that small. Easy for a Crowned Eagle to grab though. They're very powerful birds. They have to be able to pluck a fully-grown Vervet off a branch, and my God those monkeys can hang on tight. They also have extra broad wings to be able to manoeuvre between the densely growing trees with such a heavy cargo."

He poked another small and strangely shaped skull lying on the moss.

"That's a Dassie skull. They're another favourite food that the Eagles have to share with leopards. Did you know Dassies' closest relatives are elephants? Even though they look more like big rabbits – I'll show you in the book when we get home. These other bones must be legs and ribs that they've chucked out of their nest. There's been a pair of eagles raising a chick every two years in that nest as long as I can remember. Even as a small boy I heard their pee-weet pee-weet call all summer long."

I collected up as many skulls as I could carry and we made our way back down the mountainside, across the river and home. As I trotted along behind Dad I was busy making plans to tackle Evalina as soon as possible on this whole *mTagati* story.

~~~

# *26*

# Rocket

I turned nine at the end of January 1959, and had grown so tall that my legs dangled down and almost touched the ground when I rode Squib. He was an awkward little pony at the best of times, and looked very like one of those shaggy Thelwell cartoon illustrations. Dad had bought him off a Basutu – or possibly traded him for an unrideable polo pony he'd been conned into buying in a moment of weakness. Whatever the case, he'd paid a lot for old Squib with his mulish attitude and reluctant amble and the way he dragged his feet at a snail's pace on any ride out. When I turned him for home he always perked up, took the bit (he was the only pony on the place who had to wear a Pelham straight bit with a curb chain, his mouth was so hard) grimly between his teeth, and struck up the most uncomfortable bone-jarring jog that made my teeth rattle.

By the time we got home, my fingers would be raw and stinging from trying to keep his head up and stop him from bolting. His only redeeming feature was that he made me into the sort of rider who could stick onto anything. My knees had to grip, vice-like, in front of his sloping, narrow little shoulders, and his bit-snatching and head-dropping habits always kept me on full alert, ready for any eventuality.

Because my birthday was at an awkward time of the year – the very day the new school year started, and the servants were caught up in a flurry of washing, ironing, and packing my older sisters' big school trunks, my mother never had time to hold a birthday party for me. Delia was lucky as her birthday fell in the middle of the winter term. A few carefully selected local farmers' children of her age were invited over for a party on a Saturday, their parents bringing them in their farm vehicles, lurching and bumping along our rutted, pot-holed road, and the adults would play tennis all afternoon on our grass court. In the old days there had been two tennis courts. Apparently my grandmother had declared loftily that it just "Doesn't seem right to invite people all that way for tennis and then some have to sit out while others play."

So she had two courts, one below the other, measured out by a tennis expert, grassed with special 'New Zealand Brown' fine dark-green lawn grass usually used for bowling greens, and once a week had a garden boy drag a heavy roller and then push a hand mower, set very low, over both courts. The netting was chicken wire, and the nets were real ones, made from what looked like white canvas and brown hessian string, ordered from her father's supplier, WG Brown & Co in Durban.

When my mother came to the farm and took over the garden, she decided that one court would be enough, so she'd had the netting taken down, allowed the kikuyu grass to creep back into the lower lawn, and gradually she and her team of garden staff planted a border of shrubs and trees around it. On any occasion like Delia's birthday party or house parties, when my parents' friends drove up from Durban to spend the weekend fishing, everybody brought tennis kit and played until sundown, or till they were chased off the court by the sudden thunderstorms that appeared from behind the mountain as regularly as clockwork every summer's afternoon.

Then they would gather on our big front veranda to drink whisky and gin, the ice cubes tinkling merrily in their glasses while the delicious aroma of roasting lamb wafted through from the kitchen. Masango sweated under his tall chef's hat, basting meat, chopping piles of veggies from our garden and hurling them into the battered saucepans that bubbled on the stove, with such vigour that water splashed up the wall behind. He whisked up delectably sweet, fluffy banana soufflés for pudding, to be eaten piping hot with our fresh, rich cream poured over the top. Makhaye flitted silently around the dining-room in his white waiter's uniform, complete with red sash and little white cap, laying the long French-polished table with silver, and putting out crystal wine glasses that sparkled in the light from candles in scrolled silver candelabra on the Yellowwood mantelpiece, and in the middle of the gleaming table, either side of a cut glass bowl of fragrant flowers freshly picked by my mother that morning.

We children would run wild over the farm, and played in the river while our nannies (local farmers with children always brought their own Zulu nannies to *pasopa,* – caring for  – them) sat with Evalina under the gum-trees, dipping hunks of bread into deliciously strong, sugary coffee in generous, chipped enamel mugs, and gossiped tirelessly about us *aBelungu* until it was time to call us in to be bathed and given supper of creamy yellow scrambled eggs on toast, sprinkled with chopped parsley. Then the visiting children were bedded down with their respective nannies in our nursery while their parents drank wine and then port, and eventually tiny demitasses of *Nescafe* to try and sober up sufficiently to be able to tackle the treacherously slippery road home.

My ninth birthday party was quite different – a far more sedate affair. Grandpa had been invited over for afternoon tea on the Sunday before, and Masango had baked a sponge cake with cream and strawberry jam in the middle and dusted it with icing sugar.

My mother stuck nine tiny pale-blue, curly candles on top and lit them. I blew them out in one breath and made my usual wish. Grandpa put his teacup down, leaned forward in his chair and said, "Your present is in the orchard paddock."

I looked at him, puzzled. "Run down and have a look," he insisted, and I put my slice of cake carefully back on my plate and leaped off the veranda steps to race down past the tennis court.

Standing there was Lady, Grandpa's polo pony, a half-thoroughbred chestnut mare, with the sun gleaming off her glossy golden rump, and at her heels stood her latest foal. He was a long legged year-old bay colt with a white blaze down his little face and small, beautifully curved ears that pricked curiously towards me.

"Yes – he's yours," chuckled Grandpa. He'd walked down to the paddock behind me and stood now, watching my face as I stared in disbelief and then utter delight as I realised the foal was mine.

"His sire is that excellent polo pony of old Jock Mackenzie's at Fort Nottingham – the one he bought as an ex-racehorse. I got Simeon to ride Lady over yesterday afternoon, leading him, and we hid them in the apple tree field until this afternoon. He'll take Lady home now as your new colt is fully weaned, and we'll lead him to the pigsty field where the others are so he doesn't get lonely. What are you going to call him?"

I pondered for a moment thinking of Squib. "Rocket!" I said triumphantly. "It's the perfect name because he'll be so much faster than Squib." I could scarcely believe that at last my birthday wish had come true. Every year I wished for a proper pony, a real one that held his head up, ran like the wind and didn't have to be kicked along every step of the way.

"What'll happen to Squib now?" I asked, a little anxiously. After all, he'd served me, however reluctantly, for the past four years.

"I've arranged for him to go up on top," said my father who'd joined us by now and was looking my new colt over with an appraising eye. "The herd boys will ride him and you can still see him when you go up there. In the meantime you can ride Ronald or Prince. You really are too tall to be getting back onto Squib now. That foal has some Arab blood in him – look at those sickle-shaped ears."

I could hardly believe my own ears. Not only was I being promoted from my recalcitrant little beast, but I would be allowed to ride Dad's most prized, not to say valuable, polo ponies. "I'll help you break Rocket in when he's ready," said Grandpa standing there in the sun, leaning on his walking stick, and he tipped his bush hat back off his forehead with his thumb.

Grandpa was the best horseman in the district, and had on several occasions represented South Africa as the highest handicap polo player.

He'd taught us all to ride as soon as we were able to walk, putting us on the pommel of his own saddle, to meander about his smallholding in Fort Nottingham, before sitting us on old Sunny's bony back, on a special sheepskin saddle he'd had made, and leading us out behind his pony, Lady, for long rides over the farm. We'd fallen off at first of course, and landed with a bump on the hard dirt road. "No *ugazi* – no blood, no crying" was Grandpa's motto as he sat there benignly on his horse, waiting for us to remount by ourselves. He wasn't one for a fuss.

Sunny was about 23 years old and from Nicolette down-wards each toddler had been placed carefully on the sheepskin saddle, to be led plodding around by Grandpa. We'd all learned to ride on Sunny, and then gradually progressed to more adventurous mounts as we grew older. He wasn't a small horse, but he had the wonderful placid disposition that made him such an ideal child's pony. 'Bomb proof' Grandpa called him. Nicolette had fallen off Sunny and gone around with a broken arm for three days before our parents realised that she was in serious pain and needed to be taken all the way in to the doctor in Nottingham Road for an X-ray. So we had to be tough, and quickly learned to stay on our ponies as we graduated from bombproof Sunny to our various mounts.

I spent the rest of the day in a daze of delirious joy, and kept running back down to the field to look at my new colt.

"He's halter trained, so the next thing you'll have to do is put a bridle on him and teach him how to lead – the polo boys will show you how," Grandpa had told me, and I couldn't wait.

There was a soft rubber snaffle in the saddle room, which I attached to Squib's bridle and hung from a hook all ready to start on Monday morning. Over the following months, with help from the ever-patient Toto and Shorty, I gradually accustomed Rocket to the bit, the bridle, and eventually a saddle. Grandpa came over regularly for Sunday lunch to supervise my progress, and he passed on everything he knew about breaking in young horses. I was eager to hasten the procedure, longing to go to the next step – desperate for the day I could ride my new pony, but he kept me in check. "You're as green as that young horse of yours," he chuckled amiably as, once again, I was restricted to leading the colt about, this time with a sack half-filled with mealie meal on his back. "Let him get used to having the weight on his back before you try and ride him."

One summer morning, nearly a year on from my birthday, Grandpa came over for Sunday lunch as usual. I had Rocket saddled up, ready and waiting for our next lesson.

"Go and get Toto," he said. I tied my pony up and ran down the road, past the stables and up to Toto's hut where I found him sitting comfortably on a sawn-off log in the sun, enjoying a mug of strong coffee. His wife, with their latest baby tied on her back, was sweeping up the dust in front of their hut with a bundle of twigs. His other two children, both wearing only T-shirts, played with a little car they'd made out of baling-wire.

"Toto come!" I pulled at his hand excitedly. "Numzane wants you to help us with Rocket." He swallowed the dregs in his enamel mug, and good-naturedly allowed himself to be dragged to his feet. "What's the hurry? It's Sunday," he teased, but I could see he was as keen as I was to see what Grandpa was up to.

We led Rocket down to the field below the road, opened the wire concertina gate and walked in. The field had been ploughed ready to sow rye grass that would be used to feed our cattle through the three or four dry winter months. The earth was soft and crumbly, and felt warm to my bare feet. Rocket's hooves sank into the yielding soil, right in to his hocks.

"Now," said Grandpa to Toto, "get on the horse very care-fully. Hang yourself over the saddle first and let him feel your weight." Toto knew exactly what to do – he must have broken in many horses in his time. He was shorter than me as his growth had been so stunted as a child, and he was almost as light as I was.

Carefully he leaned on the saddle and then eased himself so that he was lying over it with his weight evenly distributed. Grandpa told me to lead Rocket in a big circle. My horse – he was no longer a pony as he now stood at just over fifteen hands – walked obediently around behind me, seemingly unaware of the man on his back.

"Right Toto, you can get off, and this time get on him properly. I want you sitting in the saddle," said Grandpa.

Toto did so, and once he was mounted, I held my breath. This was the most crucial moment – to see whether the horse would suddenly realise he had a rider on his back and begin to buck or rear up on his hind legs. When Dad trained his polo ponies he always got Toto or Shorty to get on first, and he never bothered to take the horse down to a ploughed field either – just told them to get mounted at the back gate. The rest of the Zulu labourers somehow always got wind of a potential rodeo and appeared from nowhere, gathering in a crowd to see what would happen.

Occasionally a new horse, or one that was being broken in, would explode into a series of bucks and pig jumps, and rear up to try and dislodge the rider, who (not Shorty or Toto – they never fell off) would hit the ground with a thump, sending up a puff of dust.

The crowd roared with delight and called out to him to hurry and remount so that they could be entertained again with another fall. There was laughter and good-natured jeers as comments were passed on the rider's skills. Not all the men on the farm could ride, and certainly none of the women or children. In Zulu custom, if you owned a horse, you rode it, and your women and children walked behind you, carrying your and their possessions in bundles on their heads.

Rocket stood absolutely still for a moment, and then, when Toto touched his bare heels to his flanks, moved forward in a brisk walk. "Perfect!" said Grandpa triumphantly. "This horse knows what you want him to do." Then it was my turn, and I swung myself as lightly into the saddle as I could, while Toto held his head. "Off you go now," said Grandpa.

"Ride him round the field in a big circle. If he bolts, he'll tire quickly in this soft ground and won't run away with you." It felt like magic. Rocket moved forward smoothly at a touch of my heels, and I trotted and then cantered him. He was as comfortable as a rocking horse, moving effortlessly under my knees in an almost silken stride. I pulled gently on the reins and he stopped immediately and stood still.

"You've got a good horse there," said Grandpa with a pleased smile. "He doesn't look as though he'll give you any trouble." For me, having Rocket was the equivalent of being given my own sports car. Unlike Squib, who moved away mutinously the minute he saw a bridle in my hand, and was so difficult to catch, Rocket came trotting and stuck his head out for the halter.

Often I didn't bother taking him back to the house to be saddled, and rode him bareback all over the farm. He had a springy, bouncy step, but his gait was so comfortable that I could ride him all day without a saddle, and when he galloped, he was faster than any of the others, polo ponies included.

~~~

# *27*

# Wakefield

I rode all over the farm, but if I rode on past the nuns, on towards Wakefield (the farm my father leased grazing on), I crossed a small stream and came to a sort of no-man's land that was overgrown with a thick, tall mass of young wattle saplings, self-seeded from an old plantation there. The stream (called *Nunu* Stream by cousins of ours who came up now and again to spend a couple of weeks' summer holidays at Wakefield) bubbled from a spring high up in the mountain range behind Wakefield and the nuns, and bounced down the steep, rocky krantzes in little cascades, to settle into its pebbled bed before joining the Umgeni River, which ran below the farm-house.

We absolutely loved it when our four cousins came up from their house in Kloof, near Durban, and spent as much time as we could with them. Our favourite game was to swipe all the pots and pans from Ezekiel's (their cook boy from Kloof) kitchen and bring them down to *Nunu* Stream to play all day long. We would spend most of the day swirling water and gravel around in them, panning for gold, and squabbled over whose turn it was to commandeer the battered aluminium colander, which we all knew was best for panning. We made mud pies and dams, using the pots to scoop out water and empty it into ponds we dredged in the shallows. It was the equivalent of playing on a beach with buckets and spades, as the stream flowed over golden yellow gravel, in ripples that danced in the sunlight, and there were little, silvery creatures like water boatmen, and various other swimming insects in the shallow stream with its crystal clear water – hence its name – *Nunu* is Zulu for insect.

Now and again we found small chips of gravel that looked exactly like gold nuggets, and we collected these in little piles on the grassy bank to take back to the house later on. Our games had to grind to a halt when Ezekiel came down to retrieve his pots as he had started making the evening meal and needed to boil up the potatoes he'd already peeled. After that, we ran down to swim in the Umgeni River that flowed below the wattle plantation, our favourite place being 'The Judges' Pool' which was a particularly big one, deep enough to dive off a shelf of rock which jutted out to make a perfect diving board. It seemed almost bottomless and there were no crabs to nip us down there. The pool had derived its name from a visiting judge who had caught an enormous Brown Trout while fishing there many years ago. He was a friend of the Lasches who own the farm and had built the house as a fishing retreat.

We would then trudge back up the long, baked red mud track to the huge, sprawling thatched bungalow that was Wakefield. The Zulu caretaker's children joined us in these activities, as they were all the same ages as we were. This was also a novelty, as Mum didn't allow us to play with "Munt children." All my own sorties with Dumi and the others had to be done clandestinely.

We would arrive at the bungalow, a mixed gaggle of children, thirsty from our day in the baking summer sun, and pour ourselves drinks from a big bottle of *Oros* (an orange flavoured concentrate), diluting it with cool water taken from the fridge. It was a huge old round-topped paraffin fridge, as Wakefield had no electricity, and it stood at the end of the back veranda, which had been covered with thatch to incorporate a makeshift kitchen. In the huge fridge door stood a few ex-gin bottles that were now used to keep drinking water cool, particularly for the adults' pink gins and evening whiskies.

# White Zulu

Fiona Ross

One hot afternoon we ran out of cold water from the fridge, and my cousin Sarah, who was about seven at the time, ran in to the sitting room to fetch another bottle. She looked around and saw a gin bottle standing nearby on a big wooden chest in which my aunt kept all their booze.

She grabbed it and ran out to the kitchen to carry on pouring water from it to dilute the juice, which had already been sloshed out into glasses and held out by our many small hands, black and white. We gulped down our drinks and then ran off to play until suppertime.

It was only when my aunt came out to call us to come in and eat that she discovered two *umfaans* lying in a deep stupor in the shade of the back veranda. She was puzzled by this and eventually discovered the reason when she went to the drinks chest to retrieve the full bottle of gin that she'd put out for my parents, who were driving over for drinks before dinner, and found it lying empty in the kitchen, among the debris of drained juice glasses and the dregs of an *Oros* bottle.

With a small half-shriek, she clapped her hand over her mouth and said, "Who's been feeding gin to the *umfaans*?" They were none the worse for wear though, and came along the next morning to join in our games.

~~~

# *28*

# Special Days

In the summer there would be a flurry of activity the day the schools closed for the long, hot, Christmas break. When boarding school Prep broke up and Nicolette came home, there had to be a reshuffle of bedrooms; I had to leave my room and move to the spare room for the school holidays, and Evalina bustled my clothing out of the end room and into the spare room. Nicolette, Dine and Delia each had their own bedroom, but I didn't.

Unbelievably from early on, I'd been the baby who didn't cry during the night and, as a reward for being so amenable, I'd been allocated to Mum and Dad's dressing room off their bedroom, while my sisters were given the three bedrooms well out of earshot. When Nicolette went to boarding school at the age of five, I was relocated to her bedroom at the furthest end of the passage, and had to move into the spare room when she came back for holidays.

Nicolette was at the Preparatory School for girls – the Prep, which is next to the College on the outskirts of Hilton. It was run by two tyrannical and dreary middle-aged spinsters – Miss Grindley and Miss Turnbull – who were strictly Victorian in their outlook.

The food was terrible, too, all of which we would discover for ourselves when we arrived there, one by one, in the years to come. Mum would drive down to Hilton, an attractive village perched on the plateau that overlooks Pietermaritzburg, the big, sprawling capital city of Zululand and Natal, to fetch her. The drive took about three-quarters of an hour and they came back at lunchtime; Nicolette's huge school trunk in the boot of the car. This was removed by our two nannies and the contents whisked off to be laundered.

She was dressed in her uniform of pale blue cotton dress, brown Clark's sandals and a white panama hat perched on her dark, curly hair, with the school badge prominently displayed. We were insatiably curious and asked Nicolette endless questions about boarding school. She was quite reticent and soon got fed up with our interrogation and would walk off. Dine and I mocked and jeered, rolling around on the grass at our own hilarious jokes at her expense, then we lost interest and went back to our games with our dolls and fairies, which we played all year round.

Nicolette found all our giggling, Delia-baiting and minor squabbles irritating. We didn't know how traumatic it had been for her at the age of five to be wrenched away from our remote farm and very isolated family, to be thrust into a big dormitory full of strange girls. Coming home to find her irresponsible, immature and extremely annoying younger sisters as her only companions must have been awful for her, and she became slightly aloof and with-drawn. At least all the girls at school were in the same boat; they could commiserate with one another about their hardships, and she'd formed close friendships with most of them. With our clowning around and never taking anything seriously, we were impossible to communicate with and simply couldn't identify with her situation. She was clearly lonely, missed her friends (although she was delighted to be away from that dreadful school), and became more and more detached from the three of us.

I was pleased when Nicolette came home, although we rather resented the fuss Mum made of her, especially on the occasions when she came back for the day on Sunday outings from school: three each term. She was allowed treats such as the best bit off the roast leg of mutton: the tail – a delicious, crispy morsel for which we all competed vociferously. "It's my turn!" I'd wail as the delicacy was put onto Nicolette's plate. I knew as well as Dine did that she'd managed to get the tail the last time, and the pope's nose of the chicken the Sunday before – I didn't even like the pope's nose.

To me lambs' tails and chickens' bums were two entirely different things, but I felt it was an infringement of my civil rights to be passed over, so I tried to kick up a fuss anyway; it's no wonder our parents made us eat in the nursery. Nicolette had immediately changed into shorts like the rest of us, and we sat down to lunch in the dining-room; usually we ate in the nursery, but on the odd occasion like this one, we were allowed to eat with our parents.

Masango often roasted a chicken – a big treat. One chicken could feed a family of six, and there would still be enough left over to make an adequate curry or stew the next day, and the flavour was quite delicious. The chickens came from our flock of fowls that scratched about in an enclosure behind the veggie garden, and Dine and I used to trail after him as he carried his big firewood axe over to the fowl run with its hen-house. This was firmly barricaded against nocturnal predators such as wildcats and Spotted Genets, which could slip through the smallest opening – "If its skull can fit through, then it can get in," said Grandpa – and slaughter the entire flock in one night. We would help an impassive Masango round up and catch a nice big cockerel, and then stand by to watch as he removed his tall, starched, white chef's hat, hung it on a fence post holding up the wire that surrounded the chicken run, and, taking a firmer grip on the squawking fowl's body, summarily lay it on a nearby tree stump and chop its head off with a single swift blow. He would then release it, and the body twitched and leaped about entertainingly, headless and spraying blood everywhere. For some odd reason we thought this was fascinating, seeing the tiny head still lying there on the tree stump while the rest of the fowl performed its gruesome dance.

We would also regularly go over to the sheds to watch one of our sheep being slaughtered for the house. One of the Zulu men laid it on its side and held its body down with one knee, its legs kicking frantically. He pinned its head to the ground and sawed at its throat with a rather blunt kitchen knife. After a lot of bleating, which finally changed to a gurgle, blood cascaded from the unfortunate creature's jugular.

When the animal had subsided into death with one final jerk of its legs, the Zulu and a workmate hung the carcass up by its back feet from a strong wire hook tied to the low branch of a gum-tree that grew conveniently next to a water tap, and the skinning began. Once they'd cut out its stomach, one of the boys took it, turned it inside out and washed off most of the chewed green, slimy looking contents under the tap. He popped slices of the raw tripe into his mouth and ate it with relish. He offered some to us, but Dine and I recoiled with disgust.

Dad loved tripe and onions, but I couldn't stand even the smell of it.

~~~

# *29*

# The Umgeni River

**H**igh up in the mountains on a plateau between two hills, is a marsh that collects various springs and becomes a stream that winds its way down into the valley, becoming bigger as other streams flow out of the dense, dark forest to become the Umgeni River (without the usual African accoutrements of crocs, hippos, bilharzia, or even a drop of pollution). The water was crystal clear, and pristine. We used the sweet, pure water for drinking as well as bathing. Grandpa had placed a pipe under a cascade high above the house, which ran into a reservoir in the pine plantation. The water was then fed by gravity down another pipe to the house below. Grandpa had shown us how to tell whether water is drinkable: we had to turn over a small rock and look underneath – if there were little may-fly larvae wriggling beneath the rock, then we knew it was safe to drink. The first time I ever tasted town water was my first day at boarding school, and the chlorine flavour reminded me of lavatories – I was so disgusted that I gagged, and to this day I can't stand the taste of treated water.

In the dry winter months, as the river fell to a trickle, its rushing sound was reduced almost to a silence, rising again to a roar during the wet season. Almost daily, this sound rose to a thunderous roar after our regular midsummer storms released a cloudburst into the valley, swelling the river so that it overflowed its banks. These floods came right up over the low, concrete bridge that spanned the river, effectively cutting us off from the rest of the world. The original bridge that Grandpa had built, had been a flimsy affair made from timber and packed with soil, and was washed away completely in the 1950s.

The Nationalist Party Government Roads Department replaced the bridge with a hideous concrete causeway, strong enough to take army tanks. The Army needed to be able to get to *Impendhle*, the Zulu location high in the hills behind our farm (Afrikaners called any African township, small or large, a location). If trouble brewed among the 'natives' up there, they wanted to be able to get tanks up there to sort the 'unrest' out immediately.

By 'unrest' they meant any uprising and rioting against Apartheid, and 'sorting it out' involved shooting rioters, and not necessarily with rubber bullets. When our parents were planning one of their annual skiing trips to Austria or Switzerland, and there was a likelihood that the water would surge over the bridge preventing them from crossing, they would book into Rawdons Hotel, just the other side of Nottingham Road, for a couple of nights ahead of departure, to ensure that they wouldn't miss their plane.

The Umgeni River formed a permanent background to our everyday lives. There'd be perennial panic, caused and fuelled by Mum's obsession with the weather, as it affected her garden – when the first spring rains were late and we'd had no rain for up to seven months. The whole farm, apart from both our huge areas of indigenous bush, was tinder dry and the tension would be palpable as Mum got up at first light every morning, long before anyone else on the farm, apart from the roosters crowing at the huts, were awake. She'd walk down to the edge of the front lawn, peering through the shrubbery to see if any of the pools in the river visible from there, had sunk any lower.

Then she'd minutely scan the skies for any signs of cloud. She would anxiously gaze at the pine plantation to check for indications of smoke, and lifting her head and standing on tiptoe, turn south to see if there were any untoward or suspicious signs of fire coming from the Nuns at Umgeni Poort in the far distance, way down the valley.

What little time Mum spent at breakfast between tearing around with a half-finished cup of coffee in one hand and a pencil in the other, making lists on scraps of paper in case someone was going into Hoosen's, she'd interrogate Dad, who'd sensibly lain in bed with his early morning tea, brought in on a tray by Makhaye, and listened to the local weather forecast on his transistor radio. Every spring this ritual and Mum's anxiety levels escalated as the entire place became more and more desiccated until one could almost hear the vegetation crackling as it dried up. The river levels sank in reverse proportion to that of Mum's blood pressure, and she'd begin to talk as though the entire farm had already gone up in smoke, especially when she heard daily reports of runaway bush-fires in neighbouring areas.

"I heard that the Baldwins' wattle plantations are on fire," she'd say despondently. "It's just a matter of time before ours goes up, too. They're too close to our boundary." And so her days were spent fretting over what she had decided was the inevitable.

Every night, throughout the years, we'd eat our three-course supper cooked by Masango, all six of us seated at the dining-room table with its full accoutrements of crystal and silver, flowers arranged, and candles lit, and each dish served to us by Makhaye, wearing his red sash and little white wedge cap. After we'd finished, if it was a clear night, the whole family would walk out onto the front lawn, us kids in bare feet, even though there was a thick frost on the grass in winter, and we'd gaze into the sky to look for signs of rain. It was mainly to appease Mum's constant anxiety, but it was also the only really pleasurable activity we did as a family. Others usually involved a trip to Durban to visit the dentist – a horrible ordeal.

The only other time we six congregated was when we sat down for our three daily meals and a slightly tense atmosphere as Mum watched our table manners like a hawk, and Dad insisted that we either made conversation of general interest or didn't speak at all. There was absolutely no light pollution in the valley, so we had the full impact of the Southern Hemisphere constellation.

There's nothing quite like the African night skies. The Milky Way actually blazes in a full, broad arc from horizon to horizon, dotted with bigger individual stars scattered here and there and the Southern Cross stands out proudly, easily identifiable and pointing towards the Celestial South Pole.

Later on, after 1957 when Sputnik was launched, over the ensuing years right up until we left the homestead at New Forest in the mid-2000s, we'd gradually see more and more flashes of sunlight being reflected off satellite solar panels as the numbers being launched increased. It was always fun to see who'd be the first to spot the give-away, intermittent flashes as one went rapidly past, rotating in its orbit seemingly among the stars. I was hopeless at this game after the age of about fifteen and before it was discovered that I was seriously myopic. I then hated wearing my thick, clunky, coke-bottle-bottom glasses so much that I'd have put them down somewhere and forgotten where.

Mum would drag our attention away from the skies (once we'd established that there were no promising signs of oncoming rain) and turn our attention to the perilously low level of the river, shushing our excited conversations so we could listen intently to hear if the water had somehow miraculously risen, possibly from a rain storm high up in the vleis up on top. As we stopped our chatter about stars and satellites to listen, the night noises of the bush took over.

There was the constant chirping of crickets in the background, interspersed by the occasional croak of a frog anticipating by the rising temperatures that spring was on its way. A male Wood Owl would give off his mournful hoot, immediately followed by his mate's "Who?" response – "the surprised owl" as we children called it. We always found every owl-call spooky as, since we'd been born, all the Zulus had dinned into us their many and various superstitions about owls in general. The Spotted Eagle Owl was the most notorious for causing havoc by setting spells on unsuspecting Zulus, possibly because it had ear tufts that looked suspiciously like horns. It had a deep and sinister (to us anyway) long, low hoot. These calls came from the gum-trees surrounding the house.

But, in the deep bush across the valley came a whole lot of different noises.

There was the volley of grunts that became faster and louder, climaxing in a series of noisy and bloodcurdling screams, which genuinely sounded as though someone was being murdered.

These came from the "bush babies" as we called them, but are actually Tree Hyraxes, the arboreal cousins to our dassies, and their hair-raising, spine chilling screams would go on all summer long and usually all night as well. Guests who were new to spending nights with us, would come ashen-faced and extra early to breakfast, asking querulously whether anyone on the farm had been murdered during the night. We do actually have plenty of Thick-Tailed Bush Babies resident in the bush, but they aren't vocal. Bushbuck rams barked occasionally, giving out their dog-like alarm call as leopards prowled the bush, or a bush pig would disturb them.

But the most alarming noise of all was when, in the pitch dark, a leopard would jump into a tree in which the baboon troop was roosting that night, and snatch one from the lower branches.

The entire troop would erupt, screaming, howling, and roaring in terror, giving off futile alarm barks as the body of a hapless young baboon was carried off in the big cat's powerful jaws, possibly still screaming, and the babies shrieked shrilly as their mothers gripped them tighter and tried to carry them higher up the already overcrowded tree. This hideous racket echoed up and down the valley for some twenty minutes before the troop would gradually settle again.

Mum quite enjoyed these *kattevrye* (cat fights), as she'd say with some satisfaction, "One less baboon. Bloody vermin!" There were plenty of other nocturnal animals in the bush, but unseen during our nightly family gatherings. Large Spotted Genets prowled the trees and hunted the forest for rodents and nestlings. There were plenty of mongooses too. Big, fluffy black Water Mongooses hunted waterfowl, and there were others; the solitary Yellow Mongoose hunted at night as did the Large Grey and Slender Mongooses. The White Tailed Mongoose, also as solitary as the others, was a common nocturnal predator, preferring the deepest part of the bush, but sadly we didn't have those enchanting groups of diurnal mongoose, like the Banded and Dwarf mongooses, which are always so entertaining to watch.

There were plenty of other nocturnal creatures roaming the 5,000 acres of varied habitats of our ranch. In the valley and on top there were Caracal, otherwise known as Lynx or Rooikat, which (along with Black Backed Jackals) carried off some of our lambs and even a few full-grown sheep, and were enough of a nuisance to farmers to have a bounty of one rand for each tail handed in to the Nottingham Road police station. In the same way that we could call in the Baboon Boy, there was a similar enterprise called the Jackal Pack, which consisted of a Zulu man with his pack of *isiGodyi* (mongrels) who would hunt down these scavengers for a price agreed between himself and the farmer.

Then there were Aardvarks (which we called ant-bears), those strange, hump-backed animals with sparse hair on their tough, leathery bodies. They have extra-long snouts and even longer tongues, and only come out at night. They dig deep holes in the veld, looking for fat, sleepy termites, and slurping them up with those extremely long and thin, sticky pink tongues. They're related to shrews and elephants, rather like Dassies are (we called Dassies rock rabbits, but they're actually Hyraxes.)

There's deep superstition among the Africans about Aardvarks because they're so seldom seen. Most nocturnal creatures have some sort of folklore or superstition attached to them, as the only evidence for them is their calls or what they leave behind in the morning. Traditionally, before cars and electricity were introduced to the country, no Africans would venture out of their kraals or *bomas* (thorny enclosures) after nightfall because of the many predators roaming around in the dark. If they were in their *bomas* all the light they could produce was a flaming torch to keep lions, leopards and hyenas off their stock, and that light only showed glowing eyes reflecting back. So it was easy for Africans lying inside their dark, smoky hut with no windows and only the light coming from the dying embers of the cooking fire, to imagine that the strange and mournfully repetitive call came from *uZavolo*, the Goat Sucker, a sinister creature that crept in, somehow magically impervious to the thorns of their *boma*, and drank milk from the nanny goats, instead of the Fiery Necked Nightjar, a small, innocuous bird that feeds on nocturnal flying insects.

Aardvarks always infuriated Dad, as they chose our airstrip to dig their burrows, leaving humps and bumps of earth everywhere, which made the little Cessnas, and other small planes that used the strip, lurch all over the place as they taxied to take off, and leap about alarmingly when landing. The other thing that made him so cross was all those hidden holes they left after digging so deep in the long, tawny veld grass; all of us, girls and grooms alike, had to watch out all the time that his polo ponies, and our own mounts, didn't put a hoof into the hole, sometimes somersaulting and throwing its rider. In our area ant-bear holes were the most common cause of a horse's broken leg.

There was the night creature the Zulus called *iMbohla*, the African Wild Cat, which was so secretive that we never got to see one. They were lone hunters, bold enough to prowl the areas near the house and sheds, where there were plenty of rats among the lucerne bales. They approached the fowl run at the back, near our veggie garden, where Mum's fowls were supposedly safely locked up each night, and occasionally managed to squeeze in through an overlooked hole in the netting to grab a roosting hen and rip its head off, eating what it couldn't carry out. Even young house and stable cats had been carried off and killed by these *isiMbohla*, much to our distress.

Among the bigger predators like the jackals were serval cats, but they seemed to leave our lambs alone, and there were plenty of smaller predators such as the White-Striped Weasel and the Striped Polecat, prowling silently around the garden and the rest of the valley, marking their own various territories with a stinking spray that drove our dogs into a frenzy of excitement, and which they'd roll in if they could find enough of it, particularly the polecat's leavings, forcing us to bath them in diluted *Jeyes Fluid* after they came back triumphantly, reeking enough to make our eyes water. They were always led by Pitz (who had the thickest coat of them all) and who struggled the most vigorously during baths.

After about half an hour of our weather watching, and when (in the summer months) the mosquitoes had really begun to plague us, or the frost nipped our bare toes in winter, we'd troop back into the house, Dad stopping briefly to tap on the barometer that hung on the front veranda, peering at it to see if there was any change in the direction of the brass arrow indicator. I always enjoyed this all year round nightly family ritual, as it was the one and only time the six of us stood as one, animatedly inspecting the skies, silently straining to hear the river in winter and having to talk loudly over its roar in summer when the clouds up and down our valley flashed continuously with silent sheet lightning long after our major daily blitzkrieg thunderstorms had rumbled away down towards the convent.

On the very hottest and most sultry nights it was too stuffy to sit in the house, so we'd switch on our *nunu* (insect) killer. This was a simple but effective wire cage surrounding a bare light bulb. It was green-coloured and unobtrusive in the daytime, but once switched on really came into its own. The bright light from the bulb attracted a variety of moths, from the huge, fat pine moths to tiny pale ones. These fluttered helplessly into the now live bars of the cage and sizzled and sputtered as they burned and fell to the red brick veranda floor. As they lay there, still twitching and smoking, large toads of every description hopped into the pool of light cast by the solitary light bulb and began to feast on their freshly grilled prey. There could be up to ten or more toads all clustered there on some nights, busily gobbling up this bounty. It was only when we saw night adders slithering in, intent on catching their favourite meal: a plump and succulent toad, that we would beat a hasty retreat back into the house, as there was no way of telling where on that dark floor we might put our bare feet on an unseen snake.

In summertime, which is the rest of the year round, the river's background sound rose to a thunderous roar after our regular daily thunderstorms released a cloudburst into the vleis, the catchment area on top of the escarpment, swelling the river so that it overflowed its banks, and then continued down into our valley, still unleashing a fury of torrential rain, thunder and lighting, which constantly struck the conductor on our tin roof.

Worst of all was when we had hailstorms with massive hailstones that shattered our windows until the mid-1960s when Mum eventually had hail shutters installed.

~~~

# *30*

# Our Valley

The only way in or out of our valley is the District Road, which was maintained by re-grading once a year at the beginning of the wet season. This involved the big yellow grader arriving, a monumentally exciting event in our (to us) monotonous daily lives, rumbling down the valley once a year. The driver was a white Afrikaner man with a pot-belly wearing a khaki safari suit, and, using the machine's powerful blade, he scraped a foot of rutted, stony winter surface off the top of the road, leaving a glassy smooth surface underneath. This ensured that all our vehicles slipped and slid on the slick red mud, frequently getting stuck in the glutinous slush as our road became more and more churned up.

As you leave the farm, there is a steep little hill just the other side of the bridge that remains wetter that the rest of the surface as it gets no sun at all, and is pure red mud. You had to take an accelerated run while still on the bridge to get enough momentum to be able to get up it, slipping with wheels churning frantically. If you didn't make it, the vehicle slid impotently backwards and into the ditch to get stuck sideways on.

Coming down that same hill caused concern as, even though you'd carefully applied your brakes to come to a complete stop, the car or bakkie simply continued to slide down toboggan-like, and sometimes sideways, out of control and only to stop when you had run out of momentum, but perilously close to missing the bridge altogether and toppling into the swollen, foaming torrents of the river. This precariously dangerous bit of road presented problems to us all right up until the late 1990s, when SUVs became available. With the comforts of regular cars and less like our basic bone-jarring farm vehicles, one could travel safely on both the tarmac and our treacherous roads, making our farm far more accessible. Going anywhere meant taking our own road off the farm, then negotiating 12 miles of appallingly bad District Road, followed by 50 to 100 miles of tarmac, depending on whether one was going to Pietermaritzburg or Durban.

The only bit that's changed since I was born, is there is a bit more tarmac from Nottingham Road to Lion's Bush, which took away the problem of another steep, slippery hill that trapped everyone but those who had farm 4x4s, but which is now so full of deep potholes that it has become a disintegrating cobweb of tarmac and almost as tricky as the dirt roads.

There were other ways out of our farm. One of them was on horseback (or possibly jeep), via the convent at Umgeni Poort in dry weather, whereby you could ride or drive to the Wakefield turnoff, then, following a track next to the Umgeni River, go through the uninhabited farm of Wakefield and onto the neighbouring farm beyond, called Stonycroft, which had a road out to the Dargle. But if our bridge was flooded, then inevitably the bridge over Poort stream, which separated us from the convent, was also covered by several feet of water, or washed away completely. That bridge had been built at the same time as our original one across the Umgeni River had been, and in exactly the same way, with gum-tree poles spanning the stream and then packed with earth. The District Road didn't reach the Convent, so theirs was declared a private road and thus they had to rebuild their own bridges every time they were washed away.

The other option was to ride on horseback, or take a 4x4 up on top, using the road Grandpa had dynamited out of the hillside, and back along the top of our farm to our airstrip, or further along the escarpment to our neighbours on the farm Ivanhoe, where they had an access road to iMpendhle. Unfortunately, there's a drift (a stream running across the road) on the way up on top, and if that was flooded, it cut off that route as well. The mountains directly behind our house, which also had a footpath that our Zulu staff used to get home, were too steep and rocky for a horse to pick its way through. Over all the years I was growing up there, I had tried it many times, even in the best conditions, going so far as to dismount and lead my sure-footed Basotho pony up the steepest parts but with no success. In very rainy conditions even a Zulu couldn't climb out of the valley that way, as the almost vertical stone track became a series of cascading waterfalls.

We could be cut off completely. If there was an emergency then it would have to be dealt with by helicopter, and only if visibility was suitable. The only problem with that was there was no way of calling one. When we had our regular, violent daily thunderstorms the first amenity to go was our electricity, immediately followed by the phone. It only took a bolt of lightning to strike a pylon or telephone pole, and bang! out went the lot. Just a tree branch blown by the high winds onto our lines was enough to cut us off.

We didn't have a generator, and the CB radio was hardly ever used, really only for Mum to respond to the weekly "radio check" at 7 p.m. every Thursday night, when a volunteer called every farm on our circuit to check their equipment was operational. This was for emergencies such as armed attacks by intruders on the many very vulnerable and isolated farmers, who relied for support on an armed response by their neighbours. It was also essential when there were runaway bush-fires, in which case the whole district mustered up all their labour, tractors, and water tanks pulled by tractors, as they possibly could, using the radio to call for help. But the radio had a limited battery life, and could not be relied upon if the electricity went out for more than five days. To date, our valley has yet to receive a cell phone signal.

In the big floods of 1987 that washed away a good portion of Natal and Zululand, Mum and Dad were alone on the farm along with their staff. They lost all power and communications immediately, and even though they still had the radio, it poured with rain continuously for five days. It gets cold up there at nearly 6 000 feet when there's no sun, even in summer, and the massive floods had occurred in springtime, so to keep warm Mum and Dad had the house-girls drag a couple of mattresses into the sitting-room where there's a big fireplace, and got them to bring in piles and piles of firewood.

"In between getting up to put more logs on the fire, I lay there listening to this strange, deep rumbling noise that we could hear over the roar of the river," said Mum. "I didn't realise what it was, and sometimes even felt vibrations on the floor while we were sleeping, when there was the loudest crashing and rumbling. It was only after we were able to leave the house and take a look at the river that we realised the noise had been from massive boulders being moved around by the sheer force of the water. The worst bit was being so cold all the time, especially at night."

"So why didn't you and Dad share a mattress to keep warm?" we asked mischievously, knowing full well what the answer would be.

"Good God, no!" she exclaimed, horrified. "Your father and I have never shared a bed in our lives and never will."

These floods changed the shape and nature of our river forever. Our favourite childhood bathing pools had gone, banks had disappeared and curves and contours had been straightened out. It was by a miracle that the old sawmill wasn't washed away, although the water had risen right up to flood the lower storey where the saw blade and giant axles were located.

We girls often treated the reservoir as our own private swimming pool, and, occasionally, when the weather was too hot to make the walk back from our usual swimming pool in the river enticing, we children walked up to the reservoir in the cool plantation and slipped, stark naked, into the deep and chilly waters of the pond, which was simply a smallish pool dug out of the earth and lined with dark green moss, ferns, and wild flowers that dipped their delicate pale pink and blue heads towards their reflections. We had to keep quiet about this activity, as we knew Mum and Dad wouldn't have enjoyed their pink gin or whisky-and-water pre-prandial drinks quite so much if they knew their daughters had been frolicking in it.

The baboons got the blame if muddy water ran out of the taps, bringing with it some of the dark, peaty silt that we'd stirred up. Sometimes the baboons did pull up the pipe leading to the reservoir in their search for roots and insects in the damp needle scattered floor, causing the trickle to run to waste into the soft earth beside the pool. "Those bloody baboons have been pulling up the pipes again." Mum would storm through the house, yelling for old Jomela to trudge up the hill and put the pipe back into its groove.

Ticks were a problem. On our walks through often waist-high summer grass to swim in the river, pepper ticks covered our lower limbs so thickly that it looked as though someone had sprinkled reddish pepper over the skin. We washed them off once we got into the water, only to pick up another load on the long hot trudge home, forcing us to try and scrub them off under an outside tap. We always missed one or two, and days later would find them, their microscopic heads buried under the skin in our groins or armpits, forming itchy, raised red weal that sometimes went septic.

They became weeping sores that Evalina treated by dabbing surgical spirit on the affected places. Pepper ticks always lodged themselves in parts of the body where it is most indecent to be seen surreptitiously scratching.

In spite of all these drawbacks all through the summer we walked down to the river as often as we could – it depended on how full the river was, to lie and sunbathe on the huge, rounded granite boulders, slipping every now and again into the bracingly-cold, fast-running water to cool off. We fished for crabs using a piece of string about two feet long with a small piece of raw bacon (purloined from the fridge when Masango's back was turned) tied firmly on the end. We dangled the bait in a pool and after a few minutes would pull the line up, with one or more crabs attached by their strong pincers.

Unfortunately, they weren't edible, even though we occasionally took some up to the house asking Masango to boil them up. He always refused to even attempt this culinary experiment, and hurled the bucket's worth of crabs indignantly into the bush where they had to make their long and arduous way back to the safety of the river.

I often went down to play in the river alone – usually when I was in some sort of trouble or disgrace. This practice was nearly my undoing. One afternoon I was climbing up a very high bank leading from the river to the paddock when the tuft of grass I grabbed to haul myself up over the cliff, came out of the soft earth, and I fell about fifteen feet into the water below. I landed on my back in the only pool just a fraction larger than my nine-year-old self and only just deep enough to break my fall.

This little pool was surrounded by big rocks, which my head had missed by a whisker. It was a miracle that I hadn't hit any of them, so, chastened and sopping wet, I trudged home, anticipating a lecture on getting myself wet. I never told a soul about my narrow escape.

In the wet season, and after every afternoon thunderstorm, the river levels would rise until the banks overflowed with clear, sparkling water. Now and again we would see big Bushbuck rams coming tentatively through the dense forest down their ancient, narrow paths that had been carved by centuries of hooves of the many and various antelope, to drink the cool, running water that raced and tumbled down over the rocks. The bulls, with their magnificently curved, almost twisted and shallowly corkscrewed, trophy horns, of which so many adorned the walls and verandas of practically every farmhouse in South Africa, were beautiful.

They carried their heads high on long necks, like the Kudu does, as both, being browsers, had to be able to reach those parts of the trees higher than the numerous competitive species. The males could weigh up to 80 kilograms and were notoriously dangerous if either wounded or cornered. Many hunters' deaths have been attributed to these big antelope, goring men or tossing them high into the air before trampling them and gouging the torso with those fearsome horns, as they can reach over half a metre with only one twist. Bushbuck have a light brown coat, with up to seven white stripes and white splotches on the sides.

The snowy white patches are usually geometrically shaped and are on the most mobile parts of their body such as their enormous, constantly twitching ears, chin, tail, legs and neck.

The muzzle is also white, and horns are found only on the males.

Early summer also brought the smaller and much lighter in colour, almost ginger, does with their single young at heel. Baby Bushbuck are enchanting and look as though they were lifted directly from Disney's *Bambi*, with their distinctive, pure white spots and stripes against the very orangey ginger background of their coats.

There was a Grey Duiker, easily distinguishable by the single black tuft of hair that stood up between its little horns, that lived near the boundary, too. When alarmed, they have the habit of taking off at high speed, giving off a loud nasal snort, a zigzag in a series of diving jumps directly out of where they lay completely hidden in the long grass, and which could spook my horse so much as to almost unseat me. Oddly, these small antelope, about the size of a whippet and substantially larger than their close relations, the Blue Duikers that lived deep in the densest part of the forest, appeared to prefer living near humans. This phenomenon had been discovered by the first white settlers to the country, who had recorded that invariably, once they'd set up a camp, and on some occasions forts in anticipation of raids or battles over territories, Grey Duikers immediately appeared to make themselves at home within a couple of hundred yards of a camp, whereas all other wild animals, apart from predators, made themselves as scarce as they possibly could. Even after bloody battles, when men picked over the corpses of their enemies, or came out to reclaim and bury their own dead, there were always these largest members of the duiker family grazing unconcernedly among the carnage. I knew of two separate Grey Duikers, always solitary, both of which could always be found near a kraal on two different parts of the farm. There was another one living near our house, which was the bane of Mum's life, as it chose every night to come out to nibble all the tender green shoots off her rose bushes.

Antelope, bush pigs and baboons alike drank from the mossy riverbanks, and Giant Kingfishers flew up and down the river, cackling like Kookaburras. Often we found evidence of Spotted Necked Otters, their polished mudslides leading into the water and their dung, consisting of turds of crunched up crab shells, was left in obvious places on big boulders as markers, warning intruders off their territory. We occasionally saw leopard pug marks in the soft earth on the riverbank, and now again found their scats, the unmistakable oddly-shaped dung they also left as territorial markers.

Dine and I spent many glorious hours playing in a big pool below the water-mill that Grandpa had built when he'd acquired the farm at the turn of the last century. There were weeping willow trees trailing the tips of their fronds in the dappled water, and it had a beach made of sandy silt covered by miniscule, many-coloured, round pebbles. We took our dolls down there to play. There was a boulder with a natural hollow in it, which was surrounded by smaller stepping-stones. We'd been to a christening once, in Mooi River, and so we poured water into the hollow with our hands then, proceeding solemnly with a doll dressed in our version of a robe, we held christenings.

# White Zulu                                    Fiona Ross

There was a magnificent big brown trout lurking in the bottom of that pool. We learned not to show ourselves as he would dart away at the first sight of a moving shape above him, so we lay down on the bank and edged towards the pool on our stomachs until we could reach him to tickle his speckled back with a thin willow twig. He became a sort of pet and seemed to enjoy the tickling so much that he'd swim forward to nestle against the bank well within reach. We lay there in the soft, sweet-scented grass in the sun, on the bank with the forest just across the rippling water and the cicadas shrieked from the willows. They liked willows best, and deafened us when we rode or drove along the bit of road where Grandpa had planted so many willows to try and stabilise the banks on either side of the old bridge. We spent a pleasant summer with our tame trout until one Sunday afternoon, when Grandpa was over for his customary drinks and lunch, and was telling us a story about singing to trout and tickling their bellies to get them to jump into our hands. Dine and I sat on the veranda steps discussing our own new pet. "I wonder what we should call our trout," said Dine, "I like it that he doesn't swim away and hide under the ledge of the mill-pool when we walk onto the bank."

"I think Old Faithful would be a good name for him," I replied.

I'd just been reading a *National Geographic* magazine featuring national parks of North America, and had been fascinated by the geyser that erupted at such regular intervals. What we didn't realise was that Grandpa was leaning forward in his cane armchair, drink in hand, and was listening to us with great interest. After lunch we disappeared to play as usual, and that night at suppertime, to our horror and utter disbelief, there was a big, familiar-looking spotted trout in a dish on the sideboard.

We both simultaneously came to the terrible realisation that Grandpa must have overheard us, got to his feet, picked up his trout rod and landing net, and strolled down to the pool. He had only to cast a fly into the water just above our unsuspecting pet, flick it once or twice to catch Old Faithful, and bring him back to the kitchen for Masango to gut and fry in butter, parsley and bread crumbs for supper. It was a salutary lesson to us – a short, sharp lesson that taught us not to reveal secrets. We'd always trusted our beloved, amenable and affectionate Grandpa – up until that evening. In our innocent discussion on the steps we'd even revealed the exact spot where the trout liked to lie.

The water-mill stood beside the dirt District Road that runs alongside the river, and had been built out of strong timber cut from the bush on its far bank. Grandpa had somehow managed to get a massive water-wheel sent up from Durban by ox-wagon.

He'd diverted a stream from the main river into a big shallow dam in the wall of which he'd put a sluice gate. When this was opened, the rush of water flowed down the narrow channel to splash into the buckets of the big wheel forcing it to turn slowly at first, then speeding up as it gathered momentum. As soon as we heard the rumble of the water-wheel we dropped whatever we were playing with and raced down to the mill to see Makhaye using the huge, lethal-looking circular saw to cut logs for firewood, or we watched NGidi grind yellow maize kernels into coarse flour, which we ate for breakfast as delicious thick mealie-meal porridge, slathered with farm butter and rich cream. We got sticky black grease on our shorts by turning somersaults on the giant, slowly-turning axles, from which wide canvas belts drove the saw and the mealie grinder.

Eventually, as darkness fell, good-natured Makhaye would allow us to sit on top of the sawn firewood piled in his wheelbarrow, and he'd push us slowly up the hill towards the house and our supper. My little dog, Pitz, jumped in on top of us and sat perched on my bare knees as we rode majestically home.

"Even after you girls had all gone to boarding school," said Mum, "Pitz would still ride home from the mill on the wheelbarrow, sitting regally all by himself on top of the wood as Makhaye strained to push the laden barrow up the hill."

Once our two older sisters had returned to boarding school, we two younger ones reverted instantly to our own normal routines, spending every afternoon with Evalina, and I'd slip quickly away on some pretext and run up to the huts to join in with whatever adventures the Zulu children were up to, like hunting for *mBiba* (mice), smoking out a wild beehive or making clay-oxen on the banks of the river, among other exciting activities.

~~~

# *31*

# The Remittance men

On my rides, when I crossed over *Nunu* Stream, I was faced with a choice: on the right the red hard-packed mud road that led up the steep hill to Wakefield House, and on the left a big, rusty metal gate that opened on to a track in the veldt, and led through fields below the house and eventually to Stonycroft, the next farm along the valley. Right next to the gate, on the left, was where the wattles grew thickest. There was nothing spookier than wattle plantations as, to start with, the trunks were all pitch black, and their densely clustered little leaves a very dark green. They grew as thick as hair on a dog's back, and even on the sunniest days managed to shut out all the light, creating a sense of gloom.

Silence added to the eeriness. In the bush, at any time of the day, there were bird calls or the clattering of doves' wings as they fluttered about in the tree tops; even the chatter of monkeys or murmurs from a troop of foraging baboons gave the impression that the place was alive with creatures. But here, because wattles are an alien species from Australia and a monoculture, nothing else grew with or under them. They rendered the ground and their surroundings sterile, and provided no food for indigenous wildlife. So there, in the deep shade, there was eerie silence.

At night, especially when the mist came down and threaded through the wattle trees, there was no place more terrifyingly spooky. Of course we never went out at night, unless it was driving home from a polo tournament, and I watched the wattle plantations from the safety of the back seat of the car, giving myself thrills of terror as I imagined what it might be like to be out there by myself.

The chill, silent, pitch-black night, the sinister trees, and the fact that there could be big wild animals, such as leopards, lurking in among the mist that swirled around those coal black trunks, made me shudder with horror. Even now, in broad daylight when the sun was blazing down, riding through the cool, dark shade of the wattles left me feeling cold and uneasy. To add to the sinister atmosphere there were, to the left of the gate, the remains of a hut, called Billy Hempson's hut.

The ruined hut, just a short walk up from the river, had young wattle saplings growing out of it, which gave me the creeps, especially as I knew the story behind it from Grandpa. Billy Simpson had been a remittance man in the 1940s, ten years before I was born, during the time that my grandparents were running the farm while my father dropped bombs on the Italians in North Africa. Remittance men were the black sheep from well-off and often aristocratic families in England, who, when their wayward antics became too much for their parents or siblings to bear, were given a one-way ticket on a steamship to The Colonies, such as South Africa, Australia and New Zealand – even India and Malaysia had their remittance men. "Filth" was a common acronym for these pariahs, meaning, "finished in London, try Hong Kong."

These outcasts – now and again there were women who'd blotted their copybooks, too – were given regular sums of money (but never enough for the return journey) to stay in their allocated colonies, too far away to be stirring up any more scandals on their home turf. In my grandparent's time there were several remittance men in our district, and it was through Grandpa that we learned the history of the Hempsons: Billy and his brother. Sometime in the early 1940s they had arrived at Wakefield; two young Englishmen who'd been educated at an expensive public school, still well-spoken but with long, bushy beards and wild hair, with a boy of roughly ten years old (the same age as I was now) who must have been Billy's son.

They built themselves a wattle and daub hut near the Umgeni river, thatched it with long grass from the hillside, and settled there, living on brown trout they caught in the river with flies they made from Guinea Fowl feathers. The two men and the young boy twisted wire-snares to trap rabbits in the veldt, and small antelope in the bush, and occasionally they stole a goat from the Zulu settlement across the river in the dead of night. They would slit its throat, bring the carcass back across the river, skin and butcher it, and put it in a big black three-legged cast-iron pot they'd brought with them when they arrived from God knows where, to stew over an open fire.

They spent their days lying up in the gullies reading novels brought by the travelling salesman, and shooting hadedas – big, raucous Ibis – for the pot. My grandparents only heard about the goat episodes through the travelling salesman. This was a man who came all the way out to the scattered ranches in our district, riding on the seat of an ox-wagon full of books that he sold to the farmers.

On the bookshelves at home we had a set of *American Illustrated Bible Stories*, which had been bought from his stock, and which had brightly coloured plates of beaming little boys and girls who had dropped to their knees in roads and muddy fields, and who prayed earnestly to Jesus, their tiny hands clasped together, their faces raised to Heaven and their eyes tight shut. The boys wore short shorts and white ankle socks, and the girls all had neat, tight pigtails or plaits, short dresses with pinnies and white ankle socks.

After paying our farm a visit, the travelling salesman continued on down to Umgeni Poort, which was a cattle ranch before the Catholic Church bought it for the nuns, and finally Wakefield, where the road eventually petered out, and where the Hempson brothers had built their makeshift mud hut.

He parked his wagon full of books, turned his team of oxen out to graze next to the river and spent a night or two there.

According to Grandpa he was more than surprised to be offered a supper of goat stew, and after the brothers had imbibed a few brandies from his stock, was told the source of the meat. I tried to picture the three men: the Hempsons, dressed in tattered khaki with home-made shoes – veldskoens – made from buckskin, their wild, bushy beards and long hair, sitting around a camp-fire, smoking their pipes, drinking brandy from tin mugs and talking, while the thin, ragged boy sat with them, gnawing on a piece of goat meat.

In order to collect their remittance money, Billy Hempson and his brother had to ride on horseback fifteen miles to the Nottingham Road Post Office, which was just a tin-roofed shed with a front stoep held up by two wooden posts. They owned (or borrowed) three small, shaggy Basutu ponies that they saddled up on pay-day, and, taking the ten-year-old boy with them, rode off at first light to make the long trek to the Post Office.

Once they had collected their money – wired there by their parents – in cash from the Postmaster, it was just a mere couple of hundred yards across the railway line to the Nottingham Road Hotel where there was a thriving and very busy bar.

Later that night, when the two men had eventually been thrown out by the bartender (who wanted to lock up and go to bed), they would be uproariously drunk, and most of the remittance money had been spent.

The small boy had to somehow load them back on to their ponies and, leading them both on a long rein, plod home in the pitch dark all the way back, beyond our farm and Umgeni Poort, and eventually down to their hut next to the river. I don't know if the young boy had any sort of lantern, not according to Grandpa anyway, but he had to ride, unarmed, with those two dead drunk men slung sideways over their saddles, through Lions Bush.

The area was no longer infested with lions after farmers like Great Grandpa had shot them all; the last lion shot was back in about

1846 by a Boer settler, Gert Maritz, who owned the farm called
Lions Bush. He was the brother (or cousin, no one seems sure), of
Piet Maritz who founded what used to be called Pietermaritzburg -
now uMgungundlovu. (There is a well-known story that Maritz and
some pals shot five lions before breakfast one morning in the vlei
below Lions Bush). There were certainly leopards about. Every
rustle in the grass in the pitch dark on his long, long trudge home
must have made the small Hempson boy jump.

My Grandmother, hearing all this from her Zulu herdsmen
and the travelling salesmen, often felt sorry for the remittance men,
especially the little boy, and she would organise for her *iNduna*
(head man) to take an ox-wagon down to the Hempsons' hut with
some mealie meal, milk, and a few groceries like tea and sugar, just
so that they wouldn't starve to death having blown all their money
on booze.

On one occasion, possibly at the end of winter, after things
had become so dire that they had run out of food of any kind and
were beginning to look emaciated, my Grandmother wrote a letter to
Billy's family in England, asking them to send some money
urgently. She told them that it was an emergency, and the family
complied.

The brothers had some money left over from their payoff,
even after their usual drinking orgy at the Notties pub, and they
threw a party for their neighbours, inviting our grandparents down to
their hut in the wattles.

They presented my Grandmother with a gift – a large solid
brass ashtray in a sort of Art Deco style, which stood on a table in
our sitting room as long as I can remember. It must have cost the
Hempsons quite a bit to buy and have sent up from our nearest town,
and no doubt they must have regretted it the next month when they
were broke again and it would be a long time before they'd receive
their next remittance pay-off. Some remittance men drifted back to
England, but nobody knows what became of Billy Hempson, his

brother or the boy after the war.

They slipped away, leaving the hut to decay and be reclaimed by wattle saplings.

~~~

# *32*

# Government School

Like Nicolette and Dine, Delia and I were destined to go to boarding school, and our older sisters had already been there several years. But there had been a change to the school's entrance exam. After the country had been slowly subjected to legislated Apartheid after the South African general election in 1948, in 1960 the Nationalist Party held a referendum among South African white voters over whether to leave the British Commonwealth and become a republic. The Afrikaner dominated Nats (Nationalist Party) won easily and we became the Republic of South Africa. Afrikaans immediately became the first official language, followed by English and, for some reason, French. No African languages were recognised. Because our school received a large grant from the Department of Education, Afrikaans as a subject became compulsory, and it had to be included in the six major subjects we would take to pass Matric (a grade somewhere between O and A level).

It occurred to my father that as we would be going to boarding school fairly soon, and could not speak a word of Afrikaans, he should enrol Delia and me in a term's crash course at the Nottingham Road Government School, so we could learn enough of the language to pass the exam.

The first I knew of this decision was early one spring morning when Evalina bustled into my bedroom and whisked me out of bed. I was hurriedly dressed in a green and white gingham dress, white socks and black shoes, given a small brown suitcase and bundled into the bakkie along with a sleepy Delia.

A dusty half-hour later we arrived at the government school: two prefab classrooms built on stilts, a tiny brick assembly hall, and a corrugated iron shed that housed the two lavatories (one for boys and one for girls), set around a dry, brown playing-field, alongside the main Johannesburg to Durban railway line. We were greeted by the headmaster, Mr Lamb, a most inappropriate name for this red-faced Irishman with his fiery temper and ferocious manner. Mr Lamb taught Standards Three to Five (9 – 11 years old) in one classroom, and his wife (a far gentler soul), taught the younger pupils, from five years old in Class One to eight years old in Standard Two.

Delia and I attracted a ripple of interest from the small group of white children of various ages that were milling around the school gate kicking a half-inflated soccer ball about in the dust. Some of the older children were barefoot I noticed enviously, as I scuffed my hard, new and uncomfortable black leather shoes despondently in the red earth. The interest was mainly in our bakkie, which was quite a new, top of the range model, and not in two neatly dressed girls with our short, dark hair and solemn expressions.

As I was in Standard Five, I was led into my classroom by Mr Lamb, where the older children were already standing to attention, and given a desk to share with a girl with long blonde plaits (whose father, I discovered later, was the station-master). Delia was to be in Mrs Lamb's class next door.

My first experience of proper schooling started when I jumped with fright as Mr Lamb gave a terrifying roar at a boy called Hamish who was looking out of the window at the soccer ball lying in the playground. "Pay attention, boy!" he thundered, and bug-eyed with terror I sat down meekly with my classmates to pay close attention to my first lesson, and try not to draw any adverse attention from our formidable headmaster. I was so afraid of him that I didn't dare do anything but hang onto his every word, and since he was an inspiring and interesting teacher, I was engrossed in every aspect of each subject he taught, and enjoyed the stimulation, as the days flew by, of learning so many new things. I found Afrikaans quite easy as I was already bilingual, and at that age absorbing another language wasn't a big step.

In the playground I made new friends and learned to play more conventional games such as hopscotch and skipping, jumping the long rope alongside my peers, while everybody took turns at swinging the rope, all chanting the traditional skipping songs and counting us in. There was a family of five Afrikaner children who stood out from the others. Their surname was Van der Berg, and their father was a 'wheel-tapper' on the railways. This was a derogatory term for semi-literate whites in South Africa, mostly Afrikaans speaking, who had no qualifications but were employed by the Nationalist Government railways to do menial work, such as oversee the gangs of Africans who did all the hard, physical labour on the tracks.

When a train pulled into the station, a white man was employed to walk its length, hitting each wheel with a little hammer and listening for cracks or other weaknesses in the metal – hence the name wheel-tapper. The Van der Bergs lived in a tin roofed railway house, with a veranda all the way around it, on the banks of the main line, and every day walked the three miles to school. The oldest was Bennie, who was fifteen and still in Standard One (Grade 3). His voice had broken; he was well into puberty and very close to six feet tall, but there he was, crouched at a desk, his grubby knees practically touching his ears, sharing his lessons with eight years old. His younger brother Dirkie, fourteen, was in Grade Two among the six years old children and I can't remember the names of the other boys, but Corrie, the only girl, and obviously the brightest member of the family, was in our class and was actually the correct age. The Van der Berg boys all had their bullet heads permanently shaved, something I'd never come across before.

"Why are the Van der Berg boys' heads shaved?" I asked

Jean during our first break-time together. Since she shared a desk with me she'd become my new best friend and, I discovered, was a valuable source of gossip.

"Because they all have ringworm," she replied.

"What's ringworm?" I asked, imagining little circles of live, wriggling worm-like maggots in their hair, rather like the colour illustrations of Blowfly infections in sheeps' nether regions under their tails, pictures of which I'd carefully examined in my father's *Sheep Management and Diseases* book – it sounded disgusting.

"I dunno, it's something dirty and very catching," she said, "so keep well away from them – we all do," and she shuddered theatrically. I looked cautiously at the Van der Bergs as they scuffed in the dust on the bare part of the playground under some gum-trees.

Nobody else was playing with them. The other children kept their distance and played their own games; the girls skipping with a long rope, and the boys were having a makeshift game of soccer on the patchy brown grass playing-field. The four outcast boys were thin to the point of emaciation, and their skin had an exhausted grey patina under the well-established dirt. Patches of dry skin flaked off in between the numerous scabs, leaving white areas and giving the impression of Plane Tree bark with its various shades of grey and white.

Their shorts were far too small, as they'd obviously outgrown their school uniforms a while back, and their short-sleeved shirts were tight across their toast-rack ribs. They reminded me of the starving jackal hounds I saw now and again on the farm when the Jackal Pack was summoned by my father to reduce the vermin population a bit. I'd never seen undernourished people before, certainly not among the Africans on our farm, rather the reverse. The Van der Bergs' bare feet were horny and so thickened and tough that they looked like well-worn leather. All the Zulus on our farm had tough feet, and even mine and my sisters' were nicely hardened on the soles, enabling us to run over gravel and thorns alike.

Jean saw me looking at Bennie's feet.

"He trod on a puff-adder last term, but it wasn't able to bite him – his feet are too tough," she said. I stared at his leathery feet and they did look as impenetrable as any veldskoens. I could just picture a puff-adder's fangs bouncing off, unable to puncture the horny layers of Bennie's feet. Corrie, on the other hand, always arrived at school in the mornings dressed in a frilly party dress – which we secretly coveted – rather than our regulation green checked uniform. Her hair was elaborately styled in long ringlets, which we immediately dubbed ringworms, and tied with brightly coloured satin ribbons. Corrie always wore pretty sandals and was scrubbed till her skin glowed.

I was intrigued by the bizarre discrepancy between Corrie's appearance and that of her four brothers, and asked Jean why she was dressed so differently. She shrugged.

"I've heard that their father hangs all the boys up, one by one, tied up in a sack from a tree branch, and beats them with a stick for no reason at all," she said matter-of-factly, as though it was normal behaviour. I was slightly horrified, but wondered if that was how Afrikaners brought up their children. I knew nothing about them other than the disparaging way in which my mother and my father referred to them as Boets, which translates to "brothers", almost alluding to them as a subspecies of the human race.

I was quickly swept up into playground politics and gave the rougher, dirtier children a wide berth. They were mostly Afrikaners, although the Nottingham Road Government School was an English-Medium school. The Department of Education had a three-tier system. In towns and villages where the majority of whites spoke Afrikaans, they built Afrikaans-Medium junior and high schools, in which all lessons were taught in Afrikaans.

Conversely, if the majority spoke English, as in the case of Nottingham Road with its large, scattered community of English speaking white farmers, it had an English-Medium junior school, but no high school as there weren't enough children to warrant building one. My fellow pupils were all destined to attend Estcourt High School, an English-Medium boarding establishment in a small town beyond Mooi River.

There were no African children in our school, nor were there in any other government schools. Indian children attended schools set aside for them by the Department of Indian Affairs, and Coloured pupils also went to separate schools somewhere in the Coloured townships near Durban. In 1953 the Nationalist Government had come under the leadership of D. F. Malan, a dyed-in-the-wool Afrikaner and one of the most enthusiastic architects of Apartheid. He was an active member of the Broederbond (The Brotherhood) a secret society with covert cells within all the crucial institutions and organisations of the entire country. Their aim was to create the Afrikaner nation – Die Volk – as a separate and superior group in terms of language, culture and religion.

The society publicly waged an energetic campaign to propagate Afrikaner cultural tradition and historical legacy at the expense of other South Africans, particularly the blacks. In 1953 D. F. Malan instituted the Bantu Education Act, putting education for Africans under a government department called Bantu Affairs, instead of the Department of Education. This establishment built and controlled schools for African children, all of which taught on a different and lower level than those of the whites. They could learn basic reading and writing, and were particularly encouraged to learn menial and manual skills. Maths and science were not taught at all, and lessons were taught in local languages, effectively barring African students from learning English.

Attending school was not compulsory for African children, and as a result a huge percentage of the population was illiterate, a situation the government advocated as being ideal because the blacks wouldn't be able to compete with whites for jobs. The whole Bantu education system ensured that the great majority of Africans had no other choice but to go and work underground in the gold, diamond and coalmines, where the conditions were unhealthy, dangerous and the pay abysmal.

White-collar jobs were reserved for whites at a far better rate of pay, and thus the South African economy grew from strength to strength.

Every morning Ben Masango made us a picnic lunch to eat at midday break-time, which consisted of sandwiches with various fillings, a hard-boiled egg or a cold chicken leg, some fruit or some homemade biscuits, and a small bottle of orange squash and water to drink. At break on my first day, I sat with my new friends on the sunny steps leading down from our classroom, and we unpacked our lunches. As I opened my small brown suitcase and pulled out the plastic boxes containing my food, I saw Corrie's eyes widen. She called to her brothers who were playing soccer nearby, and all five of them stood round me, watching every mouthful I took, their eyes following every bite.

Eventually, Bennie asked shyly if he could have a sandwich. I shrugged. "OK," I said and gave them the entire picnic, as I wasn't hungry. All the Van der Bergs fell upon the food, scrapping over it like starving wild dogs, which shocked me a little, but from that day on I happily handed over my lunch to the family, and skipped off to play instead. My mother was pleased to find that I'd polished off every mouthful, as I was a picky eater at home. I never told her the true story of where my lunch was going because it was such a convenient arrangement for us all. It made me the most popular girl in the school, too; that and the fact that I never did my homework the whole term I was at the school. For some reason, which I can't explain to this day, however scared I was of Mr Lamb, I just couldn't bring myself to sit down at home and do any homework. If my mother ever asked, I said I didn't have any, and she was too disinterested to check, so day after day I manufactured story after story, telling Mr Lamb that we'd had a storm and the electricity had been off, so I couldn't see well enough to do any work (carefully omitting to reveal that we had a back-up system of gas and paraffin lamps giving off more than enough light for Dad to read his newspapers).

There were other, numerous variations on 'the dog ate my homework'.

Somehow, he appeared to swallow these unlikely stories hook, line and sinker, and I stayed out of trouble.

It might have something to do with the fact that my mother would regularly take the headmaster and his wife fresh fruit and vegetables, and even occasionally a large chicken, plucked and dressed by Ben. In retrospect, this behaviour must have guaranteed certain favouritism for my sister and me, but we weren't aware of it at the time.

There were only about 25 pupils in the school, ranging from five to eleven, and slightly less than half of them were Afrikaans speaking. Every morning at 8 o'clock we lined up in front of the assembly hall: the smallest children at the front and the oldest at the back. Mrs Lamb struck up 'Onward Christian Soldiers' on a rickety old upright piano, her upper arms wobbling as she banged her plump, be-ringed fingers vigorously on the loose, rattling keys, and we marched into the hall, our feet stamping loudly on the wooden floor. We all sat cross-legged on the floorboards while Mr Lamb read out a short prayer, not a word of which I heard because I was too busy gazing around at all the unfamiliar white children surrounding me, and then we stood up to sing 'All things Bright and Beautiful'. He read out a few notices and we marched out again, this time to 'D'ye ken John Peel?', to start our lessons.

In retrospect, Mr Lamb must have been Catholic, and most of the children would have had parents who were members of the Dutch Reformed Church, a strict Calvinistic austere religion that had been one of the bones of contention between the Boers and the British. The main reason the Afrikaner Boer settlers started the Great

Trek into the interior of South Africa from the secure, comfortable Cape, was because the British Imperial settlers threatened their rigid religion by bringing in lax, decadent Anglican ways.

On Friday mornings, after our short tea break, we lined up again outside the assembly hall and walked in to sit on the floor.

We watched educational films (which Mr Lamb pronounced 'fillums'), about bears in Canada or seal colonies in the Antarctic or, my personal favourite, time-lapse photography films of plants growing and flowers opening. Up to that date I had only ever seen one full-length movie (at the age of seven), which was Walt Disney's *Pinocchio* at the Howick cinema.

Howick was our nearest town, a further half an hour's drive on tarmac down the N3 national highway towards Durban. More of a village than a small town, it had a hotel, quite a few shops and the Howick Grand, an ambitious name for the tin roofed, high-ceilinged building. There was the main seating, where we sat, and in front of us a low wooden screen, beyond which the 'Non White' Indians and Africans sat to watch the movies. We could just see the tops of their heads bobbing as we all waited excitedly for the *Pathe Newsreel* to begin. I remember very little about the animated film, the only impact it had on me was that I was puzzled by a scene where a villainous wolf ate an apple, thinking to myself "Wolves don't eat apples." I nudged Dine who was sitting next to me and whispered my revelation to her. "Shut up!" she hissed back.

Mr Lamb was a teacher with great passion. Being Irish, he had learned to speak Afrikaans quite late in life and his pronunciation was often rather odd, judging from my classmates' giggles. The language has many pitfalls for English speakers. For example, 'v' is always pronounced as 'f' and the short 'a' vowel is said as in 'bus', so the word for a subject such as geography is v-a-k but pronounced f-u-k. Hamish, whom, I'd discovered on my very first day there, had a talent for attracting adverse attention from Mr Lamb, unwisely started to snigger when Mr Lamb told us, in

Afrikaans, what subject we were going to learn that morning.

With a furious bellow Mr Lamb lunged over to the boy, hauled him by the collar, onto the wooden teachers' platform and ordered him to bend over. He received four sharp whacks from the headmaster's cane, which hung on a hook behind the classroom door; the strokes making the dust fly off his grey school shorts.

Red-faced, he slunk back to his desk and sat down gingerly. Nobody dared laugh after that, even when we learned the word for 'side', as in side of the room, was k-a-n-t. I, of course, had no idea what the English translations meant either, so I was in no danger of sniggering or being whacked. I did try out my new Afrikaans vocabulary that I'd learned in the playground on my mother as she drove us home every afternoon.

I casually threw Here (God), Jassus (Jesus), and Jislaaik (an expletive) into my conversation, and even remarked that my sister's new shoes were "Sexy man", but when I said I'd had to go to the toilet at break-time, my mother stamped on the brake pedal so hard that the wheels locked and the car skidded for some distance on the hard, dirt road, enveloping us in a choking cloud of red dust. She turned in her seat (this was long before head rests became standard) and yelled at me "Don't you EVER use that word again!" To her the word 'toilet' was far worse than any swearing, because it was what 'common' people called the loo.

To my shame I have very little recollection of doing schoolwork in class, apart from writing compositions, which I loved, using my fertile imagination to great success. Break-time and the games we played had far more impact on me. After Mrs Lamb had rung the brass handbell we ran outside, pulling our shoes and socks off, to throw them beneath a big gum-tree that shaded the large patch of bare, reddish earth, which was our playground. Apart from hopscotch and skipping rope, the older children played a game called 'Open Gates' which is apparently like British Bulldog, where one child is the wolf, and the rest of us lined up on one side of the playground. When the solitary child called out, "Open Gates!" we rushed across to the other side. Anyone who was caught or even touched by the wolf, became one, until we were all wolves and only one person, the winner, was left to start as the wolf in the next game. The most exciting part was when we were evenly numbered, with as many wolves as others.

There were a lot of scrapes and bruises, too, as the bigger boys, especially the Van der Bergs, who were several years older than we were, were inclined to catch us by means of a flying tackle behind the knees which brought us down to earth with a 'whump!' and we'd lie there, winded, spitting out sand and bits of dry gum-leaves. On a piece of brown, desiccated lawn to one side of the playground there were two swings and a structure of monkey bars – a sort of simple climbing frame, from which we hung, upside down, by our knees, having first taken the precaution to tuck our dresses into the leg elastic of our green gingham checked bloomers, so the boys couldn't look at our broeks.

Both the girls I shared my desk with, Jean Jackson and Helen Potter (our local GP's daughter), had long, fair hair in plaits, the ends of which trailed on the ground. Even Corrie van der Berg's 'ringworms' dangled in the dust.

We older girls sat to eat our sandwiches on the wooden steps leading up to the classrooms, while the boys played soccer. We were divided into two factions, because on the day I arrived at school, Jean had asked me, "Do you like Elvis or Cliff?" My knowledge of either was restricted to what I'd overheard from my older sisters when they came back on holiday from boarding school. Our radio reception in the valley where the farm lies, consisted of medium or short-wave. FM only arrived in South Africa in the late 60s. My sisters listened to a programme called *The Springbok Hit Parade*, which was broadcast on Saturday afternoons, and as we lay on the back lawn at home, our ears pressed to the tinny, crackling transistor, they'd squeal with delight if Cliff was top of the charts.

"Cliff," I said firmly.

There was the sharp hiss of intaken breath. "D'ya mean you don't like Elvis?" Their puzzlement was palpable.

"No," I said. Another discussion cropped up on the school steps – a political one – the Referendum. I'd seen posters plastered on walls and hanging from poles in the village. They either said, "Vote Yes" or "Vote No," and I'd asked my father what they were for.

"The Nats – the Government – are holding a referendum among the whites. We have to vote whether to become a Republic or stay in the Commonwealth."

"What are you going to vote?" I asked my father.

"No to a Republic, of course."

"Why?"

"Because I don't trust the Nats – they're too enthusiastic about Apartheid and will carry it so far that there'll eventually be a revolution. The *munts* won't be able to take any more of this extreme repression and they'll rise up in an armed rebellion, and that will be the end of all us whites, that's for sure."

"Would staying in the Commonwealth be better then?" I asked.

"Oh yes! The British Government don't support Apartheid at all and won't allow the Nats to create a republic. It's far better that those extreme Boers like our President Verwoerd, who started this Apartheid nonsense, will have to answer to Harold Macmillan's government."

At school during break-time we pulled off our shoes and socks and sunned our legs while we chatted, "Just say that if you were old enough, what would you vote in the Referendum?" Helen asked me.

"I'd vote no of course!" I said emphatically.

There was a collective gasp of horror. About six heads whipped round, plaits flying and the girls stared at me, speechless.

"Why on earth would you vote no?" demanded Jean, when she'd recovered from her shock.

I had to think about my reply quite carefully for a moment or two as I'd forgotten the reason that my father had told me, so scratching frantically in my head, I grasped at a straw. "Because I want to belong to the Queen," I said with as much confidence as I could muster. They gaped. Nobody had an answer to that comment. Apparently, they couldn't see my logic, and eventually they turned to another, safer subject like who was better looking – Cliff or Elvis?

I suspect now that I would have been labelled an outcast, if it hadn't been for the fact that I was so generous with my packed lunches. Towards the end of the term my father, having decided that there was no getting away from the fact that he was due to have four daughters at boarding school the following year, traded in his modest, medium-sized grey Mercedes saloon, for an enormous black Pontiac. The size of a tennis court on wheels, it was encrusted with shiny chrome excrescences, and had a battery of glowing, ruby coloured brake and tail-lights at the back. The rear fins gave the impression of an aircraft carrier's bow, and covered a cavernous boot. The front grill looked like a silver grimace flanked by huge, twin headlights, and there was plenty of room for our family of six on the big leather bench seats, back and front.

We arrived in this apparition one Monday morning, bouncing awkwardly down the bumpy dirt track to the school, and pulled up majestically at the gates, the car still rocking on the soft suspension for some time after we'd come to a standstill. As my sister and I climbed out, every child in the school ran up to the wire fence to have a look. Jaws dropped and eyes boggled, as my mother drove off in a flourish of dust.

"Is that your new car?" Bennie van der Berg asked, in hushed tones of awe.

"Yes – it's nice, huh?" I said proudly.

"Are you proud of your new car?" He gulped, horrified, as if

I'd declared I was the spawn of the devil.

"Yes", I said steadfastly.

Everybody gasped. Other children came up to me to repeat Bennie's question, only to look shocked at my answer. Then somebody said, "It's wrong to be proud. It's a sin!" I just shrugged and walked off. The Calvinistic beliefs of the Dutch Reformed Church were not going to impinge on my enjoyment, but after that I noticed one or two of my classmates casually let slip that they were proud of their own possessions or achievements.

The big black car was dubbed *Gigi Bia* (which was soon shortened to 'Gig') by my father after the large, stout Indian Hindu matrons who wore ornate, glittering and bejewelled saris in bright colours of scarlet, emerald green and gold, to go shopping in the Durban markets, looking like glorious birds of paradise. The enormous car coped adequately with the rutted roads in dry weather, behaving a little like a boat on rough seas, and causing Nicolette to become carsick for the first time ever, but it was a nightmare in the wet season, slipping and sliding in the slick red mud that constituted our twenty miles of dirt road from the farm into the station. If it looked as if it was going to rain my mother would get Jomela, the garden boy, to put the chains on the wide, balloon-like whitewall tyres before we left, and we'd crawl, frustratingly slowly, clinking and rattling to school.

If we were caught out in the frequent sudden spring thunderstorms, which signified the start of the wet season and which could release a torrent of rain up to several inches within an hour, my mother would have to stop, cursing, and we'd all get out reluctantly and wrestle the horrible, heavy, clanking chains onto the slippery, muddy wheels. We'd start by laying all four sets of chains out on the mire in front of the wheels, hoping they were the right way up. My mother drove cautiously onto the chains and we'd yell "stop!" when the wheels were in place.

Then we had to twist stiff heavy-duty wires, slimy with red

mud, through the chains to secure them – a tricky task because, if we got it wrong, the wire stuck up and punctured the tyre as my mother drove off, and we'd have the added problem of changing the tyre and still having to put the chain on.

Every afternoon, the minute our car pulled into the garage at home, I jumped out and ran to my bedroom to pull off my hideous dress and drag the horrible shoes and socks off and change into jeans and a T-shirt. Barefoot and followed by three excited dogs, I would run to the tack room, snatch Rocket's bridle off its hook on the wall and race to the paddock where he was grazing with the polo ponies. There I slipped the bridle over his head, swung myself onto his warm, shining back and cantered off, the dogs running a safe distance behind his heels, to help the herd boys, Petrus and Toto, and sometimes Boniface, collect the milking cows from their daytime grazing in the bush beyond the river.

Rocket jogged impatiently home behind the cows' full, swaying udders and swishing tails, while I chuckled at the antics of the calves' playful bucking at their heels. I could feel the chill of the early evening air nipping at my bare toes as they dangled down either side of Rocket's round belly. Toto and Petrus walked on either side of the cattle, carrying their long stock whips over their shoulders, and letting out a piecing whistle now and again if a cow started to wander to the roadside to snatch a mouthful of grass. "*Iyapi?*" (where are you going?), they would shout, and obediently she'd swing back to join the herd. As we made our way slowly down into the valley, I could see pale-blue smoke rising from the kitchen chimney into the still, darkening sky, and drifting downwards in the cooling air, giving off the scent of eucalyptus from the gum-leaves Ben Masango used as kindling.

After leaving Rocket in his paddock with a quick rub down and a handful of oats, I walked into the kitchen to be greeted by the delicious aroma of Ben's freshly baked bread, which had come out of the oven a little earlier. Ben was sitting on the back steps, his chef's hat casually tossed onto the woodpile, and was enjoying one of his pungent mixture of *mSango* (marijuana or dagga as it's known in South Africa) and *Boxer* tobacco rolled up in newspaper joints the size of a sausage. I was ravenous as I hadn't eaten since a hasty breakfast of porridge at six o'clock that morning before leaving for school, and I'd given away my lunch, so I furtively sawed a big hunk of crusty warm bread off the end of the loaf, spread it thickly with rich, yellow, farm butter and a generous spoonful of *mlotjezane* (wild raspberry) jam, and slunk off to my room to enjoy my feast. It was no wonder that, at suppertime a little later, I just pushed my insipid, pale-pink spaghetti and tomato sauce disinterestedly around my plate.

~~~

# *33*

# Autumn

**W**as the beginning of the dry season. Because African trees don't have to adapt to a harsh winter, they keep their leaves, but my grandmother had planted European Plane and Liquid Amber trees around the homestead garden to try and recreate an English park, and these turn to magnificent blazing orange, ruby and gold colours. Their big, star-shaped leaves flutter to the ground, eventually to be raked into big piles by the Zulu women who worked in Mum's vast garden.

As children, we would jump into the scented, dusty leaf piles, savouring the crunchy feel of the dry leaves beneath our toughened feet as we stamped them to powder. I would lie on the drying kikuyu lawn, watching tiny jewel-like Sunbirds, our African versions of Humming Birds, with their iridescent scarlet breasts and emerald bodies, hovering and sipping nectar from the scented red bells of fuchsias.

I enjoyed the loud twittering of huge clouds of Redwing Starlings that flew into the valley to feast off the berry-laden Cotoneaster shrubs. The sky is always at its bluest at this time of the year, before the haze of bush-fires that burn all through the winter, and dust storms turn it to a paler wash, and give us such spectacular sunsets.

Hay-making was another pleasure. Late in the morning, after the dew had been burned off by the sun, my sister and I would run barefoot in the dust behind the teams of oxen as they were led at a leisurely pace, up the sandy road to begin work. Every April, Dad got his labourers to mow the sweet, pale veld grass on the hillsides and stack it for winter feed for our cattle. Six sweating oxen pulled the mower, and we knew all their names: Rooikop, Satan, Ubovu, iMpondo, Donsa and uMhlope. We'd shout them out as they plodded across the hillside, led by Danda, one of the Zulu men, the other riding on the mower, sending the singing tip of his stock whip to crack over their horns, urging them on.

Two oxen pulled the rake and four more followed with the drag, a wooden three-sided gate-like creation that my grandfather had constructed, to scoop up the haycocks and take them to the main stack, where the rest of the men were lifting the hay with pitchforks.

They sang a lilting song in their deep voices as they worked, weaving harmony into the repetitive verses that matched their thrusts to the top of the stack. It was always hot and dusty, and we were allowed to ride on the drag, taking care to keep our fingers and bare feet away from getting severely pinched in the hinges that held the three sections together.

Fragrant long grass mixed with papery, everlasting wild flowers and deliciously pungent khaki weed piled higher and higher in the drag, and it was our job to yell to Toto, leading the oxen, that the drag was full and it was time to head towards the main stack.

Occasionally, our legs got scratched by the thorns of bramble that grew in the long grass, seeded there by birds that fed on the succulent blackberries.

On Easter Sunday morning my sister and I would run into the garden after breakfast and hunt for the Easter eggs the bunny had brought. Mum told us to look in a border of scarlet Canna Lilies around the grass tennis court, and occasionally we would find an overlooked tennis ball as well as the silver foil covered chocolate eggs.

Until I grew older and discovered the truth about the Easter Bunny, I would often run down the lawns to hunt through the Cannas, hoping to find a gleam of silver concealed among the cool,

## White Zulu

Fiona Ross

dark green leaves.

~~~

# *34*

# Getting caught in a storm

**W**hen I got tired of riding by myself, I would ride to the next farm, about five miles away, to visit a boy I'd met at Delia's birthday party. His name was John and he was a year younger than I was. He had his own shaggy Basutu pony, and I'd call in regularly, stopping in their driveway to wait while John saddled up his pony and rode out to meet me. Together we spent the whole day out, and raced along the dusty District Road on the straight, flat bits. I always beat him of course, because Rocket had been sired by a racehorse and could move like the wind. I'd sit there, one hand on my horse's rump, waiting mockingly while John's pony puffed towards me at top speed, then, just as he thought he'd caught up, move off at another gallop.

It was great fun, and I spent most of my time out riding with my new friend.

We swam our horses in his father's dam when it got hot, and tethered them in the shade of a wattle tree to graze on the tender green reed grass near the water, while we stripped to our underpants and splashed around in the water to cool off, stirring up fine mud from the bottom, and making the dabchicks run away on the surface, shrilling with fright.

One afternoon a great white thunderhead of clouds began building up behind the hills at midday, earlier than usual, and as the clouds billowed into an anvil shape they slowly turned to a charcoal colour, the surrounding sky darkened to olive green, and we saw flashes of lighting and heard rumbles as the storm gathered momentum on its way towards us.

"We'd better get home," said John, worried. "This storm's going to catch us out in the open if we don't hurry. You'd better come to my house as it's closer."

We galloped over the veldt to his house just ahead of the breaking storm and quickly led our horses into an open stable.

"They'll be fine here," he said, and closed the half door behind us before we ran to the kitchen door, trying to dodge through the first few big drops of rain.

"It looks as if it might hail – the sky's gone that greenish colour," said his mum who had been standing in the kitchen, anxiously watching the approaching storm and waiting for us to get into the house.

"Would you like to stay for lunch? I'll give your mum a ring and tell her you're safe, but I'll have to let the storm pass first, in case the line gets hit by lighting while we're talking."

The four of us sat around their dining-room table and ate spaghetti and mince with tomato sauce and grated cheese on top. I knew John's dad from the cattle sales. He didn't play polo and he was a quiet man, with a typical farmers' tan – his face, arms and legs burned brown from working out in the sun all the time, and when he took off his bush hat, above the brow his face was white. He didn't have a farm manager like my father did, and he worked hard, spending his days out among his sheep and cattle.

Sometimes he was on horseback with John at his side on his pony; other times I'd seen him out in his bakkie checking his stock, his sweat-stained bush hat pulled well down to keep the blazing sun out of his eyes, and John would be perched on the tailgate with a couple of their dogs running beside, pink tongues lolling out as they panted through the dust.

Mr Derwent told me to call him Jimmy, and asked all sorts of questions about my horse. Nobody did that at home, and I found myself enjoying chatting to these amicable grown-ups with John. I was used to being relegated to the nursery with my sisters for meals.

As far as my parents were concerned, children were neither to be seen nor heard. The storm raged overhead and instinctively we ducked as flashes of lightning struck the conductor on their tin roof with a loud crack, immediately followed by the explosion of thunder right there in the room. Huge hailstones rattled down on the tin roof so hard that the noise was a deafening roar.

"Look!" shouted John, pointing out of the window after one particularly violent crash, his voice only just audible above the noise, "Look at that tree!"

A tall gum-tree that stood outside the house had been struck and had split in half down the middle as the volatile sap boiled and exploded. Blue smoke and steam rose from the gashed and splintered centre where the bolt had hit and there was the same smell that came from the shotgun cartridges after my mother had taken a pot shot at the baboons. Eventually the storm moved on, and the noise gradually abated. We sat for a little while, watching it grumble its way towards Lions Bush on the horizon.

"Well! What a good thing you two weren't caught in that!" exclaimed John's mum, and she went to ring our farm. Their phone was exactly like ours; a small wooden box on the wall, with two shiny metal dome-shaped bells on top, and they were on the same party line as we were.

I watched as she lifted the black Bakelite receiver from its hook and listen to see if there was anybody using the line, then she cranked the little black handle on the side of the box twice for two short rings, and then one long one. That was our ring – there were twelve farms, including the convent, sharing that one line and we all had our own Morse code ring. It seemed that whenever my father wanted to make a call to his accountant in Maritzburg, the nuns were always on the line, talking in French.

We could hear them jabbering away at top speed every time

he picked up the receiver.

"For a bunch of women who are supposed to be in silent retreat, they spend one hell of a lot of time talking," he'd say grimly as he put the receiver down again, none too gently.

"1012? Hello, Doffie. I just wanted to tell you that Fiona's here, safe and sound, and she's had some lunch with us ... er yes, I'll tell her ... Yes, right now ... bye."

She stood there for a moment, blinking, still holding the receiver, and staring at it with what looked like dismay or disbelief, then she placed it slowly back on the hook.

"Your mother wants you to go home right now," she said to me.

"There seems to be some sort of problem, although I told her you were fine here with us. Personally, I would have like the road to have dried up a bit before you set off. It will be really slippery out there."

I had a hollow, sinking feeling in my stomach as I followed John through the puddles to fetch Rocket from their stable.

Hailstones the size of golf balls lay scattered around on the ground, and piled up like snow banks in corners of their yard where they'd bounced off the tin roof.

"I hope everything's OK at home for you," he said quietly. "Just be careful in the mud."

I let Rocket pick his own way along the road home. There'd been a couple of inches of hard rain, and in some parts runnels of churning water formed a foaming stream on either side of the slippery red mud hump in the middle of the road. Now and again his hooves slithered from under him, making him sit right down on his haunches, but he was sure footed enough to regain his step and we carried on home. The roaring, frothing river thundered down our valley, bursting with the sudden extra rain, and had overflowed its banks. The level had already reached the top of the bridge and little waves slopped over the edge and onto the concrete causeway. I felt a jolt of alarm when an uprooted tree trunk hit the middle pillar as it was washed underneath by the torrent. The impact made the whole bridge shudder, and I nudged Rocket into a canter to get over as fast as possible in case the whole thing gave way while we were still on it.

Evalina was standing on the back veranda when I got home, twisting her white cotton pinny anxiously in her brown hands. "Hau! Where have you been?" she called.

"nKosikazi is very, very angry. She's been shouting!" I paused to wash my muddy bare feet under the tap that stood outside the kitchen, and hastily wiping them on the doormat ran into the house. Both my parents were waiting for me in the *gluzeen*, and my mother turned on me as I skidded into the room.

"I've just been speaking to Mrs Derwent," she said to me in a tight voice. I could see she was furious. My father looked at me coldly from his armchair, both his hands gripped the arms and his newspaper had fallen to the floor.

"What do you think you were doing?" my mother raged. "What were you doing hanging around their place?"

Before I could answer, my father added "You have this whole ruddy great farm to ride on. You're not, and I repeat not, to go anywhere near our neighbours!" His face was red with anger. I stood there stunned, and opened my mouth to explain about the storm.

"But ... " I started.

"Do you hear me? You are never to ride anywhere but on this farm!" interrupted my father.

I nodded dumbly. I couldn't understand why, but I knew that if I argued, I'd be in worse trouble than I already was. I padded out of the room, puzzled and feeling slightly sick with fright. What had I done wrong? We knew the Derwents, and John had been to our house to a birthday party, but that was all. Neither he nor his parents had ever been invited over on any other occasion, even though they lived on the next farm. In fact, the only time I'd heard their name mentioned was when my mother described her as "that dumpy little woman next door." Why? What did they mean?

I mooched sullenly about the farm for the next few days, riding Rocket along all the boundaries. It took a day to get to the furthest hill up at the very top of the ranch, and, seething, I plodded my horse beside the fence line. I stared out at the world beyond the barbed-wire fence and gazed unseeing at locust bodies, the corpses of small rodents, and even tiny birds, left impaled on the barbs by butcher birds – the small black and white Fiscal Shrikes we knew as the Jackie Hangman. They used the fence as a larder the same way as they employed long thorns, stabbing the still twitching bodies of their prey onto the spikes and returning to feed later on.

On several of my solitary rides I saw five or six vultures circling high overhead in the blue-white brassy sky. There had to be a dead sheep, or a carcass of one of my father's animals up in the hills somewhere, and normally I'd have ridden up the pass to find the death and report it to him.

But I ignored the carrion eaters and kept on riding the boundary fences. I raged inside. Angry, puzzled, and, above all, lonely, I pondered over and over again about the blistering dressing-down I'd received for riding over to the Derwents – all I wanted was a bit of company. Both my older sisters spent most of their time at boarding school, and Delia showed no interest in riding.

Admittedly, the first ride I ever took her on, a year ago, when she was seven, she'd fallen off old Sunny at the end of the drive, just beyond the cattle grid, and broken her right arm. She'd been pretty reluctant about going riding in the first place, and, desperate for company, I'd implored her to give it a try. She toppled off as the old moke was ambling along at a snail's place behind me, and I'd given her Grandpa's treatment, sitting back complacently on Prince and telling her to get back on.

"Hurry up, or you'll lose your nerve and never ride again!" I yelled at her, repeating his old, well-tested mantra.

Howling with pain and blinded by tears, she stumbled home on foot, clutching her arm, and I sighed, leaned over and collected up Sunny's reins to lead him back to the stables. My mother was very angry.

"I'm fed up with you, the way you treat your little sister!" she'd shouted at me as Evalina helped the still sobbing Delia into the back of the car. My mother had hastily applied lipstick in the driving mirror before she rammed the gear stick forward and they took off down the drive in a flurry of dust to get to the doctor's surgery twelve miles away. Later that evening they'd arrived home, Delia's arm in a sling and set with stark white plaster of Paris. She was enjoying the drama far too much for my liking, as everybody in the kitchen fussed over her, shaking their heads and clicking with sympathy. I glared at her as she sat smugly at the nursery table while Evalina cut up her food into little pieces so she could eat using a fork with her left hand.

"It's all your fault … " she started. Having any kind of ammunition, justified or otherwise, against me was a rare occasion for her, and she wasn't going to pass it up. But I certainly wasn't going to listen to any moral lectures from her.

An apology from me was out of the question, and I wasn't even going to give her an opportunity to finish her sentence.

"It was your own stupid fault," I retorted. "You're just a useless rider – can't even stay on old Sunny." And that was that. The end of my sister's riding career.

Generally, when I saddled up my horse and roamed to the far boundaries of the farm after what I considered particularly unfair treatment by Mum or Dad, fuming at their stupidity, I would eventually be seduced by the sheer beauty of my surroundings.

It was therapeutic to pull up from a long gallop, walk Rocket down the riverbank, belly high into the water, allowing him to regain his breath and take a drink while I slipped my feet out of the stirrups and dangled my legs down his sweating flanks dabbling my toes in the swift, cool current. Then we would plod home along a cattle path that followed the contours of the riverbank.

The thud of Rocket's hoof beats in the soft dust was barely audible against the background noise of water pouring smoothly over granite boulders, rushing past rocks and tinkling as it trickled in smaller, sparkling rills to flow underneath dark green ferns that hung down from the mossy banks. The river tumbled off the edge of a plateau in frothy white cascades, to settle down, filling its rocky bed with pristine, crystal clear water, and flowed the length of the farm along the valley floor, its right bank grassy and the left covered by bush. From the forest on the opposite bank I heard occasional gwai-gwai-gwai! alarm calls from lime-green Knysna Loeries, and caught a glimpse of a pair flapping from one tree branch to another, revealing for a moment a startling flash of bright scarlet beneath their broad wings. About the size of a Toucan, they perched clumsily, and rocked comically backwards and forwards, raising their bright green crests, and cocking an eye (exquisitely outlined in white) at me.

A flock of Common Waxbills erupted from the short brown grass next to our path. Tiny, smaller even than the English Wren, in vast numbers they fed on fallen grass seeds, showing only their brown backs, and resembling nothing more than small dry brown leaves drifting across the dusty earth in a light breeze. When startled, the tiny birds whirred up in a twittering cloud to perch, clinging sideways, to dry grass stalks – only then did they reveal their crimson faces and rose coloured breast feathers. Blue-billed Firefinches, a spectacular cherry red apart from their speckled brown wings, joined these feeding parties.

Such a flurry of bright red and brown exploding from our feet never failed to take my breath away, although Rocket barely cast an ear in their direction. What made him start, snorting with alarm and enough head tossing to jingle his bit, was a Grey Heron that rose spectrally from the water's edge with a loud Quark! and sailed off indignantly, its long legs trailing behind. The noise of the river drowned out the sound of our approach, allowing us to come within a few yards of a troop of baboons resting from the baking heat in the shade of a huge Natal fig-tree growing on our side of the river. I pulled Rocket back and allowed him to drop his head, reins hanging loose as he pulled at tufts of sweet pinkish-brown veldt grass at the path's edge, and I watched quietly, leaning comfortably back, one hand resting on his glossy brown rump and the other lightly on his neck, my fingers curled around the smooth, damp leather of his reins. We were hidden on our side of the tree in dapples of shade cast by the massive fig, whose gnarled and twisted roots grew right down to the water's edge, in and among boulders on the riverbank, half-exposed like great grey ropes.

No matter how sour and resentful I felt, I had to laugh at the games the baby baboons played while their mothers dozed, heads nodding sleepily as they relaxed against the tree trunk. A little one swung from a low branch by his front paws, another jumped up to grab his tail and hang there, followed by more and more until there was a bunch of babies swinging from one tail. When the first baboon let go, there'd be a soft whump! as they fell gently onto the earth beneath the tree, sending up quite a puff of dust, then they rolled around, play-biting, squealing in mock fright, and pouncing on one another to tumble around before racing off and up the tree again. I chuckled at this tranquil domestic scene and watched until Rocket grew restless, and I rode him away from the river and through a gully where, judging from the freshly ploughed effect on grassy slopes there, bush pigs had spent last night busily rooting for bulbs and insect larvae.

For the second time that afternoon I was glad I hadn't brought the dogs. Apart from disturbing the baboon troop, they could never resist bush pig spoor, and once they'd scented them went off for hours, deaf to my calls and whistles. I jogged home, released Rocket into his paddock, and stood and watched him roll, all four legs in the air as he writhed and twisted to ease the itch of sweat on his back. He got to his feet, front legs stuck out clownishly as he sat up like a dog, before he heaved himself to his feet and shook vigorously, sending clouds of reddish brown dust flying off his coat. Then I walked barefoot up the sloping dirt track, which wound beneath a clump of massive gum-trees, to the cluster of round thatched mud huts, one of which was Lokatia's. She was always ready to drop whatever she was doing to spend time with me. I stuck my head in through her open doorway and breathed in the atmosphere I knew so well – the ever-present scent of wood smoke from years of fires in the circle of large stones on the shiny floor in the middle of her hut.

She and her daughter, Bongi, worked hard on that floor, spreading a mixture of wet cow dung and mud over the entire area with their bare hands, smoothing the paint-like mixture with their fingers and leaving it to dry. The effect was that of well-laid cement, and the pair of them polished it to a high gloss with pads of sheepskin on their hands and knees, the same way the house-girls buffed our Yellowwood floors with *Cobra Floor Shine*. The wood smoke almost, but not quite, overwhelmed the scent of khaki weed, that deliciously pungent medicinal-smelling herb with which Zulus stuffed their sacking mattresses, along with dry hay cut from soft veldt grass.

"It keeps fleas away," Lokatia said. And now and again, we had an infestation in the farmhouse – usually after I'd smuggled a stable cat into my bedroom. I'd climb in through my window clutching the struggling cat, plonk it on my bed, and stroke it until the half-wild creature submitted and settled, purring and kneading my blanket, while the fleas leaped joyfully and unnoticed into my bedding. Evalina would take her sickle out to one of the paddocks and return with an armful of fresh khaki weed to stuff under my mattress, and I could sleep unmolested by fleas, drifting off with its almost peppery, medicinal scent infiltrating my dreams.

I sat with Lokatia on grass mats, our backs resting against

her sun-baked mud wall, faces turned to the warmth of the late afternoon sun. We drank strong, aromatic coffee out of enamel mugs (topped up with creamy milk and crunchy brown government sugar), and worked doorsteps of white bread into doughy sausage-shapes (my hands still grimy with a combination of horse sweat and red dust), to *sheba* – dip them in to suck the sweet, rich coffee from it. I unloaded all my frustrations on her, and she clucked "Au nKosizana!" as she listened intently to all my problems, and clicked her tongue and shook her head in sympathy at the injustice of it all.

Between these cathartic interludes it was easy for me to avoid Mum and Dad except for mealtimes. These were bearable only by their brevity, and the fact that Dad never allowed controversial discussions at the table, so we could eat quickly and quietly, and vanish, slipping away again to roam the farm until dark.

~~~

# *35*

# The Priest

After more days of restlessly patrolling the boundaries, consumed by loneliness, I found myself on a hill overlooking the Umgeni Poort Catholic mission. I'll go down to the nuns and talk to Sister Anne, I decided – at least I hadn't been forbidden to go down there. I loved Sister Anne. She was a new novitiate that I'd met on the road as I was riding home one afternoon. We often came across white nuns walking in pairs or threes, their hands folded in front of them, deep in prayer as they took long walks along the dusty District Road that ran below our house. They nodded and smiled to us as we passed, and we knew they weren't allowed to speak. It was a retreat as well as a mission station, and, apart from the new, youngest nuns, older ones came for retreat from the main Catholic convent in Durban.

I'd seen her again when I'd ridden down to see Sister Theophane at the dairy.

Sister Anne was helping her carry a five-gallon can of cream up to the convent, and she'd apparently been there long enough to be allowed to talk. She had the loveliest face with rosy pink cheeks, which was just about all I could see of her. The novitiates wore a sort of white cotton veil on a band that covered their hair and shorter habits than the nuns, who wore full, flowing ankle-length snowy white robes, and proper white wimples, which showed nothing but their faces. They all wore brown sandals over black socks, which looked rather odd, although Sister Theophane wore gumboots when it was wet.

I had jumped off Rocket and was holding him by the reins when Sister Anne put her bucket down and came over to greet me and pat him on the neck.

"Ahh sure, but he's a beautiful beast," she said in her sweet, lilting Irish accent. "What would you be calling him?" I gradually got to know her as I often rode down there, hungry for company. She was about seventeen or eighteen years old, and had come out from Ireland to become a nun. I wasn't particularly curious as I'd always spent time with the nuns and didn't ask her any questions, such as why did she want to become a nun in the first place. But she was a strikingly pretty and vivacious girl with sparkling green eyes and beautiful dark, wavy hair that kept escaping in wisps from under her veil.

She had a delicious and very un-nunlike giggle, and a streak of tomboy in her, as I discovered when I got to know her a little better. She had been in the Durban nunnery for a year or so, and now she had to complete her second year in the back of beyond out at the Umgeni Poort mission.

"There's certainly no temptation out *here*!" she'd say mischievously now and again. But apparently she wasn't so good at resisting temptation. As soon as she heard the clip-clop of my horse's hooves on the hard ground of the driveway approaching the convent, she'd run out from the kitchen or the dairy where she was working.

"Come," she'd hiss conspiratorially in my ear as I got off, and we'd lead Rocket back down their drive and along the road that ran past the dairy towards Wakefield, until we were out of sight of anybody from the convent.

"Now, hold his head." And she'd tuck her habit up between her legs so that I could see that her black socks were actually long stockings.

She'd put a sandalled toe into the stirrup and was in the saddle in a flash. Grinning like an imp, she'd trot up the road while I sat on the bank and kept watch for any nuns that might come over the horizon. She'd come back eventually, and hand the reins to me.

"Ahh! It reminds me of home," she'd sigh wistfully. "My brothers and I – we all rode the tinkers' ponies in the fields back there."

Today, as I trotted up the drive to the back of the convent, to where the clinic stood in the shade of some gum-trees opposite the kitchen, there was no sign of Sister Anne. She must be in the chapel or down at the dairy with sister Theophane I thought, and turned Rocket's head to go and find her. A young man came out of the gloom of the kitchen onto the back veranda. I'd never seen him before.

"Hello!" I called out cheerily to him. A nun popped out of the kitchen behind him. It was Sister Theophane.

"*'Allo ma petite!*" she smiled broadly at me. She always seemed pleased to see me, however busy she was.

"This is Father Stephens." She introduced the man, who was probably about twenty years old. "He's up here to stay with us for a while." He was the equivalent of a novitiate priest, I discovered, in training to become a real priest. He had a boyish, Mediterranean look, and I eyed him curiously. He wasn't wearing a dog collar like Father Tertius, but had on a silky sort of black shirt and black trousers. Father Tertius was the resident priest, and I only knew him vaguely – he had a grey beard and drove a Volkswagen Beetle at a hundred miles an hour along our dirt roads.

My father called him, 'Holy Smoke', and said darkly, "He's a bloody danger to the rest of us. One of these days one of us is going to meet him on a blind rise, and that'll be that. Perhaps it'll be that doctor," he'd add with some satisfaction. Our GP, Doctor Potter, also drove at top speed, tearing along in the middle of the road with a great plume of brown dust flying from his wheels.

"I've been meaning to come and see your father," the young man said to me. "I want to buy a horse so that I can ride out to places like iMmpendhle over the mountains there, to extend the work of the mission."

"I can help you buy a horse," I said with all the confidence of a then nine-year-old. After all, I knew everything there was to know about horseflesh from Grandpa. "I'll tell all the boys on the farm that you want a horse, and they can bring them down from iMpendhle for you to look at and choose one." My father didn't like priests of any kind, and he despised Catholics, and I knew for a fact he would have given this one short shrift.

"Well, that seems like an easy solution," he replied, and that's exactly how he got his horse. It was a Basutu pony, like Squib, but a bit taller, and with my help Father Stephens looked it over carefully and took it out on a long ride, with me beside him on Rocket, giving him advice, before he bought it. We didn't want another Squib with all his bad habits.

I rode down to the convent every day after that, and I had to fit our rides in between the chapel and church services he held three times a day with Father T, for the nuns and the local Zulu women. Father Stephens would be waiting for me wearing blue denim jeans and a white shirt with the sleeves rolled up. He'd be holding his pony, Duma, all saddled up and ready, and we'd ride off together. I took him over to Wakefield, the farm beyond the nuns. There was a Zulu caretaker, called Velapi, living in his kraal, hidden out of sight under the gum-trees behind the main house, with some wives and lots of children, and I knew him well.

"*Saubona nKosizana! nomFundisi! niahambapi?*" ("I see you, Chief's daughter and priest, where are you going?") he'd call, and I'd wave back and ask him how his family was, and whether there were any new calves I should see.

Father Stephens rode at my side as I took him further, through Wakefield and on to Stonycroft, the farm beyond. There were white people living there, but I didn't know them at all. They would use the Dargle District Road to get to places like Lions River and Howick, and we'd not be likely to come across them.

They also had big dogs, which raced towards us, barking madly, making Duma toss his head nervously and fidget at his bit.

"We'll go past this lot," I said, and showed Father Stephens the single track that led up over the hills to iNhlosane and iMpendhle, the settlements where all our Zulus had their huts and families, and where they went when it was their time off. The only way there was on foot or on horseback as the mountain pass was too narrow for a vehicle.

Beyond Wakefield house, on the open green veldt, our path meandered round big sinkholes, where the stream coming off the mountains behind us had dived underground, causing subsidence. They appeared as great round deep holes, lined with rich dark green moss, and out of which grew monster tree ferns with their strange trunks covered in a unique brown, papery substance.

Rare Blue Swallows nested under the mossy roofs of these cave-like holes and appeared suddenly, as if by magic, from the long grass at our horses' feet, the sunlight flashing off their cobalt blue backs as they shot out of their hidden, subterranean nests.

We could hear water trickling in little rills as the invisible stream continued its way to the river below.

We talked as we rode over the veldt for hours and hours.

Father Stephens came from an Italian background, which explained the olive complexion, although he was South African, and had been born in Durban as had I. He was very good-looking in an almost movie star way, with long dark eyelashes and hazel eyes. His hair was pitch black, thick and glossy, and he wore it slightly longer than any of the men I'd ever come across. He was very keen to learn as much as he could about horses and their behaviour, and learned to ride very quickly. I liked him. He had a boyish enthusiasm about everything, especially as I began to point out various birds to him and taught him their Zulu names.

He exclaimed with joy when I showed him where the Cape

Weaver birds made their nests over the Judge's Pool, and he saw the bright yellow birds popping in and out of their basket-like nests.

He also enjoyed the Red Bishop birds with their scarlet heads and the wonderful Sakabula birds – the Red Shouldered Widow birds with their long black tails that trailed behind them as they fluttered about in the courtship displays.

We rode together in this happy fashion for nearly two years.

By the age of nearly twelve I was semi-educated. I had read every book on the huge shelves that covered almost every wall of the big old farmhouse, (several of which were encyclopaedias), and as a result had an extensive general knowledge, but I could only count up to ten, which was all that was required for sorting sheep with the herd boys. I counted in the Zulu fashion, using my fingers and thumbs (I still count that way). The name for thumb is *uStupe*, which is also the number six in Zulu – the other numbers, up to ten, are the same names as the relevant fingers. None of the staff on the farm had ever been to school, and anyway, in old Zulu custom, there was never any need to count. Being originally cattle herding hunter gatherers, they had few possessions as they used what was available around them in the bush, and discarded items such as bowls made from leaves, and rush baskets.

Even their dwellings were simple wattle and daub huts with thatched roofs, and could be left to dissolve back into the soil, to be reclaimed by nature. They took their animal skins with them, for clothing and blankets, and of course their main source of wealth – cattle.

They certainly kept a careful tally of their precious stock of the rangy, big horned Zebu beasts that they grazed over the veldt. These provided them with milk and meat but, most importantly of all, were exchanged for new wives as lobola. But Zulus keep track of their cattle by their colours and thus there are many different names for the colour brown in their language.

Late one morning, as Father Stephens and I were riding back

towards the convent, I saw my father's *Land Rover* approaching from Wakefield. He drove slowly past us and glared at me as I sat on Rocket. He gave me his glittering, cold, hooded-cobra eyed stare as the vehicle passed and completely ignored Father Stephens's polite greeting.

"I see you've been out riding with that priest!" He spat the word out. I'd been summoned to the *gluzeen* where he and my mother were savouring their first pre-lunch gin. I braced myself for another tirade, but it never came. Instead, my father said abruptly,

"It's a good thing you're going to boarding school in a week's time. That should put a stop to your shenanigans."

This was the first I'd heard of these plans. While I'd been out, roaming the hills with Father Stephens, my parents had received a phone call from Boarding School Prep saying that they suddenly had a vacancy as one of the girls had run away. My life was about to change – and it didn't sound promising.

~~~

# *36*

# Prep School

**I** looked like a stick-insect in my over-large navy school blazer, which I had to wear over a blue cotton dress. The Boarding School Prep. uniform was pale blue (the Virgin Mary's blue) and navy, and I had on white ankle socks and clumpy brown lace-ups.

'Famine Coolie' was one of the more complimentary names given to me by my older sisters, and referred to those starved Indian outcasts labouring in paddy fields they'd seen in photographs in books at their school. My parents called Indians by the derogatory 'coolies' as a matter of routine. Not to their faces – they were always polite to the Hoosen family who ran our gold-mine of a general store in Nottingham Road – but about them in general.

I had shot up to five feet seven and a half inches in the space of eighteen months, and I'd had severe growing pains in my legs, particularly at night. On one occasion, they hurt so badly that I'd resorted to creeping, whimpering in agony down the passage to my parents' bedroom and woken my mother. Uncharacteristically, she'd given me a couple of aspirin rather than a bollocking for disturbing her.

My long, skinny legs were hinged by knobbly, scabbed knees, and my arms appeared to belong to a skeleton. I felt awkward and clumsy in my uniform, and hunched lowering my head.

"Stand up straight!" snapped my mother as she held the old Box Brownie-type camera impatiently down in front of her, trying to fit in as much of her garden as she could. She'd posed me in front of one of her best borders, which radiated with every shade of pink, red, blue and cream, in the early summer sunshine, and I'd been told to drape Miss Bun, my pyjama-case rabbit, over the little brown suitcase that held my overnight stuff. My great big trunk had been packed by the servants and was already in the boot of the car.

I was not looking forward to going to the Prep. It didn't bode well that I was taking the place of a girl who'd run away, and I sat in the car with butterflies in my tummy all the way to Hilton.

The next morning at six, I sat bolt upright on my narrow iron bed in the dormitory, jolted awake by the deafeningly loud clanging of a brass handbell. Miss Grindley (Grindlebug) bustled through the long dorm, her laced-up, sensible shoes clomping on the bare wooden floors. She jangled the bell vigorously as she went, and I could hear her progress right through to the next dorm in the cavernous Victorian red brick building. I looked around to find that all the other girls had already leaped to their feet, grabbed their sponge bags, and raced off to the big echoing bathroom. There they formed a line, and groggily I joined the end, my bag in my hand.

The bathroom was divided into about a dozen wooden cubicles with a half-size enamelled bath standing on ball-and-claw feet on the chilly red concrete floor in each one. Grindlebug had run an inch of tepid water and then splashed a liberal amount of *Dettol* in. The stink made my eyes water as I stood and waited while the girls ran into the cubicles and shut the door. My turn came and I was hustled into my lukewarm bath, cloudy with disinfectant. I got in gingerly and began to wash. As I was about to finish, a head popped over the adjoining cubicle wall and a tall girl with curly brown hair and a pale, speckled face stared at me.

"Why are you washing yourself there?" she shrieked, a nasty, grimacing expression on her face. Another head appeared over the other cubicle wall.

"What are you doing, Colleen?"

"She washing herself down there!" repeated the girl with a

squeal. "It's so rude!" I looked up at them, nonplussed. What was going on? The two faces continued to stare accusingly at me. Then, "Why are you spying on her anyway Colleen?" The second girl turned on the first, screaming at her in disgust. "Are you some kind of lezzy?"

At this stage Grindlebug started yanking the cubicle doors open and the faces disappeared. I hunched over my raised knees, puzzled and frightened by this encounter. Even my sisters didn't behave like this.

I was chased from dormitory to breakfast and classes in what seemed like breathless haste. I was the only new girl and had no idea what was going on, but ran frantically with any gaggle of other girls – they all looked the same to me: so many pink faces and blue dresses. I always bolted in the wrong direction whenever the bell rang, inevitably ending up in one big hall or another, surrounded by the starling chatter of fifty-odd other girls, mostly younger than I was. Even the smallest ones seemed to know what they were doing and carried the right books and pencil cases to their classes.

I was given a desk at the back of a classroom, and a whole lot of books and pencils, including a fountain pen that squirted bright blue ink merrily and indelibly over my hands, dress and books. Everything was out of control and I never had the right things for our various classes. A mentor would have been nice, just to explain to me where the gym class was and that I was supposed to wear the black bloomers for that. Blue bloomers for everyday, white bloomers for Sundays.

Miss Turnbull (Turney) with her grim mouth, mottled old face and wispy grey bun, pushed a trunk full of uniform at me to unpack and put away neatly in a footlocker. Evalina had always done everything for me. I had no idea how to fold even a T-shirt – I'd never done it in my life. I had to make my bed – a mysterious challenge of hospital corners and stuff I'd never heard of. Furiously, Turney stripped it and shouted at me to make it again, properly this time. We could have discovered perpetual motion if we hadn't had to get to morning assembly, and I hastily dragged the bedding back on as she stamped away, and slunk after her at a safe distance, like a wary mongrel.

Meals were in a long dining-hall, and I was given a place on the right-hand side, at the top end, right next to Grindlebug. They made us eat everything on our plates, and this was a hideous ordeal. I had no interest in food, particularly stuff that looked even more insipid and overcooked than Masango's nursery meals had ever been. The stringy vegetables lurked in watery puddles, and the meat was flat slices of unidentifiable origin. They gave us 'riced' potatoes every day. These were boiled potatoes put through a mincer, and utterly dry and tasteless. On Sundays, we had roast meat, allegedly beef, and the same vegetables, but this time with anaemic, leathery roast potatoes.

Unfortunately for me, Sundays was when Dot came to eat lunch at the Prep, too. She was Miss Dorothy McEwan, headmistress (or more correctly Lady Warden, which gave her the more accurate sounding title of prison wardress) of Boarding school Diocesan College, the senior school. She struck terror into the hearts of parents and pupils alike, and nobody ever wanted to incur Dot's wrath. I didn't know any of this however, although I'd vaguely heard my sisters mention Dot in their conversations about school, usually accompanied by a shudder. So when she arrived after I'd been at school for just two days, there I sat at her right-hand side. She was tall, sat bolt upright and had icy, piercing, pale blue eyes, rather like I'd read the Gestapo had in Dad's war books.

"How are you enjoying your first days at school?" she asked me, after a long silence as I struggled with my rubbery grey meat.

"It's OK so far," I replied casually. There was the hiss of intaken breath as all the girls and staff at the table fell silent, outraged at my insolence. Every face turned to me, and then to Dot, who also remained silent, taken aback for the first time in her life probably. Nobody had ever spoken to her in that offhand manner.

I'd lost my appetite, such as it was, and put my knife and fork together on my plate. "What do you think you're doing?" demanded the Lady Warden. "How dare you leave good food on your plate. Now eat those peas!" I looked at the yellowish-grey round things lying there, swilling about in what looked like dishwater, but could have been gravy.

So that's what they were. I decided to make an early stand for my rights. "I don't like peas." By now the other girls had finished their meals and were passing plates up to be stacked. I quickly picked up my own plate and lifting the top one on the pile, slipped my uneaten meal in, and replaced the top plate, squashing those hated peas flat.

Dot glared at me. She looked as if she was going to make me take my plate back from underneath the others now piled on top, and force me to eat what I'd left, flattened as it was, but then decided not to.

"You will have no pudding, you disobedient little girl." That was fine by me, as pudding at the Prep was a succession of repulsively slimy, whitish, wobbly stuff like tapioca, or frog-spawn as the girls called it. That was one less dish that I'd have to sabotage. Unfortunately, it turned out to be vanilla ice cream, my ultimate favourite, as a special treat on Sundays. I'd certainly started off on the wrong foot, since I was to have five years to serve under Dot. I'd sealed my fate.

Underneath the main buildings at the Prep was a warren-like dungeon of music cells. I was told to go to the music mistress to be tried out for the choir. Once I'd found the right room, I found Miss Lodkin waiting for me. She was a frightening sight. She was a head shorter than I was, and fat, with a mass of frizzy pitch-black hair. It looked suspiciously as if someone had sprinkled white talcum powder on the roots, I noticed, and she had a bosom that jutted out from under her double chin, which made her look as if she had two torpedoes strapped there. She was also wearing a yellow polo neck jersey with horizontal black stripes that did her no favours at all. She looked like a very bad-tempered bumblebee.

I was quite confident that I was an excellent singer. After all, I'd spent my life riding around alone, singing at full volume the songs that I'd heard from my older sisters' records or the short-wave radio. She asked me if I knew 'All things Bright and Beautiful', and I nodded, yes, we'd sung that at Mrs Bannatyne's. Miss Lodkin played the introduction, and I let fly. I sang lustily, my mouth wide open, and my head tilted back. I was astonished when she stopped after the first line, quietly closed the piano lid and folded her hands on her lap.

"I don't think we'll be needing you for the choir," she said curtly, and sent me away. I was crushed. Mortified that all this time I'd thought I could sing. Why hadn't anybody told me? And then I remembered that, yes, my sisters had thrown objects at me whenever I'd sung, but I thought that was because they were just jealous.

I had yet another blow to my already withered ego when in class one day we were asked to write a composition in Afrikaans.

I enjoyed writing and did a nice long piece about a small boy who had an adventure with a big fish. When it was my turn to read out my work, I walked confidently up to the platform and stood there.

"Die naam van my story is 'Frikkie en sy Vis'," (The name of my story is 'Frikkie and his Fish') I began. The entire room full of girls instantly erupted with laughter. I was surprised, as my story did have some amusing bits in it, but not in the title.

"Carry on," said the Afrikaans mistress. Her face emotionless.

"Frikkie ..." I had to stop as the girls were now howling with laughter, and a couple of them had dropped books and pencils onto the floor in their mirth. I looked at the mistress again. She smiled at me, an odd sort of a smile, and told me to carry on.

To the accompaniment of screams of laughter, some of my

fellow pupils dabbing at their streaming eyes, I soldiered on to the end.

"Thank you," said the mistress, and I went back to my desk at the back, to sit down.

"What was all that about?" I asked the girl who sat next to me.

"Why did you call the boy Frikkie?" she gasped, still in paroxysms of laughter.

"Because it's an Afrikaans boy's name," I said with all the dignity I could muster.

"It's the word for a French letter, you fool, didn't you know?" she said. I looked at her blankly. She turned around to smirk at the others. "She doesn't know what a French letter is!" she cackled mockingly.

She was quite right, I didn't know what a French letter was, and nor was I going to expose my ignorance by asking either.

I was even more isolated after that. Ostracised by the others as I was such a misfit with my limited English vocabulary; I was far more fluent in Zulu. Also my utterly hopeless lack of knowledge of apparently the most basic words such as 'lezzy' and 'French letter' was getting me nowhere. So I spent a lot of the time playing 'donkey' with the younger girls, leaving my own classmates to play the same two Elvis records, 'Blue Suede Shoes' and 'Wooden Heart', over and over again, and snigger loudly when the pair of school guinea-pigs squealed out during their constant and noisy mating marathons. If they could catch my eye, they'd nudge each other and shout, "Hey! Frikkie!" across the playground.

The term dragged on. I made no progress with my hospital corners, and my foot-locker always looked as if a racoon had been rummaging through it. Often there was evidence to make me suspect that my dormitory fellows had sabotaged it, but I had no proof as I never actually caught them at it. I loathed mealtimes, and somehow got away with pushing my food around without actually eating any of it.

I was quick enough to shove it under the stack as it came my way, and acted with lightning speed, so that the stack was gone, with my food squashed in there somewhere, before Grindlebug or Turney had a chance to look my way.

I was sent up to the school doctor for a medical examination during my first week at the Prep. He was called Dr Mackenzie, or 'Strip Mac' by all the girls, since he was rumoured to tell all the girls to strip, even if they went in with a sore toe, just so that he could look at their bare bosoms. I was petrified, horrified by the thought of being alone and naked in front of a strange man.

Turney accompanied me up to the San, a building on the College grounds, and left me there with the school sister. A gimlet-eyed, middle-aged woman with a starched nursing sister's cap on. She looked at me suspiciously, weighed me and measured my height, and then sent me through to the examining room, where Dr Strip Mac was waiting.

He was an old man with glasses and a grumpy expression.

"You're very thin," he said accusingly. There was no answer to that, so I kept silent, while he examined me in my dress.

Obviously I wasn't worth being told to strip, as I had no bosom. I was as flat as a board. "You have curvature of the spine," the doctor said eventually.

"I'm ordering the matron to confiscate your pillow." And I was dismissed.

I was so relieved that I wasn't going to be made to take my clothes off, eat extra food, or be given a vile-tasting tonic from the huge bottle of black liquid I'd seen in the San (this was long before the days of vitamin supplements), but I was to have a tablespoonful of cod liver oil and malt extract every morning after breakfast instead. I loved the cod liver oil and malt, as it reminded me of the molasses we poured over the silage at home.

It smelled delicious, and we'd always stick our fingers in the black, gooey substance while it was being trickled over the freshly cut green hay in the autumns at home.

I was puzzled about having my pillow taken away, though, as I always slept on my side, and it didn't make any sense to me that being without a pillow would make any difference to my spine. I stooped because I'd grown so quickly and towered above all the other children of my age. It was just poor posture, not curvature of the spine.

Time seemed to stand still. I missed home. I missed my Zulu friends most of all, as I couldn't identify with these strange girls with their coded, incomprehensible language, and the way they always stopped talking when I joined the group, and stared at me, and then elbowed each other. They giggled and turned their backs on me and left me standing there. The younger girls tolerated me playing with a tennis ball against the wall of the assembly hall. Donkey was a good game that involved a tennis ball and as many players as you liked. We threw the ball up against the wall and had to jump, straddled over to where it landed, for the girl standing in line behind to catch it and throw again. We hitched our dresses up into our bloomers and jumped over that ball until we lost it in the gutter on the tin roof, or the bell rang for classes, or meals, or anything that involved them all racing off, and me following them, hoping I was going to the right place.

Mum came to visit me one Saturday afternoon, after her weekly social tennis game at the 'Maritzburg Country Club was rained off. She stayed for ten minutes, asked me how it was going, didn't wait for an answer, but thrust a small packet of *Mint Imperials* (her favourite peppermints) at me. She hadn't thought to bring me any tuck, as all the other parents regularly did. Most of them bringing boots full of picnics with roast chickens and cakes and bags and bags of sweets and chocolate. I stood there in the school drive with a lump in my throat, clutching my packet of mints, as I watched Gig lurching off down the drive in a cloud of dust.

I went into the music dungeons and sat there in the dark, on my own, and ate the whole packet. Crunching up sweet after sweet, until the packet was empty. Then I started to feel really nauseous and thought I was going to be sick. I spent the whole of the rest of that Saturday lying on the lawn behind the big old fir tree in the playground, near the swings, wondering if I was going to throw up.

My feet were giving me terrible trouble, too. I was not used to wearing shoes, and they'd immediately begun to rub blisters on my heels that very first day I put them on. The blisters became raw patches, and then I had to ask for sticking-plasters from Grindlebug, and permission to wear the hated brown Clark sandals that had been sent along in my trunk. These caused a whole new set of problems, as I sweated into them in the summer heat (it was now December) they began to stink. I'd never had smelly feet before, and at first I wondered where this stench was coming from. When I identified the sandals as the cause, I was then at a loss as to what to do about it. The only thing I could do, was to swap them for my shoes and socks and risk the blisters again, as my hard, leathery outdoor feet continued to fester.

I missed the farm, and the dogs. If I went to the farthest boundary of the Prep, I could just see the mountain range with the iNhlosane on it. This was a mountain exactly the same shape as the iNhlezela on the farm. I sat on the dusty ground and stared and stared at the peak, wishing myself there so that I could walk into the lovely warm kitchen, which always smelled deliciously of roasting meat and potatoes or freshly baked bread, to be greeted with utter joy by the servants. I wished I could run away like my predecessor had, but I knew that Dad would find a worse punishment for me.

Things began to look up as the term passed, and the end began to become a reality, rather than a distant, shimmering mirage. In the space of three weeks I grew a bosom. This created yet another problem for me.

"You need a bra!" sneered the girls in my dorm, mainly the

same two who had originally and continued to torment me in the bathroom. It was true, I did suddenly need a bra. I had sprouted quite a substantial bust overnight. It was most uncomfortable, and made me hunch my shoulders even more, to try and hide it.

This drew shouts of, "Stand up straight Ross!" from the matron and teachers alike, as I stood in line for assembly and the dining-hall.

I wasn't going to see Mum until the end of term, so there was nothing I could do. We had to write letters home on Sunday afternoons, but the letters were censored by the two matrons so I didn't mention my new bosom to my parents, especially if Dad was going to read the letter as well. I wanted Mum to take me out and buy me a bra, since she came past the school every Thursday to play tennis while Dad played his eighteen holes of golf, but I was too frightened even to mention the word in a letter. She might stick her head in if I was lucky, if she was rained out, but otherwise I was going to have to tough it out until the end of term.

We had gymnastics twice a week, and swimming at the college pool every other day, and I had to manhandle these two new bosoms into my gym shirt and bathing-costume, neither of which had any room now. The rest of me was skin and bone, since I wasn't eating, so my black gym bloomers looked enormous on me, but my bust had to be squashed into the top, a little, white cotton shirt. Running around the tennis courts, and the pool changing rooms, were full of pitfalls for me, and I did my best to hide myself in a corner and undress as furtively as possible. I was still suffering from the odd growing pain, and was also very tender in my new, budding bust, so I didn't feel that well, especially having to tear about after a tennis ball. I had to stop playing Donkey with the more amenable younger girls, as I was so uncomfortable.

Term ended with a blur of carol service and some sort of school play, but neither featured as high on my own private list of priorities as having to keep my head down and manage all my personal problems. Finally, the day came when I could climb thankfully into the car, already crammed with my two older sisters. I could have kissed them with joy, as they were the old, familiar enemy, the one I could cope with. But, we greeted each other with grunts and, "Move over idiot, get off my dress," and other such pleasantries. The car started and we were off, through the gates and on our way home.

I began to regale Mum and my sisters about the horrible time I'd spent at the Prep, when Nicolette turned to me and said, "Shut up, stupid – you're going to see all those girls next term, as they're all going to college with you."

I had a glorious six weeks of summer holiday riding by myself, and swimming and playing tennis with my sisters to look forward to. Now fully aware of how they'd felt, having been thrust into the Prep in the same way I'd been, I could empathise with them. Sadly, their bitterness at having been sent away so young had become so ingrained that we couldn't form any kind of relationship. I could no longer play fairies with Dine – she had become a teenager, and was interested only in boys, clothes and pop music. They also went off to stay with friends in order to go to dances and tennis parties, leaving me behind again with Delia, who was still at the Government School.

I went off to look for my Zulu playmates, only to discover that they had all gone back to iMpendhle. Sent away by their parents to get a bit of schooling of their own, if they were lucky or to herd goats or cattle (if they were boys), or fetch water and firewood and do chores around the hut if they were girls. There was nobody left of my own age, although there were still some babies and toddlers around, with their mothers, at the huts at the back of the house. I suspect it was Dad's policy to insist that his labourers get rid of their teenage children, unless there were jobs open for them. "Having young, idle *munts* around the place only causes trouble," according to him.

# White Zulu

The previous winter two boys (neither of whom were my special friends, I was glad to say) had set fire to a haystack, drawing Dad from his after-lunch doze in his comfortable armchair next to the heater in the *gluzeen* when somebody came to raise the alarm one quiet Sunday afternoon. Mustering a trailer full of labour from the Zulus available, Dad had driven crossly to the far field on the boundary, next to where our silage pit was, taking the dogs with him in the back of the jeep.

In fact, I'd just clambered into the jeep when the dogs scrambled up hoping I wouldn't be noticed in the mêlée. Once we'd got there, bumping over the veldt, I saw the bright orange blaze as the entire big stack burned fiercely. nGidi stood there with the two umfaans next to him – the culprits.

"Where did you get the matches from?" Dad asked them, and when there was no reply, as they both hung their heads in shame, he drew back his walking stick and gave each of the boys, both my age, 11, three hard whacks across the backside. Dust flew off their ragged khaki shorts as the stick made contact. I was staggered as I'd never seen Dad hit anyone before. It was Mum who meted out our punishments, smacking us on the bum with the back of her *Mason and Pearson* hairbrush imported from London. But Dad never hit us. I'd never seen either of them ever lay a hand on any of the Zulus before that day. Once the punishment had come to a swift end, Dad dismissed the two perpetrators, and got nGidi to keep a team of firefighters next to the smouldering stack, to see that the wind didn't whisk any sparks off and set fire to the rest of the farm.

There were still the adult Zulus though, and I spent time with all of them, trying to explain how awful school was. To the Zulus an education was the only way out of poverty and squalor, so I received very little sympathy. They'd been so impressed to see me in my smart uniform, going off with a huge trunk full of clothes. It was a dream come true to them.

Back to my own company, I spent most of my time on

horseback, roaming the farm, and nipping down to the nuns to see my friends there. My priest had gone back to Durban, so there was nobody free to ride with me anymore. Sister Anne had pledged her vows over Christmas and become a proper nun, and it was odd to see her in her snowy white habit, looking just like the older nuns. She wasn't available to slip away to have secret rides on my horse any longer, although I was given a warm greeting by all the nuns.

My loneliness became a bit more obvious to me now, and I realised that I should have had friends at school like my sisters did. It worried me that I hadn't found even one single girl who'd even remotely taken a kind interest in me. They'd all turned their backs on me – the odd new girl.

~~~

# *37*

# Second Form at Boarding School College

29 January 1962, and, along with a lot of yelling at the servants from Mum about packing our trunks and getting ready, my twelfth birthday. And for the next six years I was to go back to school on my birthday, as the first day of term always started on 29 January. For those six years I had to celebrate my birthday a week early – a hollow mockery of a celebration. Every year, when my parents wished me a happy birthday and gave me a present, the other three spent the whole day saying, "But it isn't your real birthday, so we don't have to be nice to you!" And spoiled it for me anyway.

The four of us would leave the farm in Gig (our capacious Pontiac): Delia to go to the Prep, and me, Dine, and Nicolette to go to the College. Mum would dump us unceremoniously in the drive at boarding school, and take off again as fast as possible. She and Dad were going skiing in Val-d'isère in the French Alps and then taking a Mediterranean cruise for six weeks, and were leaving the following day. If any of us felt unhappy about being left at a new boarding school, it was too bad; nobody was going to get any sympathy from her. Other parents tearfully embraced their daughters in front of the Chapel: our mother turned the car round with indecent haste, and bolted.

I was in Macrorie House, a ramshackle old double-storey wooden building with huge, open-raftered dormitories, partitioned into cubicles of two, four and five for the lower forms, with curtains that had to be pulled back in the daytime to reveal our beds and lockers in long rows. The head and vice-head of house each got a wooden cubicle with a proper door.

There was a disinfectant-smelling big communal bathroom upstairs, with the one and only loo, which was exclusively reserved for sixth-formers. The rest of the house of fifty-odd girls had to go down a precipitous staircase and use the two loos in the main passage of the old building, near the gym. That and our common room were situated underneath our dorms.

I had a curtained cubicle for second formers, shared with four other new girls. Two of them I recognised from the Prep, both of whom ignored me as not worth the effort of a simple hello, but the other two girls were new. One of them, a girl called Mary, had the bed next to me, and when I saw her putting a couple of china horse ornaments on her locker (which we were allowed to do), and a photograph of herself with a dog, I knew I might have a good chance of making friends. She came from Underberg, a small farming village in the Drakensberg Mountains, was the second to youngest of four, like me, (although she was lucky enough to have a brother) and was the Underberg GP's daughter.

Best of all, I discovered that she spoke pure Zulu as fluently as I did. Most white South Africans speak a little bit of 'Kitchen Kaffir' or 'Fanagalo', a bastardised, pidgin African language that was invented when the (mostly Afrikaner) gold, diamond and coal mine bosses had to communicate with several different tribes, all speaking their own languages, among the masses of African men who poured onto the Reef to work for them. It was only the whites that'd grown up among them, like Mary and I had, that spoke the language properly. It wasn't taught in government or private schools, nor did it appear on any road signs. This was because Zulu is a spoken language, and it was only the missionaries, who came with the settlers way back in the late 1700s who had started putting the words down on paper, and translating the Bible into a written form of the language.

All the different clicks made the African languages very difficult to write. People who had tried to learn Zulu from textbooks never got as far as we did who picked it up by ear.

Having said that, I can neither read nor write Zulu. Mary and I became best friends. It was nice to have somebody who was as at sea as I was, and the difference now was that, because we were a whole form of new girls, we had mentors from the third form who showed us around and taught us the ropes.

College had a more gruelling schedule than the Prep. We had early morning prep every day. The rising bell rang at six and we had to jump up, get washed and dressed, and rush off to the classrooms. As Macrorie was one of the houses furthest away from them, we had to really run to get there in time. After an hour of prep, we ran back to eat breakfast in the huge dining-hall.

There I found a pleasant change, as nobody cared whether you ate or not. We sat at tables of 12 in our houses, each table with a prefect at either end, who dished out the food. The only strictly enforced rule was that we had to talk; to eat in silence resulted in punishment from the prefects. So there we all sat, gabbling away frantically, trying not to talk with mouths full, but terrified that if we stopped talking, we'd get some sort of detention.

I couldn't find anything to talk about, as the subject was always boys, clothes, or dances and tennis parties the older girls had attended in the holidays, which boy they'd fancied and so on. I ended up having to learn the whole of 'The Rime of the Ancient Mariner' in my first week there, for remaining silent for two minutes. To add insult to injury, the fifth formers were allowed to give out punishments, and it was extremely insulting for me to be dressed down by one of my sisters, when what I really wanted to do was kick her.

The other ordeals were church and chapel. For both we had

to wear white cotton squares, called veils, to cover our hair, like nuns did. My first church service, on our first night at College, something called Evensong, was as confusing as everything else was turning out to be. We had to wear our white dresses, veils, and brown shoes and stockings. Since I'd just spent six weeks running barefoot around the farm, my feet had quickly reverted to their tough, leathery state, and I was to go over the same anguish as I'd been through at the Prep, with re-training my feet to wear shoes and sandals again, with the same results, a choice of blisters or smelly feet.

We lined up in houses in the main passage, and traipsed off to the little Hilton church, which stood just outside the school.

There we sat in pews and waited. Suddenly, everybody stood up, recited something, and dropped to their knees, shut their eyes and bowed their heads. A man in a white smock over a long, voluminous black dress came up the centre aisle with a solemn boarding school girl holding a big silver cross walking slowly in front of him. He said something and everybody scrambled to their feet and sang a long hymn, reading the words from a green book.

After that there was a lot of chanting in Latin (this was a high church apparently), and lots more singing and more praying. I stared around me in bewilderment. I had no idea what it was about. My parents, both openly and vociferously atheist (Dad's pet hates were the church, religion and priests), had never told us about God or Jesus, or even primed us that we'd have to attend church.

Boarding school, being a Diocesan college and therefore high church, didn't just stop at holding Evensong: we had an hour of compulsory communion early on Sunday mornings, an hour of chapel every morning instead of assembly, and another hour of chapel every night, except on Sundays, when we had to go to church. That meant we had to attend church or chapel three times a day on Sundays, and chapel twice a day, every day. I never learned the *Lord's Prayer*, even though we recited it six times a day, as we had grace before every meal as well. I simply blanked the whole hour out each time, and spent that time daydreaming and becoming more and more bored and resentful that I had to spend so much time devoted to something mysterious that I didn't even remotely believe in.

What further astonished me, was that the girls around me seemed to be taking the whole thing on board. They appeared to be praying earnestly, or listening intently to the interminable sermons given by Dot or Father Somebody. I just couldn't get it. What did they see that I didn't, and why couldn't I comprehend what it was all about? I stared at the sun blazing in through the stained-glass windows and wished I was out on a hillside on my horse. This continued for the six years I spent there. Bunking church or chapel was one of the worst offences you could commit at boarding school. The prefects always knew who was missing and why, because we had to sit in the same place in the same pews each time, so if there was a space, the one leaving it had to be either sick and lying in the San or bunking.

Later on that year I became highly allergic to house-dust mites and suffered from constant hay fever in the dorm and every other building. Apart from streaming, itching red eyes, and sneezing until my nose was red raw, I often had nosebleeds, which was a sure way of being escorted out of chapel, and down to the San if it was a bad one and couldn't be stopped. I became quite good at pinching my nose and blowing out my sinuses so that I got an instant nosebleed, and could spend the rest of chapel with a tissue clamped to my nose while sitting in the sun in the gutter outside.

Even this, to me, was time better spent than the utter and sheer boredom of the meaningless services. The hay fever continued to plague me at home, but instead of having it investigated and perhaps some antihistamines prescribed, Mum just shouted at me in exasperation, "If you sneeze again, I'm going to kill you!" as if I were doing it to annoy her.

At my first meal in the dining-room I had another shock. The food was served up by Zulu men in white uniform, and, when a black arm came past my ear holding a great big tin trough of some watery, pale, macaroni cheese with chunks of tomato in it, I turned and smiled at the man, exactly as I would have done with Makhaye at home. I greeted and thanked him in Zulu, and he replied with a grin. The prefect on whose right I was sitting, and the second former I was sitting next to both shrank away in horror. "You talk to those people?" they both gasped simultaneously.

I nodded, "Yes. I always do. They're my friends."

The two girls, as well as the rest of the table, who'd realised what was going on, goggled at me. "But we hate them. They're all savages!" exclaimed the prefect, and the rest of the girls joined in to agree.

"How could you?" someone shouted at me from down the table.

"Are you a Kaffirboetie (Kaffir lover)?" I didn't know what they were talking about, but didn't want to attract any more adverse attention, so I kept quiet, while the girls turned and whispered things to each other. I wished I'd been at one of the other tables, where my sisters were, and might get some kind of support, but they were both at different tables. Afterwards, I went to see them, individually, in their sections of the dorm, and asked what a Kaffirboetie meant.

"Shut up and bugger off. Whatever you do, don't come running to me if you get into trouble," was more or less the reply from both of them, so I realised that I'd get no help from that quarter. I decided to keep my affection for Zulus to myself. I'd come across my first taste of the casual racism that I was to be bombarded with from then on from every quarter – the girls and staff alike. My parents were openly racist too, but I saw how they spoke to and treated the Zulus on the farm, and I hadn't made the connection that it was apparently all Africans who were terrible savages, not just the ones they read about in the newspapers.

Apart from having a few friends of my own age, and happily a really good best friend, Mary, with whom I could share my love for horses and dogs and be able to speak Zulu with, I detached myself almost completely from school life and created a world of my own. I discovered the library. A little building all by itself at the bottom of the grounds, on the way to the swimming pool. I immersed myself there every moment I wasn't being harassed into doing things like lessons, sport or the relentless hours in chapel and church. I was allowed to take two books out at a time, and I read voraciously, like a starved animal, picking books out at random, and devouring them from cover to cover. I tried to read in class, and got into trouble and regular detention on Saturday mornings, where I was made to write hundreds of lines, or compositions on different subjects. I did the same in Prep and was caught by the prefects who unsportingly patrolled our classroom for an hour early every morning and for an hour and a half in the evenings, checking to see what we were doing. My punishments from them varied, from cleaning their shoes to reciting poetry I'd had to learn off by heart, or writing lines.

As second formers we had to 'fag' for the prefects. This meant doing all their little chores, like cleaning their shoes, their hockey pads, and tidying and cleaning their wooden cubicles.

Luckily for me, neither of my sisters made it to sixth form, and they both dropped out of school without taking their Matric (final exams that allowed you to get into university). Otherwise I can't even begin to imagine how awful it would have been to have to fag for either of them. I was fagging for the head of house, a sturdy, bossy, unpleasant girl with a hooked nose, who played goalie for the first hockey team. I was nearly always late for my fagging duties, and running in late, one afternoon, having just remembered that I was supposed to be cleaning her shoes, I managed to concuss our head of house by flinging her wooden door open just as she was bending over facing it tying up her shoelaces, and slammed the door into the top of her head. The loud crash brought the entire house full of girls over to see what had happened, and the prefect had to be taken to the San while I slunk off to detention, followed by the accusing eyes of the entire house full of prefects and girls.

Swimming was horribly different from the pleasant splashing around in the heat of the summer sun we'd done in the river, in the sea at Salt Rock, and in Knysna Lagoon. Swimming was overseen by the Games Mistress, Mort (Miss Mortimer), a butch lesbian with cruel little bloodshot red, hung-over eyes. She reeked of stale Bourbon, or some similar kind of strong liquor, chain smoked Texan unfiltered, and wore either divided skirts or a tracksuit. She even wore the grey flannel skirts on Speech Day, when everyone on the staff wore their best. We never, ever saw her in a dress. She had thin, tanned brown, hairy legs and a leathery face like a bulldog's, and her lank, greasy hair was cut in a salt-and-pepper Eton Crop.

Mort lived in a tiny, two-berth caravan in the school grounds with the singing mistress, who looked a bit like, and had modelled herself on, Julie Andrews in *The Sound of Music*. Their caravan was parked in the driveway, near the chapel, next to the staff house, and was the first thing one saw as one drove into the College. I don't know what the powers-that-be were thinking of when they allowed this set-up.

We, as girls, didn't have any real idea of what was going on.

There were rumours that these two were lezzies, but not many of us would have known what one was. But there the caravan sat, and we who had to walk past it to get to early morning prep, or early church services, couldn't help but notice that the windows were always all steamed up on the inside, or that there were several empty *Klipdrift* half-jacks (bottles) among a sea of cigarette-butts on and around the caravan doorstep early every morning.

At swimming lessons Mort stood under the diving board and made all the new girls dive in head first, first from the low board, and then from the high diving board, which was terrifyingly high.

We stood and shivered up there, teeth chattering with fright as she stood there, hands on her hips, whistle in her mouth and cigarette spiralling smoke from her wizened knuckles in the chilly six o'clock morning air.

"Dive, Ross!" she'd yell in her hoarse, ginny voice, as I trembled there, the water looking as though it was a mile down.

When I finally took the plunge, I hit the water clumsily, filled my sinuses with vile-tasting over-chlorinated pool water, and had to drag myself out onto the side, spluttering and choking, while Mort looked at me scornfully, and crossed me off as a possible diver on the clipboard in her hand. This was on a Saturday morning.

Although Boarding school was a private school, it still received some sort of grant from the Afrikaner Nationalist Government, and we were forced to learn Afrikaans so as to follow the national curriculum, and pass the national Matriculation Board's exam in order to get a university pass. We had four slightly shorter terms than the government schools got, and minimally longer holidays, as our school opted to work on Saturdays. We were allowed out from ten until six on three Sundays a term. That meant out after church or chapel, and back (in my case) sunburned and smelling of horse sweat. With our white dresses, we had to wear lisle stockings, which had shrunk in the school wash so badly that they barely came over my very long legs and only just reached my knees. To hold these up, we had suspender belts, with a sort of rubber knob and metal loop thing that we'd have to somehow hook our stockings into, to make them stay up. I had to let my suspender belt dangling pieces down to their utmost length in order for them to be able to reach my knee-length stockings, which meant I had a bare expanse of exposed skin, which got splinters in it from the wooden schoolroom chairs, and of course the pews and dining-room chairs, too. The knobs of my suspender belt also bit into my flesh as I sat down anywhere, and pinched me with the little metal loops.

My love for religion didn't increase when, after a wonderful day out on the farm, eating roast lamb, ice cream and galloping Rocket over the veldt, with the dogs running behind, their pink tongues lolling out in the heat, I had to force myself back into my uniform and spend an hour on my bony knees, praying to some remote and completely mysterious deity. The uniform (including my new, cheap WG Brown bra – Mum bought everything she could from there as we got a discount being shareholders) – scratched my newly burned skin, and the new shoes hurt my feet. I was full and sleepy, and I knew the rewards of my evening were an hour more of this, and then the usual Sunday night supper of a small square of cracked and sweating cheddar, the size of a matchbox, a bowl of dish-watery soup, and bed, with the unlovely prospect of having to get up the next morning at six when the early morning bell shrilled in my ear, and thus the week would go on, the next ray of hope in sight being another Sunday, far, far away in the foreseeable future.

In my second term I became depressed and exhausted, unable to find any reward in the daily grind of prep, chapel, lessons, meals, more prep, and finally more chapel or church. I hated it all equally, and sought the odd half-hour I could snatch here and there to read my precious library books. I was still having bad growing pains, and since I was eating virtually nothing, I had absolutely no reserves of energy, which made me lethargic at the best of times. I longed to lie in bed or in a warm, sunny place and be left to read in peace.

I turned out to be reasonably good at tennis, although not good enough to be picked for anything other than reserve for the inter-house tennis match. Again, I found the difference from playing barefoot on our nice slow, cool grass court at home a far cry from tearing around in the baking heat which blasted off these forgivingly fast concrete courts, wearing thin-soled tennis shoes. I got a migraine on my first day playing in the middle of the summer heat (it never got as hot on the farm as we were nearly 6 000 feet up in the mountains) near Pietermaritzburg, one of the hottest towns in Natal. Although there were taps strategically placed for that very purpose at each court, Mort never allowed us to have a drink of water or wet our steaming, sun-baked heads in between sets. It was my first migraine, and I felt as if somebody had hit me over the head with a sledgehammer, accompanied by severe nausea. Mort made me play on, even though I was so obviously blinded from the headache, and staggering around in agony.

Gymnastics was easy. All my tree climbing skills came into play as I swarmed easily up the rope and touched the ceiling. while other girls in my form dangled and sobbed from the ropes below me. My reward from Mort was her slashing at my bare skinny legs with the string of her whistle, leaving a red weal on my skin. I was supple and light, and could do the gymnastics well, leaving her to concentrate on my more lumpen classmates, who struggled with vaulting over the horse as she pretended to catch them, but I saw her step smartly back as they flung themselves over, leaving them to crash onto the mat on their backs, completely winded.

I was also quite good at athletics, and could run fast, hurdle, and jump fairly long and high. But I had no competitive streak in me. It had been whipped out of me by my sisters, who never liked to be beaten at anything, and one's reward for winning at whatever competition we had going on, was a pounding. So I hung back and didn't give anything like my full effort. Ingrained in me was the prospect of a beating from somebody, not praise.

Mort's attitude didn't help. She had her little clutch of favourites. Not unsurprisingly, they were the girls who were good at the various forms of sport, and these she nurtured in her creepy way, spending far longer coaching them than was entirely healthy to the rest of us, who actually needed the input.

The rest of us were left to sink or swim, and got berated by her, even if we'd put all our full effort into doing something. She never gave out praise unless we were one of her pets, and no encouragement if she saw us doing our best, not even a grunt.

By far my worst moment with Mort was my first ever hockey lesson. There, at the edge of the field lay a pile of sticks with one flat, curved end. Mort handed out some red and white vests, divided us into two teams, blew her whistle and pointed at the sticks.

We picked them up, and glancing around I saw what end to hold. Then she issued orders. "Ross! You play right wing!" she yelled hoarsely at me. I looked around and saw the girls who'd been at the Prep and had already learned to play hockey, jostling around each other. The other new girls seemed to know what to do as well.

Then, when the whistle blew again, all the girls started to run towards one end of the pitch. I ran with them, and when they turned to run back, turned back with them. I had no idea what else to do. The whistle shrilled again.

"Ross! What the bloody hell are you doing?" Mort bellowed at me. "When the ball comes your way, stop it!" I never caught on to the rules, and continued to run with the ball, while Mort swore at me from the side-lines.

We had science lessons in a wonderful dungeon-like science room that had exciting little Bunsen burner taps at each desk. On the walls were skeletons and huge jars containing the pickled remains of various creatures, including some foetuses. One afternoon, after the pickled things had become so cloudy that one could barely see them, the science mistress instructed us to pour out all the formalin and put fresh liquid in from some drums she had ordered. Without gloves or masks, and entombed in the basement classroom, we did as we were instructed. It was quite a pleasant task, as it didn't involve taking down copious notes from the blackboard, so I thought nothing of it other than feeling a bit odd afterwards.

That evening we had fish in white sauce, one of the few dishes that I could bring myself to eat, and had two helpings, as I was hungry. At about two the following morning I was suddenly and copiously sick. I hadn't time to run to the upstairs loo, so I was sick on the wooden, slatted floor, and again and again, until all I could heave up was bile. Somebody called the house-matron, who glared at me and told me to clean up the mess, handing me a mop, some disinfectant, and a bucket. Once I'd sort of managed to clear up the worst of it (I'd never seen a mop before in my life) I sank back dizzily on to my bed and stayed there till dawn, when the bell rang. I continued to lie still, my stomach heaving, until the matron came to inspect the dorm for tidiness and found me still lying there.

"If you're sick you belong in the San, not here," she snapped at me. And I dragged my weak, aching body off the bed, and all the way to the San. The sister looked at me, said nothing, but took me to a chilly looking single bed ward, told me to undress and put on a San nightie.

"I'll get someone to bring your night things down," she told me coldly, and left.

Nausea came over me again, just as suddenly as it had during the night, and as I couldn't find a receptacle to be sick in, nor could I find the bathrooms as she hadn't shown me where they were, threw up on the floor again. Sister was furious.

"Who do you think is going to clean up that mess?" she shrieked at me. "Don't you dare think it's going to be me, because I don't do that sort of thing." So once again I was handed a mop and a bucket, and groggily tried to clean up. I could barely stand by now, ill, dehydrated and exhausted from the long walk from Macrorie to the San, I felt half-dead. When I was finally allowed back into bed, I fell into a delirious sort of half sleep, only to be woken by Sister, who thrust a half glass of water and a bitter-tasting pill at me. I drank the water greedily, thirsty from dehydration, and managed to keep it all down.

I was kept in the San for three days. I was allowed only a plastic mug of unsweetened black tea and two *Marie* biscuits (flat, dry, cardboard-like), three times a day, and my strength didn't bounce back. I was given a tiny portion of poached white fish in parsley sauce on my third and last evening, and, half-starved, I wolfed it down. It stayed down, and I was released back to the hurly-burly of school life. During my three days in the San I'd been allowed to pick a couple of books from the small library (a few bookshelves of novels) to read while I languished in bed. This brought my dream of being left alone to read true, and I found it an unexpectedly pleasant surprise amongst all the physical misery I was going through.

I was still weak and dizzy from my mystery illness and had lost ill-afforded weight on the austere diet (I never discovered whether it was the formalin or the fish, or just a tummy bug that got me) but none of the other girls became ill that night, just me, possibly because my resistance was down due to my already fragile state of health. I had to catch up with the others, get my missed work from Mary, and generally cope with day to day life in the fast lane, now at the disadvantage of feeling weaker and having even less energy. I had never learned how to learn. Since I'd had such poor grounding, I didn't know how to revise or take notes as the other girls seemed to be doing. The method of teaching was for our teachers to write copious notes on the blackboard out of our textbooks, and we'd copy them down in class. Or they would dictate out of our textbooks, reams and reams of work, which we had to write into jotters, and then copy neatly into our notebooks for homework.

Sometimes the teachers passed out roneoed sheets with sections of our textbooks copied onto them, or they just told us to copy out pages and pages from our text books – even the drawings in the case of Geography and Biology. I laboriously copied down everything, and when told to 'revise' part of it for a test the following day, didn't know what the word really meant. So I'd sit and stare at the work, none the wiser.

In class, if we weren't taking notes, I would sit and daydream, tuning out the teacher's droning voice and gaze out at the school grounds where I could see a Zulu gardener pushing a lawn-mower over the kikuyu grass next to the San. Oh, how I envied him his freedom! There he got to be out in the glorious sunshine, with the scent of flowering jasmine in the air and that delicious smell of freshly cut green grass, while I was trapped, cooped up in the cold classroom, with nothing to do except wait for the bell to ring and release me to go to yet another boring lesson, or lunch.

Ironically, given the chance, I would have gladly changed places with him, and, unbeknown to me, he would have done the same, rather than face what was left of his life (Africans don't have nearly as long a life-span as Europeans do) doing hard manual labour.

Lunch went like this: Mondays, beef stew and boiled potatoes with stewed pumpkin. The meat was sour and so over-cooked it had become grey string held together by gristle. It had also stuck to the bottom of the pot and got burnt, so had a bitter taste. The vegetables had also been boiled for so long that they had become string and yellow water. Pudding was frogspawn.

Tuesdays was cottage pie minced from the leftover stew, and had exactly the same sour taste. The potato topping had developed a mysterious pool of yellowish, transparent grease floating on the top. The same vegetables, and pudding was 'dead dog', a long pastry rolled up, with jam oozing out of the sides, and lumpy, tasteless custard.

Wednesday was the best. Sausages, although they'd been cooked for so long that they were merely tough, hard mahogany-coloured skin with the tiniest amount of edible sausage inside.

These at least came with mashed potatoes. Just mashed, there was so seasoning, no milk or butter to make it palatable, and a fork full of them was like taking a mouthful of wallpaper glue.

Pudding was 'mud and toenails': a tasteless, glutinous dark brown-coloured 'blancmange' covered in grated coconut.

Thursday was that sour, scorched beef stew again, or sometimes meatballs, which the girls said with glee, had been rolled under William's (the Zulu head cook) sweaty armpits.

These were accompanied by rice (like at the Prep) or plain boiled potatoes, and the same old veggies inevitably 'boiled to buggery' (as Mum sometime called Masango's veg when he was having an off day and concentrating more on his fat, rolled up spliff than his cooking). With that came a pudding called 'syrup mattress': a large square of sponge-cake baked in a tin, turned out and had golden syrup poured all over it.

Fridays was fish, deep fried in extremely greasy, ill-drained batter, and soggy chips with a slice of lemon. Pudding would be frogspawn again, or one of the others. Saturdays we had steak-and-kidney pies, bought in from the 'Maritzburg bakery, which were quite nice, and were accompanied by salads of grated carrots, beetroot, tomato and lettuce. Pudding was a permutation of the ones I've mentioned Sundays we got roast beef (flat, hard, stringy grey meat like we'd had at the Prep) the same leathery, anaemic roast potatoes and watery, stringy pale grey cabbage with a bit of thin, transparent gravy poured over. The best pudding of the week was a small scoop of vanilla ice cream, which was plonked into the bowls far too early, and by the time we got it, had completely melted, and become warm, sweet milk with a froth on top.

Breakfasts from Mondays to Saturdays were lumpy mealie meal porridge, bread and bananas. Perfect food for adolescent girls, most of whom were already trying to stick to a slimming diet.

Suppers were a range of watery macaroni cheese with chunks of stewed tomato in it, hard-boiled eggs in an insipid cheese sauce, Welsh Rarebit (a slice of brown bread under that same sauce) or, my favourite, steamed hake in a parsley sauce. We always had an apple for afters. The girls always seemed to be hungry and, as a result, talked incessantly about food. They said their portions were too small, but I felt the opposite, and always pushed mine around my plate until the handbell to signal the end of the meal was rung by the mistress on duty, and the dining-hall full of girls rang with the sound of chairs being scraped back as we all stood up for grace. What with all the talking we had to do, and the short time we were allocated our meals, the other girls had to wolf down their food before those sinisterly perceived black hands whisked their plates away.

# White Zulu

Fiona Ross

Towards the end of the term I became ill again, nothing other than a very bad cold, but I felt awful, and took myself down to the San, hoping for a lie-down in the day sickroom. It was a lovely big room, with one side of French windows, which allowed the room to fill with sunlight that warmed the half dozen or so beds in there. The bedspreads were a cheerful yellow, the pillows soft and inviting, and there was usually a girl or two in there who was suffering from bad period cramps, or a migraine.

Sister gave me a huge dose of her very own 'cold mixture'; some vile concoction based on eucalyptus which I'm sure was for external use only, but which she watched sharply while I worried it down, gagging and spluttering. As my eyes watered from the fumes it gave off, she led me to a single bed ward which looked onto the brick wall of Francis Baines (FB) house.

"I don't want you giving your cold to any of the other girls here," Sister told me, and left me there, to climb, shivering into the hard hospital bed. Later on, bored out of my mind, I asked her if I could have a book to read from the day room, and she grudgingly fetched one for me, throwing it onto the end of my bed with a snort of disgust, while I snuffled my thanks.

The only ray of sunshine in the San was when the Zulu San maid brought me my tray of 'food'. She reminded me of Evalina, as she was plump and motherly and just as cheerful. She'd be amazed at my command of her language to start with, and then she'd cluck and click with dismay on hearing my symptoms, genuinely appearing sorry to hear how awful I felt. Then, if the San wasn't busy, and Sister wasn't lurking nearby, the maid would settle on her plump haunches and regale me with a little about herself. Invariably she'd know somebody from iMpendhle, or would have come from there herself, and knew Evalina or Lisha, or anyone of our farm Zulu's tribe well, and we'd chat about them, my horse, how many cattle and sheep my father had and other various subjects so important to both of us.

I say 'food,' because the San policy was to starve the girls, no matter what ailed them, so, even with a head cold, I got watery, unsalted *Bovril* soup with the inevitable dry cardboard like *Marie* biscuits. If you dunked your biscuit into the weak black tea or *Bovril*, it turned so sloppy that the wet piece fell instantly back into the drink, leaving you to try and fish the tiny, soggy bits out with the plastic teaspoon provided. It was a very high price to pay to lie in bed while the rising bell went, or to stay snug and warm while the girls clattered to class and chapel. The rewards were free time to read books, but the downside was Sister and her unforgiving suspicion that I was putting on my illness, as well as the distant way the other girls treated me once I got out.

Mistrustful of me at the best of times, they automatically (and sometimes correctly) assumed that I was spending time in the San to get out of doing any schoolwork. The San was seen, rightly as it turned out, to be the last place on earth one went when one wasn't feeling well. Shamming was one of the most scorned weaknesses one could succumb to, and I was looked upon as the biggest shammer in the class, if not in the school.

Once back in my classroom, I was hopelessly out of my depth as there were huge gaps in my notebooks and jotter where I'd missed lessons and hadn't had a chance to catch up, or, more accurately, read my library books in my spare time rather than copy out the missed work from Mary's neat handwriting.

I went back to daydreaming in class. Every time a small aeroplane buzzed over, above the school, I gazed up at it, yearningly, as it made its slow way across the vast burning blue sky, wishing I was in it, flying it. I had always been fascinated by planes of every description, inspired by the fact that Dad had been a pilot, and by reading all his war flying books. I became more and more obsessed with flying. I found a beautiful big book in the library, *Serengeti shall not die*, written by a man, Bernhard Grzimek, who had a beef and game ranch alongside the Serengeti Game Reserve in Kenya.

They'd had a son, Michael, who'd been mad about flying and photographing game, and owned his own little Cessna two-seater, painted in black and white stripes exactly like a Zebra's coat. The book had the most wonderful full colour illustrations, photos taken by the son, of various big game animals, as well as herds of zebra and wildebeest; and best of all it had a full-sized photograph of Michael himself, in the frontispiece.

Tragically, the book was dedicated to him by his parents as he'd died in his own plane in a crash on the Serengeti at the age of 20. The plane had collided with a vulture. This made me very sad, and I fell in love with his image, there, tanned and with his sun-bleached hair blowing in some warm Kenyan breeze. He was leaning against the zebra striped plane, his blue eyes crinkling attractively against the glare of the African sun. I was mesmerised by his beauty, captured there for eternity, and in some way I felt I owned him, as there would be no girlfriends for him, nor a family life in the future with a wife and children. All this made it safe for me to fall in love with him.

I began to shelve my veterinary ambitions, and started reading every book on flying I could find in the school library. Like Dad and Grandpa, they also had a collection of the old Second World War heroes, such as Douglas Bader, among many others, and I devoured them all. I found encyclopaedias, and read them from cover to cover too, drinking in all the knowledge they contained.

I found one that described Morse code, and had all the coded alphabetical signals written down. I copied these out carefully and memorised them. I also found and learned the air alphabet with far more care than I ever put into any of my schoolwork.

Our airstrip on the farm was occasionally used by friends with planes, and one, a cousin of my father's, Dave Carlisle, had been a pilot in the war alongside Dad. Dave had kept up his licence, however, and flew a small plane owned by WG Brown & Co.

The small trading stores in every town in Zululand and Natal were scattered so far and wide that the aircraft was the ideal vehicle for Dave to go around checking that his customers were receiving their orders; our family, including all our cousins, called him 'The Flying Grocer'. I'd changed my mind about my future, and decided that I was going to be a pilot – preferably a fighter pilot.

I kept my aspirations to myself after having mentioned them to Dad during one Sunday out and found that he scoffed at the very idea. "All you'll end up as is a glorified bus or taxi driver," he sneered. "And the South African Air Force certainly wouldn't take women (he spat the word out) as pilots!"

Dad had never got over the fact that women had been admitted into Cambridge after he'd left there sometime around 1938. He was utterly disgusted when he received the news in his Jesus College Old Boys' magazine. Apoplectic with rage, he went on and on about it at the dining-room table, right up until we'd grown up and left home and had children of our own. So instead of listening in class, or doing my prep, I stared out of the window and watched every plane go by overhead, mentally grasping the joystick, my feet operating the rudders. I daydreamed happily about owning my little two-seater zebra-striped Cessna, practised assiduously at my Morse and Alphabet codes, and did no schoolwork whatsoever.

In Second Form we did quite a wide range of subjects, including Maths, Science and Art, but later on we'd have to choose the six subjects we would need for Matric. At the time I was learning Latin and French as well as English and Afrikaans. I loved Latin and French, and picked them up very easily as I was already bilingual in Zulu and English – well – my English had improved enormously now that I was in among fellow speakers, but there were still occasions when I only knew the Zulu word for things, like parts of the body, as we only used the Zulu words for those at home, even to my mother. I had no English words for bodily functions either, which could have been a problem except that Mary helped me out a lot as her English vocabulary was far better than mine, having not had quite such a haphazard upbringing as I had. She had normal parents who didn't treat their children as a nuisance as ours did.

My maths was a joke. Mrs Bannatyne had taught us absolutely nothing, I'd learned to count sheep the Zulu way, and that was the sum total of my knowledge of arithmetic. I could neither add nor subtract, divide, or any of the other tricks one was supposed to perform with numbers. The whole subject was a blank to me, and being shouted at by Miss Park-Ross (mercifully no relation) didn't teach me anything other than to get into a blind panic and put down whatever figure came into my head. I 'see' numbers and letters in my head anyway, as apparently some people do, and I don't know if that was a help or a hindrance. The number five, for instance, is a chunky character, large and light green in colour, and ten is a shiny silver, like those little dragée beads on a birthday cake.

Because boarding school is situated about ten miles out of 'Maritzburg, our capital city, it was just too far for teachers (all women) to commute to work, so we had a staff house (a bungalow as old as Macrorie), where they could live, and a staff dining-room in the main building. This type of accommodation attracted middle-aged (elderly to us) spinsters, or young women fresh out of Teaching College or university, most of whom taught the junior classes, but all of whom got married and left after just a couple of terms.

We also got stuck with grim, humourless unmarried matrons who lived in their own bed-sits in our houses, and to me our teachers, headed by Dot, were all a prime example of thin-lipped, stick-dry old hags who encouraged the girls who were already doing well in class, and either berated or ignored those who weren't. I far preferred the latter.

Naturally these women failed to bring lessons to life, they simply regurgitated the facts and figures in indigestible chunks. I could be wrong, as there were girls who thrived on lessons, and worked hard and did their best to absorb their teaching with no trouble at all, but since my experience with Mrs Bannatyne, I had built up a strong resistance to being taught, unless the lesson was delivered in the same way as Mr Lamb had, with emphasis and enthusiasm for the subject whatever it was. It was also assumed, in my case, that I had done at least some of the ground work, but unfortunately not so, so I was immediately out of my depth, particularly when it came to arithmetic, and, since I couldn't understand what was going on in class generally, I lost interest and stared out of the window.

Five years into my time at school, I reached the form taught by a very good English teacher. She was a married woman who lived in Hilton Road, and thus was able to commute in her little Volkswagen Beetle. She was wonderfully encouraging towards us all, and especially me in my compositions. These were invariably done in extreme haste, because I had forgotten that I had to write one during prep, and had to frantically scribble one out during our morning break, while the others were lining up in the courtyard for lukewarm, pre-sweetened milky tea and a dry sandwich.

The sandwiches had the margarine scraped on and then scratched off again, and a microscopic bit of cheap fish-paste smeared afterwards by the unsupervised Zulu kitchen staff. We suspected, correctly as it turned out, that William, the head of the Zulu kitchen staff, was selling the school's butter, along with other commodities, to a freelance Indian salesman, who'd then sell it to local trading stores.

The tea was poured into scratched, evil-smelling and most unhygienic plastic mugs, and was utterly revolting. Our only other choice was to drink the heavily chlorinated water out of the taps if one was thirsty, however cold the weather was.

Our patient English teacher always managed to decipher my inky (we still used fountain-pens, ball-points were forbidden as it 'ruined our handwriting', and my pens always leaked profusely) compositions and read it out to the class, who applauded. She always put my writing, both poetry and essays, into the school magazine, which came out annually, and impressed Dad. I wrote an essay on 'Falling Asleep when One Shouldn't' and made it sound so realistic that Mum insisted that I be taken to see a specialist endocrinologist. No amount of trying to explain to her that it was fiction could sway her.

"But you sound like a dormouse! There has to be something wrong with your glands or something," she insisted, as Dad and I told her repeatedly that I'd made it all up. Eventually, Dad put the idea out of her head somehow (although I wished they'd done something about my hay fever as well as the utter exhaustion and lethargy I was constantly struggling with). That essay might have been a forecast of how my life would eventually turn out.

The water had been another shock to me. Used to the sweet spring water that was piped from the little reservoir surrounded by ferns and wild flowers, up in the plantation behind our house at home, I opened a tap into a washbasin in the Macrorie bathroom and was once again met with a blast of chlorine in my face, bringing back the association I have with public lavatories. Hilton Road Municipality had such a problem with their water treatment that Dine caught diphtheria in her first year there, and had to be quarantined in the San while they did swabs and confirmed that it was definitely the disease. This led them to over-chlorinate the water even more, making it completely undrinkable.

At last that first term ended. Six weeks and several snowy postcards from Mum later, she came to fetch us for our Easter holidays. All the way home the four of us moaned bitterly about how dreadful school was, and Mum took no notice, other than to pour herself an extra gin and tonic before lunch once we'd got home and the servants had unpacked the car of our overnight bags. It was only when it came to Evalina and Lisha unpacking our trunks the next day that Mum discovered that I'd packed my hot-water bottle still full. She went on and on about how stupid I'd been to do such a thing. Personally I didn't see what all the fuss was about.

The other problem that made Mum go on about, was how much stuff was missing from the list of uniforms we'd taken with us. The school laundry staff were notoriously light-fingered, but Mum couldn't see this, and harangued and blamed us, especially me as I was the most careless about losing expensive garments that she'd now have to replace, which she insisted they could ill afford on a farmer's income. She seemed to have forgotten that she'd stepped off a ski slope and onto a private yacht in the Med a couple of weeks before.

Admittedly, I was always leaving my things lying around. I was in a perpetual daze, constantly had my nose in a library book, and absent-mindedly (this gave rise to my nickname 'The Professor' or just 'Prof') left my jerseys, blazers, and library books wherever I'd put them last. The school had a 'lost property box' which was filled with garments, and the head girl used to stand at the top of the stairs while we lined up in the gym for our meals, chapel, or church, and call out the items she held up from the box. Each time, five times a day or more, I had to traipse up, in front of the school, and reclaim my clothing. If one had lost items more than once a week there were punishments of detention and more poetry or lines to be completed.

My library books were always giving me heart failure, because if they were late I had to pay a fine, and if lost it, pay for the book. Since Mum was such a bad sport about my losing things anyway, she'd have had apoplexy if I (she) had to shell out for lost books on a regular basis, but fortunately there was a system whereby kind-hearted girls would pick up missing books from under a tree in the grounds, or a bench in the corridor, where I'd been reading, and return them to the library on my behalf, leaving me to pay only the fine.

The second term ended, and we had a lovely July holiday of three weeks. Me out on Rocket with the dogs every morning and a lively set of tennis in the early afternoons with the rest of the family.

My third term came and reluctantly I dragged myself back

into the school routine. We'd been back at school about four weeks when I was called out of class by one of the staff. In the main walkway, near the Chapel, I found my two older sisters waiting for me. Apparently, Mum and Dad had arrived and wanted to tell us something. We got to the car, which was standing in the driveway, and Mum and Dad told us that Grandpa had died, and then, having nothing else to say to us, they drove away. The three of us turned to go back to our classes, and then it hit home to me. I was twelve, and my best friend in the whole world was dead. I burst into tears, and began to sob quietly. My oldest sister hissed at me.

"Shut up! Stop crying! People like us don't cry!" I stopped, shocked at her tone (and I didn't want a slap, which she would have given me if I hadn't). So we walked along in silence, me giving the odd hiccough now and again. Back into class and to carry on as though nothing had happened. I didn't understand why I hadn't been allowed to cry. Other girls cried when their pets died, what made us so different? Grandpa's death affected me so badly that I began to sleepwalk, sometimes waking up from a vivid nightmare, to find myself outside Macrorie, and in the main corridor.

It was the winter term, and like at home there was frost on the ground outside. Hilton was also in the mist belt, and had a similar climate to ours, but there was much more mist, and no snow at all, although we could see snow on the iNhlosane mountain range where iMpendhle and our farm was.

Early morning swimming was replaced by rehearsals for the inter-house gymnastic display, and Macrorie held their practices on Saturday mornings on the hockey field. We rolled around in the dark, at six o'clock, in the frost, getting our black bloomers and thin cotton T-shirts muddy, while our coach, a prefect, shouted instructions to us through a bull horn. After that we had to get changed and go to breakfast, our teeth chattering with cold. I kept getting one head cold after another and then had a terrible dose of 'flu which sent me into the San again for another few days of starvation, Sister's vile concoctions, and blissful rest with unlimited access to the day room bookshelf.

Second formers had to have their baths in the afternoons, as bathing at night was strictly reserved for the Sixth formers. I spent my evenings getting colder and colder until bedtime came and my feet were like blocks of ice. We had hot-water bottles, but for some reason (the cheapest Mum could find, I suspect) mine always seemed to spring a leak at the beginning of term and had to be thrown away. I lay in bed shivering, and my feet seemed as if they'd been amputated from the knees down.

Nothing I tried warmed them. I put clothes around them, trying to improvise a pair of bed socks, but to no avail, I'd inherited Dad's poor circulation.

We had Michaelmas holidays, two weeks in the spring, and then back for my last term in Second Form. Several weeks into the term, during lunch, just before grace was said, when Dot read out the names of girls she wanted to see after lunch, she called out, "Ross, F see me after lunch." I froze in shock, frantically searching my mind for what reason she wanted to see me. I cast my mind all over, trying to remember how many detentions I'd done, how many punishments I'd performed for the prefects, and the fact that I'd knocked out the head of house some time back. The fact that Dot, of all people, wanted to see me was the most terrifying one, as it would never bode well for the girls whose names were called out. The other girls around me eyed me, some with curiosity and others with contempt. Mary looked at me with pity. My sisters turned to look the other way when I gazed at them beseechingly to try and get an inkling as to why I was being called up to see the headmistress. Perhaps I was to be expelled? Oh, God! That was it. Now Dad would come and take me away in disgrace and none of my family would ever speak to me again.

Lunch seemed to take forever, and my mouth was bone-dry with nerves, so I didn't touch my food. When grace was said to end the meal, I walked over to Dot's study in the main corridor and stood there, my heart fluttering in my chest like a trapped bird.

I could hardly breathe with fright. I knocked timidly and when the green light came on over her door, indicating that I open it, I pushed it open slowly.

Dot was seated, looking at something on her desk by the big sash window, which overlooked the front lawn. This was the first time I'd ever been in to her study. "We have decided," she said coldly after a long pause and with no preamble, "that you are to stay another year in Second Form, so we are keeping you back a year." I stared at her dumbfounded. Trying to understand the words. My first and only reaction was massive relief that I wasn't in trouble.

"Thank you," I stammered. And stood there dumbly.

"You may go," she said with the same chilly detachment with which she'd given me the first bit of news.

I backed quickly, found the doorknob without really looking, and left the room, closing the door very carefully on my way out, just in case she'd changed her mind and had a punishment for me after all. The news that I was to spend another year in Second Form didn't sink in at all, and I carried on to the end of that term, and the school year, without giving it another thought.

During the lovely long Christmas holidays out on horseback and playing tennis and swimming again, not a word was said by either of my parents or even my sisters about this bit of news, so it slipped to the back of my mind. Years later, when I did ask Mum and Dad why I was kept down a year to repeat Second Form, they said dismissively, "Oh, you were too young for your class, as you went to school on your twelfth birthday, and all the others in your form were at least six months older than you. Also you'd missed so much work by being in the San that we thought it was better that you repeat the year."

That was it. Neither they nor my form mistress, not even Dot, had thought to discuss the matter with me, or even tell me what they'd planned. But that was so typical of the way our parents and the school staff handled things.

Nicolette had dropped too many subjects to be able to write Matric, so she left in Fifth Form, the year after I arrived at the College. Dine was crafty and quietly dropped so many subjects that, only after she'd done it, and the school wrote to Mum and Dad to tell them of the fact, did they and the staff realise that she wouldn't be able to take Matric either, so she also dropped out in Fifth Form, a year later. There was a lot of shouting about Dine's trickery, but the deed was done, and all they could do was yell at her for a bit, and then complain over a gin and tonic about the shoddy quality of the teaching at the college.

~~~

# *38*

# Second Form again

**O**n my thirteenth birthday, Evalina once again packed my trunk, and Delia, Dine and I went to back to Boarding School College – Delia for her first year there, and Dine for her last. Nicolette went to a small residential finishing school in a small town called Kloof, near Durban.

Arriving back at College on my birthday meant I missed my school birthday. There was a tradition of the girls giving each other little gifts if their birthdays fell during the term. I'd seen the presents being exchanged, and had myself given presents.

The current rage in Second Form was tiny China animals, especially horses, as we were allowed those on display, and I'd chosen the lovely little white horse ornaments that came with the crates of *White Horse Whiskey* Dad ordered by the dozen. I had about six of them, and had wrapped them up in birthday paper purloined from Mum's drawer in Dad's huge desk. I never received any China ornaments though, or anything else for that matter at school on my own birthdays, as there was far too much going on, with unpacking trunks and saying goodbye to parents for the extra-long term that lay ahead.

Mum and Dad went overseas again, to ski with friends in Switzerland.

I was pleased to see all the old, familiar faces, like Mary's, and we greeted each other with warmth. But then the shock hit as the school bell rang for us to line up for chapel. All my classmates lined up in Third Form, and I had to go and line up with the Second Formers, all of them strangers, except for my cousin, who was a year younger than me, and had come from Jo'burg. Feeling like a total loser, I slunk off to the back of the line and stood there. The enormity of what had happened to me – another year at the college in Second Form, with all the fagging still ahead of me – hit me like a sledgehammer. I whimpered to myself, but there was nobody and nothing to console me.

After chapel and supper, when we were settling in the dorm, my old classmates popped their heads in to say hello and the new girls looked at me with new eyes. I seemed to know a lot of girls, and I also knew what was going on, and which bell meant what. Suddenly I became popular, and all the new girls latched on to me as if I was their mentor. I also had a good, friendly relationship with most of the Third Formers, so I had a foot in both camps. This gave me enormous confidence and I began to show off, and clown around, making everybody laugh. Their positive attention was manna to me, and I thrived on it, adding more and more daring to the practical jokes I played on prefects and staff alike.

For example, I managed to catch a young bantam rooster when, bored and looking for mischief, I was mooching around the African staff compound (somewhere we were strictly forbidden from going). I managed to corner the fowl and threw my cardigan over it as it crouched, trapped in a corner of a chicken wire fence on the ash pile. Filthy with ash, feathers, fowl dung, and a new hole in my jersey, I smuggled the bird into the school dining-hall and hid it under the stage-like platform where the headmistress and staff ate. There was a deep space between where they sat and where they put their feet, and it was so dark down there that the bantam lay quite still and no one could see it. I nipped out again, just as the bell to line up for lunch rang. The effect during grace was extremely satisfying, when the bantam, startled by one of the teachers putting her foot onto it, flew into the air shrieking with fright, and the stiff, staid old spinsters scuttled about in all directions screaming as it fled out of the hall squawking and flapping its stumpy little wings. Only the girls in my form knew who the culprit was, and nobody turned me in, so it was another triumph for my ego.

For a change, I was surrounded by friends wherever I went, and I really enjoyed the sensation of being, if not popular, at least accepted as one of their peers. The fagging was a bore, but I was so used to it by now that it didn't really bother me; I did it all so badly anyway, and I think the new prefects began to despair of me, because they had lots more, brand new and fresh victims. I got away with a lot in my second year as a junior. The work was all repetition, and I had all my notes written out from the first year, so I just coasted. It was a poor reflection of the staff and their standards of teaching then that they didn't keep an eye on me, but let me stare out of the window again.

I carried on clowning around to amuse my fellow pupils, as well as immersing myself back in all my favourite library books, especially the one on the young man from the Serengeti. He haunted me and took over my thoughts on every occasion there was to daydream. And there were plenty of opportunities. I'd grab a seat at the back of the class for myself, and stay there, not participating in anything unless called upon. If I was asked a question by a teacher, I always knew the correct answer, as I'd heard it all before, and must have absorbed the knowledge by osmosis. I still didn't know how to learn, and simply sat and stared at pages of my so-called prep, with my mind far away, flying over the bush veldt in my tiny two-seater Zebra-striped Cessna. I was blessed with a photographic memory, so I could look at a page and see the thing as a picture, including the contents, and if I'd applied myself just the tiniest bit, I would have been top of the class every time.

I was stilled called 'the Professor' due to my absent-mindedness, and also because I always had my nose in a book while the others played together, or socialised. Now and again, I popped down to the San for a break from the hectic school life. I was still having my exhausted-cannot-get-up-days, but I'd learned that, if there was something going around be it a tummy bug, or 'flu or whatever, I'd present myself to Sister complaining of those symptoms. She'd check me over, take my temperature and pulse and find nothing wrong with me, but to be on the safe side, because I insisted that I had that same sore throat, swollen glands or headache or tummy ache, that she'd better keep me in overnight anyway and starve me just in case. I suppose her opinion of the San was the same as that of the rest of the school: you really had to be desperate to admit yourself.

So I'd have my couple of day's bed-rest and manage to summon up the strength to get back to school.

It was odd that I never had those exhausted days during school holidays, but although I rode and played a lot of sport in the way of swimming and tennis, none of it was competitive, and I also rested a lot lying on a rug in the shade, out of sight of Mum and everybody else, to read for hours on end; the sort of rest I never got at school.

At the end of my second year in Second Form, during the summer holidays, I woke up one morning feeling very peculiar.

My head was hot, my eyes ached and my body felt as though I'd been hit by a truck. It was the day that we were all supposed to be going out to see a film in Howick that night, and I'd been looking forward to it immensely. I tried to drag myself to breakfast, but I must have looked sick because even Mum noticed, and sent me back to bed. "Stay there and I'll come and take your temperature after I've finished my breakfast," she called out to me from the dining-room. I went back and sank my burning head gratefully back onto the cool pillows. Dine followed me.

"Don't you dare mention you're sick now!" she whispered, seething with anger. "You'll make us all miss the film! If you tell Mum you're sick I'll come and punch you!" I knew she meant it.

Mum came in shaking down the glass thermometer she kept in her first-aid cupboard. She stuck the cold tube under my hot dry tongue and said, "I'm just popping out to show Jomela where to mow the lawn. Don't touch that, I'll only be a minute." I lay there and listened to her shouting to Jomela, and then the petrol mower starting up, and I waited, and waited.

About half an hour went by and nothing happened, so I took the thermometer out and peered at it. I couldn't read any little line among the strange numbers there, so I shook it like I'd seen her do, and cracked the glass bulb end on the edge of my bedside table as I brought my arm down sharply as she'd done. There was a loud 'snap', and a little silver ball of mercury shot out of the broken end and landed on my blanket.

I was fascinated, and poked it with my forefinger. It wobbled and broke up into tiny balls that rolled around the blanket and then joined back to the main ball again, just like magic. I spent a happy hour or so playing with my new toy until it was grey with blanket fluff and I was starting to feel really sick. I ran to the loo across the passage from my room and was sick.

I felt absolutely terrible and lay on the cold bathroom floor for a while, resting my feverish forehead against the cool porcelain. Then I dragged myself back to bed, forgot about my silver ball and kicked it off the blanket and onto the floor where it disappeared within the grass matting that served as my bedside rug. I threw the two bits of broken glass out of the open window, into the hydrangeas that grew there, and lay back in bed, my aching head spinning.

I fell into some sort of doze, because I woke to find Mum standing there. "Do you want some lunch? I'll get Evalina to bring you a tray."

She'd completely forgotten that she'd left me in mid-temperature-taking, got herself immersed in her garden, as usual, and completely lost track of time. Luckily for me, she'd also forgotten about the thermometer.

I was really ill, and after a lot of discussion and eventually a rather reluctant phone call to our local GP, I was diagnosed as having measles. Dine was livid with rage as she'd already pulled out her outfit, a sleeveless cotton dress with a stiff petticoat, and hung it inside out in a stocking, to fluff up for the big evening. Mum cancelled the evening out, and there were a lot of sullen faces coming around the furtively opened crack of my now closed bedroom door, and threats to my life from my sisters.

I was too ill to care. Mum's gesture to my measles was to shut the curtains in my bedroom, as recommended by the doctor, and give me her small transistor radio to amuse me. I was forbidden to read at all times for the next five to ten days, and all books were removed from my room. And then she left me alone, quarantined from everybody else, to get on with it.

Evalina brought me food on trays, whatever was being dished up for the rest of the family for their meals, but I didn't want to eat. I was dehydrated and crept to the bathroom to drink from the tap whenever I could muster up the strength to do so.

Nobody had thought to give me a glass of water next to my bed.

The servants had been told to stay away from me as well, just in case they hadn't had measles, as Mum didn't want an epidemic, leaving her with no staff to work in the garden.

There was nothing on the radio worth listening to, as the broadcasts were strictly half and half English and Afrikaans, which I didn't understand (or want to – we had been taught to hate the Afrikaners and everything to do with them first by our parents, and then at school). The English programme was divided into talk and classical music, which I'd also learned to hate. Every Saturday at school, for two hours, our classes were forced to sit absolutely still in the main assembly hall on hard chairs, for 'Musical Appreciation'. Our backs had to be straight, our hands in our laps, and ankles crossed, like ladies, and we had to listen to classical music. Not light stuff either, but chamber music and operas, composed by Purcell, Handel, Gluck and the like. We weren't allowed to take in any knitting, embroidery or any form of handwork either, which made it all the more boring.

We were in our very early teens and had ears only for pop music. The utter tedium of having to sit so uncomfortably still for so long, and be made to listen to such heavy classics, like all the religious stuff, and too much chapel and church, had put me off for life.

So I tried to listen to the radio, but there was nothing on it for a thirteen-year-old, other than the beef market prices and mutton and wool sale figures that Dad listened to on his own transistor at the lunch-table every day anyway.

I turned it off and lay there for hour after hour, feeling terrible and running a fever, with severe headaches and very sore eyes. Eventually, I could stand it no longer, and after listening carefully to hear if anyone was about, crept out of my room into the passage, grabbed a book from the shelves that lined it, and shot back into bed, my head spinning and my heart pounding with the effort.

After the dizziness faded, I opened my book, one I'd read many times before, Enid Blyton's *Island of Adventure*, and began to try and read. The fact the curtains were drawn shut and I was hiding my book under the bedclothes made the light so poor I could hardly see through my aching, watering eyes, but I persevered and read on and on.

Only when somebody came by did I whip my head out from under the blankets and pretend I was dozing. My head throbbed, my eyes stung and sometimes I had to wipe the wateriness away with the edge of the sheet to clear them enough to be able to continue reading, as the letters swam in front of them. But I carried on for the five days, and most nights I was shut in the room with no light. When one book was finished, I'd nip out and grab another one. Once five days were up, and Mum had decided I was well enough to have the curtains open, she let me have a bit more light, but I was still forbidden to read. I was also still to be left in quarantine, although the extremely itchy spots had come out and I was covered from head to toe in them.

My scalp to the soles of my feet were a mass of raised red measles, which drove me nearly mad with the constant itching and even though I was forbidden to scratch them, I did, and made my skin bleed. On one occasion Mum put some calamine lotion on the worst ones, and that was bliss, as the coolness as the stuff soothed the fieriness of the rash, and she left the bottle out on top of the medicine cabinet, meaning to tell Evalina to apply it again whenever I needed it, but got side-tracked in her own world of her garden and forgot, even though I asked her on the few occasions I saw her.

Mum's nursing skills remained as remote as the rest of her mothering instinct. Days would go by when the only person I saw was Evalina, who hurried in to change my bedding, wash me and bring me food. Even then, she'd been told not to linger in case she caught this dreaded disease. Measles did kill a lot of Africans, as it was a disease brought in by the settlers, and the indigenous people had no natural immunity to it. German and ordinary measles, mumps, smallpox, and so many other European illnesses killed many of the native population, particularly the very young, the very old, and the weak ones. So Evalina was quite rightly frightened to either catch it herself, or take the infection home to Impendhle to cause havoc there.

My sisters were also banned from coming anywhere near me, as nobody else had had the disease yet either. Since we'd been so isolated from other white children right up until we went to boarding school, I and my sisters had missed out on all the routine childhood diseases like measles, mumps and German Measles, and I must have picked it up from the San just before I came home for the holidays. I was really very ill with it at the age of thirteen, and can't remember ever being that sick, for so long, with anything else. I stayed in bed (and read furtively) for the required ten days, and was then allowed up. I was feeling so much better by then, and was more than ready to resume my normal life of riding and swimming and everything else we did in the holidays, but I found I was terribly weak, and could barely shuffle to the front veranda where I sat in the deep shade in a cane armchair and read books, legitimately this time.

My eyes had not recovered from their prolonged strain of reading while ill, and under such bad conditions, and they still ached after a while, but I kept quiet about that. I didn't want to have my books confiscated and be forbidden to read again. It was easy for Mum to tell me not to read, but with no other stimulation, what could I do?

~~~

# *39*

# Third Form

**B**ack to school again, this time it was my fourteenth birthday; as usual Mum and Dad went skiing again. Finally I'd broken through the Second Form barrier and had reached Third Form and no more fagging. Third Form was nicer, as we were no longer the juniors and picked on by girls and staff alike, nor did we have any responsibilities either, so we were pretty much free to get on with normal school life. I fell in with a bad lot.

There was a small group of girls, some of whom had arrived as new girls this year, and the others I'd had as friends from the year before. A couple of these were Jo'burg girls, and had never known the discipline of boarding school before. They kicked at the traces, and so did I. Two of them were expelled that year for running away.

One night our house-matron came to us just after suppertime and asked me and a few of the girls I was with, if we'd seen these two recently. I'd heard them discussing something about taking a knife from the kitchen after supper, for something, but hadn't known what they wanted it for. I kept quiet. I wasn't going to shop anybody. The following morning Dot told the school at breakfast, while all kinds of exciting rumours flew around, that the two girls had been caught by the police sent out to search for them while they were trying to catch a train to Jo'burg at a small station near Hilton Road, in the middle of the night, and they'd both been asked to leave – in other words, they were expelled.

That left fewer of our little gang, but we made up for the lack of our numbers by our attempts to entertain ourselves, the others in the class, and try, not very hard, not to get into too much trouble.

My very best friend, a daughter of one of the masters at Hilton College, the boys' private boarding school about five miles away from boarding school, was particularly full of mischief. She managed to pack an air rifle and a box of pellets in her school trunk, and, since we shared a two-bed cubicle, of course I was in on her secret. We borrowed another girl's inflatable teddy bear, a huge thing that she'd won at the Durban Beach front arcades, and had proudly brought back to school to inflate and put on her bed.

Third Formers were allowed a couple more additions to their cubicles than just the china ornaments. We were allowed a soft toy to keep on our beds.

We took the bear down to the back of the school bogs. This was a row of about eight outdoor corrugated iron lavatories, standing on their own behind the gym, which were for the whole school to use when we weren't in class or in our dorms. We set our purloined target up against the back of these foul-smelling outdoor loos and let fly with the pellet gun. Lying like snipers on our bellies in the grass we took turns to fire at the bear, to see who could pop it first. My friend and I were happily thus occupied when we heard screams and quickly got up to look and see what was going on, hiding the rifle in the long grass. What we hadn't realised was that the pellets that missed the bear were hitting the back of the lavs and pinging off the corrugated iron walls, and that a troop of Second Formers had been sitting there, answering the call of nature (we never went to those loos alone – they were just too spooky) and were screaming about the noise.

"Should we use them for target practice?" my friend said, indicating the Second Formers, as they raced back to the safety of the gym, some of them still pulling up their bloomers.

I thought for a while and said, "Why not?" and we re-situated ourselves in a better position, still hidden in the long grass, to lie in wait for the next lot who came. Sure enough, another little gaggle of girls eventually came to the bogs for a wee before the bell rang for afternoon prep, and my friend fired the first round.

The result was even more spectacular as the little girls shrieked with fright, and bolted back the way they came. Then reason suddenly came to us both, as one of the girls screamed, "Somebody's shooting at us!" and ran off to the Sixth Form Common Room, which was dangerously close by.

We both ran for our lives, trying to hide the rifle against our bodies, and somehow made it back unnoticed into Macrorie and the safety of our cubicle in the dorm. She hid the gun away and we sat on our beds and stared at each other wide-eyed with horror, realising now quite what trouble we could have got into.

We would have both been summarily expelled for bringing a gun to school, let alone being caught blatantly shooting at anybody.

After that episode I tamed my anarchistic activities to a bit of scrumping for green oranges from Dot's orchard, and cooking a dead pigeon we'd found in the gum plantation in the grounds near the hockey pitch (that's why my friend had brought the gun to school in the first place – to shoot us some nice plump rock pigeons). We took the dead bird along to the science lab and sort of gutted it, and then tried to roast it over a Bunsen burner.

The smell of it wasn't the delicious flavour of roasting bird, but that of rotting, long-dead pigeon, so we threw it away in the dustbin.

Again, if we'd been caught, we'd have been in serious trouble as nobody was allowed near the science lab, let alone loose with the Bunsen burners, at any time, whatsoever.

The year came and went fairly uneventfully after that. I didn't seem to have recovered fully from my measles though. I was still very weak, and had even less energy and stamina than before, and had had to spend a fair bit of time in the San again, resting with some made-up ailments. Sometimes I was lucky and got the day room, other times I had the single, cheerless and ice-cold solitary ward, designed for quarantined patients. This happened if I'd been a bit too imaginative with my symptoms.

By now I'd started my periods, too. The first time it happened took me completely by surprise. About a year previously, Mum had called me in to her bedroom in the middle of the day. I was immediately suspicious and on my guard, as I had a far from clear conscience about many things, and thought I was in for a dressing-down. But instead she said to me something about having babies. I had no idea what she was talking about. She ummed and ahhhed and said something about white pads "down there."

I suddenly twigged and said, "Oh yes! I've already got one!" She looked surprised and said, "Surely, not?"

I ran to get my new school bathing-costume, and showed her the little bit of white material sewn into the gusset, "There!" I said triumphantly "That's one."

"Oh, no. I mean proper pads. Anyway, when it happens call one of your sisters, and she'll show you what to do." And that was that. No other information.

I'd been feeling extra depressed in my first term of Third Form, and had started to get horrible sharp pains in my lower belly. The next thing I knew, I was bleeding. I stared at my stained white bloomers with dismay. What was happening? I called my older sister, who was in her last year there, and she briskly handed me, from her own locker, a paper bag full of soft pads called *Dr Whites*, with loops on either side, an elastic belt with two hooks, and a couple of pairs of rubber pants. She showed me briefly and wordlessly what to do and left me to it.

In those days the subject was absolutely taboo, and even though it was an all girls' school and a completely natural monthly event, everybody treated that 'time of the month' as if it were a horrible, secret disease, and, if you had 'the curse' you had to keep absolutely quiet about it, and pretend you didn't. The disposal of the pads had to become a subterfuge, even at home Mum made us walk right around the back of the house to *shisa* (burn) the 'things' in the *biyela* outside, so that the servants didn't see us.

I had dreadful monthly cramps from the word go, and used that time to go to the San and drink Sister's hideous cocktail heavily based on castor-oil to ease the pain. All that happened to me was that I got terrible diarrhoea every time I took her 'mixture' which only added to my problems. But, I did get a note from her, too, excusing me from swimming. Mort never took these notes seriously. She looked upon them as a complete con, getting us out of swimming whether we were 'on' or not. She'd look at the note with her rheumy red eyes and snarl, "I don't believe you for one minute. You've just gone and told lies to Sister. I know you!" and made those of us who had notes duck-walk all the way around the double hockey pitch, ensuring that we had a different set of aches for the next three days. Our thigh muscles were always stiff and painful after an hour's duck walking at a full squat each month.

A couple of times that year at the end of term, Mum would come to pick us up and find me lying in the San, my trunk not packed, and me not dressed or ready. There was a lot of shouting at me to get up and get myself up to the dorm to get washed and dressed and into my suit; and at a reluctant, and surly, sister and a flapping Matron to help throw all the things from my locker into the big trunk. Invariably, items like my new costume and brand new towel, which were kept in my gym locker, and my tennis shoes and racquet, got left behind, and there was hell to pay at the other end when the loss was discovered. Everything that was left at school disappeared during the holidays, filched by the Zulu cleaners for their own use, or their children's.

Mum raged about the cost of keeping me in new replacement bits of uniform. One winter term my jersey disappeared in about the first week I was at school. I'd probably left it lying around somewhere, but number 71 didn't get called out during 'lost property' for a change – my nice warm jersey had gone. I was freezing cold, so I wrote to Mum and asked her to buy me another jersey. She refused point blank, to teach me a lesson to be more careful, and I spent those five weeks shivering and wearing my flannel pyjama top under my long-sleeved white shirt under my navy gym dress.

Another time, I lost my blazer, and the same thing happened, and finally, when the school introduced capes – lovely long, warm, lined capes that wrapped right around one like a cosy blanket – Mum refused to buy me one.

"You'll just go and lose it," she said flatly, and she was probably right, but I didn't feel any happier about it when I was the only one without a nice warm cape during those icy cold days when the frost was thick on the grass.

I got chilblains. Bad circulation inherited from Dad (I still had the ice cold feet all-night problem) and my habit of trying to thaw my hands out by holding them in warm water run into a washbasin brought out chilblains in all my fingers so badly that each hand looked like a bunch of split sausages. The chilblains swelled up and burst and became open sores, and I suffered trying to write neatly with these hands oozing pus everywhere.

Magically, they disappeared during the holidays, even when I rode out first thing in the morning, when the valley sparkled white with frost like diamonds all over the grass in the rising African sun.

I didn't have gloves, nor did I wear shoes, and I felt the cold nip on the end of my toes, but no chilblains. I'd come home in the evenings with the milking cattle, helping herd the cows and calves from horseback just as the frost was settling again, and the smoke from the *biyela* chimney rose vertically, blue and fragrant with the smell of scorched eucalyptus.

I'd help with the polo ponies, putting each one to bed individually, calling their names softly and kissing each one gently on his or her velvety nose, and rubbing my own nose into the soft fluff in their ears.

They nickered contentedly and carried on munching their delicious-smelling scalded oats and bran. I'd run barefoot back over the crunchy white kikuyu grass to get into a warm bath afterwards, and still never got chilblains at home.

~~~

# *40*

# Fourth Form

**A**nother birthday and another year at College. I was in the Fourth Form and had a couple of privileges – like our own territory, called the Fourth Form Lawn, an area where we could drag our rugs and lie with our backs against the trunk of a big fallen gum-tree, and listen to somebody's records on a battery-operated gramophone (another privilege). We were now allowed a transistor radio, and I was lucky enough to have a very kind and generous Godfather. Martin, my cousin's father, had always given me the loveliest presents. He was head of *American Express* in Jo'burg, and travelled a lot. One year he'd sent me a darling little miniature travelling clock that folded neatly into a beautifully enamelled case, and which had luminous hands and numbers on its tiny face. They were radioactive of course, but I loved my clock and took it to school with me, secreted in my pyjama case, and I took it out at night and held it in my hand against my ear to hear the faintest ticking sound, or lie and gaze at the green, lit-up hands on its face.

The following year, just before my birthday, Martin sent me a state-of-the-art, latest-model transistor radio. Smaller than a book, it was a thing of beauty, and best of all came with a set of earphones, so I could lie at night with it under my pillow (strictly forbidden) and listen to the Beatles and Frank Sinatra's 'Strangers in the Night' while the others slept.

Fourth Formers were allowed to sleep in the Annexe. This was a bedroom off the main dorm and out of sight and earshot of the prefects. We were supposed to be mature enough now to be trusted to spend a term there on our own, unsupervised.

Knowing we were to sleep in the annexe, my three friends and I had organised to smuggle in some tuck in our trunks. I was in charge of tinned goods, since we didn't live anywhere near any shops. I packed tins of condensed milk, sardines, bully-beef, Vienna sausages, baked beans, and anything else I could purloin from Mum's store cupboard. One of my sisters had managed to find out that the combination of her padlock was 'pilot', and so when the household was asleep, I sneaked down the passage from my room at the end, held my breath as I opened the swing doors outside Dad's dressing room, and off to fetch my goodies.

I included a tin opener of course, a lethal thing that left a jagged edge on the tins we opened.

Others had brought perishables like sweets, chocolate, biscuits, crisps, and other treats. We pulled up a couple of the floorboards and hoarded our spoils down on the rafters below.

Later on, we'd invite the rest of our house classmates to a 'middy' (midnight feast). They would tiptoe out of the main dorm one by one, and if caught, would say they were going to the loo. Then, when everybody was there, we'd have our feast.

We left it for a few days, as there was a lot going on during the beginning of term, and anyway it took a bit of organising with messages being passed around, and a lot of whispering. It must have been about ten days later that I was woken by a huge rat running over my face while I was fast asleep. I sat bolt upright, thinking it was a dream, then I heard the sound of crunching coming from under the floor. I woke the others and we got out our torches and whipped up the two loose floorboards. Rats scattered everywhere – there must have been at least ten of them gobbling up all our tuck. The other girls screamed and then clamped their hands over their mouths. They were terrified of the rats. I wasn't so much, as I was used to them.

There were rats aplenty in the sheds on the farm, and we

often saw them, either in the mouth of one of the stable cats, or on the end of a pitchfork after our labourers had sprung the trap the manager kept baited in the storeroom.

The other girls were torn between running out into the corridor, and abandoning the Annexe and all its perks, but I persuaded them that rats weren't so bad, and at least we still had all the tinned food. After a bit of hysteria and panic, my friends saw reason, and we hid the tins in a trunk, threw away all that remained of the treats (just the packaging), and told Matron that we had a rat infestation in the Annexe. She organised the place to be baited and we had our middy with the tinned food, an unusual combination of flavours interspersed with swigs from the tins of sweetened condensed milk.

ANDY – R.I.P.

My friends had now begun to show an interest in boys. I only knew one boy. His name was Andy, and he was Delia's age but my friend. His mother was a friend of Mum and Dad's and lived in Jo'burg. She often came to stay on the farm and brought Andy with her. Andy hero-worshipped me as I was such a tomboy, and he was anything but. Slightly plump with puppy fat, he loved cooking, light classical music and hair and flower arranging. I liked Andy. He gave me a wonderful unconditional and adoring friendship, something I'd never had before. He was the brother I'd never had, and although he was too terrified of horses to ride with me, he would walk or run, red-faced and puffing, beside me when I went for a ride. He was as faithful to me as my beloved dog, Pitz, and they were sort of similar in a way.

Totally unsuited to their surroundings, they would both put themselves through anything to be with me. The year after I went to college Andy went to Michaelhouse, the brother school to the college, and he wrote me long and amusing letters about school. He was miserable at boarding school as well, and I'm sure he was bullied unmercifully, something that I hadn't suffered. But he didn't com-plain, and I loved getting the fat envelopes from BG (Balgowan – the nickname for the school) with his handwriting on them. I wrote back to him just as prolifically.

In prep I'd write him long letters in my jotter, leaving out the 'Dear Andy' bit so that to any nosy prefects who cruised the classroom looking for trouble, it looked like I was writing an essay. Naturally, we were forbidden to write letters during prep, so I'd tear the pages out later and address the envelope to him.

The fact that I was receiving lots of letters from a Michaelhouse boy didn't go unnoticed by my friends, and there was another ritual that brought me more, and the most surprising, attention.

It was the tradition at boarding school, near Valentine's Day, for the prefects in charge of our post to confiscate anything that might look like a Valentine's card. These were then held back until 14 February, when the head girl stood on the steps of the courtyard and, accompanied by catcalls and shrieks and whistles from the rest of us, called out the names of all the girls who'd received cards. To my amazement, I became the girl from Fourth Form to receive the most Valentine cards in the school. This was simply because my birthday was at the end of January, and people like aunts, Godparents, and relations overseas, sent my cards to the school. These were collected up as Valentine cards and withheld until the much-looked forward to distribution. Andy added to this astonishing pile of cards by sending me lots of proper Valentine cards with a Michaelhouse postal stamp on, to boot.

So I had to traipse up and down the courtyard, as each card was mockingly held up high by the head prefect, my name was called out again and again, and I had to run the gauntlet of whoops and cheers. Some years I got about ten cards when other, older girls received no more than one or two.

# White Zulu                                              Fiona Ross

On a couple of memorable occasions, when Andy's mum took him home, she took me up to stay with them. I was his only friend, and I had the most wonderful time. Mostly his parents ignored us, but I was used to that so I didn't mind, and sat there happily in their sunny study on the thick pile carpet, reading their *National Geographic* magazines, my absolute favourite, and Andy cooked up a delicious, extraordinarily well-presented salmon mousse, with transparently thin slices of cucumber for the scales, and half a pimento-stuffed green olive for the eye.

Or I sat with him at his baby grand piano while he serenaded me with 'The Shadow of Your Smile' and show tunes he'd learned to play. Music was Andy's first love; he had lessons and played with precision and passion. Now and again his mum would drive us in her Jag to Hillbrow or Rosebank, and drop us off to have dinner at a smart restaurant and go to a movie afterwards. I loved this glittering lifestyle, and Andy and I, aged thirteen and fifteen, ate at the top of the President Hotel, in a revolving restaurant, while we were waited on by Indians in long white aprons, and a live band played in the corner. We went to see films like *The Sound of Music*, and Andy cried when the old nun sang 'Climb Every Mountain', and I didn't.

Back at school I had to decide what subjects I wanted to take for Matric. None of them looked particularly inviting, so I looked at them from another angle. I would have taken art, but I showed no talent whatsoever. I had to drop maths anyway, because I still couldn't count past ten, and I dropped Latin so that I could do French. I chose three languages as they were easy. I took geography because I quite liked the subject; it looked as though all I needed to do was draw a few maps and mountains. That left history, which I knew I could waffle through, and one other. So I chose domestic science as it looked like a bit of cooking and we could eat what we made, and how hard could it be?

The Domestic Science Block was next to the San and consisted of a big room, full of stoves, with a locked pantry off one side.

The first thing we learned, was how to pick the lock on the pantry with a hairpin (the same way we'd learned how to get into the Sacristy next to the chapel and drink the Communion wine kept in there), and eat all the raisins and drink the cooking sherry.

Our textbooks were so out of date that the illustrations showed girls wearing mobcaps and long dresses preparing the food. The subject hadn't changed much since the Voortrekker days, and some of the skills we had to learn for Matric were how to make a water filter (with all the big stones at the bottom and the fine sand at the top); how to make our own soap using caustic soda and glycerine, and invalid cookery, which involved rennet (the stuff from a calf's stomach that thickened the disgusting milk puddings we had to present to those vulnerable invalids), along with beef broth.

The very first invalid dish we had to make was poached white fish in parsley sauce, and I excelled myself by finely chopping a small green caterpillar into the parsley that I'd forgotten to wash, and then having hysterics because I've been terrified of caterpillars all my life, ever since one sunny afternoon on the farm when a young male cousin of ours pulled back my T-shirt, and stuck a large handful of those prickly, grey, hairy, venomous caterpillars that sting, down my back. I had been badly stung as they released their little hairs with the venom in them into my skin, and I couldn't get them out.

When I discovered that the green parsley wasn't all parsley I collapsed with a lot of shrieking of genuine horror, and had to be sent out of the building to calm myself down and get the inevitable punishment.

Domestic science also involved sewing, something I'd never, ever, done in my life, and at fourteen was told I had to make a pair of shortie pyjamas. I was given the pattern and told to choose some material. There was an ugly, pond-slime-green gingham check cotton there, and I chose it out of sheer indifference. I then cut the pattern out all wrong, tacked the paper to the material and cut that out wrong as well; I never got past the tacking. The teacher, a young woman who'd taken an instant dislike to me on sight, never even looked at my work.

She'd walk past my desk without turning her head and say, "Ross. Tack that again, it's all wrong." I had no idea what was wrong and she didn't show me, so I never got past that tacking stage.

While other girls in my class made padded Ottomans in upholstery class, I picked moodily at my piece of green gingham, and never got any further than the tacking. Cooking wasn't a great success either, and I made the odd lopsided, half-burnt and half-raw sponge cakes. But somehow I passed all my subjects, and scraped through my exams with Ds and the odd E, but never enough Fs to actually fail and stay down, or abandon that subject as both my sisters had done.

When our reports came, just after we'd broken up for the holidays, and I heard Mum shouting for me, I called the dogs and took to the hills, where I stayed until dusk, and slunk back home hoping Mum would have calmed down slightly from her rage at reading words like 'insolent' and 'lazy' on my school reports.

'Could do better' was about the highest praise I ever got from my exasperated teachers. I tried to point out that my sisters had been allowed to drop out of school, Delia didn't have a hope in hell of getting her Matric as she was struggling far more than any of us had, and did Mum get a Matric? She took off at this question, evaded the answer, and went on and on about how bright I was, and how I did no work at all. I was to stay on and write Matric and that was that.

~~~

# *41*

# My first dance

**R**ocket's hooves made a crunching sound as he plodded over the newly burnt veld, which wore a fuzz of green now that we'd had our first spring rains. The afternoon heat hung over the baked earth, and my horse's neck stretched out low and relaxed as I rode, daydreaming, with my bare feet dangling. I was looking for some stray cattle on the far bank of the river that runs alongside the edge of the dense indigenous forest. Our cattle wintered in the bush where they were able to graze on grass that remained green throughout our dry season, and browse on the evergreen and varied indigenous trees and shrubs. I caught a glimpse of a cow with her calf in the deep shade of a Yellowwood tree. She was a pitch black Aberdeen Angus, and it was only the movement as she swung her horns at a troublesome fly that gave her position away.

I turned Rocket's head towards the shadows and kicked his flanks. As I rounded up the pair, along with two more cows grazing further back in the bush, and started urging the cattle back to the river, I looked around uneasily. The previous afternoon, our Zulu herd boys had seen leopard spoor in the soft earth on the riverbank, and our neighbour Mike had lost a couple of sheep to leopard recently. Even though baboons are favourite prey and cattle too large for the big cat to take, I still felt uneasy as I jostled the reluctant cows back over the rocky river-bed and into their fenced paddock to wait for the count tomorrow.

I hopped off my horse and slung the reins over my shoulder

as I wrestled with the barbed-wire gate. Rocket, normally a placid horse, suddenly started and, shying away from me, wrenched my shoulder and trampled on my bare foot with his sharp, unshod hoof. I held his bridle tightly as he circled me nervously and looked around, expecting to see the amber glowing eyes or hear the sawing cough-like growl that would precede a leopard attack.

Nothing. Just the zeep-zeep of cicadas, and the blowing snorts of my terrified pony.

I wished now that I had the dogs with me, but they were a nuisance on cattle round-ups because now that most of the cows had calves they charged any dogs running at the pony's heels, so I'd left them behind, tied up on the back veranda of the house. I quickly finished tying up the wire loop on the gate and, grabbing a handful of his mane, swung myself onto Rocket's shining, sweating back. I turned his head for home, and he exploded into a gallop, my head low on his neck as we bolted up and over the brow of the kopje and onto the dusty red track that led back home. We settled to a steady jog and as we re-crossed the river at the ford startled a troop of baboons. Their lookout was gazing at his reflection in a pool and the sound of rushing water had drowned out the noise of our approach.

I was a few yards from him when he looked up and gave a bark of alarm. The rest of the troop burst away from the water where they'd been drinking and fled for the safety of the trees. The lookout male, rather sheepishly I thought, made his way in the inimitable nonchalant, tail cocked, front paws crossing swagger that only a baboon can achieve.

As we clattered up to the back gate, Evalina was hurrying from the kitchen, "nKosizana, we've been looking for you. *Checha!* (Hurry!)." As she puffed her ample, white pinafored bulk towards me she yelled for Toto, one of our grooms to take care of Rocket. I slid off his back, puzzled by her urgency. She bustled me along the kitchen veranda and down the long passage towards my bedroom. There, hanging on the wardrobe, was a dress. Pink and satiny, it was freshly pressed and next to it hung a froth of stiff net petticoats. Then I remembered. I was going to my first party that night.

I bathed in the big tub with ball-and-claw feet, pouring a generous handful of geranium-scented bath salts into the soft, slightly silted water. I inspected my foot closely. It still throbbed where Rocket had trodden on it, but the skin was unbroken and the toenail still intact. I dried myself and scrambled into the dress. My older sister had worn it to a school dance the term before, and Mum had arranged for it to be laundered, ready for me. I struggled into the petticoats and slipped my bare feet into a pair of pink satin bridesmaids' shoes that Evalina had put out for me. I hurriedly dragged a brush through my short, dark hair and clip-clopped my unsteady way down the passage to the kitchen.

Ben Masango was sitting on the kitchen steps, taking a break from cooking and smoking his pungent *Boxer* tobacco cigarettes, his white chef's hat in its usual place on top of a pile of logs in the wood box. Evalina was working at the sink, shoulder to shoulder with Lefina, peeling vegetables together and chatting softly. Both women turned as I clattered into the kitchen, dropped their knives and covered their mouths with their hands. "*Hau!* nKosizana!" they exclaimed. With appreciative whoops, they made me twirl again and again around the big kitchen. With clicks of approval they fingered the net petticoats and stroked the satin dress.

I tottered through the house to the front veranda where my parents were enjoying their whisky sun-downer. Mum looked at me. "You really ought to have stockings on. You can't go like that."

Dad looked over his newspaper. "I'm leaving in two minutes, so you'd better be ready."

Slipping out of my shoes, I ran back to my sister's room, rummaged through her underwear drawer and found a pair of nylon stockings and a suspender belt.

Dad was waiting in the bakkie as, shoes in my hand, I ran over the kikuyu lawn, followed by three delighted dogs who, having heard the engine start, assumed they were going for a ride. I fended the excited dogs off with my foot as I scrambled into the cab and we sped off down the drive, eventually leaving them panting in our dust. Dad drove the twenty miles to our nearest village in silence.

As we left the dirt road and turned onto the tarmac, I looked at Nottingham Road (such a pretentious name for a filling station, a railway station, and a cluster of stockyards). There was also Hoosen's Store (a general dealership owned by a gentle Indian family), and a ramshackle tin shed with fly specked chicken wire nailed over the windows that served as our butchery. The party was at the stockyards. There's a big room behind the auctioneer's stall that serves as a hall. On sale days the corrugated roofed building with its wooden floors was an exciting bustle of farmers who'd brought their cattle and sheep for auction. Their wives stood behind a trestle table, pouring tea from huge enamel teapots and occasionally one would slip a buttered scone into my hand as we shy, overawed country children stood and gaped at all the activity.

Tonight there were blue and white crepe paper streamers festooned from the rafters, and balloons tied in bunches on the walls. French chalk covered the floor and there was a radiogram set up in a corner with a stack of LPs piled on a table next to it.

Dad dropped me at the door and went to Notties Pub to while away the evening with other parents who'd brought their teenage children in from remote ranches in the district.

Our hostess bustled me into the echoing hall and I stopped at the edge of the dance floor in horror.

I had been pleased with my party outfit. In the mid-60s, from what I'd heard from my older sisters, everybody wore stiff petticoats under their dresses.

As some half dozen girls turned slowly to stare at me, I realised fashion had moved on. They were all wearing neat little tight-fitting shifts and flat pumps. It was typical of Mum not to have realised either. Immersed in her life of gardening, she'd suddenly noticed that the party was due, grabbed a vaguely suitable dress from my sister's wardrobe, and given it to the servants to press and freshen up for me.

I slunk off to the girls' powder room and pulled the voluminous petticoats off, bundling them under an upholstered bench. Then I tugged the dress down and close around my thin, tall frame and walked back to the dance floor with as much dignity as I could muster. Early Beatles music at full blast soon had dancers twisting and bopping on the wooden boards. A shy, handsome boy I had been eyeing from a distance, clumped awkwardly over to me. Wearing shoes was as unfamiliar to him as it was to me and I'd already shed my high heels under a nearby chair. Most of the girls were now dancing in stockinged feet. He gruffly asked me to dance and we made an attempt at a slow foxtrot. As he steered me across the dance floor he trod heavily on the same foot as Rocket had trampled earlier that afternoon. I was undismayed, feeling nothing but the strange bristle of his adolescent cheek as he held me close, and his heavy breathing as he concentrated fiercely on his footwork. I was in heaven.

My worst fear had been that I'd be left a tall lonely wallflower, sitting among the unfortunate few girls who sat primly on chairs against the wall, tapping their feet, looking aloof and pretending they didn't care. After midnight, Dad came to fetch me, grumpy now, as, when we reached the dirt road again, it had started to rain and he had to put chains on the tyres of the bakkie. He lay on a sack on the muddy road, laying the chain strips out for me to drive forward when he shouted the command, and swearing in his whisky befuddled state when the sodden chains wouldn't lock. I realised I'd also forgotten to tell him about the leopard, but this wasn't a good time.

~~~

# *42*

# Fifth Form

**B**ack to school, and into Fifth Form on my sixteenth birthday.

We had a few more privileges: a lawn to ourselves and not too much hassle from the prefects. The work got harder, as the pressure was on. We were all going to take our Matric, and the subjects we did and all the work, applied to that final goal. I coasted along as usual, and wrote lots of letters to Andy, and enjoyed myself to the best of my ability when I felt well enough.

I was still having to slip away to the San for a rest now and again, and I had got so used to the routine down there that I lay in my narrow little hospital bed in the isolation ward and stared out at the mellow brick wall of Frances Baines House and pretended I was a princess, and that those were the walls of my castle. I worked up quite a saga in my head, and imagined myself as chatelaine of this wonderful big castle in the English countryside, with servants, footmen and a butler – and of course a handsome young prince as a husband. My ideal prince was the young, dead pilot in that library book; blond hair and blue eyes and a tanned face from all that flying. My heart raced at the very thought of him. I still had my pilot ambitions, too.

In class, I found I was becoming more and more bored and gazing out of the window all the time. I lived in my own fuzzy world. One day our geography teacher called me up to the front of class after the bell for lunch had gone. We were alone as the others clattered off down the corridor to eat sausages.

"Have you ever had your eyes tested?" she asked me not unkindly.

"No," I replied.

"Well, I think you'd better ask your parents to organise an eye test, as I think you might have a problem copying things down from the board," and she left it at that.

During the holidays I mentioned the test, and it was arranged for first thing the next term. I went to the San to see Dr Strip Mac and he told me to put one hand over my eye and read from the chart with the other eye. I looked for the chart. He pointed and I saw the first two lines. After I'd called out the letters he said, "Next line," and I was flummoxed. There was nothing but a blur. The other eye was even worse. I was seriously myopic, short-sighted with an astigmatism in both eyes, and was sent on the San transport down to 'Maritzburg to the optician who prescribed a huge, heavy pair of thick, bottle-bottom glasses for me. The fashion in the mid-sixties, in South Africa, was quite a heavy, square black frame, about the most unflattering, nerdy glasses you could ever have, and that's what I got.

The optometrist was a kind man, and saw my disappointment at having this massively heavy prescription handed to me. "Will I be able to fly?" I asked him. When I'd explained that my ambition was to be a pilot, he shook his head sadly.

"Not a hope," he said. "Not with the problems you have with your weak eyesight." I was crushed. Devastated. I'd been waiting all this time until I became old enough to go down to Oribi Airport to get my learner's licence. Now I'd failed at the first hurdle, the eye test.

I was stuck with these hideous things, and all it did was add to my absented-minded professor look. I hated the glasses, and tried to take them off at every opportunity, but couldn't see a thing without them. Whether it was all that reading during my bout of measles, and I'd strained my eyes irreversibly, or I was just destined to be myopic at puberty, I'll never know. I suspected the former, because of the amount of eye-watering pain I put myself through.

In the July holidays we went as a family to Durban to stay with friends on the coast. We spent quite a bit of time on the beach-front there. Dine had turned into a very pretty, flirty girl, and I trailed in her wake as she mixed with Post-Matric Michaelhouse boys who'd started the newest craze – surfing.

These eighteen-year-olds were just old enough to have their first beaten up old cars, like Volkswagens and Deux Chevaux, and they cut the roofs off so that they could drive around with their long surf-boards sticking out, or they bought roof racks and tied their boards on top, fins up. These demigods paraded along the golden sands and flicked their sun-bleached hair at the girls.

We were mesmerised, and I stuck to Dine like glue.

We met up with other boarding school girls and wore our tiny bikinis to sunbathe in little groups, lying out and baking ourselves in the winter sun. One of the girls was a year ahead of me, and thus had been in the same class as me in my first year in Second Form. She had an older brother, two years older than I was, at Michaelhouse, and he often joined our group, chatting to Dine in an easy manner, while I looked on enviously.

This boy was gorgeous. He had blond sun-bleached, slightly curly hair, twinkling blue eyes, and a lovely way of laughing by throwing his head back to expose his long, tanned throat. Dine had several guys interested in her, and she had a knack of putting them at their ease, and attracting lots of their avid attention. Another young man, a school friend of the gorgeous one, was a brother of Dine's best friend, and we became a group of six, with the two of us and the two brothers and sisters. We had a great time in the evenings walking along the Marine Parade and visiting all the lovely, tacky arcades that used to festoon the Durban beachfront. Dodgem cars, tombola stalls and all kinds of games where you threw things and won a prize. The good-looking boy threw a tennis ball at a pile of tat, and won a beer mug, which to my greatest surprise, he handed to me. I was taken aback as I was the skinny, ugly duckling trailing along in the wake of my infinitely better-looking older sister, with my huge, heavy, thick glasses falling off my nose all the time.

After a wonderful holiday of this, we got back to school. I went up to my dorm, and Joan, the sister of the boy I'd fancied so much, came running up to me. She drew me aside and said, "Tell me – do you like my brother?" I was rendered speechless by her question for a second, as she finished by saying, "Because he likes you."

To 'like' somebody meant that they wanted to go steady. Oh, my God! It was me he had liked and not Dine. The beer mug had spoken the truth. "Oh yes!" I exclaimed, and she wrote to him, as was the custom, and he began to write to me. I had my first boyfriend, and he was a Michaelhouse boy and a spitting image of my imaginary prince too.

~~~

# *43*

# Sixth Form and Matric

Another birthday spent on my first day back at school. But things were different now. I'd broken the record for any known generation of Ross girls reaching Matric, and there were a whole lot of new treats I could enjoy. We were allowed to bring in tinned instant coffee and drink it in our own Sixth Form common room – a corrugated iron shed on breeze blocks opposite the gym. We spent all our free time in there, making cappuccino by whisking lots of sugar, coffee powder, and a drop of water, in our own mugs (no more slimy, scratched plastic mugs for us) and we could have all the tuck we liked. Biscuits, sweets, and chocolate were stashed away on our own shelves, safe from rats, as, like the Voortrekkers did before us, we kept them in old biscuit tins.

Best of all was that we could have a bath at night and get straight into bed. For the first time in six years, I didn't have frozen feet all night, every night. Everybody, except me and two of my best friends, were made prefects, heads of houses and head girls. I was a bit disappointed that I didn't get a cubicle with a wooden door, which my younger cousin had as Vice-head of House, but at least I had a cubicle to myself, with a little study desk and a small goose-necked lamp. I used this to read my library books most of the night. No studying for me.

I took advantage of all the privileges and accepted none of the responsibilities that the other girls had – of disciplining the younger girls, or, indeed, setting a good example for the rest of the school. Rather the reverse. I could, and did, do my own thing. I was the bane of my classmates' lives, as I broke all the rules and they weren't able to tell me off, let alone issue punishments. They didn't like my behaviour, and took every opportunity they could to tell me I was a bad reflection on the sixth form in general, but I didn't care. I was my own master.

There was a lot of fuss from teachers and classmates about how hard Matric work was, and how important it was to apply oneself to passing the final exams, but I cruised along, neither revising nor learning anything new. I'd had to abandon my aspirations to be a fighter pilot, and had long ago forgotten about wanting to be a vet. I had no ambition other than to sit out my last year of confinement in this meaningless prison, extracting as much enjoyment as I could under the circumstances.

With my new-found freedom I could read a now unrestricted quantity of library books to my heart's content – and that's what I did. I wrote letters during prep to my two boyfriends at Michael-house. I was hopelessly in love with my surfer. He loved me, too, and we wrote long, soppy letters to each other every other day. I still wrote to Andy on a daily basis, now telling him every detail of my new boyfriend, Greg. Andy, the good sport that he was, was thrilled for me, and loved to share all the romance I was enjoying. He was genuinely pleased for me and not in the least bit jealous, as I think he knew that we'd never be more than best friends. I didn't know Andy was gay, and neither did he. I think his parents and brother knew, but it was never mentioned in front of me. They didn't accept him as he was, and spent all their time trying to change him. I loved him the way he was.

Greg managed to come and see me as much as he could as a Post Matric pupil. He was taking his A levels and aimed to go to Cambridge at the end of the year. He was eighteen and had his driver's licence, and his friend, the other surfer, who'd left school by now, had his own car, a battered old Peugeot, embellished with a rusty roof-rack to carry their long surfboards – the very pinnacle of looking cool. They sometimes came up to visit me at school, and, as we sat in the car, parked in the driveway next to the chapel, the friend played gooseberry at the wheel while Greg and I smooched in the back seat, keeping one eye open to see if anyone came out of the staff house and saw us. The friend had to keep cave! as well, poor guy, and got nothing out of the whole exercise.

Ever since Boarding School had been founded, the school had held an annual formal dance, arranged by the Fifth Formers and attended by the Sixth Form girls. Unfortunately for us, Dine's year (three previous to mine) had behaved so badly that all school dances had been banned for good. As a consolation, the staff had organised an informal braai, inviting all the Michaelhouse Matric boys to attend. The braai was held down by the swimming pool on a piece of lawn surrounded by a big, thick hedge on three sides. The area was floodlit, and some Fifth Formers enlisted to play music over a loudspeaker system. The meat, buns and salad were brought down by the Zulu kitchen staff who cooked the meat, and served it to us on paper plates.

The house mistresses from all five houses prowled around among us to see there was no hanky-panky going on as we danced on the concrete area between the pool and the changing rooms. Once the food had been eaten and everything taken away, one of the kitchen staff switched off what he thought was the spotlight over the grill, but turned out to be all the lights, plunging the whole area into pitch darkness. The music played on in the dark, but by the time the matrons had realised what had happened and were fumbling in the dark trying to get the lights on again, everyone, including my partner, who had grabbed me by the arm and run off with me, had disappeared behind the hedge and were busy snogging. I had no idea of the name of the guy I was dancing with, nor what he looked like but I joined in as enthusiastically as the rest of the girls apparently were. Suddenly, the lights were turned on again and we were exposed to the full view of the house mistresses, all of us crammed in behind the hedge in interlocked couples.

This, of course, put paid to any future (even informal) socialising between boarding school Matric girls and any boys' schools forever. It seems we could not be trusted either.

The year passed in a blur, as I was having plenty of rest, and felt quite well for a change. The rest time was supposed to be time set aside for studying for these monumental exams at the end of the year. I read library books and spent a lot of time working on my tan for the school leavers' dance, also at the end of the year.

Matric Trials arrived out of the blue, and I found myself sitting in the school gym with a teacher as an invigilator, and staring helplessly at reams of questions typed out on thick wads of paper. I failed the Trials by failing Afrikaans. The Afrikaner Nationalist Government insisted that all Matriculants passed Afrikaans, otherwise we failed in spite of getting good grades in all our other subjects. I'd never even heard the language until I'd gone to the Prep at the age of nearly 12, so was at an extra disadvantage.

To me the miracle was that I'd passed anything at all. My results were abysmal, and I'd only just scraped through the other subjects with the minimum marks required. My parents were furious. The fact that I'd failed Afrikaans, "Such an easy language – after all, it's only a bastard form of Dutch," was anathema to them. They booked me into 'Boetplaas' (Afrikaans farm), a boot camp specifically for those who'd failed the subject, for two weeks in the July holidays. I was horrified, as I'd made plans to spend the entire month on the beach with Greg. Now I had to go to a dismal farm outside Lion's River, where the Michaelhouse Afrikaans master had orga-nised a live-in cram school.

It was a horrible place – dusty and bleak. There were about fourteen other girls, and only one of them from the college. But they were all like me – totally disinterested in learning Afrikaans; we were supposed to speak nothing else all the time, but we bunked off and did as we pleased. There were some scabby old horses available to the guests, and one wild, half-broken young stallion with wall-eyes and a vicious way of getting its bit in its teeth, arching its neck around in a bow, and bolting. I was the only one who rode it, and I had several frights with it running away, plunging down the steep banks and trying to throw me into the freezing cold Lion's River. One big consolation was that the farm was right opposite the Lion's River polo ground – and it was polo season.

Dad had given up playing polo by then and sold all the ponies, keeping only old Ronald and Prince to live out their retirement days loafing around in the paddocks eating, or standing in the shade of a tree, nose to tail, switching absently at the flies on one another's faces, or as my hacks when I felt like a change from riding Rocket. Our next-door neighbour, Mike, still played and he was extremely kind as I hung around the polo ground all day, and lent me his ponies one by one, to take out on lovely gallops with the other girls. I cantered past the thatched hut where I was supposed to be sitting and writing some Afrikaans test, and merely put my bare heels to the pony's flanks, to accelerate and get out of there before somebody spotted me and called me in. There was certainly no discipline at Boetplaas as I don't recall ever spending any time in the classroom with the swots.

One day, the three girls I shared a *rondavel* (round, thatched hut) with, got bored and walked up the old main road to the railway station, then hitching an illegal ride on the timber goods train to Howick, where we pooled our money and bought a gallon of cheap sherry. Then, realising it was getting dark and we had no way of getting home, I used my Zulu on an old man driving a tractor and trailer, and persuaded him to drop us off, back at the farm turn-off.

Clutching our bottle of sherry, we bumped our way back to Boetplaas at the speed of five miles an hour, and were very grateful for the ride. I shudder to think what would have become of four white teenage girls, out in the middle of nowhere, in the pitch dark

African night. That night we drank all the sherry, and then put stockings over our heads and ran around the entire resort, banging on all the doors of all the rondavels. There must have been about ten of them, and we crashed into the last one, thinking it was ours, only to switch the light on and find a middle-aged couple sitting bolt upright in the twin beds, blankets clutched to their chins and looking at us in horror.

We slunk off, glad of the anonymity of the stockings on our heads, but still giggling and stumbling drunkenly about the place. There was a complaint to the management from a *dominee* (Pastor) and his wife about us the following morning, and we got a dressing down from the hotel manager, as well as the Afrikaans master. How did they know it was us?

I went back to school, and suddenly the Matric dance was upon us. I'd asked Mum about getting a dress, and she merely pulled out a wine-stained old cocktail dress of my aunt's and handed it to me. It had seen better days, as Dine had worn it to several parties already. I was aghast. Most of the fun of the dance was planning our dresses, having them bought or made up, and discussing the accessories. I felt so left out, as all the other girls chattered about their plans, drew sketches of their dresses and shoes and compared colours and styles. I was definitely the only one to be wearing a stained old third-hand dress.

I wasn't able to ask Greg to the dance as he had already written his A levels, left school and gone back to Jo'burg where he lived, only a block away from Andy's parent's house. I asked the only other boy I knew, the brother of my air rifle friend, and he good-naturedly accepted my invitation. At least I had a partner.

Matric loomed ahead of us, and all the other girls descended into a sort of mild hysteria at the amount of swotting we had to do. I felt a bit left out, so one Saturday night, the day before my parents were to take me out on the Sunday, I sat up the whole night, as the others were now doing, and stared at my text and notebooks. Nothing sank in, so I gave up and read a novel from the library instead. On principle, I refused to read the three set books we'd been given for Matric English. Apparently, according to others, they were quite good.

One was *Venture into the Interior* by Laurens van der Post, a cousin on Mum's side of the family, and "that Lefty Pinko" to Dad. I didn't open it, even though it had been recommended as excellent by everybody who had. I could have read all three set books instead of anything I could lay my hands on in the library, but it was the sheer cussedness in me that prevented me from reading them. The following day I ran to the car to show my parents how pale I was and had even rubbed a bit of newsprint under my eyes to create that exhausted, sleepless look.

"About time," was all I got from them. Then it was the big event, and we were back in the gym, this time with a Government teacher invigilating at the top table. I was completely taken aback by the set of questions for each subject on the desk in front of me. For the History Exam I put my name and number on the paper, the date and very little else. The exams lasted three hours, and I found that I'd finished mine within twenty minutes, and spent the rest of the time worrying why everybody else was hunched over their desks, writing away furiously. I eventually found myself sketching my aunt's cocktail dress to pass the time. The bell finally rang, the invigilator told us all to stop writing, and with sighs and groans the other girls reluctantly put down their pens.

I felt a lot happier as we were released back into the sunshine and I could slip into my swimming costume and spend a couple of hours lying in the pool, on a lilo my best friend had thoughtfully brought from home. The others spent their time frantically comparing notes as to what they'd written and what they'd left out. I'd left out just about everything. I'd stopped thinking beyond the end of my nose years before, and simply couldn't see the importance of it all.

The exams finished, and it was our last night at school. We went carol singing and had a party in the house common room, given by the Fifth Formers. It was wonderful. By that time I'd had a brief discussion with Mum and Dad as to what I'd do when I left school. The subject of passing my Matric was avoided by everybody, especially me, and Dad said, "You'll go to finishing school in Switzerland just like your sisters did."

"What if I wanted to go to university, like all the others in my class are?" I asked.

"No. University is full of communists," said Dad firmly, and that was the end of our discussion.

Now that I wasn't to be allowed to go to 'Varsity' like my peers, I suddenly decided to reclaim my yen to be a vet.

"I want to go to university and be a vet," I told Dad during a Sunday out.

"The only veterinary college in this country is in Pretoria, at Onderstepoort, and it's full of Afrikaners. Forget it," I was told. "It's not ladylike to be a vet anyway, it's a man's job."

I decided to lower my sights and asked to attend the more local English Medium Natal University in 'Maritzburg, but no – any university was out of the question because there had been some protests against Apartheid held by university students across the country. Paradoxically, Mum and Dad despised the Afrikaner Government, but couldn't bear the though of our country being run by Africans either.

Teaching and nursing were out as well – "Too common for the likes of us." I was puzzled. Why all the fuss about making me take my Matric and then sending me off to the same place my sisters had gone. It wasn't fair. They'd dropped out of school and left in Fifth Form. At least, I thought they could allow me to use my qualifications. Secretly though, I was quite pleased, as I didn't have much hope of passing the university entrance exams with the paltry amount I'd written on my papers.

On our school-leaving day, we were milling around the main corridor, saying goodbye to everybody, staff included. I found myself in front of Mort. I said goodbye to her, and out of politeness, she had to ask me what I was going to do when I left school. All the other teachers were being very nice and showing an interest in our future, so she must had felt obliged to ask me.

"I'm going to finishing school to learn French and skiing," I replied. Mort snorted with disgust before she realised that she had to be civil, gave me a final bloodshot glare and shook my hand with her leathery, nicotine stained paw.

We had our Sixth Form Dance, and I enjoyed myself with the friend's brother. He was a genial boy, a year older than I was, and had been at Hilton College. At the end of the dance, when he dropped me off at our cousins' home in Kloof, where I was staying, I didn't know what to do. He wasn't my boyfriend as I already had Greg. To the merriment of my cousins who were watching furtively from the front veranda, I was teased mercilessly by all of them for not kissing my date – I'd shaken hands with him instead.

~~~

# 44

# Flying to Lisbon

**O**n Boxing Day, a month before my eighteenth birthday, Dad and I set off to fly to Rome and Madrid, before he left me with my new Swiss family. I was dressed in a tweed suit, cream blouse with stockings and matching black leather low-heeled court shoes and handbag, and carrying a thick camel-hair coat over my arm, boarded a South African Airways Vickers Viscount bound for Lisbon, our first stop. It was one of Durban's hottest summer days, with a humidity of 100% and no different from a sauna, but that's how one travelled in the '60s. It was still the smartest form of transport, far more up-market even than a first-class cabin on the Castle Line mail ships, and everybody wore their very best for the occasion.

Dad was in a dark, winter Savile Row suit, and just as hot, sweaty and uncomfortable as I was. He was longing for his first pink gin, and was as grumpy as I was excited.

By no stretch of the imagination was Dad my ideal travelling partner for my first trip overseas, but realistically, if I'd been sent off on my own, God knows where I'd have ended up – in white slavery probably, as that was one of the big fears doing the rounds in the 60s. Apparently, there were dealers in disguises lurking everywhere, with the sole aim of snatching young white girls to be sold on to rich Arabs in the Middle East.

I would have been a perfect target as I was hopelessly under-equipped to be let loose in the world outside boarding school or New Forest. I still hadn't yet crossed a street by myself, and I was nearly eighteen.

I was still living in my own little world as well.

To survive the mind-numbing boredom of the lonely life that I'd spent on the farm when my Zulu playmates had been banished back to Impendhle in 1961, and I'd been sent to the Prep and six years at boarding school, I'd created my own pleasant world in my head. With my lively imagination and plenty of uninterrupted time on my hands while I sat in class, chapel or prep, even when I rode my horses out on the hills with just the dogs for company, I'd given myself an unlimited future, which included flying a fighter-jet once I'd somehow got around my myopia problem.

I'd decided the Fleet Air Arm would be perfect for me, as it involved battleships, another of my favourites, as well as aircraft (this was before aircraft carriers became the standard method of landing planes at sea). As far as marriage went, I still had my prince in his castle even though I was in love with Greg and he didn't have a castle yet, but that didn't seem to pose any problems. I'd kept my veterinary dream and had amalgamated that with piloting a small zebra-striped singled-engined Cessna into the Serengeti to tend to sick and injured wildlife. I would hand-raise sick, injured, and orphaned wild animals and birds in my own locally built, thatched home there, bottle feeding the youngest baby mammals, while predators prowled the premises at night. Eventually I would set all the creatures I'd saved, free and back into the wild.

I had whiled away the six weeks of Christmas summer holidays in these delightful daydreams, embellishing them as I roamed the farm on Rocket. I'd also entertained the idea of being a prima ballerina after reading some of Nicolette's novels about famous ballet dancers like Margot Fonteyn, particularly as I loved the costumes; all those spangles and the gorgeous frilly tutus. I'd once or twice had a couple of ballet lessons at the Mooi River Farmers' Association stockyard hall, driven there by Mum after she'd picked us up from the Government school on the odd afternoon, and had absolutely loved them. Sadly, there were no sequinned net tutus, and we had to wear plain black leotards, pink tights and black pumps, but I had applied myself to all the beginners' feet and arm positions, as well as the barre exercises with all my heart. I was graceful and could have been a good dancer if it hadn't been for two problems: one was my growing to five foot seven in less than a year and thus becoming incredibly skinny and gangly, but with a D-cup bosom, and the other was Mum getting fed up with having to hang around for the hour or so that our lessons took, instead of being in her beloved garden.

The final straw had come when we had to drive home in a torrential thunderstorm, forcing us to put chains on the recalcitrant and cumbersome Pontiac (so hopelessly unsuitable for those mud roads), and getting two punctures as a result of Jomela's habit of always mending the broken links of all our chains with barbed wire. Delia and I crawled around in the ankle deep, gooey red mud under the car, in the pelting rain, which was interspersed by blinding bolts of lightning striking terrifyingly close to us, followed by deafening cracks of thunder, trying to fit the chains, only to be rewarded with an explosive pop and a loud hissing noise coming from the tyres on both occasions, while Mum yelled at us to hurry up. Our ballet outfits were ruined and her temper was way beyond breaking point, and that was the end of our dancing lessons forever.

I read books about famous show jumpers, and wonderful novels like *Jump for Joy* about girls like me who lived for their ponies and eventually became Olympic competitors in show jumping. I knew this was definitely a pipe dream, as I couldn't even get Dad to take Rocket to a gymkhana in the horsebox, when he still had one to ferry his polo ponies around in.

On the plane all my questions were met with monosyllabic grunts, but Dad perked up enough to point out to me that the pilot wore more gold bands on his jacket sleeves than the co-pilot, as we watched them do their pre-flight check though the open door of the cockpit. That was long before the days of security, and, after checking our baggage and showing an official our passports, we simply strolled out of the terminal and across the lava-like heat of the runway, and climbed the steps into the aircraft, our small overnight bags, with our coats, over our arms.

There was no in-flight movie, but plenty of free drink to keep Dad mellow, and after a fairly decent supper, I spent the rest of the time gazing out of the porthole at the pitch-blackness of Africa beneath me. We landed for refuelling at Luanda, the capital city of Angola, having had to circle the airport for twenty minutes or so while someone chased a few stray camels off the runway before we could land. The Angolan heat blasted us in the face as we climbed out to stretch our legs while the airport authorities sprayed the entire interior of our cabin with a noxious insecticide (mainly to eradicate killer mosquitoes, which carried both Yellow Fever and Malaria. We'd had to have all kinds of inoculations two weeks before we left South Africa, none of which exist today), which made me sneeze and my eyes water for the rest of the journey.

We arrived in Lisbon on a grey, overcast day, and as we stepped down onto the tarmac the ice-cold air hit me in the face like a bucket of freezing water. I couldn't get my coat on fast enough, after having silently cursed having to carry it in the Durban heat. We were proceeding through Immigration, to transfer to a flight to Rome where Dad had arranged for us to spend a few days, when the most extraordinary sight met my eyes.

It was a white woman pushing a broom across the floor. I was flabbergasted, and stood and stared in disbelief; I'd never in my entire life seen a white person sweeping a floor.

The journey continues in Part Two.

\*\*\*

Tel: 076 320 8407
www.worldwidebooksandart.com
E-mail: info@worldwidebooksandart.co.za

Unit 104 Oasis
Disa Road
Gordon's Bay
Western Cape
7410
South Africa